PENGUIN BO

THE PENGUIN HISTORY OF BRITAIN
GENERAL EDITOR: DAVID CANNADINE

NEW WORLDS, LOST WORLDS:
THE RULE OF THE TUDORS 1485–1603

'[Brigden] has told her story with superb narrative flair, and has given her readers a vivid picture of beliefs and aspirations widely held among the Tudors' subjects . . . a brilliant work of chiaroscuro . . . it will make a deep impression, and doubtless help to shape perceptions of the Tudor epoch for years to come' Ralph Houlbrooke, *The Times Literary Supplement*

'Susan Brigden's profound grasp of her period is here brought to life with a wealth of significant details, contemporary voices and her own apt commentaries and comparisons . . . deserves to become a classic' Jane Dunn, *Literary Review*

'Brigden's final achievement is her evocation of Ireland . . . Ireland's troubles down the centuries always make heartrending reading: but here they have something of the power of a Greek tragedy – Irish style' Antonia Fraser, *Sunday Times*

'A thoroughly convincing picture . . . rich and thoroughly well informed. A distinguished book which will give a lot of pleasure' Diarmaid MacCulloch

'Admirable . . . Brigden is just as concerned to examine the life of the ordinary people during this period. She chillingly recounts the lot of the poorest classes in the century that gave the world the phrase "Poor Law", and the modern parallels are striking' David McVey, *Scotland on Sunday*

'Brigden has written a book which is not only in masterly control of its subject, but which is a thing of beauty and feeling . . . *New Worlds, Lost Worlds* expresses on every page a sense of fascinated wonder . . . We shall not have to hesitate any longer when asked, as we sometimes are, to recommend just one book on the history of our own country in the sixteenth century' Patrick Collinson, *London Review of Books*

THE PENGUIN HISTORY OF BRITAIN

Published or forthcoming:

SUSAN BRIGDEN

New Worlds, Lost Worlds

THE RULE OF THE TUDORS
1485–1603

PENGUIN BOOKS

PENGUIN BOOKS

Published by the Penguin Group
Penguin Books Ltd, 80 Strand, London WC2R 0RL, England
Penguin Putnam Inc., 375 Hudson Street, New York, New York 10014, USA
Penguin Books Australia Ltd, 250 Camberwell Road, Camberwell, Victoria 3124, Australia
Penguin Books Canada Ltd, 10 Alcorn Avenue, Toronto, Ontario, Canada M4V 3B2
Penguin Books India (P) Ltd, 11 Community Centre, Panchsheel Park, New Delhi – 110 017, India
Penguin Books (NZ) Ltd, Cnr Rosedale and Airborne Roads, Albany, Auckland, New Zealand
Penguin Books (South Africa) (Pty) Ltd, 24 Sturdee Avenue, Rosebank 2196, South Africa

Penguin Books Ltd, Registered Offices: 80 Strand, London WC2R 0RL, England

www.penguin.com

First published by Allen Lane The Penguin Press 2000
Published in Penguin Books 2001

6

Copyright © Susan Brigden, 2000
All rights reserved

Title page illustration adapted from Miles Hogarde's *Mirroure of Myserie* (1557/8?)
perhaps intended as a New Year's gift for Queen Mary, reproduced courtesy of the
Huntington Library, California (HM121, fol. 6); 'The House of Tudor', after John Guy's
Tudor England (Oxford University Press); 'Henry Tudor's March to Bosworth Field',
after Ralph A. Griffiths and Roger S. Thomas's *The Making of the Tudor Dynasty* (Sutton);
'Anglo-Irish and Gaelic Lordships in the Late Fifteenth Century' and 'Sixteenth-Century
Plantations in Ireland', after Moody *et al*'s *A New History of Ireland* (Oxford University
Press); 'The Battle in the Narrow Seas', after Mattingly, *The Defeat of the Spanish
Armada*; 'A General Map' after Humphrey Gilbert's *A Discourse of a Discovery for
a New Passage to Cataia*, in the British Museum (photo © Photomas Index)

The moral right of the author has been asserted

Printed in England by Clays Ltd, St Ives plc

For Jeremy

Contents

CONTENTS

List of Illustrations

Preface

First among the new worlds with which this book is concerned are the English Renaissance and Reformation. In offering an alternative path to salvation, the new religion broke the unity of Catholic Christendom and shattered a world of shared belief. For England, the lost worlds were those of past certainties, of traditional religion, and of all that was destroyed in the name of faith. People in the past thought differently. Almost no one doubted then that there was a God, that He intervened constantly in the world which He had made, and that He had purposes for His people. Yet despite this, religious conviction was not often manifested in lives of ceaseless devotion, spent in undeviating obedience to Christ's Great Commandments. On the same page of a copy of Thomas More's *The Supplication of Souls* (1529) two messages are written in the margin in contemporary hand, one an insult, the other a pious invocation:

> Thomas is a knave, by God.

> In the name of God, Amen.

Even in a religious age, God's name could be invoked in different ways. Yet the old world was a society in which sanctions, worldly and otherworldly, were imposed upon those who did not give witness of their faith, and in which obedience to the Church and its teaching was a fundamental duty. At the Reformation, as individual conscience came to be asserted and the Church's authority was shaken, the Christian was confronted by choices. This book concerns the making of those choices, and their consequences. With the Reformation came division. Wars of religion were fought throughout Europe in the sixteenth century. England and Ireland were deeply involved in them, but not always on the same side.

As the throne of England passed to the King of Scotland in 1603, England and Scotland were at last united, after centuries of enmity and mutual threat. But during the sixteenth century Scotland was a foreign country, an independent kingdom. Ireland was another matter. It had been conquered by an English king centuries before. Macaulay said, much later, that to write of Ireland was to tread upon a volcano on which the lava was still glowing, and every English historian must feel the same trepidation. But in the sixteenth century the histories of what then became the two kingdoms of England and Ireland are inseparably bound together. For Ireland, the lost worlds and new worlds are not the same as those for England. Ireland saw the passing of the Gaelic order, and the arrival of the Counter-Reformation and of the New English colonists. The tragedy of Ireland under the last Tudor monarch helps to explain why peace has been so hard to find there since.

As Henry Tudor came to the throne, the islands of Britain and Ireland were isolated, on the edge of Europe, and little regarded by their greater neighbours. So they were still as his granddaughter Elizabeth died. 'This empire is a world divided from the world,' wrote Ben Jonson in 1604. Yet England's enemies now looked to Ireland as a bridge for invasion, and by 1589 England was powerful enough to send an Armada against Spain as vast as that which Spain had sent against her in 1588. Elizabethans aspired to travel, to discover, and to colonize in the New World, and they began to build an empire of their own.

Many of their discoveries and rediscoveries were intellectual. They looked to the classical past for lessons about how to live. The literature of the English Renaissance appears very often in what follows; not only because of its brilliance, but because so many of the writers were at the heart of the new world of power: at the court, where life often followed art. Their works of imagination reveal their private thoughts and their political ethics and preoccupations in a way which other sources cannot. Some of the figures who appear and reappear in this book are hardly typical of their own age, or of any other, but their voices were insistent.

We cannot understand the past without imposing patterns, but should always remember that there are other ways of seeing it. This book is more about kings, and queens, than cabbages; even so, it has little to say about the constitution or institutions, about the workings of Parliaments and Councils. There is much about religion, but little about the institutional Church and the clergy. The economy, trade, agriculture – upon which everything else rested – are left for other histories. More is included about going to war than about paying for it. What Elizabethans thought of as 'the fourth sort of men who did not rule' (and they did not think to include women) are not here given the say which their overwhelming number deserves. Most of the people of the past remain, as individuals, beyond history, unknown and unknowable. Many of the century's great discoveries and transformations may have passed by those who, working for what they hoped would be their daily bread, simply had no time for them. Every parish and precinct, ward and village had its own political life, and its own history, but in this book most of those local histories are subsumed within a larger whole. Even Wales, although set apart by its own history, language and culture, has not been given its separate, national history under the Tudors, the dynasty which was partly Welsh in blood, and first ventured its claim there. During the sixteenth century Wales increasingly participated in English politics, government and religion and came to adopt its institutions – the common law, Parliament, the established Church, the apparatus of local government – while in Ireland, the Tudors' other Celtic dominion, the estrangement grew.

The awe and excitement I felt when I was first asked to write this book never quite left me as I wrote it. Following S. T. Bindoff's classic *Tudor England* in the original Pelican History of England would give any historian pause. This book is not like his; his guiding themes are not always mine. After half a century, and with the vast increase of scholarship about the period, the vision is bound to have changed. Yet I hope that I have written in the same spirit; with the intention of telling the story to those who do not know it already, and of recovering something of the experience of those who lived in that time, of their certainties and uncertainties, hopes and terrors.

In the Renaissance people thought often about friendship, and so have I in writing this book. It is a product of the University of Oxford, of its particular community and system. I thank the Rector and Fellows of Lincoln College for fellowship, and for the support which a college provides. I am grateful to Paul Langford, best of colleagues through two decades, for steeling my resolve to accept Penguin's invitation, and to Perry Gauci for endless cheerfulness and support. This book might have been finished sooner had it not been for hours spent with undergraduates, but I thank them for their company and for all they have taught me. I greatly valued Rosamund Oates's help and encouragement as I was finishing this book. I have learnt a great deal from those with whom I have shared University classes, and I particularly thank Ian Archer, Cliff Davies, Steven Gunn, Christopher Haigh (my undergraduate tutor), Felicity Heal, Judith Maltby, Scott Mandelbrote, Peter McCullough, Jonathan Woolfson and Jenny Wormald.

Many people have generously answered my questions, sent me references, found me books and taken pity on my ignorance: Andy Barnett, Jeremy Catto, Thomas Charles-Edwards, Jason Dorsett, Roy Foster, Hiram Morgan, Pat Palmer, Fiona Piddock, Claire Preston, Mike White, Nigel Wilson, Lucy Wooding, David Wootton, the staff of the Bodleian and History Faculty Libraries. Bridget Smith kindly typed the bibliographical essay. I am grateful to them all.

I have often thought of my late supervisor, Geoffrey Elton, as I wrote this book, and profoundly wish that he could have read it and put me right. He taught me very many things; not least that I should not expect writing history to be easy.

For Elizabethans, books were like bear cubs, formed by licking. This 'bear's whelp of mine' was finally handed over to friends and scholars, whose acute reading and wise criticisms have improved it immeasurably: Toby Barnard, Steven Gunn, Diarmaid MacCulloch, Scott Mandelbrote, Peter Marshall, and Sandy Sullivan. I thank them profoundly for their care and consideration and absolve them from any blame for the faults that remain, which I claim for my own.

To Blair Worden, whose support and inspiration have been constant, who has given me so many ideas, who has read this book more than once, I am, as in the sixteenth century they said in gratitude, 'bounden during life'. My parents were my ideal general readers.

No one could have found a more patient, knowledgeable and encouraging editor than Simon Winder. He had faith in this book when mine faltered. I owe grateful thanks to Jane Birdsell, my acute and vigilant copy editor, and to Felicity Bryan for her advice.

At crucial moments in the writing of this book, Joanna and the late Angus Macintyre, and Vivian and Richard King, rescued me. I am very grateful.

My horse helped me to understand why Philip Sidney would begin *The Defence of Poesy* with a horse.

To my husband, Jeremy Wormell, who deserves a better book, I dedicate this one.

Lincoln College, Oxford

January 2000

About Dates and Names

The dates in this book are all, unless otherwise specified, Old Style – that is, according to the calendar introduced by Julius Caesar in 45 BC. In February 1582 a new calendar was established by Pope Gregory XIII in a bull which prescribed that the day following 4 October 1582 should be 15 October, and that the new year should begin on 1 January instead of on Lady Day, 25 March. England, having repudiated papal authority, ignored the new calendar and, until 1751, English time marched ten days behind that of the Catholic states of Europe. Old Style was the official calendar in Ireland, yet some Gaelic lords, loyal to the papacy, soon adopted the Gregorian calendar. In revolt against the English crown, the confederate lords used New Style when they wrote to Spain or Rome, and this is indicated (n.s.). The year, for both England and Ireland, is taken to begin on 1 January.

Irish names, proper and common, have for the most part been anglicized. So Hugh Roe O'Donnell is not here given the name by which he called himself, Aodh Ruadh Ó Domhnaill.

All quotations are in modern English spelling.

Prologue

NEW WORLDS, LOST WORLDS

In 1515 Thomas More, then under-sheriff of London, wrote an elusive work of fiction, *Utopia*. He presented an imaginary vision of Utopia, an island state far beyond the equator and out of contact with Europe for 1,200 years. As the story begins, an imaginary traveller, the philosopher Raphael Hythloday, steps into the real world of More, who is on an embassy in Antwerp and has just come from attending Mass. Hythloday has travelled with Amerigo Vespucci on his later voyages to the New World, and in his travels has encountered the Utopians, with whom he has lived for five years, sharing his knowledge and their lives. More places himself in his fiction as the character Morus, and presents the plodding Morus in debate with the brilliant Hythloday. Morus implores Hythloday to describe all that he has seen. And so Hythloday does. In writing *Utopia* More was inspired by classical authors, especially by Plato, but Plato had devised only a theoretical Republic. As More recounted Hythloday's tale he brought a just and happy society to life, as though he had walked in its gardens and dined with its citizens.

Here in Utopia was 'the best state of a commonwealth', thought Hythloday. Utopian society was a true commonwealth; founded indeed on common wealth. The Utopians' abolition of private property, their holding of everything in common – as friends should and early Christians had done – guarded the Utopians against the malign tendencies of human nature to pride, greed and envy. In Utopia nothing was private. Labour was a communal, universal duty. There was no money, no ownership, yet everyone was rich, for there could be no greater riches than to live happily and peacefully, without worries about making a living. The Utopians were freed to concern themselves with the common good. Once they had been ruled by a king, but now they elected their governors, choosing them for their virtue. Tyranny was an evil Utopians so far condemned that, although they hated war, they would intervene to save their neighbours from oppression. Their society was pacific and benevolent, tolerant and temperate, and, said Hythloday, capable, so far as anyone could tell, of lasting forever.

Utopia was an artificial state, the creation of an enlightened despot, King Utopus. Rescuing the island from the chaos of religious schism, he had left the Utopians under the necessity only of believing that the soul is immortal, that there is a divine providence at work, and that eternal reward and punishment await in the afterlife. The Utopians of More's imagining were evolving a natural theology through the processes of reason, and far surpassed European Christians in matters quintessentially Christian. They lived lives of virtue, wisdom, justice and charity, in the way that Christ had commanded. Yet they did not know Christ, and had not received the illumination of the Gospel. When Hythloday and his fellow travellers revealed Christ's teachings, the Utopians recognized them as truths to which they already aspired, and were eager to be converted to the faith of the Old World, believing that the life of apostolic purity was to be found among the truest society of Christians. And where was that? Certainly not in More's own society.

Hythloday knew not only Utopia, which was, for him, the best state of a commonwealth, but also England, which was not. The fantasy, ideal world of Utopia is set starkly in More's work against the society of contemporary England and Europe, which was neither just nor happy. The imaginary traveller recalled a debate in 1497 at the table of Cardinal Morton, Lord Chancellor and Archbishop of Canterbury, at which a dismal catalogue of England's social evils had been rehearsed. And no one had listened. Hythloday presented a picture of European society chained to custom, incapable of reform. While Utopia was a society without hierarchies save of virtue, where deference was given only where it was deserved, England was obsessed by honour, ruled by a wanton aristocracy whose title to govern was not virtue but birth and wealth. Those whose wealth rested upon their daily exploitation of the poor made laws to justify that oppression, and then sat in judgement upon the poor whom they had ruined. In England, law was not justice, and the penalties went beyond justice. A lawyer at Morton's dinner had boasted of the strict penalties meted out to thieves, who were hanged twenty at a time. He wondered why so many stole. No wonder in such a society, judged Hythloday. The poor found themselves under a terrible necessity: first to steal, and then to die for it. The nobility, Hythloday thought, were doubly guilty: they lived like drones on the labour of others, demanding more and more from the tenants of their estates, and then corrupted the crowds of servants they took into service by making them live as idly as they did themselves. A circumstance unique to England made the plight of the poor more desperate: the landowners enclosed land for pasture, driving poor farmers from the soil and families from their homes to wander and beg – sheep became 'devourers of men'. The very fertility of England was a reproach, for it was exploited by the wealthy as a monopoly, leaving the common people destitute. When Hythloday surveyed contemporary European society he found nothing but a 'conspiracy of the rich'.

Whence should remedy come? From kings? Unlikely. The account of the wise and holy institutions of the Utopians is set against a debate between Morus and Hythloday – either of whose invented characters More himself might have played; now one, now the other – about the nature of counsel. Hythloday was a philosopher, perfectly qualified to serve princes, urged Morus. But Hythloday knew that such service was not freedom, and that it was folly to believe that princes would listen to truths that they did not wish to hear. Worse, the wise, the honest counsellor would become a screen for the wickedness and folly of others. This was precisely the debate that the real More had had with his friend Erasmus, and within himself. When Hythloday described the counsellors to the king of France in secret session, devising strategems for foreign conquest, his imaginary picture was tellingly close to the contemporary diplomatic reality. All their destabilizing schemes were ones which any Renaissance prince, set on glory rather than peace, would use, not least More's own real prince, Henry VIII. Who could provide an example and restrain the warlike princes of Europe? The Pope, Christ's vicar? Hardly. When Hythloday told of the Utopians, who needed no treaties because the fellowship created by nature sufficed, he referred to their happy belief that European treaties, sanctioned by the justice of kings and universal reverence for the Pope, were inviolable. Here was desperate irony, for More wrote at a time when the Pope was leading a martial Holy League, which was neither holy nor a league.

As More dreamt of Utopia and thought upon the creation of political and social institutions which would restrain the human propensity to sin, he was accustoming himself to the prospect of entering royal service. He knew as well as Hythloday that service was near to servitude, and that princes were not inclined to listen. But he accepted the duty to sacrifice private liberty for the public good, and he needed to support his growing family. At certain times the relationship between scholars and rulers is re-conceived. So it was in the Renaissance. Those who were educated believed themselves to be educated for public service, believed that they could persuade princes, in Church and state, to reform. Scholars left the retreat of their studies to guide the will of princes and thereby change the world. *Utopia* was written and published for those who advised princes. Reform was dependent upon power, but power was vested precisely in those institutions most resistant to reform, where reform was most urgently needed. Thomas More chose, in *Utopia*, to write not a political treatise, but a satire, hoping perhaps that fiction might achieve what philosophy alone could not. He hoped that by presenting an ideal, and confronting this ideal with lamentable reality, reform might be generated. The Utopians themselves were eager to learn and to improve, yet Hythloday doubted that his own society would even remember the Utopians, let alone try to emulate them. At the end of the book, when the fictional More leads Hythloday to supper, he admits that there are many features of the Utopian commonwealth which he would like to see in his own society, yet he never expects them to be introduced.

Even as More wrote *Utopia* he had already begun to conceive his other great political work, *The History of King Richard III*. This was history, not chronicle, and history with clear moral intent. It was also a parable and a tragedy; its theme the nature of power and its abuse, of tyranny and the sin that made it possible. In *The History of King Richard III* the Devil is a real presence, as he had not been in *Utopia*; the progress of Richard of Gloucester to his kingdom is accursed and execrable. More's Richard was a parricide and unnatural uncle, a Judas who broke all the ties of kinship, like the figure of Vice in a morality play. A Protector who was no protector, a dissimulator and a plotter, he contrived the murder of his nephews, Edward V and Richard of York, the young princes who stood in his way to the throne. He was abetted by an ambitious Duke of Buckingham, by a nerveless clergy, and by the common people, who looked on as sullen spectators, powerless to prevent the tragedy played before them. More's Richard and the historical Richard are not one and the same, for More's purpose was to present a narrative of evil rather than an impartial account. But Richard III has never been free of the guilt of the massacre of the innocents in his reign.

More presented here a 'green world'; green because it was primal and chaotic, and because of the new-minted opportunism of the principal conspirators. It might also have seemed by the time he wrote, in 1514–18, a lost world; the world of his early childhood (More was born in 1477 or 1478), when the realm was shadowed by civil wars, gripped by fear, fought over by overmighty nobles; where political rivals were driven to seek sanctuary and the uncertain protection of the Church. But More knew that the tyranny which had existed in his own childhood might come again; that in England, unlike Utopia, political institutions could not prevent it. More's history, both dark and brilliant, was left unfinished, unpublished; perhaps because he was unwilling to allow his royal master to use the history of the last Plantagenet to sanction and celebrate the Tudor rise to power. The memory of Richard III's reign – of usurpation and tyranny, of the fragility of the succession, of a world which was not altogether lost and might return – haunted the century.

More's imaginings in his *Utopia* and *History of King Richard III* were prescient, even tragic. He lived to regret publishing his fictional *Utopia*, with its devastating account of his own society. He had been inspired by contemporary accounts of the people of the New World living lives of primal innocence, holding all in common. Fortunately for him, he never lived to see his ideal society appropriated by Elizabethan adventurers to inspire and justify colonization and expropriation, not only in the New World but also in Ireland. More, whose indictment of English law was, in *Utopia*, comprehensive, became Lord Chancellor in 1529, and presided over the system which Hythloday had condemned. The English, inured to the brutality of the law's punishments, soon saw even more terrible penalties inflicted for religious heresies which the Utopians might have tolerated. In 1515 it had been possible for More to write, with seeming approval, of the imaginary tolerant society of Utopia, a pagan world aspiring to perfectibility, but this was just before his own world was cleft by religious divisions deeper than any Europe had yet known. Christian renewal would come from a direction which appalled More and his friends. When he wrote of the Utopians, religious and austere, living like a single family, he described a world close to the world of the cloister, a religious life which would soon be desolated. Hythloday had warned of the dangers of serving a vainglorious prince; of the prince's aversion to listening to counsel which displeased him; of the moral contagion and delusiveness of life at court. More's own experience vindicated Hythloday's advice, and he learnt the truth of the political maxim, 'The wrath of the prince is death'. More's *Richard III* would be used by those who came after him, not as a warning against contemporary misrule, but as a history of tyranny which was past and not to come again, and as a celebration of the Tudor accession.

I

Rather Feared than Loved

HENRY VII AND HIS DOMINIONS
1485–1509

Only Richard III's usurpation of the throne, his murder of the young princes in the Tower – alleged against him but never proved – and the violence of his subsequent rule made Henry Tudor, an obscure and exiled claimant, a likely contender for the throne of England. In August 1485, after long years of precarious exile, Henry landed in South Wales to challenge the throne with a motley army of French and Scottish troops and English fugitives. Presenting himself as the unifier of the warring Houses of York and Lancaster, and as heir to both dynasties, he promised to free an oppressed people from Richard Plantagenet, 'homicide and unnatural tyrant'. At Bosworth Field in Leicestershire Richard charged into the midst of the usurper's army and, abandoned by his supposed allies and by the God of battles, was cut down. He lost his kingdom and his life and left Henry Tudor, for the while, without a rival. The Tudor adventurer found himself king by right of conquest, by inheritance and by acclamation, of a country he neither knew nor understood.

Henry Tudor was born in Pembroke in 1457, and had fled there once before, for shelter, in 1470–71. It was to Pembroke and to Wales that he returned in 1485, hoping for popular support and promising to restore lost freedoms. As he marched through the coastal lowlands and northwards he saw at first a landscape of mixed farming, where the furrows of ploughland traced agricultural progress. Making his way through the centre of the principality, he entered a bleaker territory of mountain and moorland, of rocky, barren heath where sheep and cattle grazed, but where otherwise signs of cultivation were few, for the people accepted the constraints of nature. Perhaps 200,000 people lived in Wales then, bound by a strong sense of national identity, made clear in their use of the name *Cymry*, 'people of one region'. Most of these people lived in the lowlands, in villages, while in the pastoral uplands there were single farmsteads in lonely valleys. Henry Tudor's forced

The House of Tudor

John of Gaunt m. Catherine Swynford
Duke of Lancaster, King of Castile
(d.1399)

John Beaufort m. Margaret Holland
Marquess of Somerset
(d.1410)

HENRY V m. Katherine of Valois [who m.(2)
(1413–22)   Owen Tudor
                         ex.1461]
(d.1437)

John m. Margaret of Bletso
Duke of Somerset
(d.1444)

Edmund Tudor m. Margaret Beaufort
Earl of Richmond   (d.1509)
(d.1456)

HENRY VII m. Elizabeth of York
(1485–1509)   (1461–83)

EDWARD IV

Catherine m. Arthur
of   (d.1502)
Aragon

HENRY VIII
(1509–1547)

(1) Catherine
of
Aragon
(m.1509 a.1533
d.1536)

(2) Anne Boleyn
m.
(m.1533
ex.1536)

(3) Jane Seymour
(m.1536
d.1537)

Philip II m. MARY I
of   (1553–1558)
Spain
(d.1598)

ELIZABETH I
(1558–1603)

EDWARD VI
(1547–1553)

Margaret Tudor
(d.1541)
m.

(1) James IV   (2) Archibald   (3) Henry
of Scotland   Earl of Angus   Lord Methuen
(d.1513)   (div.c.1526)

James V   Margaret Douglas m. Matthew
(d.1542)   Countess of Lennox   Earl of Lennox
m.   (d.1578)   (d.1571)

(1) Madeleine
daughter of
Francis I of France
(d.1537)

(2) Mary of Guise
(d.1560)

Mary
Queen of Scots
(ex.1587)
m.

(1) Francis II   (2) Henry, Lord Darnley   (3) James Hepburn
of France   (d.1567)   Earl of Bothwell
(d.1560)   (d.1578)

James VI of Scotland
JAMES I
(1603–25)

Mary Tudor
(d.1533)
m.

(1) Louis XII   (2) Charles Brandon
of France   Duke of Suffolk
(d.1515)   (d.1545)

Henry Grey m. Frances Brandon
Duke of Suffolk   Duchess of Suffolk
(ex.1554)   (d.1563)

Jane Grey m. Lord Guildford Dudley
proclaimed Queen   (ex.1554)
1553 (ex.1554)
m.

Catherine Grey
(d.1568)
m.

(1) Henry   (2) Edward
Lord Herbert   Earl of Hertford
(diss.1554)   (d.1621)

Mary Grey

a. marriage annulled
d. died
diss. dissolved
div. divorced
ex. executed
m. married

march into England led across the mountains of mid Wales to the lordships of the Welsh Marches, to Welshpool and the Shropshire plain beyond. He marched over Long Mountain down the Roman road to Shrewsbury, into the English Midlands, and to victorious battle with Richard III on 22 August.

Henry's passage from Wales to Bosworth Field in the heart of England showed him the diversity of the dominions he now claimed. Nature had defined the patterns of terrain and soil, of lowland and hills, of the prevailing wind and rainfall, which human labour could exploit but never change. The landscape determined the patterns not only of cultivation, but also of inheritance and social relations; as the landscape changed, even within counties, so did the character of settlement. The fenlands and marshlands and wild upland dales each created their own distinct agricultural and social worlds, and with transport slow and laborious, every region was highly localized and fragmented. In Leicestershire, where he took his crown, Henry was in the heart of open-field countryside – ploughland, where land was intensively cultivated according to communal rules. Here he could survey a patchwork of green and gold, furlongs of corn and crops in hedgeless fields. There was forest there also, Charnwood Forest, and tilled fields might always revert to forest. The people of England had waged war upon nature – clearing, felling, ploughing, draining – but with more energy at some times and in some places. The retreat of the population after the devastating plagues of the mid fourteenth century, and the continuing epidemic illnesses and stagnation of the population through the next century, had brought a retreat in cultivation. As Henry entered this kingdom he claimed, there were perhaps two and a half or three million people in England and Wales. Within a generation the population began to rise dramatically, and with that rise came great alterations to the seemingly immemorial, changeless character of rural society.

Describing the landscape, contemporaries distinguished not between highland and lowland, but between champion (open) ground and woodland, between a pattern of arable farming and a pastoral landscape with isolated farmsteads set amidst their closes of pasture. In fielden country there were numerous villages and towns, surrounded by their common fields, with houses and hovels clustered around parish church and manor house. In woodland areas towns were few and far between, settlement dispersed. The distinction between arable and pastoral was moral as well as topographical: where the land was uncultivated so the people

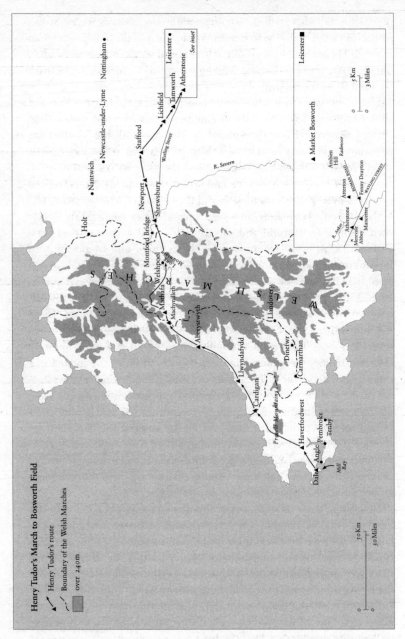

Henry Tudor's March to Bosworth Field

Henry Tudor's route
Boundary of the Welsh Marches
over 240m

were believed to be also. Forest and pastoralism were associated with a more primitive, barbaric state.

As Henry surveyed his realm, he saw more sheep than people; those sheep which More would characterize as 'devourers of men'. Vast areas of open-field arable land were being converted to sheep and cattle pasture in the later fifteenth century, and where before a hundred arable labourers had tilled and harrowed, now a few shepherds watched. In most of England – the south-east, south-west and north – the countryside had been fenced and enclosed before, often long before, and these anciently enclosed lands had their own character. Nearly a century later, in 1572, the Duke of Norfolk defended himself against the charge of planning an invasion through Harwich by asking rhetorically who would choose to lead an army through an area so wholly enclosed by hedges and encumbered by narrow paths. In the Midlands conversion from tillage to pasture was taking place as Henry Tudor came to the throne, as lords of the manor and great freeholders took commercial decisions with devastating consequences for communities, evicting tenants who were powerless to oppose when lands and lives were determined at the lord's will. Enclosure was caused by decay and depopulation, as well as causing them, for population decline had led to labour shortage. But now the population began to rise, and with that rise came a drive to cultivate in order to feed.

The new king could see the patterns of landscape and cultivation as he passed. He knew that all lordship, influence and status rested upon land, and understood the sanctity of landed property, which no king must violate. His seizure of the crown had made him the greatest landowner in England, and he would become greater still. Yet what neither he, nor anyone else, could tell just by looking was how the land was held; who held freehold as free tenants, and who held land at the lord's will as customary tenants and copyholders, owing him fees and fines and duties. The nature of ownership dictated where power lay and determined or disturbed the peace of the countryside. Some land was left 'waste', in its natural state, for the common grazing which was vital for the whole economy, and especially for the landless poor. This common land was about to become overstocked and under threat. If the King had cared to observe them, the social inequalities, and the poverty, were manifest, even in the fertile landscape of the east Midlands. Here about one third of the male population were cottagers and labourers, with little hope of acquiring their own farms, and facing a hard struggle even to defend their common grazing. A quarter of the personal wealth of Leicestershire villagers in the early sixteenth century was held by 4 per cent of the people. Such inequalities were taken as part of the divine and natural order, which no one should question. As the first Tudor king passed by, the common people looked on, their lives affected more by the fecundity of the harvest, which happened to be good in 1485, than by any change of dynasty.

Henry had been crowned on the battlefield with the crown of the fallen King, and acclaimed by his troops. Taking oaths of allegiance from the towns on his way, he marched on slowly towards London, the capital and centre of trade, and nearby Westminster, the heart of government. London was England's largest city, but its population was only about 50,000. The population of Paris was three or four times as large. The citizens of London boasted of their worldwide trade, but they lived in a city of one square mile, bound still within its ancient and defensible walls. London was a great franchise, proud of its freedoms and wealth, arrogant in its claims. The City's loyalty must be won and its conformity assured, but it had in its long history often shown sympathies quite different from those the Crown required. London was small enough for news to travel fast, and for causes to be swiftly followed; it was large enough for a formidable volume of support or resentment to grow and for fearsome numbers to gather. Its citizens had acquiesced sullenly at Richard III's usurpation, and regretted it; they welcomed Henry Tudor at his accession, and came to regret it.

The towers and steeples of London's hundred parish churches and its many religious houses dominated the skyline, for none of the laity aspired to build to rival the Church, and only the Guildhall, the seat of the City's governors, and the daunting Tower could compare in grandeur. To the north door of St Paul's Cathedral the new king came to offer his battle standards in thanks to the giver of victory. One bore the red dragon of Cadwaladr, symbolizing Tudor descent from the ancient British kings who had defeated the Saxon invaders. Another banner carried the symbol of St George of England; another the Lancastrian and Beaufort emblems. On 30 October Henry VII was crowned, swearing the oath sworn by kings long before him to keep the peace to clergy and people, to do justice in mercy and in truth, and to maintain the laws: an oath which few had been able to keep. His marriage in January 1486 to Elizabeth of York, Edward IV's daughter, sealed his pact with the Yorkists, merged the Yorkist claim with the Tudors, and promised an end to the civil wars between Lancaster and York. A prince was born within the year. They called him Arthur, with evident promise, recalling the Arthurian past and ancient British blood of the Tudors, and looking to the future of the dynasty.

'Britain' was an ancient land of myth, not a political reality. When Henry Howard, Earl of Surrey wrote in his last poem of the blood which he had shed 'for Britannes sake', he used a term of art, for the lands of England, Wales, Ireland and Scotland were very far from being united as 'Britain'. Henry was acclaimed 'by the grace of God, King of England and of France, Prince of Wales and Lord of Ireland'. Until only a generation earlier the English monarchy had also ruled Gascony and Normandy. Now only Calais was still in English possession, a military outpost, but the claim to the throne of France and the Angevin empire lived on. It was France and French ways of governing which Henry knew best, after long exile in France and ducal Brittany: it was England which this inexperienced, stranger king must now rule. England was an ancient, unified and intensively governed realm. Compared with the other kingdoms of late medieval Europe, it had remarkable governmental coherence and lack of provincial autonomy and custom. There was a common law, a common language (save in distant, Celtic Cornwall) and a common coinage. A sophisticated and intrusive bureaucracy, centred at Westminster, through proper forms and channels sent tens of thousands of parchment directives every year into the shires. This was an administration which meant to keep the peace even down to village level, and to protect the property of the king's free subjects. In war, it could marshal and provision forces. Taxation was freely granted in Parliament and duly collected. And yet this *public* authority, its administration of justice, its maintenance of peace and order, was upheld – and could be subverted – by the *private* power and personal lordship of the king's leading landed subjects: upon their consent and cooperation the whole system of governance depended. The king, as the greatest of lords and of landholders, had his *private* following (or affinity), but in his *public* role as king he had hardly any paid officials and no standing military force. He must rely upon the private forces of his magnates for the maintenance of order during peace time and for troops to wage war.

The magnates, the great nobility – the tiny group of peers who alone had titles of nobility and who were the king's natural counsellors – ruled in their 'countries', as they called them, as the king did in the realm. Through their personal lordship they maintained the peace and protected the interests of their dependent gentry and peasant tenants. The nobility had great power and wealth, and might have paramount influence in their 'countries', but no lord could exercise a local tyranny. After the demise of Richard III no noble held the awesome regional hegemony that he had done in his great northern territory. In a firmly hierarchical society the knights, esquires and gentlemen looked to nobles for patronage and protection, and expected them to maintain and restore social peace by arbitration and reconciliation. Yet the gentry were also increasingly independent, self-regarding, and capable of managing both their own affairs and those of their county commonwealths, in which their collective wealth and land gave them so large a stake. The nobility, in their turn, looked to them for local support and the Crown looked to them to run the shires. The county gentry were entrusted with great and wide-ranging authority: as Justices of the Peace, assessors of taxes, arrayers of troops, commissioners of many kinds, and as county representatives in the House of Commons. Lesser gentry served as coroners and tax collectors, and beneath them, in manors and villages, husbandmen (poorer farmers) too sought a share in the activity of governing, acting as constables and jurymen. Despite intense competitiveness and frequent feuding, local society had a will to peace and stability. A wise king understood that, lacking the power to compel and enforce, he must inspire and lead; he must command the loyalty of a political nation deeply versed in government and anxious to participate.

As in all personal lordships, the character and ability of the king was vital. The realm was not only his kingdom and personal estate, but a commonwealth, a polity, and he must rule in his subjects' interests. Kings who had failed to do so had been deposed. It was the king's duty to listen to the counsel of his greater subjects, and to hear in it the voice of local society. He must defend his subjects in war and keep the peace at home; and ensure that the law was respected. That the king himself should observe his own law in his dealings with his subjects was a fundamental principle, enshrined in Magna Carta. Where a king was unjust or partial, public justice must fail, and the will of his subjects to obedience and allegiance would be violated. The consequences of Henry VI's inadequacies as king, of his failure to rule at all, had been a breakdown in both public and private authority and, finally, civil war. A wise king must trust his nobles to rule their regions justly in his name, and keep their confidence, but it was not in Henry VII's nature to trust; his tendency was to treat them as enemies rather than as allies.

Not all the King's dominions were so coherent, so stable, so bound to the monarchy as the lowland South of England. To the west, England shared a frontier, a March with Wales, and on this borderland, as on others, an older world of feud and violence remained to disturb the peace, even though the wars between the English and Welsh nations had ended centuries before. Wales had finally been conquered by Edward I in 1282–3 and the lands of the native Welsh princes had been annexed to the English Crown. Wales was divided between this small principality and a large number of Marcher lordships along the frontier with the English shires. In the principality itself the native laws of Wales remained alongside English laws; in their lordships the almost autonomous Marcher lords continued to exercise extensive rights delegated to them by the Crown, even though the original military justification was long gone. Each of these feudal enclaves had its own legal, fiscal and political processes. The fragmented authority in the Marches and the unfettered power of the lords, many of whom were absentee, allowed criminals to escape justice by fleeing from one lordship to another. Marcher society was perennially seen as turbulent and lawless. The Welsh were still regarded as a race apart; by the English and by themselves. Welsh national identity was based more upon their own language and memories of past glories than on common political organization. That Welsh inheritance might be revived by a new king of Welsh name and Welsh descent. As he entered Wales in 1485 Henry promised to deliver the people of the principality from 'such miserable servitudes as they have piteously long' suffered. The Welsh poet who praised Henry Tudor for setting the Welsh free was not mistaken: in a series of charters of enfranchisement granted to communities of North Wales in 1504–8 he released his countrymen from the legal restrictions imposed upon them by Henry IV after the revolt of Owain Glyndwr.

Its people usually thought of England as an island, as a watery fortress walled by waves. Yet England shared that island with another independent kingdom with which it had been intermittently at war for two centuries; that war interrupted only by a series of broken truces. Scotland, under its Stewart kings, had its own patterns of lordship and power; of law-making and peacekeeping, of kinship and clientage, quite different from those of its southern neighbour and enemy. Despite failing kings and factious nobles Scotland maintained its independence, challenging the continuing claims of the English king to overlordship, and, potentially in alliance with France or with the Gaelic lords of

Ireland, posed a constant threat to England. Between England and Scotland lay a military frontier, its precise boundaries still disputed in the 'Debateable Land' between the two kingdoms. That the Scots had not penetrated south of the Tyne since 1388 did not mean that they could not come again, and the pervasive fear of invasion was given tangible form in the continued building of tower houses, of peel towers surrounded by barmekins (defensible walls). The English Borders, lying in the remote uplands of Coquetdale, Redesdale and Tynedale, were divided into three Marches, East, Middle and West, and here royal authority was delegated to wardens charged with defending the frontier in war, and maintaining law and order in time of peace. Law and order were relative in the unique society of the Borders, where the 'surnames', kin groups which had formed for mutual protection as a response to war against the Scots, lived by raiding, mainly cattle (known as reiving). The March had its own archaic laws, its own entrenched customs shared by the English and Scottish Borderers, who often had more in common with each other than with their own compatriots beyond the March. To southerners their customs seemed antediluvian, exotic, dangerous. When, in 1535, Henry VIII wished to watch the ghastly execution of traitors in London he came disguised as a wild 'Borderer'.

On 24 September 1485 Henry had offered pardon to those in the 'north parts' of his land who had fought in the field with 'the enemy of nature', Richard III. The 'north parts' – which he specified as the counties of Nottingham, York, Northumberland, Cumberland, Westmorland and the bishopric of Durham – were recognized as a separate 'country' in the later fifteenth century, formed in part by the particular duty to defend the rest of England from the Scots. The royal writ did not run in almost half of the far North. The Bishop of Durham ruled in the lands 'between Tyne and Tees', a palatinate where he exercised powers which, elsewhere, were monopolized by the Crown. The Archbishop of York ruled at Hexham. Annexed to the Borders were 'liberties' where royal authority had effectively been granted to Border barons, who held quasi-royal power. Unable to rule the far North without the greatest regional lords, kings granted sweeping military and civil powers to men whose wealth and power were already great, and then found themselves unable to control them. The great and deadly feud between the most powerful magnate families – the Nevilles of Middleham and the Percys – not only dominated the political history of the North in the mid fifteenth century but also drew in the conflicting parties at Henry VI's court and became a moving cause of the Wars of the Roses. The support of Richard Neville, Earl of Warwick, and of his great northern affinity (his personal following of dependants, allies, tenants and servants) had helped at the Battle of Towton in 1461 to establish Edward IV on the throne. The Percys were, for the while, routed, and the Nevilles seemed set to become unchallenged lords of the North East. But a decade later Warwick 'the Kingmaker' had fallen at Barnet, fighting not for, but against, the King he had made. The vast Neville lands, with their powerful affinity, were entrusted by Edward IV to his brother, Richard of Gloucester, with malign consequences for the Yorkist dynasty and the whole kingdom. In 1485 the Nevilles were eclipsed, and Richard's lands were in the new King's hands, but the great regional power of the Percy Earls of Northumberland remained to alarm a wary king.

*

In Ireland also several distinct societies shared the same island. Ireland was a land of many lordships, with many marches in between them. Once there had been high kings of Ireland, invested by sacred rites in hallowed places. The Anglo-Norman invasion of the twelfth century had usurped these kingships and intruded the claims of another king, the king of England, who as Lord of Ireland claimed jurisdiction over the whole island and thought to be high king himself. If Henry VII had visited his lordship of Ireland – though no Tudor monarch ever went there – he would have encountered a world remote from anything he knew. The island was divided – not neatly, for nothing here was straightforward – between the *Gaedhil* (the native Irish) and the *Gaill* (the settlers). To the Irish, the English of Ireland – the Anglo-Irish descendants of the first invaders of the twelfth-century conquest – were *Gaill* (foreign); they were bound by the same statutes and to the same allegiance as the English of England, and spoke English, yet they were also clearly distinct from the English of England, for they were born in Ireland, and most also spoke Irish. The English of Ireland lived in close but uneasy proximity to a culture profoundly different from their own.

The *Gaedhealtacht*, or Gaeldom of the native Irish, had its own ancient language, laws and culture, its own Christian traditions. And even hostile foreign observers in the late middle ages allowed that the Irish, though 'wild', were also good Christians. Hereditary bards were custodians and celebrants of the royal past of the Gaelic ruling dynasties.

Anglo–Irish and Gaelic Lordships in the Late Fifteenth Century

BREIFNE   Lordships

O' Malley   Ruling families

CO. LOUTH   Administrative areas

– – – –   Boundaries of provinces

———   Boundary of The Pale as defined by a statue of *1488*

INISHOWEN
O' Doherty

THE ROUTE
MacQuillan

MacSweenys

THE GLENS
Macdonnells

O' Cahan

TIRCONNELL
O' Donnell

KINEL MOAIN

CLANDEBOYE

O' Neill Boy   Carrickfergus

DUFFERIN

ARDS

ULSTER

TYRONE

Ballyshannon   O' Neill
Dungannon

KINELARTY
MacCartan   Savage

Armagh   Down   *IVEAGH*   *LECALE*

FERMANAGH
Maguire   THE
FEWS   *MOURNE*

Sligo   O' Rourke
O' Dowda   *ORIEL*
MacMahon
DARTRY   FARNEY

TIRAWLEY   MacDonaghs   *IOCHTAIR–CONNACHT*

Dundalk
CO.
LOUTH

MacJordan   *MOYLURG*
MacDermot   *BREIFNE*
MacRannell   Cavan

CLANCOSTELLO
MacCostello   O' Reilly

CLANMORRIS   *MAGHERY–CONNACHT*
MacMorris   *ANNALY*
O' Connors   O' Ferrall   Kells   Drogheda

O' Malley   MacDavid

MacWilliam   *CLANCONWAY*   Roscommon   CO. MEATH

CONNACHT   Dalton   Mullingar
HY MANY   Dillon   Trim
IAR CONNACHT   O' Kelly   Athlone   *MEATH*   CO.

O' Flaherty   O' Maghlin   *KINELEAGH*   Maynooth

Galway   Athenry   MacGeoghegan   Bermingham   Dublin

CLANRICARD   *SILANMGHY*   *OFFALY*   DUBLIN

Loughrea   O' Madden   *FERCALLO*   Connor   CO. KILDARE

O' Molloy   O' Dempsey

Macwilliam   *ELY*   *UPPER*   O' Toole

THOMOND   *ORMOND*   *OSSORY*   *LEIX*   O' Byrne   Wicklow

O' Brien   O' Carroll   MacGillapatrick   O' More

MacNamaras   *ARRA*   *ODOGH*   Carlow   Arklow

OWNEY   Mac I Brien   O' Brennan

MacMahons   Limerick   O' Mulryan   Kilkenny   Leighlinbridge   *Kinsellagh*

CLANWILLIAM   O' Duryer   CO.   *IDRONE*   MacMurrough

O' CONNELL   Burkes   *LIBERTY OF*   KILKENNY   Kavanagh

CO. LIMERICK   MacBriens   *TIPPERARY*   *LEINSTER*

CLANMAURICE   White   O' Morchoe

FitzMaurice   *MUNSTER*   Knight   Clonmel   Ross   *LIBERTY OF*

Tralee   LIBERTY   *FERMOY*   Carrick   *WEXFORD*   Wexford

OF KERRY   *DUHALLOW*   Roche Condon   *DECIES*   Powers   Waterford

Dingle   MacDonogh
MacCarthy   Dungarvan

MacCarthy Mór   *MUSKERRY*

DESMOND   Barrett   Cork

O' Sullivan Mór   *KERRYCURRIHY*   Youghal

IMOKILIY

O' Sullivan   *CARBERY*   *KINALEA*

BEARE   Barry Oge

MacCarthy Reagh   Kinsale

Barry Roe   Courcy

O' Mahony   O' Driscoll

Miles   50

Km   80

Using poetic conventions five or six centuries old, the bard evoked and eulogized the hospitality, piety, justice and martial prowess of his Gaelic lord and patron, and the fertility of the land during his rule. Historians recorded the genealogies and descent of the chiefly families. Hereditary judges were guardians of immemorial, seemingly unchanging laws.

The late medieval Gaelic world extended beyond the land of Ireland to the highlands and islands of western Scotland, divided only by the narrow North Channel. Gaelic Scotland and Ireland shared a common language and culture and, regardless of whether they lived in Scotland or Ireland, the people might be termed 'Irishry'. The inhabitants of Gaeldom recognized a common identity, and saw themselves as surrounded by *Gaill*. The MacDonald, John of Islay, fourth and last Lord of the Isles, whose great lordship stretched from the glens of Antrim in Ulster, along the west coast of Scotland from Kintyre to Glenelg, and through the Hebrides, had aspired to be high king of all Ireland. When in 1493 the Scottish Crown annexed his troublesome lordship and divided MacDonald's lands among his dependent chiefs, waves of migrants left Scotland for Ulster. Another wave followed in the 1540s after an abortive attempt to resurrect the lordship. The presence of so many Scots in north-east Ulster unsettled the province through most of the sixteenth century. The attempts by the government in Dublin to prevent intermarriage between Gaelic Scots and Irish, to contain the employment by Ulster lords of Scottish redshanks (mercenary foot soldiers), and to drive the Scots from Ulster perennially failed.

The land of Ireland was not easily delineated between highland and lowland, for broken rings of mountains arose in unexpected places, and even the lowland heart of Ireland, still undrained, was interspersed with lakes and bogs. Scrubby woodland covered half the island. To English observers the wildness of the terrain and the wildness of the people were all one. Where the country was 'nothing but woods, rocks, great bogs and barren ground', all untilled, the inhabitants were bound to live 'like wild and savage persons', by robbery and rustling. True, in many parts of the island neither the terrain nor political conditions encouraged patient tillage, but the English view of the Irish as semi-nomadic herdsmen and barbarians was a travesty. Corn was cultivated where the land suited. Yet those crops were often laid waste and burnt in the raids between Irish lords; incendiary methods which were indigenous but would be adopted by the English in time.

Every observer noted the transient nature of Irish society: the scattered settlements, houses which were easily erected and as easily abandoned, fields with temporary fences, the mobility of the great cattle herds which were the movable wealth of the lords and their dependants, and which could be driven to places of safety, or raided by enemies. Such transience was conducive to the growth of neither wealth nor population. The economy of Gaelic Ireland was primarily one of subsistence, and while coinage was known and used it was not central to its system of exchange. Taxation was exacted in the form of food and billeting of troops. There were probably less than half a million people in later medieval Ireland, and the population, unlike that of England, was not set to recover in the course of the sixteenth century. Much of the island was impenetrable and inaccessible; not only because of the difficulties of the terrain, the lack of roads and bridges and maps, but because of the dangers of ambush and attack unless travellers had the protection of the lord through whose territory they ventured. The lords themselves rode with armed bands.

To the English governors, Gaelic Ireland was 'the land of war' and the Irish were 'Irish enemies'. This was not because there was a state of open war, but because of the radical estrangement between the Gaelic Irish, beyond the Pale, and the English of Ireland, the Englishry, who lived in the 'land of peace', where English laws, civility and customs were preserved. The English lordship in Ireland had, by Henry VII's accession, contracted to the coastal plain between Dublin and Dundalk – the four loyal (or half-loyal) counties of Dublin, Kildare, Louth and Meath – plus the towns of Drogheda, Wexford, Waterford, Cork, Limerick and Galway and the royal fortress of Carrickfergus in the northeast. In the late fifteenth century a Pale was established, as in Calais, ringed around with a system of dykes and castles. In Dublin the institutions of English central and local government, and the concepts of authority which underlay them, were replicated: there was a Parliament, there was the king's Irish Council, there were the four courts of King's Bench, Chancery, Exchequer and Common Pleas. The law here was the common law; the language English, albeit of an archaic kind.

The Gaelic Irish were effectively banished from English Ireland, save as peasant labourers, disabled at law from holding land or office, beyond appeal to English law. On the edge of the English colony was a border world, which was hardly defensible. Even Dublin itself suffered predatory raids from the circling Irish; from the O'Byrnes of the Wicklow Mountains, the O'Mores of Leix and the O'Connors of Offaly. At the northern boundary of the Pale the Benedictine abbey of Fore was aggressively fortified in the mid fifteenth century against Gaelic incursions. In County Louth the families who paid both 'black rent' (protection money) to the Ulster chieftains to ransom their safety and taxes to the government of the Pale were recognizing the bewildering reality of lordship in Ireland.

The towns of Ireland were the heartlands of the Englishry. Their citizens spoke English, wore English dress, lived in houses like those in English towns, had well-ordered civic governments, prosperous trade and thriving religious institutions. There were about fifty towns of any size in early sixteenth-century Ireland; their inhabitants composing about one-tenth of the whole population of the island. Dublin, the royal capital, and the home of two cathedrals, was the largest city in Ireland and included most of Leinster in its hinterland. By the late sixteenth century its population was perhaps 6,000. It was the main port for the whole east coast. Like other Irish towns, Dublin was governed by a wealthy patriciate which dominated civic life through its ascendancy in the merchant guilds and its monopoly of office holding. A few families, closely tied by intermarriage, seemed to pass the city offices of mayor, sheriff, and alderman among themselves, although they were duly elected by the citizenry. In Galway, the second city of Ireland, fifteen merchant families formed so powerful and self-perpetuating an oligarchy that from 1484 until the mid seventeenth century only one mayor was elected from outside the group. Within these small, closed communities a strong sense of civic identity grew, fostered by a deep awareness of their difference from their Gaelic neighbours. By 1500 many of the coastal towns were isolated behind their defensible walls, dependent upon the sea for trade. It was usually easier for towns to send goods beyond Ireland than to each other, such were the difficulties of travel, but town merchants – 'grey merchants' – did buy and sell among the Irish. Inland towns were often overawed by local lords, as Galway was by the Clanrickard Burkes. Athenry in County Galway and Kilmallock in County Limerick were both razed and rebuilt during the sixteenth century. In the towns municipal and private philanthropy provided almshouses, hospitals and schools. In 1599 Sir John Harington wrote of his escape from the rigours of the army camp in Roscommon and of his arrival in the town of Galway, where his English translation of Ariosto's epic romance, *Orlando Furioso*, was being read by the young ladies of the town. Tudor governors in Dublin and Westminster always looked upon the Anglo-Irish of the towns as upholders of civility against the forces of Gaelic barbarism.

The Gaelic Irish lords had been driven back at the twelfth-century conquest, but that conquest had never been completed; the lords had reclaimed much of what had been lost, and most of Ireland was still theirs. Power in Gaelic Ireland was highly fragmented; there was no collective central authority, no governmental institutions. Each lordship was its own small society, with its own particular history, celebrated by its bards. Gaelic Ireland was ruled by lords whose power was dynastic and particularist, tribal rather than territorial, and lay in their personal headship of their own clans. The chieftains of the Gaelic ruling dynasties were always seeking to extend their overlordship and to become provincial kings once again. To the English king's claims to overlordship they were oblivious, and he could never be sovereign where the Irish chieftains held their lands and lordships and administered their own law without reference to him. In Gaelic Ireland lordship lay in the control of people rather than of territory: where a chief of a lesser sept (a branch of a clan) feared a lord sufficiently to rise with him, seek his protection or pay him tribute, then effectively he was subject. Yet he could appeal over the head of his own immediate lord to secure the protection of a more powerful lord, as indemnity against the lesser lord's oppression or neglect. In Ulster the O'Neill was lord of all the septs within Tyrone, but claimed authority also over the *uirríthe* (sub-kings) who were over-lords over their own people: over O'Cahan, MacMahon of Oriel, Maguire of Fermanagh, and O'Reilly of Breifne.

It was the intense competition between and within the Gaelic dynasties which had invited invasion in the first place. That competition continued, and it was not only the Yorkists who had a parricidal history. Between the O'Neills of Tyrone and the O'Donnells of Tirconnell lay an old contention over the tribute of Inishowen and for overlordship of Ulster. And within the clans of O'Neill and O'Donnell there was intense rivalry too. One sept of O'Neills was habitually hostile to the ruling O'Neills and consequently allied with the O'Donnells. In 1493 Conn O'Neill was murdered by his half-brother, Henry Óg, who made himself chief – the O'Neill – with the support of another branch of the family, the Sliocht Airt. Henry Óg was in turn murdered in 1498 by Conn's sons, 'in revenge of their father'. There was civil war too among the Maguires of Fermanagh, after long peace. In 1484 at the altar of the church of Aghalurcher, Gillapatrick Maguire, the chosen successor to his father, the chief, was slaughtered by his own five brothers. Almost every page of the Irish annals tells of murder within the ruling dynasties. Internecine struggles and raids between lordships were frequent; the consequence of a Gaelic inheritance system where succession was not the automatic right of the eldest son, and of the lack of any institutions of central government to control the warfare and violence which characterized political relations between lords who were concerned not only to extend their power but to defend their rights. But there was instability and rivalry too among the Anglo-Irish feudal lords who lived on the borders of the Gaelic world. In 1487 the 9th Earl of Desmond was murdered 'by his own people', allegedly at the instigation of his brother John Fitzgerald.

The first Anglo-Norman conquerors had been granted great lordships upon the ruins of the Irish supremacies. In Munster the Fitzgeralds became earls of Desmond in 1329 and possessors of palatine jurisdiction in Kerry, and they came to rule as independent princes over County Kerry, Limerick, Waterford and North Cork. At the same time the Butlers received the earldom of Ormond. They had extensive possessions in the south, especially in Tipperary, which they held as a liberty palatine, and in the area around Kilkenny, a 'second Pale'. In the late fifteenth century the Butlers and the Fitzgeralds held these areas still, against the extreme hostility of neighbouring Gaelic lords and of each other, and by means fitting to a rough border world. The Fitzgerald Desmonds maintained private armies of hired kerns (foot-soldiers) and gallo-glasses (professional axemen) ready to march against rival lords; not only against the Gaelic MacCarthy Mór but also against the Earl of Ormond. The feudal barons had to defend the vast lands and liberties they had gained. They had little help, and little interference, from their overlord, the absentee king in England, who depended on their power while disapproving of their methods. In this marcher society, conditioned to war, they were the arbiters and keepers of peace. In England, war was the king's war, peace the king's peace; not so in Ireland where Ormond and Desmond waged private war into the later sixteenth century.

To English government officials, who saw a chasm between how things were and how they thought they should be, these feudal lords had, by making so many accommodations with their Gaelic neighbours, become Irish themselves. It was true that the earls of Ormond and Desmond used Irish law as well as English law; and that in the north-west the Anglo-Irish Mayo Burkes were inaugurating their chiefs after the Gaelic manner. From the beginning, there was intermarriage between Anglo-Irish and Gaelic families; feudal lords took pledges and hostages, and fostered chiefs' children, as the Irish did; spoke Irish as well as English; employed Irish bards and wore Gaelic dress. But life on the edge of the 'land of war' entailed compromise: Gaelic allies were needed to overawe Gaelic enemies. And while bureaucrats safe in Dublin and Westminster saw the Anglo-Irish as 'degenerate', fallen from their race, they saw themselves as quite distinct from, and superior to, their Irish neighbours, for they held their lands and titles by feudal tenure and succeeded to their estates by primogeniture, a world away from the Gaelic system. When in 1488 Sir Richard Edgecombe tried to make the Anglo-Irish nobility accept certain conditions of pardon, they obdurately refused: they would rather be Irish, they said, appalled.

The Fitzgerald earls of Kildare, the feudal magnates who became ascendant in Ireland under the first Tudors, the bringers and the beneficiaries of English recovery there, had not been pre-eminent through the later middle ages. The 7th Earl (d.1478) had begun to restore the Kildare estates during a long period as chief governor for the king. In their perennial absence, the English kings, as Lords of Ireland, delegated their authority to their viceroys – their 'lieutenants' or 'deputy lieutenants' (for simplicity the term 'chief governor' will hereafter be used throughout). The position of chief governor was one of extraordinary power and autonomy. Pre-eminent in Ireland and isolated from the king in England, he had remarkable freedom to act. Garret Mór, the 8th Earl, attained huge power through his personal lordship over Palesmen, his clients, vassals and allies in Leinster, and also over many Gaelic and Anglo-Irish lords far beyond the Pale and the bureaucratic control of Dublin, who paid tribute to him in return for his protection. Though he might have looked like a high king come again, his lordship depended on the powers eventually entrusted to him as governor by the Lord of Ireland, Henry VII, a king who was always unwilling to send those whom he trusted and to trust those whom he sent.

*

At his accession Henry Tudor was in many ways fortunate. He was a king with few rivals. Richard III was dead with no child to succeed him. Henry had gained his throne because Richard had alienated most of the landed community of Yorkist England by his plantation of the southern counties with his northern followers, by breaking his own bonds of fidelity, by his usurpation and his presumed murder of the princes. 'Men of honour' had been uncertain where to give allegiance and, according to the *Great Chronicle of London*, most would as gladly have been French, subject to the ancient enemy, as ruled by Richard. Henry was the inheritor, if tortuously, of the Lancastrian claim, but as the vast royal affinity transferred allegiance to him, he also became the Yorkist claimant. He had support from Edward of York's former household and was married to Edward's daughter. Henry had no brothers and there was no focus among his kindred for political discontent. There was a kingmaker, and kingmakers were often dangerous to the kings they had made, but this one, Lord Stanley, soon to be elevated to Earl of Derby, was safely married to the King's redoubtable mother, Lady Margaret Beaufort, Countess of Richmond. The destruction during the last few years of the greatest English magnates – Clarence, Neville, Buckingham, Hastings – had left the major noble families leaderless, powerless to set up petty kingdoms in the regions, even if they had so wished. Whole regions were without traditional local rulers. In East Anglia, the de la Poles and Howards, loyal Yorkists, were displaced by John de Vere, Earl of Oxford, a stalwart ally of the new king. Henry chose not to give any one noble a commanding position in the Midlands; instead he allowed second-rank magnates to compete for regional dominance. The consequence would be a failure of law and order. In the South-West, royal favour was given almost exclusively to Giles, Lord Daubeney. Yet royal favour could not always guarantee loyalty; either from the lord who had been rewarded, or from the local political community, who might show a greater allegiance to their lord than to the King. A redistribution of patronage followed Bosworth, but it could not, of course, please everyone, and some thought themselves ill rewarded.

Richard's supporters were in disarray, not knowing whether to resist or to make terms with the new order. Some fought on, some were imprisoned, some were executed, some fled, but most made peace. And still Henry felt acutely threatened and insecure. He would never be free from the fear that a challenger would arrive with a stronger claim to the allegiance owed to blood. The mystery surrounding the disappearance of the young princes left the way open for hopes and promises of their return. Since foreign intervention had secured a change of king and dynasty in 1470 and 1471, and had helped to put Henry himself on the throne, foreign powers might intervene again, and for a rival contender.

Rebellion soon confirmed the sense and reality of the King's vulnerability. In the North, where allegiance to Richard had been strongest, there were disturbances in 1485 and 1486; risings stirred by the commons, not by landed society which showed a prudent loyalty to the new regime. At the end of 1485 Henry released the Earls of Northumberland and Westmorland, the leading lords of the North, but he restored them to their offices only during his pleasure, conditionally. From the first months of his reign Scotland showed its potential for disruption. In Ireland, the Earl of Kildare and the political community which he led held Parliament in October 1485, but still in Richard's name, not acknowledging the change of state.

A boy arrived in Ireland at the turn of 1486–7, claiming to be Edward Plantagenet, Earl of Warwick, nephew of the Yorkist kings. No one seemed to doubt him. In Ulster the annalist Cathal MacManus Maguire believed that of the two kings of England this boy, not the one 'of the Welsh race', was the true heir. But the real Earl of Warwick was captive in the Tower, and the 'feigned boy', Lambert Simnel, had been set up by irreconcilable Yorkists; the plot was led, if not instigated, by John de la Pole, Earl of Lincoln, and backed by Margaret of York, dowager Duchess of Burgundy, whose court was a perennial centre of Yorkist intrigue. By May 1487 Henry knew that a rebel fleet had sailed westward to invade Ireland. On 24 May the boy was crowned 'Edward VI' at Christ Church Cathedral, Dublin, with a diadem borrowed from a statue of the Virgin Mary. The Earl of Kildare was kingmaker, with the whole Anglo-Irish political establishment concurring. Only Waterford protested. Henry thought of leading an army into his rebellious Lordship, but on 4 June the rebels came to him. The rebel army landed in Cumberland and advanced through Yorkshire. The Earl of Northumberland, with the largest private army in England, moved, not south to aid the King, but north. At Stoke by Newark-on-Trent on 16 June great armies met in what was to be the last battle of the Wars of the Roses. It was a decisive victory for Henry, whose loyal supporters heavily outnumbered the rebels. Perhaps 4,000 Irish kerns, who fought dauntlessly but without armour, were cut down.

In 1485 a new and terrifying epidemic had swept through England, and only England. This was the sweating sickness; *sudor Anglicus*, the 'English sweat'. The people, who were addicted to prophecy, interpreted this as a portent presaging the harshness with which Henry would 'sweat' his subjects. This heavy lordship took various forms. Henry, raised in penury in the luxurious courts of foreign princes, determined from the first to be rich, for wealth brought power and security. In England there was a tradition that taxation should be raised only by consent, the consent of the representatives of the community of the realm in Parliament. That principle was stated more and more insistently through the later middle ages, and was the reason why demands for non-parliamentary taxes were couched in appeasing terms: a 'loving contribution', a 'benevolence' (or to Henry's increasingly cynical subjects, a 'malevolence'). In peacetime kings were meant to be self-sufficient, to 'live of their own', and the prudent remembered how, in the Peasants' Revolt of 1381, half of England had risen against a novel and exorbitant tax. French kings imposed taxes arbitrarily; English kings did so at their peril.

Henry was, from his accession, the greatest royal landowner since the Norman Conquest. He held five times more land than Henry VI had done and learnt from his predecessor's disastrous example: what he gained he held, never alienating these vast possessions. To Henry came the duchy of Lancaster, the whole estates of the duchy of York and the Mortimer earldom of March. A ruthless efficiency marked the administration of these royal estates, especially under Sir Richard Empson, Chancellor of the Duchy of Lancaster 1505–9. Since the King had few scruples about disinheriting lawful heirs, he confiscated other noble estates, like those of the Berkeleys. Such affronts to the sanctity of landed property and inheritance had been the downfall of kings before him. With land came power; not only wealth but lordship, that lordship over men which ensured service in peace and war. The King gained a greater fund of patronage than his predecessors had ever held, and with it came an advance of royal government in the shires. Retaining followers and dependants among local gentry, who would then owe the King loyalty and service, by grants of local offices was a vital way of expanding and maintaining the royal affinity. Where the great nobility had upheld their ascendancy in the provinces by grants of the offices of stewards, surveyors, receivers of lordships and constables of castles, now these offices were in the royal gift. In 1489 indictments in Warwickshire for the offence of illegal retaining – that is, the assembly of a force of 'mean men' of low rank on a short-term basis – gave warning not only that landowners should not raise forces for their violent confrontations, but also that the only retaining there must be by the King. Local officials became the King's own men, and offices were used to forge a new and politically vital relationship between the Crown and the gentry which would mark the following century.

Throughout his reign Henry pursued a policy of exacting every penny of his fiscal rights. The King was the head of the feudal system of land tenure, and much of his income derived from his rights in the lands of his tenants-in-chief. To discover these rights Henry instigated a great series of investigative commissions from early in his reign. But the King's relentless pursuit and exploitation of his prerogative rights and revenues was to confront the private interests and personal security of his leading subjects and their families. This was an exercise of royal power which, although within the law, became so extreme and invasive that the people affected came not only to resent and to fear it but to doubt its legitimacy. If the ways which the King sought to find security in wealth became too oppressive, or arbitrary, or of dubious legality, then he was in danger of undermining that security. In *Utopia* More's fictional character Hythloday recalled a series of fiscal dodges: suppose a king and his councillors recommended increasing the value of money when they paid debts and devaluing it when they collected revenues; suppose they unearthed moth-eaten laws, long unused, which no one remembered and everyone had transgressed. Such dodges could be made to wear the 'mask of justice'. All of these were practised by Henry and his councillors, though More named no names.

In 1496 a Florentine observer noted that 'the King is feared rather than loved'. Harsh necessity drove new rulers, for new regimes were full of danger. Henry, anticipating Niccolò Machiavelli's advice in *The Prince* (written in 1513) – which would so shock and so intrigue the English – as he was forced to choose between being feared and loved, decided that it was much safer to be feared. He devised and developed particular ways of having 'many persons in his danger at his pleasure'. From early in his reign he collected bonds from his greatest subjects. Those fined – perfectly legally – for offences committed, or made to enter bonds for future good behaviour, bound themselves to pay large – sometimes huge – amounts of money. But as long as they retained his royal favour Henry would graciously demand only a little of the debt, year by year. By this means not only the offender, but also his kin and friends who stood surety for him, were linked in a chain of obligation. Descendants, too, were held in awe and in obedience. The bonds were used not only – though perhaps principally – as a way of augmenting royal revenue, but as a way of guaranteeing submission and allegiance.

Edmund Dudley, President of the King's Council by 1506, and with the best reason to know, believed that the King intended them only as a threat; 'verily his inward mind was never to use them'.

In the last years of his reign Henry's use of bonds to restrain his greater subjects became more oppressive. Between 1502 and 1509 two-thirds of the English peerage lay under financial penalties, either on their own behalf or as sureties for others. The most extreme instance was his dealing with George Neville, Lord Abergavenny, who was indicted in 1507 for retaining a private army of 471 men, and fined £70,000. That vast sum was commuted to a fine of £5,000, payable over a decade, but there were oppressive conditions: that he should not enter Kent, Surrey, Hampshire or Sussex, the area where his estates and power lay, without royal licence, ever. He was the only peer put on trial for the offence of retaining, which was widespread. But his real offence was far graver. In 1497 he had, allegedly, incited Edmund de la Pole, Earl of Suffolk, to desert the King and join the rebel army; the supreme disloyalty, the epitome of treason. That his leading nobles, upon whose military power a king without a standing army must depend, might revolt was a spectre which continued to haunt Henry. The Florentine observer who judged in 1496 that Henry was 'rather feared than loved' believed then that 'if fortune allowed some lord of the royal blood to rise', and Henry had to take the field, his people would abandon him.

*

In 1491 a new and more dangerous pretender, foretold by prophecy, had appeared. Richard Plantagenet, Duke of York, so it was claimed, had providentially escaped the Tower and murder at his uncle's hands, and had been secretly conveyed abroad. Now he returned to claim his throne. In this brilliant impostor, Perkin Warbeck, Yorkist sympathies and hopes were revived; testimony not only to the claims of blood but to growing alienation from Henry VII. Support for the pretender came not only from the disaffected in the country, but from the heart of the King's own household. For six years Warbeck was welcomed in the courts of Europe – by Maximilian, King of the Romans, James IV of Scotland, Charles VIII of France and Margaret of Burgundy. For Margaret, he was truly her nephew returned to life; for the others, the perfect instrument for the pursuit of their diplomatic and territorial ambitions. This pretender, the Yorkists' 'puppet' and 'idol', several times threatened a Yorkist restoration and renewed civil war.

Peace with Scotland had been preserved, at first. War had threatened in October 1485 and again early in 1488, but a three-year truce concluded in July had held, surviving the death in June 1488 of James III in battle against his rival lords at Sauchieburn. That further truces were made in 1488, 1491 and 1492 signalled not amity, but lack of it. With France, England's other ancient enemy and Scotland's old ally, Henry had at first attempted neutrality while Charles VIII sought to annexe Brittany. Henry tried to arbitrate a settlement between the kingdom and the duchy which had harboured him in exile, but he failed. In 1489 and again in 1490 he sent forces to protect Breton independence, and planned a third expedition. Such provocative intervention was buttressed by parallel alliances concluded with Maximilian, Holy Roman Emperor at Dordrecht in February 1489 and with Ferdinand of Aragon and Isabella of Castile at Medina del Campo in March. When Charles VIII married Duchess Anne of Brittany in December 1491 Brittany's independence was lost, and with it so much English expenditure. It was in the midst of this intense diplomatic activity, and as an instrument of it, that Perkin Warbeck appeared.

As before, the pretender came first to Ireland. Arriving at Cork in November 1491, 'Richard Plantagenet' received the allegiance of Desmond and with him, of Munster. Kildare offered no support: neither did he oppose. Forces were sent from England to secure the midlands and the south of Ireland, and in the shadow of this military presence in June 1492 Kildare was removed from the office of chief governor. Kildare's disgrace and the King's patronage of the Fitzgeralds' Butler rivals inexorably renewed the old feud, and fighting between their retinues followed. Abandoned by Kildare, the English colony lay open to plundering and burning by the Irish. Warbeck left Ireland, but would return.

Warbeck's removal to the French court in the spring of 1492 spurred preparations for a campaign against France. Great forces and taxes were levied for a war which was hardly fought at all. After postponing the expedition three times, Henry crossed to Calais at the head of an army of 15,000 in October 1492, and in November was effectively paid by Charles VIII to go away: the price of his freedom to pursue grand designs in Italy. In *Utopia* More's Hythloday recalled a king and his council devising a make-believe war so that a fortune could be raised on the pretext of waging it, and then when the money was collected a ceremonious peace would follow. Certainly this was how the more cynical of Henry's subjects regarded the French campaign. At Étaples in November

1492 Charles promised to expel the pretender. Warbeck was bought and sold. From France, he migrated to the court of Margaret of Burgundy. Relieved of foreign war, Henry was more ready to meet any challenge from home, and he would need to be.

Now Henry turned to pacify Ireland; not only to tame the disloyal colony but also – so he told the French king – to conquer the 'wild Irish'. Rebellion in Ireland posed a double danger, for it opened the way for the King's enemies to use the island for the invasion of England. At Trim in September 1493 a great Council was held to seal the reconciliation of the Anglo-Irish lords with the King, and with each other. Kildare and fifteen other lords entered massive bonds to keep the peace and to relinquish Gaelic customs. A year later a new lieutenant was appointed: the King's younger son Henry, Duke of York, aged four, with Sir Edward Poynings as his deputy, the chief governor. Poynings' mission to Ireland that October – intended to curb the disruptive tendencies of the feudal lords and to prevent the subversion of royal institutions of government – left a lasting political legacy. That winter the Irish Parliament, meeting at Drogheda, enacted measures which affirmed Ireland's constitutional inferiority, the subordination of Crown government in Ireland to that of England. 'Poynings' law' provided that no Irish Parliament could meet without royal licence and that all measures to be submitted to Parliament had first to be approved by King and Council in England. English officials replaced Anglo-Irish ones in high offices of state and in the judiciary. Early in 1495 the restive Kildare was arrested, charged with treasonable contact with the King's Gaelic enemies and with conspiring with the Earl of Desmond and James IV of Scotland to overthrow English rule in Ireland. He was sent captive to England.

Far from there being peace in Ireland, universal rebellion threatened. Forswearing allegiance to Henry, Desmond rallied support throughout Munster for Warbeck. Gaelic chiefs of the north – O'Donnell of Tirconnell and O'Neill of Clandeboye – declared for Warbeck, and so did Clanrickard Burke in the west. In August 1495 O'Donnell sailed to Scotland to form a league with James IV. That the real ambitions of the Irish lords were for their own dynasties rather than that of York made their hostility and confederacy no less alarming. In July 1495 Warbeck – cast back from a disastrous invasion attempt in Kent – landed at Youghal, and the rebel army besieged Waterford, but without success. Desmond withdrew into the wilds of Munster, and Warbeck fled to refuge at the Scottish court. Henry, always suspicious, always reluctant to trust his magnates, had particular reason to distrust the Anglo-Irish lords who, distrusting him, had been manifestly disloyal. Yet the King now determined to rest his rule in Ireland upon Kildare and to use the Earl's personal lordship in Ireland to strengthen his own. Kildare returned to Ireland as chief governor in October 1496.

More dangerous than any shadowy conspiracy abroad or any disloyalty in Ireland were the discoveries of Yorkist plots in England and of the defection of those who had seemed most loyal. Spies and double-agents sent terrifying reports of conspiracy, and Sir Robert Clifford, a Yorkist fugitive, turned king's evidence. By the end of 1494 Henry believed what he had suspected before; that Sir William Stanley, his Chamberlain, and John, Lord Fitzwalter, his Steward, men who had great power and much to lose, were secret Yorkist supporters. Even the allegiance of those who had received the greatest favour was still not secure. Betrayal at the heart of the royal household offered the possibility even of assassination. Early in 1495 great show trials were held, and among those indicted were leading figures in the realm: Stanley; Fitzwalter; Sir Simon Mountford, a leading Warwickshire landowner; William Daubney, Clerk of the Jewels; Thomas Thwaites, ex-Treasurer of Calais; and even the Dean of St Paul's and the head of the English Dominican friars. Their alienation from Henry's policies was clear. Simon Mountford, who had once held high office in Warwickshire, had been consigned to the outer circles of power. He had watched the serious crisis in order engendered by the King's mismanagement, while the King's own men, responsible for much of the disorder, went unpunished but not unrewarded. Maybe Stanley and Mountford were indeed guilty of conspiracy, but they may also have been sacrificed as a terrible warning to others and to quieten the turbulent Midlands, where their lands and power had lain. Stanley had allegedly said that if Warbeck were Richard Plantagenet then he would not oppose him. This was a denial of his fealty to the King, but to hold that York had a better claim than Tudor was no more than was generally believed. The atmosphere of pervasive suspicion intensified. In October 1495 Parliament passed the *De Facto* Act, testimony to the deep insecurity that still existed a decade after Bosworth: those fighting now for Henry could not be charged with treason by some future king, just as Henry would not account traitors those who had fought for Richard. This indemnity was granted just as Warbeck sought support in Scotland and the most dangerous stage of his conspiracy began.

At the Scottish court James IV received Warbeck as Richard Plantagenet, and married him to Lady Katherine Gordon ('the brightest
ornament in Scotland', according to the smitten Warbeck). Preparations
began for 'Richard IV' to challenge Henry's throne. After the murder in
1489 of the chastened but doubtfully loyal and awesomely powerful 4th
Earl of Northumberland, Henry had allowed no local magnate to rule
as a northern prince. Instead, he had given personal responsibility there
to Richard III's supporter, Thomas Howard, Earl of Surrey, who, after
having fought for Richard at Bosworth, had all to prove. The Howard
estates and power, only gradually restored to him, lay in distant East
Anglia. As the Stewart and Plantagenet army laid waste the Border and
prepared to invade in the autumn of 1496, Henry feared the enemy but
also feared his northern nobility and gentry. But they armed for the
defence – perhaps more against the traditional enemy than against the
Yorkist challenger – and the invasion of Warbeck inspired no answering
rebellion in the North. Honour demanded retaliation. War was declared
against Scotland, and massive forces arrayed to strike. The Stewart–
Plantagenet host crossed the border at Coldstream on 20–22 September.
When there was no uprising in his favour, 'Richard IV' withdrew, and
James IV, too, made a swift tactical withdrawal rather than face English
forces.

As a great army marched north towards Berwick, beyond recall, news
came of a rising in the West, to which all England lay open. The rebellion
began in mid May in Cornwall, the Celtic western tip of the kingdom: a
popular protest against an exceptionally heavy and ubiquitous levy of
direct taxation, and an indictment of Tudor rule by the whole community
of the West. Lord Audley, with at least twenty-five members of the
gentry communities of Dorset and Somerset, once the heartland of Henry
Tudor's support, joined the revolt. The proclamation of 'Richard IV'
against the 'misrule and mischief' of an oppressive King, against the
'crafty means' whereby he levied 'outrageous' sums, had found no
response in the North, but the West shared his views. And the revolt
was not simply about taxes. The rebels' intention was to march to
London, to free the captive Earl of Warwick from the Tower, and restore
the Yorkists. They marched, unopposed, through southern England
from Cornwall to Kent, and news of their advance caused many to
question their allegiance. At Ewelme in Oxfordshire, Lord Abergavenny,
who was sharing a bed with Edmund de la Pole, Earl of Suffolk, asked
him, 'If a man will do ought [anything], what will you do now it is time?'

The nobility might, if they had chosen, have renewed the Wars of the Roses. Even as the rebel army advanced to Blackheath, on the edge of London and close to the Tower, they were at first unopposed. Their hope was that the men of Kent would join them. Lord Daubeney, Lord Chamberlain and commander of the royal forces, held back from engaging the rebels whose leaders were his own allies in the South-West. Yet at this great crisis for the Tudor dynasty, the political nation of central southern England rallied to Henry, and the rebels were cut down at Blackheath on 17 June. Warbeck landed at Land's End on 7 September; he had missed his chance. For years after, inquisitions probed the extent of the disloyalty. Henry's victory was followed by no sense of security, by no relaxation of his policies, but rather by a darker period of repression.

The cause of the White Rose would not die while claimants lived. Warbeck, the 'may-game lord', who had played his part so well, was executed in November 1499, and with him the dangerous, but guiltless, true Earl of Warwick. That Edmund de la Pole was allowed to flee abroad, not once but twice, was an uncharacteristic and expensive failure of vigilance by Henry. From 1501 de la Pole found refuge at the court of the Habsburgs, and their control of the fugitive allowed Emperor Maximilian and Archduke Charles to extort vast sums from Henry, in the guise of loans. Henry paid in order to ransom the peace and security of his faltering dynasty.

*

By 1503 the heir to the throne was a ten-year-old boy, raised among women in the Queen's household, untutored in the arts of kingship: Henry, Duke of York, the future Henry VIII. The death of Prince Arthur in April 1502, and the advancing age and ill health of the King, offered once again the alarming prospect of – at best – a royal minority. In the Calais garrison, some time between 1504 and 1506, leading figures talked of the succession. Some expected Edmund de la Pole to succeed, some Edward Stafford, Duke of Buckingham, both of the House of York, but even two decades after the Tudor accession no one mentioned the King's son. There was deep anxiety about the future, and some were trying to secure their own positions 'howsoever the world turn', in case the dynasty were overthrown. It was at the first succession that a new dynasty was most vulnerable, and the fate of the sons of Edward IV was never forgotten. Prince Henry was taught by the poet John Skelton, who told him sad stories of the deaths of kings.

A sense of impermanence and unease was still pervasive in Henry's last years. All his great achievements – the vast acquisition of royal land and wealth, the defeat of internal enemies, peace with Scotland and European neighbours, English recovery in Ireland, the brilliant dynastic marriages for his children: Arthur to Catherine of Aragon, Margaret to James IV of Scotland – were the consequence of his own political wisdom and mastery. Yet the very strength of his royal position, resting as it did upon his intensely personal control, might prove evanescent. Henry's deep circumspection, his suspicion and secretiveness, led him to trust few and to listen to few. There was little faction in his reign, for this king, unlike his son, set himself apart and was not easily manipulated. The nobility, traditionally the natural counsellors to a king, were summoned to illumine and magnify the magnificence of his court, and gradually given greater trust in the localities in his later years, but they were eclipsed at the centre of policy. When Warbeck issued his proclamation as 'Richard IV', complaining that the King favoured low-born councillors, he was not entirely wrong. Henry chose men whose authority stemmed not from their lands or titles, but from his choosing of them.

Contemporaries, chroniclers and rebels all attested to the King's independence of judgement, and named the same names of those who had some influence with him: great clerical officers of state like Cardinal Morton, Archbishop of Canterbury and Richard Fox, Bishop of Winchester; household peers and knights like Giles, Lord Daubeney and Sir Thomas Lovell; common lawyers and administrators like Sir Reynold Bray, Sir Richard Empson and Edmund Dudley. Their status was diverse, but the basis of their authority was common: it lay in their membership of the royal Council. The Council, with its judicial, administrative and executive function, omnicompetent under the King and at the centre of his government, gained a new supremacy during this reign. Under Henry VII the Council was a large, undifferentiated body with multiple roles, yet the councillors attendant upon the King constituted a vital 'inner ring' of government. Members of the Council were closely associated with the King in the daily conduct of government, not least because the King was usually present at its meetings. The crisis of 1497 had consequences for the Council. The Spanish ambassador wrote that Henry had shaken off the influence of some of his Council, and would have liked to reduce it still further. Increasingly, power was given to inner councils within the Council – such as the Council Learned in Law (from 1498 or 1499) – in the hands of fewer men, mainly lawyers.

The position of councillor gave the opportunity for bribery, personal aggrandizement and profit. The attacks upon Edmund Dudley and his agents were vituperative, and in 'A Ballad of Empson' William Cornysshe of the King's Chapel accused Sir Richard Empson of extortion and corruption.

> And whom thou hatest, he was in jeopardy
> Of life and goods, both high and low estate
> For judge thou were, of treason and felony.

Yet government should be a matter not of expediency but of morality. When, in 1501, Sir Robert Plumpton lost a law suit to Empson, Dame Elizabeth de la Pole besought 'the good Lord that redeemed me and all mankind upon the holy cross' to be Plumpton's helper and to give him power to resist the 'malicious enmity and false craft of Master Empson'. The accusations of intervention in legal suits where the King had an interest were not without foundation. Critics of the Crown's policy traditionally gave the blame to 'evil councillors', yet everything Henry's councillors did was in the King's name, and almost nothing escaped his close scrutiny and surveillance. Even Empson's own petition for a grant of stewardship in 1507 was amended in the King's own hand from a grant for life to a grant 'during pleasure'.

As the King's Chamber, rather than the Exchequer, came to gather and control ever more income, Henry extended his personal hold upon government. This was far more than simply a means of amassing revenue; it was at the centre of the administrative system and a source of the King's political as well as financial control. Francis Bacon, a century later, wrote *The History of the Reign of King Henry the Seventh*: it was an account of 'this Solomon of England' – 'for Solomon also was too heavy upon his people in exactions'. He told a story of a monkey set by a courtier to destroy a notebook in which Henry recorded secret observations and memoranda about particular people; whom to reward, whom to be wary of. The story, which was probably apocryphal and borrowed from *Utopia*, was nevertheless revealing of the manner of this king's rule; so intensely personal, so minatory.

On 24 April 1509 Edmund Dudley, the most ruthless agent of the King's harsh legalism, who had been most relentless in exacting forfeiture and fines, was sent to the Tower. Henry VII had died three days earlier. Dudley and Empson, who were held most responsible for the 'briberies and tyrannies' of the reign, were charged first with extortion, then with treason. Whether they were guilty of conspiring against the new King, as they were accused, was doubtful, but it was true that they had marshalled armed retinues in March and April 1509 to preserve order in the City, which the King's mortal illness threatened, and to save themselves. Awaiting the penalty for treason, 'a dead man by the King's laws', Dudley prepared a list of all those persons whom Henry VII, his late master, had wronged 'contrary to the order of his laws'. To these Henry had by his last will ordered that restitution be made. The list was a long one, of more than a hundred names, including some of Henry's lesser as well as his greater subjects. Dudley remembered how the Bishop of London had sworn by his priesthood that the charges against him were untrue. Henry had treated bishops with the same harshness as temporal lords. Dudley admitted that people had paid huge fines or lingered in prison for 'light [trivial] matters', upon 'light surmise'; that they had been 'hardly treated and too sore'; had had a 'very hard end', 'to their utter undoing', 'contrary to conscience'. The bonds of obligation had been drawn up 'because the King would have them so'. The policy was the King's and he, as a devout Christian, must repent it.

After Henry's death, the chroniclers, remembering his many politic virtues, remembered too the avarice that undermined them. Avarice was no venial failing, but one of the seven deadly sins. Sinning Christians must be penitent and make restitution. Where penitence and restitution failed, kings too might become subject to a tyrant – the Devil in Hell.

2

Family and Friends

At midsummer in many English towns and villages in the later middle ages, pageant wagons rolled through the narrow streets, stopping along the procession way. On these wagons actors played God, Christ, the Virgin Mary, Noah and his wife, and, dressed as demons, they danced among the people. The mystery plays, put on by the craft guilds of the towns, were the most popular drama ever staged in England. Most towns played only a single biblical scene, but in some, like York, Chester and Wakefield, the greatest cycles of the mystery plays told the whole of salvation history from the Creation to the Last Judgement. Play by play, all day long, the divine plan was revealed, the events of the Old Testament prefiguring the New. This was a society in which devotion to God and belief in the elements of the Christian faith were assumed; in which there were sanctions, worldly and otherworldly, against those who did not give visible witness of their faith; in which membership of the Church and obedience to its teachings were profound social duties. These plays spoke to the unlettered, the unlearned, and to all Christians, and taught them what they must believe.

The mystery plays begin and end in heaven. First, God the Father appears and defines Himself: first and last, without beginning or end, maker unmade, Three in One, Almighty. He creates heaven. Enter Satan, the fallen angel who, in his pride, has rebelled against God and is cast out of heaven. Creating the world by His Word, God sets in an earthly paradise the first man and the first woman, Adam and Eve, formed in the divine likeness. In the Garden of Eden, Eve is tempted by the serpent and eats the forbidden fruit of the tree of knowledge and she tempts Adam to do the same. For their disobedience, the original sin, they are cast out of Paradise and from the divine presence, and their first sin is transferred to their descendants forever. The Fall of Man is complete when Cain kills his brother Abel. From this abyss of evil, mankind can be saved only by God's intervention and mercy. He sends the Flood to drown the sinful world, and then from the destruction saves some. Noah, his wife and family, and two animals of each kind, board an ark as the waters rise. Noah is a man who walks with God, obedient to His command. So is Abraham who agonizingly, unquestioningly, prepares to kill his innocent son, Isaac, a willing sacrifice and prophetic of the greatest sacrifice in the world.

In the East Anglian 'play called Corpus Christi', which was written down sometime after 1468, a debate is staged in the parliament of heaven. It enshrines the understanding of man's salvation and redemption prevailing at the end of the middle ages. According to the figure of Justice, man's offence against God is endless and so must be the punishment. Should man be saved? 'Nay, nay, nay!' Yet according to Mercy, 'Endless sin God endless may restore.' Man cannot be restored to divine favour until satisfaction has been made, but in his wretchedness he has nothing to offer to compensate for so great an offence, and all that he has is God's anyway. Only God has the power to satisfy the debt, but it is mankind that owes it. In the play a council is held among the Trinity, and Christ offers Himself, willing self-sacrifice, to atone to His Father for mankind's offence and redeem mankind: 'Father, he that shall do this must be both God and man . . . I am ready to do this deed'. Archangel Gabriel is sent to tell Mary, blessed among women, that she, although a virgin, will bear God's son – mother and maiden. His salutation – 'Hail Mary, full of grace' – is the one that all Catholics will use to her forever after. The Christ-child is born in a stable, poor and lowly, and shepherds and kings come to adore Him, their joy suffused with sorrow as they contemplate His suffering to come.

The late medieval preoccupation with Christ's human nature led to a devotion to His mother, the Virgin Mary. The plays tell in parallel the story of her life, and that of the cousins and aunts, family and friends whom Christ gained when He was made man. All the mystery plays lead to 'such a sorrow' that will pierce 'even through his mother's heart'; to a mother grieving at the foot of the Cross. At the heart of the mystery plays was the Passion Play, for it was above all Christ's Passion which was the focus of late medieval spirituality: not Christ in majesty, but Christ in His vulnerable humanity suffering on the Cross, His body broken, bleeding, dying. The plays depicted the extremity of Christ's suffering, and showed Him tempted, betrayed, mocked and tortured; hanging on a cross, crowned with thorns, His arms outstretched in compassionate self-immolation. Since Christ has taken upon Himself a human nature, He suffers human doubt and desolation; feels Himself forsaken. Without sin Himself, he has come to take mankind's sin upon Him and to redeem the human race. He tells His mother from the Cross:

> And, woman, thou knowest that my Father of heaven me sent
> To take this mankind of thee, Adam's ransom to pay.

He dies to save those who torment and crucify Him, the sublime example of loving one's enemies. From the tragedy of His Passion comes mankind's salvation.

The cycle of plays enacted, scene by scene, and brought to life the events narrated in the Apostles' Creed, which all the faithful were taught from an early age. In church windows, on rood screens, on altars the twelve Apostles were portrayed, each carrying a banner with the article of the Creed attributed to him. St Peter bore the first: '*Credo in Deum, Patrem Omnipotentem* [I believe in God, Father Almighty].' The text was made available in English to assist the devout to a fuller understanding. In the fourteenth-century *Lay Folks Mass Book* the Creed was written in verse:

> Under Ponce Pilate pined (tormented) was He,
>> us to save
> Down on the ✠ and dead He was,
>> and laid in His grave.
> The soul of Him went to hell.

Moving from the past to the future, the play cycle ends in heaven, with God in judgement. At the Last Judgement, the collective end of time, men and women will be judged not by what they have promised, but what they have done. The saved will be those who have obeyed Christ's great commandments – to love God and one's neighbour as oneself – and seen Him in the poor and wretched. The rejected, the damned, will be those who have disobeyed. The plays end with the vision of hell's mouth gaping and the sound of the interminable lamentation of the damned.

In the plays the audience saw the profane amidst the holy, and witnessed the real world intruding into the Gospel story. Alongside the figures of Christ and His Apostles were shepherds portrayed as turbulent adolescents; unjust judges; Noah's shrewish wife; a jealous Joseph in a May to December marriage; raging tyrants – figures, in their frailties, closer by far to the audience's own lives than were the Holy Family. There were quarrels among the players about who should take each part, and who should pay for the production. The plays were staged by the craft guilds of the towns, often with particular appropriateness to their calling: at York the shipwrights presented the building of the ark; the fishermen the scene of the Flood; the bakers the Last Supper. The rich mercers put on the most expensive and last play: the Last Judgement.

The plays, written in English, probably by the clergy, were intended to teach, to inspire, to admonish, so that the audience might remember that they were subject to the same human frailty, the spiritual blindness and lack of charity which made Peter deny Christ, or Thomas doubt the Resurrection, or even made Judas betray and the soldiers crucify Christ. They were left with a vision of judgement. But compellingly, through pity and grief and love for the Virgin and her divine Son, the audience could understand the price of salvation, the depth of divine love, the sublimity of Christ's sacrificial death for mankind, the need for sorrow and repentance of sin, the joyful possibility of heaven at last. Before Christ's Incarnation and Passion all men were judged guilty of Adam's sin and had lost heaven. Thereafter, there was hope of salvation. Eden would be restored, but not in this world.

*

Why was the 'play called Corpus Christi', the body of Christ? Because this narrative of salvation through grace was originally performed at the great liturgical feast of the later middle ages, Corpus Christi. With Corpus Christi, in May or June, the great cycle of feasts of the Church commemorating the Redemption was brought to a close. Yet it stood apart from the liturgical sequence which narrated the events in Christ's life – from Christmas, which celebrated His nativity and the mystery of the Incarnation; His presentation in the Temple at Candlemas; through Easter which celebrated the Resurrection; to the feasts of His Ascension and Whitsun or Pentecost, which recalled the descent of the Holy Spirit and the foundation of the Church. Corpus Christi was the time to celebrate the whole work of God, the redeeming power of Christ, rather than to sorrow for His Passion, which was particularly remembered, in deepest mourning, on Good Friday. The feast of Corpus Christi had been instituted to celebrate the sacrament of the altar, the Mass, which was divine miracle and mystery, God among men, the focus of the hopes and longings of all Christians.

The Mass was offered by and to God, for the living and the dead. In every church and chapel, on every altar at every celebration, Christ's redemptive sacrifice was re-enacted, and the blood of forgiveness made endlessly available to Christians. At the words of the consecration, Christ's own words to His disciples at the Last Supper, the elements of bread and wine were transformed, transubstantiated, by Christ's own working, through a priest as channel of divine grace, into the very body and blood of Christ. To the eyes of faith, God had transcended the laws of nature. Bread was no longer bread, wine no longer wine; the consecrated Host elevated above the priest's head was not what the eyes saw, but Christ returned to earth. The believer gazing upon the Host, thinking of Christ's Passion, was transported to Calvary. Now bread, now God, the host was the promise of satisfaction for sin, deliverance from evil, safety from danger, the promise of reconciliation with God. As the body of Christ, it represented the Church itself, and was the centre of the entire religious system, the focus of popular allegiance and devotion: Corpus Christi.

The full public sung Mass included these events: an account of the predicament of fallen man and confession of sin; the declaration of redemption in the hymn *Gloria*; readings from the Epistles and Gospels and the Creed; the offertory, during which the priest prepared the bread and wine for sacrifice, and the congregation prepared itself by prayer; the canon, the consecration of the bread and wine; the elevation of the Host; the communion by the priest and – very occasionally – by the people; the post communion, and priestly blessing of the people which imparted salutary protection. All the while, the priest celebrated apart, at the high altar, separated from the people by the rood screen, whispering low and in Latin the words of the rite which were too sacred for the laity to know. Yet they, praying their own prayers, knew that a miracle took place before their eyes and, seeing, believed. As the sacring bell rang and candles were lit, they knelt, hands raised, as the priest elevated the Host. At that moment grace was imparted and special blessings flowed: they would not go blind or suffer sudden death that day, angels would count the steps they took to the Mass towards their merit. This was a moment of intense private devotion, the way to individual forgiveness and sanctification, but it was also the bond of human charity, the source of Christian fellowship. Communion was common union; the unity of Christ and His Church. Corpus Christi.

The faithful made sure that they witnessed the miracle of the Mass often. The parish Mass, celebrated on Sundays and holy days at the high altar, following the order specified in missal, breviary and processional, was not the only Mass which the faithful experienced. There were daily celebrations besides: dawn or 'morrow Mass', 'low' Masses, votive or requiem Masses, Masses in honour of Our Lady, or of the name of Jesus, or of special saints. These were celebrated at side altars, by guild or chantry priests, and here the people could worship close, even very close, to their priests, and to their 'Maker'. Henry VIII heard three Masses daily on hunting days and sometimes five on other days. But although the laity attended Mass frequently, they received communion rarely, perhaps only once a year, at Easter, after confession in Holy Week. Christ had commanded His followers to love one another, to love even their enemies. The institutions of the Church as well as the teachings of Christ demanded that Christians be 'in charity'. The priest warned all communicants not to come to 'God's board, but if ye be in perfect love and charity, and be clean shriven, and in full purpose to leave your sin'. Loving one's enemies was always a counsel of perfection, but there were powerful imperatives to Christian unity. Within the Mass there was a ceremony of peace (although sometimes distinctly uncharitable disputes arose over who should kiss the *pax* board first). There were sanctions against asking for divine forgiveness without giving or deserving human forgiveness. Enmity was an obstacle to the reception of the Mass. Some did have scruples about receiving the Easter sacrament while out of charity with neighbours and refusing to be reconciled. The Mass was the symbol of peace, and as a symbol of awesome power, could bring peace. In April 1459 there was a great riot in Fleet Street in London during which, it was said, many might have died had not bishops processed with crosses and 'Our Lord's body' to restore peace.

At Corpus Christi the blessed sacrament which the feast honoured was consecrated at a special Mass, then carried by priests in a precious vessel, under a canopy, along a processional route strewn with grass and flowers. Unity was the theme of Corpus Christi; a social ideal of holy togetherness, worked out in the Mass of the feast, its hymns, its great procession. Here, in this feast, so intensely popular, so universally observed, embellished so spontaneously with plays and pageants, lay, if anywhere, a demonstration of a Christian community. Yet community in Christ's saving sacrifice never meant social equality. In practice, this festival of unity also celebrated power and privilege; the precedence of the powerful, who walked closest to the Host, over the powerless.

The poor, women, children, servants – most people – watched from a distance. Yet although the celebrations sometimes became *dis*cordant, *dis*ordered, they were held in the name of the sacrament, which bound the Christian community as nothing else could.

What was the Christian community? Christians thought of themselves as one society, sharing in baptism with their 'even Christen' throughout the world: Christendom. Though torn by war, faction, doctrinal dispute and family quarrels, Christendom was one. Or, Latin Christendom was one. The Church in Rome had long been divided from the Orthodox Church of Byzantium by deep questions of doctrine and authority, but hopes of reconciliation had never been abandoned. The fall of Constantinople to the Ottoman Turks in 1453 was a profound blow to the West. Moscow had become the 'third Rome', and Eastern Orthodoxy seemed infinitely distant. Founded in Christ, the Church in Rome which revealed His message, claimed to be 'one, holy, Catholic, and apostolic', universal and unitary, timeless. Catholic means universal, and for the West there was as yet no question about which Church should claim universality. The Christian community was defined by its membership of the Catholic Church. Since this was a militant, missionary faith, people everywhere, including Turks and Saracens, infidels, and the pagans in the New World might eventually be incorporated. Christendom, by its nature, could have no conceivable frontiers. Though the worlds of most people were bounded by the hills and fields of their horizons, still they knew that Jerusalem was the cradle of the faith and Rome its capital. Many must have dreamed of travelling there, and some did.

Greater than the community of the whole Christian world on earth was the community of the dead. The Christian community extended from this world to the next and included all those who had ever lived, the faithful departed. The souls of dead family and friends seemed to the living scarcely less real and needy than their own bodies. Between the living and dead an intricate passage existed of love and fear. The Mass was not only a service for the living, visible congregation, but for a ghostly company of the dead, still in search of eternal peace, for whose souls the living prayed. The saints were with God already, enjoying the everlasting peace of heaven. Some of this 'blessed company' were sanctified because, like the Apostles, they had been chosen by Christ Himself during His life; others because they wore a martyr's crown; others because in their own lives they had transcended the frailties of the human condition. They were friends of God, and friends, in turn, to the human race.

The damned – unrepentant and unconfessed, beyond help, human or divine – were consigned to hell after death. There they became servants of the Devil, the tyrant of hell, condemned eternally to suffer the torments which he and his evil spirits had prepared for them. Punishments were devised to mirror sins on earth. So John Mirk, writing in the early fifteenth century and still read a century later, warned that worms ceaselessly devoured those who 'eat their even christen here in earth with false back biting'. Some had visions of hell. The visionary Nun of Kent, Elizabeth Barton, claimed to have watched the disputation of devils for the soul of Cardinal Wolsey. Infernal spirits were believed to have the power to rise from hell to tempt the living. The torments of the damned were terrifyingly portrayed in sermons and in the doom paintings above every chancel arch. Anyone foolish enough not to believe in the afterlife would discover in a terrible and irreversible way that hell was not a fable: so they were warned.

It was a defining belief of Christians of the later middle ages – a belief that the Church finally endorsed in the late thirteenth century – that a third other-worldly place existed beyond heaven and hell. This was purgatory, through which the sinful soul must pass on its journey to God. To the faithful in the later middle ages purgatory was real; they could even visit St Patrick's Purgatory at Lough Derg in the north-west of Ireland, an outlet of purgatory on earth. Purgatory was a place of fire and torment, incessant pain and seemingly endless languishing, but also of profound hope and consolation, for the torment was not endless; the dark fire was a cleansing fire. Like hell in its pains, it was contrary to hell in its promise, for the soul freed from purgatory would at last see God. Only those without sin could escape purgatory, but anyone who felt the least penitent, even if not until their dying moment, could hope for a penitential stay in purgatory and for heaven at last. The greater the sins on earth and the greater the penance unperformed by the living, the longer the stay in purgatory; perhaps thousands of years, when every moment seemed endless there. The faithful should perform due penance while on earth, in the time of grace, for after death, the time of justice, penance for sins was harder; yet where they failed, their family and friends could work by intercession for the ultimate redemption of their souls.

The faithful believed and the Church taught that merit could be transferred by the faithful on earth or the saints in heaven to those who were paying for their sins in purgatory. Kinship and fellowship did not end with death, nor were family boundaries circumscribed by mortality. 'Your late acquaintance, kindred, spouses, companions, play fellows and friends' had special claims, wrote Thomas More, but a duty in charity was owed to all Christian souls. The belief that the living could hasten the soul's release from purgatory held late medieval Catholics in thrall, for would it not be unforgivably cruel to abandon souls who were suffering so dreadfully? 'What heart were so hard . . . that it could sit in rest at supper or sleep in rest a bed, and let a man lie and burn?' asked Thomas More's imagined souls in his *Supplication of Souls* (1529). But they had found the old saying true: 'Out of sight, out of mind.' Ghosts returned to describe the horrors, haunting not places but people, appearing to those who through allegiance of blood had a duty to obey their commands. So Shakespeare's King Hamlet, murdered unshriven, 'cut off even in the blossoms of my sin', called upon his son to avenge him. Christians on earth owed a duty to their fellow Christians departed: to remember them in their prayers. Gravestones and memorial brasses bore messages adjuring passers-by 'of your charity, pray for the souls of . . .', as they would that others would do for them, later. To friends, people left rings inscribed: 'Have pity on me'. The faithful prayed for their own dead, and they prayed for 'all Christian souls', those they did not know, on All Souls' Day.

Most powerful of the intercessors between God and men was the transcendental society of the saints. Their intercession healed the breach between God and the fallen world. Jesus was the most eloquent advocate to His Father, and Mary, the first of the human race to be redeemed, had special influence. Heaven, it was popularly believed, was ordered like this world, with God as ruler, Christ as prince, Mary as queen, and the saints, like courtiers, acting as 'holy patrons' in the 'blessed court of heaven'. The saints were figures of awe and power; powerful enough to atone for the sins that called down destructive forces in the natural world, to ward off the disasters that daily threatened their supplicants. They were believed to protect against fire, flood and disease; to bring travellers safely home, and to save them from shipwreck. Their aid was often invoked for reasons which hardly seem Christian, because the safety of votaries might depend on the destruction of enemies. So unhappy wives prayed to St Uncumber when they wished to be rid of their husbands. In 1487 Henry VII prayed before the image of Our Lady at Walsingham to be delivered from his many enemies, and after his victory at Stoke sent the battle standard to her in thanks. Rulers prayed to the Virgin for victory in war; the poor prayed to her for daily favours and protection.

Stories of the saints' holy lives, their spectacular torments and their miracles were told in the *Golden Legend*, translated by England's first printer, William Caxton, in 1483, and reprinted often. Particular saints were believed to have particular powers: St Sebastian, because of his many wounds, protected against plague; St Barbara, killed by her angry father, protected against thunder and lightning and sudden death (she was the special patron of soldiers and gunpowder makers). As figures of transcendant power, saints could be angered and must be placated. Yet the tenor of the devotion to them was not fear, but love. At one time the saints had lived, as their votaries did now, on earth; 'Wherefore', wrote John Mirk, 'they have compassion of us.' The devout looked upon them as heavenly friends. One woman left money to edify the image of St John the Evangelist, 'whom I have ever worshipped and loved'. Everyone venerated the Virgin, but from among so many, many saints each Catholic chose one specially to honour; a patron saint. Thomas More's was St Thomas the Apostle, doubting Thomas, who did not believe until he saw the wounds of the resurrected Christ. Although honouring one saint privately, the faithful should honour them all; the Church enjoined them to do so on the feast of All Saints.

Saints were venerated through their images and at their shrines. Miracles were performed at shrines to reveal divine power to the faithful. In 1482, in Ireland, a figure of the Holy Cross removed itself to the shores of the lake of Baile-an-Chuillin, 'and many wonders and miracles were wrought by it'. A miracle occurred in Cheapside in July 1507 when a girl was run over by a cart and lay lifeless; reviving, she said that the image of Our Lady at Barking had lifted up the cart. Pilgrims travelled to see St Cuthbert at Durham, St Thomas Becket at Canterbury and Our Lady at Walsingham and Ipswich. At the tomb of St John of Bridlington little silver ships were left as votive offerings by merchants who sought protection for their ships at sea. Wax and silver models of afflicted parts of the body – legs, hearts, hands, breasts – were presented at shrines in expectation of or thanksgiving for cures. Images of saints – painted pictures and carved statues, gilded and adorned – looked down protectively from altars, screens, walls and windows in every church. The saints were instantly recognizable by their symbols: St Anthony had his pig, St Barbara her tower, and St Catherine her wheel. The holy was served by art, often works of numinous beauty, paid and cared for by parishioners. Images were dressed in gowns and wore little silver shoes which the faithful kissed. In public streets and private houses there were images to be daily reverenced. The rich had paintings and tapestries depicting saints' lives; the poor, little wooden crucifixes and single-sheet woodcuts: rich or poor, the object of the devotion was the same.

Communion with the saints through contemplation of their images was, for late medieval Christians, central to the experience of the holy. Art might excite people to devotion more readily than words. For the illiterate, images were 'poor men's books'. Like sacraments, images represented higher spiritual truths. Believers gazing upon an image of the Virgin saw, in their mind's eye, more than a statue; they saw Our Lady herself and found an intimate exchange. Defending images, Thomas More insisted that the simplest, most credulous believers could distinguish between the image and the saint it represented, just as they could tell the difference between a real rabbit and a painted one. Yet there was a danger that images might be considered holy and worshipped for themselves; that the believer would serve the image rather than the image the believer; that people would seek in them what should be sought from God alone. More himself had written wryly to his friend Desiderius Erasmus of the London women who prayed to the image of the Virgin by the Tower and imagined fondly that it smiled back at them.

The quintessential image of popular devotion was the rood, the figure of Christ crucified. High above the congregation in every church, between the people and the priest, was the great rood of Christ, with the Virgin and St John the Evangelist at either hand, to move the people to remembrance of the Passion as the priest celebrated the Mass. Some roods inspired particular devotion. In 1503 German de la Pole commended Sir Robert Plumpton to the 'blessed Rood of Radburn, who save you in His blessed keeping'. With the advent of printing, images were made widely available as objects of devotion and prayer: the Image of Pity – Christ on the Cross as the Man of Sorrows – or of Our Lady of Pity – the Virgin at the foot of the Cross with her Son in her arms, surrounded by the instruments of the Passion. Some of these images promised devout beholders indulgences of release from tens of thousands of years of purgatorial suffering. To contemplate the Image of Pity, or a picture of the five wounds of Christ, was to think not only of divine love but of divine judgement. At the Last Judgement, so it was believed, Christ would show His wounds: to the saved as promise of redemption and to the damned in reproach. Banners of the five wounds were carried on pilgrimage and became rallying standards for rebellions.

For all the impassioned devotion to Christ in His suffering, pitying humanity, the adoration of Christ as the Man of Sorrows, the new feasts and Masses popularly dedicated to the holy name of Jesus, to the five wounds, to the crown of thorns, it seemed as though His mercies were not available to the faithful without mediation. The incessant invocation of saints implies a belief that the sinner could never reach God without ceaseless intercession. All the intercessions of family and friends, on earth and in heaven, could never bring souls to God without the mediation of the Church. Belief in the redemptive power of Christ was central, but the pathway to salvation also led through the seven sacraments, obedience to the teachings of Holy Church and penitential good works. The authority of the Church was fundamental; authority which lay not only in the hierarchy of the Church but in the sources on which the faith rested. For Catholics, the foundation of faith was not only scripture but also the 'unwritten verities' which Christ had confided to the Apostles, the decrees of General Councils of the Church, the writings of the Church Fathers, the pronouncements of popes. These only the Church could interpret.

The Church had huge reserves of spiritual power which it dispensed through the sacraments and through indulgences. Christ by His sacrifice had won such an amplitude of merit before God that it might make satisfaction for sin for sinning Christians forever. This, so the Church taught, was the treasury of merit. And who should control it? The Church itself, came the answer; especially its hierarchs, especially the Pope. Though the doctrine of indulgences was complex and disputed, by the end of the middle ages popes were granting remission from all temporal punishments. This was plenary indulgence. The merits acquired from a plenary indulgence could also be applied to benefit souls already in purgatory. Popes declared that plenary indulgences gave remission from both *culpa*, guilt, and *poena*, satisfaction for sin; and not only in this life. By the end of the fifteenth century the Pope was claiming jurisdiction over souls in purgatory as well as over Christians on earth. Some priests were preaching that he could free souls at will. Such indulgences came at a price, spiritual as well as financial.

The hierarchy of the Church mirrored that of the secular realm; with the Pope as monarch and General Councils as Parliaments; bishops and cardinals as the nobility; through a series of lesser clerical orders down to the priest with cure of souls in the humblest parish. The Church had its own law which intervened widely in people's lives; its own courts and judges; its own massive administration. Tensions might exist between the institutional Church and the church of believers, the community of the faithful. The religion of the Church and the religion of the people might diverge and, in the cases of the definition of purgatory or the creation of new saints or new feasts, the Church might follow the people as well as the people the Church. Yet none of the faithful could challenge the Church or repudiate its practices without cutting themselves off from the sources of salvation and risking damnation.

Priests lived among their congregations, their 'ghostly' children, in the world and of it. Yet they were set apart from the lay society into which they were born by their sacred vocation, by their ordination. Through the sacrament of holy orders they were empowered, by the working of grace, to celebrate all the other sacraments; in the sacrament of penance they could bind and loose from sin; in the sacrament of the Mass they celebrated a sacred mystery. Mediators to God for men, given secret knowledge denied to the laity, they had died to the world in order to imitate Christ and His Apostles. In the Mass there was a resemblance between Christ and the celebrant. Such was the high view of the priest-hood, and it had consequences for the laity. The clergy, so Dean Colet reminded them in 1511, were the light of the world, and if their light darkened, so much darker was the rest of the world. By 1530 recruitment to the priesthood in England had reached high levels not seen since the Black Death of the mid fourteenth century. In More's *Utopia* the priests were of an extraordinary sanctity; it followed that they were very few. In England, they seemed countless. More's moral was clear. Perhaps 4 per cent of the the total male population was 'priested'; the only other occupation which employed so many was agriculture (the employment which many joined the priesthood to escape). Whether quite so many had truly died to the world may be doubted.

Priests, with the cure of souls, as guides of moral and spiritual life, preachers, teachers, confessors and celebrants, were supposed to be educated, chaste and charitable themselves. Yet although the Church had a divine mission, as an institution it was profoundly human. Priests were sworn to celibacy, never to have families of their own, but the flesh is weak. The laity revered the vow of celibacy and were shocked when it was broken, especially when the breaking of it involved the deflowering of a daughter or the adultery of a wife. Since he taught the idea of Christian life as community, and warned of the sins that would fracture it, a priest's own fall from grace was likely to break the peace of his parish.

In Gaelic Ireland, expectations were different. The Church there had developed in virtual isolation and had never succeeded in transforming marriage and family life to the Catholic pattern of the rest of Europe. In Gaelic society the major professions were hereditary castes, and that included the clergy. Ireland had been resistant to the ethic of clerical celibacy, and here sons followed fathers into the clerical profession. Seeking titles to benefices, the sons needed papal dispensation for their illegitimacy, and were granted it. Between 1449 and 1522 twenty-two sons of bishops were recorded in the lists of dispensation. And Welsh priests had long taken 'wives' in defiance of canon law.

Everywhere the relationship between parishioners and priests was likely to be ambivalent, for the relationship was personal and, like other personal relationships, subject to the vagaries of personality, the strains of proximity and complications of financial obligation. The laity were obliged to provide for their priests, and might object where they thought their pastor unworthy. Yet the unworthiness of the priest could never affect the validity of the sacraments, since the true minister was Christ. Because of the sacrament of ordination even the best and wisest layman must always yield place to the most ignorant and venal priest, and clergy had powerful sanctions. In confession, the priest sat in judgement and enjoined penance; at Mass he could exclude those he thought unworthy. The Church might be criticized, its clergy found wanting, but for the faithful there was no salvation outside it, and without the priesthood admitting the laity to the sacraments, immortal souls were lost.

Christian rites and sacraments were central to people's lives. They created and validated relationships, made new affinities, and sanctioned the passage from one stage of life to another. The sacraments of baptism, marriage and extreme unction sanctified a believer's birth, marriage and death. Confirmation marked the end of one stage of childhood. The sacrament of ordination allowed the priesthood to celebrate the others. All these sacraments were celebrated only once in a lifetime, but two others – penance and the Mass – regularly brought the sinning Christian closer to God. Baptism and marriage were celebrations, accompanied by feasting, to which kin, friends and neighbours came as witnesses as well as worshippers. Sacraments were a unifying bond of the community. Or once they were. At the Reformation, the nature and the number of the sacraments changed. Only baptism and the Eucharist stayed as sacraments which were a means to grace, and even their significance was more cautiously defined. Yet the human need for sacraments remained.

*

The first sacrament in the life of a Christian was baptism. Baptism was the rite that incorporated the newborn child into the Church and Christian society (Christendom), and it was a sacrament of faith. Without baptism there was no salvation, and the unbaptized child was consigned to limbo, forever denied heaven and the beatific vision. Every child was born innocent but with a proclivity to sin which was the inheritance of the Fall, and if unprotected by baptism, a child was prey to the Devil. And the Devil was believed to be a real, not a metaphorical, presence of evil in the world. Within the rite of baptism was a rite of exorcism in which the priest cast out the Devil from the child. Exorcized at the church door, the child was carried into the church to the font and there immersed in baptismal water, anointed with holy oil, and marked on the forehead and breast with the sign of the cross, becoming a member of Christendom, endowed with the promise of salvation and with the duties of the faith. Since baptism was essential for salvation it could in an emergency be administered by anyone. The midwife – the 'gracewoman' – knew the effectual words of baptism: 'I christen thee in the name of the Father and of the Son and of the Holy Ghost.'

At baptism, the child was handed by the priest to his godparents as his Christian kindred or *godsibb*. They made vows on the child's behalf and bound themselves to bring up the child in the 'ways of God and godly living'. Priests were sometimes asked to act as godfathers, in the hope of true spiritual guidance for the child, but godparents were often chosen more for the help they could give in the ways of this world than of Heaven. Choosing godparents was a way of creating affinity and formalizing friendships, for at baptism not only the child but the child's parents became related to the godparents. A christening was a time for celebration and thanksgiving, a time to invite friends and neighbours to feast. Another sacrament offered grace to the child: the vows of baptism were reaffirmed in the sacrament of confirmation. Time was when the child had waited until the age of spiritual discretion before confirmation, but by the early sixteenth century the child was brought from baptism to confirmation as soon as the bishop was available, and long before he or she could rehearse the elements of the faith. Princess Elizabeth, the daughter of Henry VIII and Anne Boleyn, was baptized and confirmed when three days old. That a tiny child needed to be protected by a double sacrament shows how much people believed in the power of the sacraments and in the immanence of evil.

One person was notably absent from the christening in church: the infant's mother. Since before the child's birth she had been secluded among her women friends, at a lying-in as luxurious as she could afford. Great excitements, or great disappointments, attended the birth of a child. In January 1537 it became known to her friends and servants that Lady Lisle was expecting a baby; a 'man child', a Plantagenet heir, they hoped. Night gowns, bonnets, cramp rings and a cradle were ordered. In March John Hutton, governor of the Merchant Adventurers in Flanders, wrote asking her 'to recommend me to your little boy in your belly, the which I pray God to send into your arms, to your comfort and my lord's'. By July the baby had not arrived, nor by August; the pregnancy was a false one. Lady Lisle's 'very friends' were sad, and she was distraught. Her servant consoled his mistress in this private tragedy: 'If it be His pleasure He spareth neither empress, queen, princess nor duchess ... good madam, put your whole trust in God, and leave these sorrows.' Women friends, neighbours and midwives were with the mother at her delivery. In the agonies and danger of labour, a mother implored 'Our Lady [to] help her in her most need' and perhaps borrowed a girdle supposedly worn by Our Lady herself; she called upon pilgrimage saints like St Anne of Buxton and, to ease her pains, leant upon the staff of St Modwyn of Burton-upon-Trent. Since every childbed might be a deathbed for both the mother and her child, the mother should be contrite and have confessed, and water must be ready for the urgent christening of the child. Baptism was believed to be essential not only for the child's soul, but as a preservative to allow the baby to survive and thrive. The newborn child was wrapped tight in swaddling clothes and tucked in a cradle, as though to exchange one womb for another.

The new mother remained secluded, still among women, until a few weeks after the birth, when she was taken, veiled and gazing downwards, by her women friends for her churching or purification. Taboos, usually unspoken, were associated with pregnancy. When, just before Christmas

1553, Anne Williamson dared to enter St Mary Magdalen, Old Fish Street in London 'unchurched', 'contrary to womanhood', and refused to leave, she horrified the 'most devout and worthy' of the parish. The vicar-general ordered her to undergo purification, to sit in the churching pew and to do public penance. The Church might insist that the ceremony was for thanksgiving not for purification, but many people believed otherwise.

Thanksgiving for a safe delivery was certainly due, for at every childbirth the sense of mortality was acute. Making his will, a Somerset husband bequeathed five marks to 'the child in my wife's womb, if God fortune it to have christendom and live'. A woman's risk of death in every pregnancy was perhaps one in a hundred, and she might expect to be pregnant six or seven times in her life. Her child's prospect of dying in the hours and days and weeks after birth was even greater. There was a name for baptized infants who died within a month of birth; they were called 'chrisoms' after the cloth which was tied around the anointed cross on their foreheads. The first year of life was the most dangerous. Between one in six and one in five of all children died before reaching their first birthday. In the unhealthiest times and places infant mortality was higher still. In the crowded slums of St Botolph Aldgate in London in the late sixteenth century of every hundred babies born only about seventy would live to see their first birthday. Endemic infectious diseases – bronchial in the winter, enteric in the summer – carried off the most vulnerable. Perhaps a quarter of all children born between 1550 and 1649 failed to reach the age of ten. Death was not reserved for the old.

Newborn children at any time are most vulnerable, most constantly in need of care if they are to survive. Mothers were advised to breastfeed their own children, in order to inculcate virtue along with their milk, but richer mothers chose to send their children to wet-nurses – often for years, because a child was not weaned until the age of two. Women were taught to keep their children from all danger, not to lay them in their own beds 'while they be of tender age', nor leave them near water or fire. Records of coroners' inquests testify to childhood catastrophes – toddlers falling into fires or wells, falling out of windows – sometimes through parental neglect, but more often not. The experience of infancy and childhood was conditioned by the circumstances of the parents. Children brought up in homes deserted daily by fathers who had to go out to work, and looked after distractedly by mothers who worked at home, spinning or knitting, or in the fields, had a different upbringing from those children cared for in households where the whole family, and their servants, lived and worked. Children grew up in families, but not in extended families for it was rare for relatives to live together; they were brought up with their parents, brothers and sisters, but not with grandparents, aunts, uncles or cousins living in the same house.

Despite their vulnerability, children under the age of ten constituted a quarter of the entire population of England in the mid sixteenth century. Though hardly silent in their own time, they have almost no voice in history. Others wrote for them, or about them, when they remembered them, but no children, even the most precocious, even King Edward VI, quite spoke for themselves. Certain statistics about their lives are telling. Children, whether rich or poor, had brothers and sisters, for in marriages where births could hardly be planned one child followed another. Many brothers and sisters were step-brothers and sisters, because perhaps as many as 30 per cent of all those marrying in the mid-century were widows or widowers, and many brought children from the first marriage to the next. Children lived to learn the sorrow of the deaths of parents and siblings.

The pain experienced at the death of a child reaches down the ages. The Church taught that the child was a gift of God whom God might take back again, and bereaved parents wrote conventionally of their departed children enjoying the 'joys of Heaven'. Ben Jonson, at the end of the century, dutifully acknowledged at the death of his first daughter: 'All heaven's gifts being heaven's due/ It makes the father less to rue'. Yet he recollected the loss of his first son, dead of the plague in 1603, with less tranquillity:

> Farewell, thou child of my right hand, and joy;
>   My sin was too much hope of thee, loved boy.
> Seven years thou wert lent to me, and I thee pay,
>   Exacted by thy fate, on the just day.
> Oh, could I lose all father now!

Parents loved their children and, loving them, they had to chastise and warn them of the spiritual danger that surrounded them. Children were taught from an early age that there was hell as well as heaven, and that the Devil waited to tempt them. As a child John Stow, London's chronicler (born in 1525), was told often of the terrible apparition that bell-ringers saw at St Michael Cornhill during a storm on St James's Eve: it was the Devil. Stow poked feathers in the clefts the Devil's paw had raked in the tower. Children were taught the dangers of sin because they were not invariably regarded as innocent, as Christ had seen them, but as tainted by the Fall and ready, as Bishop Bonner wrote, to 'take and embrace vice, unthriftiness and all manner naughtiness'. They must be kept from that sin to which their nature impelled them. Freedom in a child was not seen as an inalienable right but as wantonness. John Johnson, a London merchant, wrote to his brother-in-law, to whom he had sent his four-year-old daughter Charity to safeguard her from the plague: his wife feared that 'you will make Charity a wanton in suffering her to have her will'. This was no favour; it would 'cause her to have strokes [be spanked] thereafter. I pray you, therefore, let her be kept in awe'.

Children must, above all, remember the Fourth Commandment: 'Honour thy father and thy mother.' In a society which was founded upon obedience, obedience began with a child's duty to parents. They learnt to ask, kneeling, for their parents' blessing: 'Mother, I beseech you of charity, give me your blessing.' And parents should respond, making the sign of the cross and saying, 'In the name of Father, Son and Holy Ghost, Amen.' The duty remained while the parents lived. Discipline, obedience, manners: these were inculcated early, when the child was most amenable, and by force where persuasion failed. Tudor parents were taught that 'who spareth the rod, hateth the child', though the correction must be given 'in charity'. 'Let not the feminine pity of your wives destroy your children', wrote Edmund Dudley; 'pamper them not at home in furred coats and their shirts to be warmed against their uprising ... Dandle them not too dearly lest folly fasten on them.' So constant were the admonitions against spoiling and pampering ('cockering') children that we may imagine the ambivalence of parents torn between tenderness and duty. Sabine Johnson, the same mother who wished little Charity to be 'kept in awe', asked her husband: 'I pray you, cast away a little money for some baby [doll]', for their son. The same parents who could bear to send children away to be nursed for two years showed the greatest solicitude for their welfare. Some teachers, at least, knew that beating was not the best way to lead a child to study. The Abbot of Reading, tutor to six-year-old James Basset, 'playeth him to his learning, both to Latin and to French'.

By the age of seven, children became helping hands in a peasant household; both boys and girls were expected to work. Girls helped their mothers, fetching water, building fires, cooking, and watching younger siblings; boys herded cattle, tended geese, sheep and pigs, gleaned in the fields, collected firewood and fished. In a census of the poor in Norwich of 1570 children as young as six, if they had no particular occupations, were called 'idle'. Children might become the main breadwinners of pauper families. An Italian observer in about 1500, who charged English parents with want of affection, and with sending their children away from home at a pathetically early age, was correct, at least in his second charge. For the poor, there was little choice. In families living in cottages crammed with children, with too many to a bed and too many mouths to feed, a boy or girl who reached the age of ten or twelve left home by necessity to seek work as a servant or labourer. The vulnerability of young people setting out alone can be imagined, and sometimes proved. In 1517 a man returning from a pilgrimage to Our Lady at Willesden encountered a young girl by the wayside, seeking honest service in London. She entrusted herself to the man's protection, but he took her to the Bankside stews, London's notorious brothels, and engaged the 'maiden' to service with a prostitute. The girl implored a waterman's wife 'for Our Lady's sake' to save her, and so she did. Others were less fortunate. Yet most children, sent away from their families to find work, and rarely returning to them, found new homes of a kind with their masters and mistresses.

The sons of the nobility were also sent away: in the early sixteenth century to be brought up in another noble household; and a century later, to go to school. Girls of noble and gentry families went as ladies-in-waiting to other households, or might be contracted in marriage very young and sent to be brought up in the household of their future family. Elizabeth Plumpton was only three when in 1464 she was contracted to marry John Sotehill, and went to live in the Sotehill household. When the Italian observer asked why people sent their own children away from home and received the children of strangers, 'they answered that they did it in order that the children might learn better manners'. Manners were part of the larger duty to 'reverence, honour and obey' superiors.

When they left home, children were expected to have received the last sacraments of childhood: penance and the Eucharist. Little children were supposed to attend church – quietly – with their families, to learn the paternoster (the Lord's Prayer) and Ave Maria (Hail Mary) as soon as they could talk, and receive the benediction of witnessing the elevation of the Host. Some time between the ages of seven and fourteen they were judged to have reached the age of spiritual discretion, the age at which they could tell right from wrong and appreciate the mystery of the Mass. A true understanding of sin, of penitence, and of salvation was needed before they could confess, be absolved and be worthy to receive Communion. God knew every sin already. 'You are always in the presence and sight of God . . . He seeth and is not seen,' as Sir Thomas Wyatt, Henry VIII's courtier and diplomat, reminded his fifteen-year-old son in 1537. Sorrowful penitence alone would restore the sinner to God, but only contrite repentance expressed before the priest in confession could restore the sinner to the body of the faithful.

The seven deadly sins – pride, envy, wrath, covetousness, gluttony, sloth, lechery – all had malign social consequences and were transgressions against the community. Forgiveness and absolution depended upon tangible restitution for wrongs. The priest was empowered to impose penitential exercises and pronounce penitents absolved from sin and reconciled to the community of believers. In the confession, which was secret, the priest should comfort the penitent, telling him that Christ had died for our sins, reminding him that he was not the first in the world to sin, and that the greatest sinners had been saved through repentance and calling upon Christ. Much better to confess sins in this world than to come to universal judgement in the next, 'when no man of law may speak for us, nor any excuse may serve'; better to perform penance now, in the time of grace, than in purgatory. The sinner was questioned in detail concerning his failings: of the five senses; of the seven deadly sins; against the twelve articles of faith in the Apostles' Creed, the seven sacraments of the Church, and the seven corporeal works of mercy (feeding the hungry, giving drink to the thirsty, clothing the naked, housing the homeless, visiting the sick, aiding prisoners and burying the dead). Confessional manuals were full of advice regarding youthful failings, especially concerning that sin that most obsesses adolescents. Confession brought consolation, freedom, and a lifting of the burden of sin, but it also imposed its own burdens, of ecclesiastical discipline and social control. The duty might have seemed more evident than the liberation.

Adolescence – third of the seven ages of man – was judged to last between the ages of fifteen and twenty-four, and was recognized as an age which must be ruled, for 'lusty iuventus' (youth) was by nature ignorant, ill-disciplined and savage. Against adolescents 'the Devil doth lay all his ordnance and use all his engines against the soldiers of Christ,' warned Erasmus. Living in households together as servants and apprentices, adolescents shared their lives, their rooms, their beds. Richard Whitford, monk and moralist, counselled spiritual exercises upon waking – making the sign of the cross from head to foot, from left to right – but he knew how some 'who lie two or three sometime together, and in one chamber divers beds and so many in company' would be mortified by the jeers of mocking bedfellows if they practised such devotions: 'O Jesu, what hear I now?' Adolescence was not usually a time for vaunting piety. Boys were notorious for swearing. Curses are chosen because they shock; so in the sixteenth century they would always be religious: 'God's passion, God's wounds, God's nails, and ever His holy and blessed blood.' There was a cautionary tale of an apprentice. He swore so often by God's bones that his own bones cleaved through his flesh; a mirroring punishment for such blasphemy. This was a society in which the young were allowed no authority. For young men to command was against the law of nature: they must obey until they had achieved mastery of their baser desires. The prevailing ideal was gerontocratic; only the old had *gravitas* and wisdom enough to rule. Not until the age of twenty-four were men considered ready to be ordained to the priesthood or emancipated from apprenticeship; only then could they set up independent, single households. Adolescence was ended by another rite of passage, another sacrament: marriage.

Marriage brought profound transformations: new privileges, obligations, freedoms and restrictions. Sons became patriarchs; women exchanged duty to fathers for duty to husbands. Men became householders; women housekeepers. From being dependants – children, apprentices, servants – they became masters and mistresses and bore authority. Women vowed at marriage to be 'bonere [gentle, courteous] and buxom [compliant], in bed and at board', acknowledging the sexual duty of marriage. They would bear children and become matrons themselves. And the transformation was irreversible, 'till death us do part'.

A marriage was easily – too easily – made. The Church had long allowed that the free exchange of vows before witnesses – it did not matter where – followed by sexual consummation constituted a valid, sacramental, marriage. When, in 1553, Mary Blage and Walter Cely told Edmund Parker that they wished to marry, he said, 'Well, I will play the priest', and invited Walter to take Mary by the hand and say these familiar, binding words: 'I, Walter, do take thee, Mary, to my wife; to have and to hold until death us do part, and thereunto I plight unto thee my faith and my troth.' Their story, like that of many others, came before the Church courts, as at least one party repented at leisure and asked ecclesiastical judges to find a way to dissolve a union which was virtually indissoluble and which the Church's permissive doctrine had allowed. Women found themselves married to men who had seduced them but would not stay with them; men married women who deceived them and had plighted troths elsewhere. In the highly charged atmosphere of the royal court, Lady Margaret Douglas, Henry VIII's niece, and Lord Thomas Howard dared in 1536 to contract a secret marriage. It led Lord Thomas to the Tower, where he wrote some of the most tragic, if stilted, of Tudor love poetry, and where he died.

> Oh, ye lovers that high upon the wheel
> Of fortune be set, in good adventure,
> God grant that ye find aye love of steel
> And long may your life in joy endure.
> But when you come by my sepulture
> Remember that your fellow resteth there,
> For I loved eke [also], though I unworthy were.

Clandestine marriage often ended in tears. It excluded parents, family and friends, whose presence to witness the new union celebrated and sanctioned a new affinity. It banished the clergy, who objected to the laity 'playing the priest'. Marriage without public spousal rites seemed anarchic, not a sacrament in the sense of a social institution. A marriage – wedding – which the whole community affirmed involved the reading of banns, a solemnization before a priest, the exchange of vows, the blessing of the ring, a public pledge at the church door, and ideally the blessing of a nuptial mass inside the church. Marriage feasts and revels followed. The solemnization of marriage was forbidden during Lent, Rogationtide and Advent, and the prohibition was respected. Nor did weddings take place during the busy harvest season, but followed the rhythms of the agricultural year. The most popular period for marriage was at the time of the annual hiring fairs, after the harvest, when young farm servants received their wages and left their masters' houses to seek new opportunities. This was a time of relative prosperity after harvest, a moment to celebrate at church and bride ales (feasts).

Marriage for love was usually the dubious privilege of those with little to lose: the poor. For the rest, love in marriage was its consequence rather than its cause. Marriage was too serious a matter to be left to sentiment and passion, for it not only altered the lives of the couple, creating new duties towards each other and their children, it also forged family alliances, ended or exacerbated local vendettas, and might be a means to political and tenurial aggrandizement. The warring Houses of York and Lancaster were united by the marriage of Henry VII to Elizabeth of York. Royal children were used as pawns in international diplomacy. Gentry families tended to make marital alliances within their localities, binding other families to their own.

The Church insisted that marriage be made by free consent, and recognized no parental right to determine children's choices, but utterly dependent children, especially daughters, brought up in obedience and deference, were unable or unwilling to gainsay obdurate fathers and mothers, whose duty it was to marry them off. Henry VIII's sister Princess Mary dutifully married, and buried, Louis XII of France. Bravely, she told her brother that she had married once to please him, but should he refuse to allow her now to marry Charles Brandon, 'I will be there whereas your grace nor none other shall have any joy of me': in a convent. They married in 1515, without his consent. For girls of gentry and noble families, there was little alternative to marriage. Sir William Ayscough 'covenanted' with his Lincolnshire neighbour, Kyme, 'for lucre' to marry his daughter to Kyme's heir. This proved to be a hellish marriage from which Anne Ayscough [Askew] sought consolation in religion.

A couple were fortunate if love led to a match which accorded with prudence. In March 1497 Edmund Plumpton wrote in a fever of excitement to his kinsman, Sir Robert Plumpton. 'Lovers and friends' of Edmund's in London had introduced him to a widow 'good and beautiful, womanly and wise ... of good stock and worshipful'. Her name was Agnes. She and he were 'agreed, in one mind and all one', but her friends demanded a jointure of 20 marks a year, and Edmund needed help in order to marry her. 'It were otherwise my great undoing forever.' This courtship contained many of the ritual elements: friends and 'lovers' as matchmakers, the exchange of gifts (she gave him a cross set with rubies and pearls), financial negotiations. Their marriage took place, but the couple did not live happily ever after. In 1501 Robert Tykhull, a gentleman of Holborn in London was pardoned for the murder of Edmund Plumpton on the grounds that he had acted in self-defence.

Complicated financial negotiations attended the making of marriage for the nobility and gentry. Sir Francis Lovell wrote to Lord Lisle in September 1534, hoping that 'your noble blood and my poor stock shall be by the grace of God confedered together' by the marriage of his elder son to Lisle's second daughter, Lady Elizabeth Plantagenet. If Lisle would provide a dowry of £700 in cash, Lovell would ensure an income for Elizabeth of £100 each year for life; her jointure. This was a typical financial arrangement. The immediate cost of the dowry might be huge, but it was the provision of the jointure which was the greatest gamble, because the widow could live long and independently, to the ruin of her husband's family's estate. Sir John Bassett of Devon sent two daughters, Anne and Thomasine, aged about ten and twelve, to live in Giles, Lord Daubeney's household, intending that one should marry Daubeney's son and heir; whichever of them Daubeney – rather than his son – chose. Should these daughters die, or fail to please, Bassett promised by indenture in 1504 to deliver another. Transactions such as these seem to tell more of property transfer than parental devotion, but parental love was not expressed in legal documents. Rather than being heartless marriage brokers, parents were finding ways to provide for children who might easily be left orphaned.

Poorer couples, too, waited until they could set up an independent household before they married; and they waited a long time. Peasant couples needed a farm or smallholding and a cottage (a half-yardland, a farm of about fifteen acres, was the minimum holding upon which a family could support itself without other employment); artisans a craft; and labourers a steady demand for their labour. The wealthy, taking pity upon girls without dowries condemned to long spinsterhood, often left bequests towards 'poor maidens' marriages'. In times of particular deprivation and dislocation – as in the 1550s and 1590s – the rate of marriage declined altogether as people lacked the confidence and resources to marry and begin families. In mid-sixteenth-century London Robert Trappes and Ellen Tompkins 'made merry gently and lovingly together' and wanted to marry, but Ellen was a 'poor wench and liveth only on her service' and Robert was an apprentice, 'a poor young man', though with a rich father, with no certain prospects. How could they marry? Both men and women married very late, usually in their late twenties. And this was at a time when people were taught that all 'fleshly meddling' outside marriage was a deadly sin. Early in the century, another apprentice, Anthony Pountisbury, a mercer's son of Cheapside, had 'an inward love to a young woman', and tried to marry her, but his master had him arrested on his wedding day. Anthony claimed that this prohibition of apprentices to marry 'causeth much fornication and adultery'.

In early modern England the illegitimacy rate was remarkably low – perhaps as low as 2 per cent – and illegitimate children were often born after broken betrothals, each one a private tragedy for mother and child. Illegitimacy was rare, but bridal pregnancy very common. Trial marriages were not countenanced in England, but they were in Gaelic Ireland, where marriage and divorce remained secular matters, determined by secular rules, not ecclesiastical ones. Sir Thomas Cusack, Master of the Rolls in Dublin, complained in 1541 that the Irish lived 'diabolically without marriage'. Gaelic law was relaxed about marriage and divorce, and took little account of legitimacy. In the Gaelic lordships men and women might have a succession of partners, and women could 'name' children as sons to men with whom they had had fleeting liaisons. These children were accorded the same status and same relationship to their father as children born within wedlock, and the same claim upon the patrimony. In England, too, fathers who could afford it might show affection and care for their illegitimate children, whom they acknowledged during life and at death. William Ayloffe, a lawyer in Hornchurch, dying in 1517, left his lands and goods to his legitimate children, but remembered also 'William, my supposed bastard son', who was to be apprenticed, 'John, my supposed bastard', who was to be kept at school to learn grammar and become a priest, and a daughter Dorothy, who was to be 'put into a close nunnery, considering her sickness and disease'. A less relaxed attitude to illegitimacy appeared by the end of the century.

A marriage is a secret place, a mutual society, an emotional world entered only by the couple. In their private letters and public wills husbands and wives wrote of 'dearly beloved' spouses, as though the devotion was real as well as conventional. After nearly five hundred years, how are we to tell? Elizabeth Grey, widow of the 9th Earl of Kildare, nightly kissed his portrait. Were we told that because such devotion was uncommon? Human emotions – love, grief, rage, jealousy – exist immemorially in marriage, but ways of expressing, or not expressing, them change. For the upper orders, emotion was fettered by convention, by the need for property and procreation. In 1537 Sir Thomas

Wyatt wrote a letter of advice to his newly married fifteen-year-old son, describing an ideal of fellowship in marriage:

Love well and agree with your wife, for where there is noise and debate in the house, there is unquiet dwelling. And much more where it is in one bed. Frame well yourself to love, and rule well and honestly your wife as your fellow, and she shall love and reverence you as her head. Such as you are unto her such shall she be unto you.

Some turned ideal into reality. Not Wyatt. He wrote from the desolation of his own marriage:

And the blessing of God for good agreement between the wife and husband is fruit of many children, which I for the like thing do lack, and the fault is both in your mother and me, but chiefly in her.

Wyatt looked for love elsewhere, and, fleetingly, found it. Testament to his search is his most beautiful and despairing love poetry. Romantic love was, for the upper orders, often reserved for the mistress or the lover. But to love elsewhere than in marriage was forbidden, and in Wyatt's case punished by his sanctimonious king.

Adultery was regarded by the Church as a sin, and treated as a crime to be formally punished. Bishop Latimer dared to send Henry VIII a New Year's gift of a New Testament and the message 'The Lord will judge fornicators and adulterers'. The breach of marriage vows angered God, sundered families, and broke the peace of the community. Because this was a society which insisted upon the 'good and Catholic' behaviour of its members, neighbours brought accusations of sexual misconduct before the Church courts for trial. Midwives would demand of single women in labour the identity of the child's father and report his name. Convicted adulterers were ordered to perform public penance. Penitents, barefoot and bareheaded (a state of shocking undress in a society where heads were always covered), dressed in a white sheet and bearing a candle to present to the priest at the high altar, declared their guilt and shame before the congregation and sought forgiveness.

Before the Church courts, too, came a torrent of defamation suits, increasing as the century progressed, the overwhelming majority concerned with imputations of sexual misconduct. Women – especially women – stood at doorways, arms folded, arguing from different premises, and hurling abuse at their neighbours. The insults, often remarkably graphic, were usually variants on a single theme: 'arrant whore', 'privy whore', 'stewed [brothel] whore', 'priest's whore', 'Lombard's whore', 'hedge whore', 'burnt [venereally diseased] whore'. The imputations might be true, or they might spring from malice festering among neighbours living at close quarters, gossiping obsessively. The victim of the slander would take her case before the judge, often bringing neighbours to court with her to swear their belief in her innocence. Women had to guard their reputation for sexual 'honesty', not least because they feared being charged with adultery themselves. The most common insult for men was 'whoreson'. Husbands were often called 'cuckold' – the logical counterpoint of their wives' alleged infidelity – and taunted by signs of horns. A double standard prevailed. When, in 1601, Sergeant Harris proposed in the House of Commons (all male, of course) that the penalty for women taken in adultery should be lowered to equal that of men guilty of the same offence, 'all the House cried "Away with it" 'and 'gave a monstrous great "No"'.

Death, not divorce, was the quietus of a marriage. Only in the rarest cases would the Church annul a marriage; where it was judged invalid from its beginning. Every way was sought to bring reconciliation. Priests would ask soul-searching questions in confession, because they were ordained to be parish peace-makers, the arbiters of quarrels. In 1527–8 the wife of Peter Fernandez, a London physician, came often to her confessor, telling him of her husband's threats. The priest sought to make peace between them, unavailingly. The Church could not grant divorce on account of infidelity or cruelty, but could offer a decree of separation which allowed neither party to remarry. Happily or unhappily, a couple might be a long time married, for those who lived to be old enough to marry might expect to live on for another three decades. Till death us do part. In Ireland, however, divorce was lightly granted under the secular custom of the brehon law. When Richard Burke of Clanrickard died in 1582 he left five wives behind, and a sixth had predeceased him.

Catholics were exhorted constantly to remember the four last things – death, judgement, hell and heaven; 'in all thy works remember thine ending day'. Inscriptions on tombs adjured passers-by to consider 'I am what you shall be. I was what you are. Pray for me, I beseech you.' Woodcuts showed angels and demons at the deathbed, vying for the sinner's soul. Death was the last chance to repent and make amends for a life misspent, to cast off sin. All Catholics were taught the art of dying well, although not everyone learnt the lesson. 'Some have I seen,' wrote

Thomas More, 'sit up in their deathbed underpropped by pillows, take their playfellows to them, and comfort themselves with cards.' They gambled with their immortal souls. Yet even the wicked would be saved, if penitent at the last, for God's mercy is infinite. Shortly before his execution in the aftermath of Bosworth, Richard III's counsellor, William Catesby, made a last will full of requests for prayers for his sinning soul and pervaded by a spirit of repentance and remorse for wrongs done during a ruthless and treacherous career.

All Catholics prayed that death would not take them suddenly – they prayed especially to St Barbara for this grace – so that they might have time to repent and confess. Desperate deathbed confessions were made to priests hurriedly summoned. The priest carried the Blessed Sacrament and a crucifix through the streets to the dying, and hearing the last confession gave final absolution and ministered the last rites – the sacraments of unction, confession and Communion. At this rite of departure dying Christians were expected to forgive all who had wronged them and seek forgiveness of those whom they had wronged, affirming their faith and hope for reconciliation with God and the world. Never was the need to be in charity so urgent. The desperation that good Christians should die reconciled with the Almighty was clear at Alice Grisby's deathbed in Aldermanbury, London in 1538. While she lay dying, too ill to speak, her curate and women friends sat anxiously about her, imploring her to look upon the blessed sacrament, to remember the passion of Christ. They pleaded, 'What, will ye die like a hellhound and a beast, not remembering your maker?' At the last, Alice lifted her eyes and held up her hands 'until the extreme pains of death'. So she died a Christian death. The inordinate relief of her friends at the propriety of her manner of dying says much about the anxiety of the community for the Christian life of others as well as about the obsession with dying well.

Paintings of *The Dance of the Dead*, like those at Hexham Abbey or on the north wall of the cloisters of St Paul's, showed the ghastly figure of Death leading the ranks of humanity, grand and lowly, in a grotesque round. Sermons and plays taught that with death comes judgement, and that Christians would be judged not according to who they were, but how they had lived their lives. Yet nothing distinguished the life of a prince from that of a pauper more than the ceremonies at the leaving of it. Magnificent in death as in life, the lord processed for the last time at his funeral, attended still by his household and retinue who wore his badge, and with a brilliant display of heraldic banners. Priests, his poor neighbours and tenants, russet-liveried beggars who had never known him, followed his hearse, bearing lighted candles and praying for his soul. The lord's funeral demonstrated the honour and continuity of his family, surviving the death of its head, but it also celebrated the spiritual affinity between dead and living, rich and poor, the aspiration of the whole community to collective salvation as it prayed for the lord's soul and all Christian souls.

The magnate, for all his great wealth and power, depended upon the goodwill and intercession of his fellow parishioners, just as they depended upon his charity and protection. But perhaps his spiritual need was greater, for had not Christ pointed out the special difficulties for the rich in entering the kingdom of heaven? Any contradiction between the pursuit of wealth and honour in this world, and hopes for salvation in the next, might be reconciled by making restitution and by works of charity. Alms-giving could aid the soul of the donor in the afterlife as it relieved the plight of the poor in this. Doles to the poor were called 'devotions', crumbs from the rich man's table 'Our Lady's bread', for such gifts were believed to lay up treasure in heaven. Doles were given at funerals in exchange for the grateful prayers of the poor, which were believed to impart a special blessing. A bequest of £20 for a penny dole for the poor provided no fewer than 4,800 mourners for the needy soul. In their last wills and testaments the lifelong devout and the belatedly repentant made the same testimonies of devotion.

In every church, every day, masses were sung for the souls of the dead. The requiem mass was first sung at the funeral, but masses continued long after death; for the wealthy sometimes for ever, or so they intended. Perpetual chantries were founded in the late middle ages to provide for a priest and his successors to celebrate requiem mass daily for the repose of the founder's soul, and for the well-being of the living. The multitude of masses celebrated in a parish church – even hourly in some – brought not only intercessory prayers for the souls of the departed but intercession for the salvation of many. The rich endowed prayers for ever; the poor, too, needed and asked for prayers, as many as they could afford. Sharing the same spiritual aspirations and hopes for intercession as their lords, poor craftsmen left a few pence to the high altar in restitution for forgotten tithes or to the fabric of their church; they hoped to share in the benefit of perpetual chantries by joining guilds which would bury them and pray for them; they bade their kin, friends and neighbours to funeral feasts as lavish as they could offer. Feasting was important in binding the community fractured by the death of a member and as a way of keeping the friend in memory. But some had no memorial, and a pauper's grave.

*

Peasants and great nobles alike were born into a family; the tiny society of the nuclear family – a husband, a wife and their children. No bonds in society were stronger than these; no love greater, but no quarrels more bitter, than among those tied by blood. On earth, as in heaven, the society of the family was patriarchal, headed by the father, who was to be feared as well as loved; who ruled and judged his family, as well as caring for it. The figure of the father was central to all authority: monarchical, papal, clerical. Society was strongly patrilineal, defined by the father. When a woman married she took her husband's surname. She left her own patrilineage, her father's family, and entered another family, another patrilineage. The children of the marriage were, in most essential matters – before the law and to her friends and family – his children rather than hers. In the family, founded upon the monogamous marriage, the wife was the necessary, cherished, but subordinate partner. A woman, even a wife, was always inferior, second best. As a sister she was inferior to her brothers, as a wife inferior to her husband. Only as a widow could she, sometimes, escape this depressed condition.

Rich or poor, the legal definition of the family was the same. Then as now, English kinship was bilateral: that is, individuals traced their descent from both father and mother and were equally related to female as to male cousins, to nieces as to nephews. There was kinship by blood (consanguinity) and kinship created by marriage (affinity), for marriage made the in-law's family kin also. When a family chose godparents, spiritual affinity was established, for through baptism not only the child but the child's family became related to the godparents. Children were usually named after their principal godparent, and this – not parental carelessness – was why two children in a family might share the same Christian name. The Church had introduced elaborate canonical prohibitions on marriage by degree of kinship. Those whom one could not marry were one's kin, and vice-versa. Marriage was forbidden between men and women related in the fourth degree of kinship – that is, descended from the same great-great-grandfather – nor could a widow marry the brother of her former husband. Affinity was a bar to marriage.

Adulterous alliance created kinship also, as Henry VIII would forget, when it suited him to forget, and remember when it suited him to remember. Yet the Church rarely intervened to annul the marriages of those married within the forbidden degrees. In small and insular societies the rules had to be suspended or ignored if women were to find husbands and men wives. It was said that 'all Cornish gentlemen are cousins'. The citizens of Cork, according to the chronicler Richard Stanihurst, 'trust not the country adjoining but match in wedlock among themselves only'. In 1537 complaints came from Dublin that no jury could be empanelled because of 'challenging of consanguinity and affinity within the ninth degree'. At that degree, all of Anglo-Irish society was related.

To what extent did people recognize their wider kin, and did kinship create bonds of alliance, loyalty, friendship, duty? In Gaelic Ireland kinship lay at the heart of society, of politics, of justice; it was the primary social bond. There, ancestral piety and a preoccupation with the cult of the dead were even more deeply entrenched than elsewhere in Europe. People were defined by membership of their clan – literally, 'offspring', a corporate family claiming descent from a common male ancestor – and of their sept, a branch of the clan. Still in 1589, as centuries earlier, annalists recorded the death of a lord thus: 'Turlough, the son of Teige, son of Conor, son of Turlough, son of Teige O'Brien of Bel-atha-an chomraic, died; and his death was the cause of great lamentation.' The obligations and loyalty due to kin, this natural affinity, were fundamental. This was a world which knew the extent of kinship, even to the most distant cousins, because there were advantages to knowing it. Knowledge of kin was no mere genealogical curiosity: power and inheritance depended upon it, and kin made real claims on each other, on their possessions, even on their lives. Succession to lordships was elective. It passed, in theory, to the eldest and worthiest among the descendants of former lords within four generations – the *derbfine* group of early Irish law. The whole system of justice in Gaelic Ireland was predicated upon the principle of 'kincogish', the responsibility of the clan for the actions of its members.

Kinship was a powerful force in the extreme instability of late medieval and early modern Ireland. So it was also on the borders with Scotland, in Cumberland, and in Redesdale and North Tynedale in Northumberland, where the 'surnames' – kin groups organized for the mutual protection and security of near neighbours related by blood – had formed, perhaps in the fourteenth century, perhaps earlier, to contain the effects of constant warfare between England and Scotland. In Weardale the unity and strength of the family groupings of the upland kin gave the communities power to mobilize against external aggression. In all these regions, where pastoral farming was practised, the custom of partible inheritance was widespread. Here this pattern of inheritance – gavelkind – promised sons a share in family lands, and encouraged them to stay at home. Nowhere else in England were the ties of kinship so binding; certainly not among the lower orders.

In the restricted society of the nobility and gentry of England, the sense of lineage was vital to its members' self-conception. Seeing themselves as part of a line, with a future and a past, they recognized a compelling duty to the family that came before and would come after, and to the land which was the source of the family's wealth and power. The present head of the family was steward of the patrimony, and it was his responsibility to pass this inheritance to his descendants. Laws of property and laws of entail ensured that estates were not lost to the male family line in the event of a failure to produce children. When William, Lord (later Marquess of) Berkeley (d. 1492) sacrificed the interests of his brother and heir to his own, his seventeenth-century biographer condemned his unnatural behaviour: 'This man was born for himself and intended his house and family should end in himself.' A noble needed to assert the family 'honour' and 'worship', and to maintain the wealth and authority of the family commensurate with its inherited status and right. To exercise 'lordship' was the natural prerogative of the leading lineages and to the lord was owed the service and fidelity of servants and tenants who held the family's lands, and of the dependent gentry who made up his affinity. In uncertain times, the affinity might rise in arms for the lord and the kin be called upon. Yet by the end of the sixteenth century kinsmen were no longer bound in loyalty to name and blood to act; especially not to act against the Crown. For the nobility and gentry, as the century wore on, the sense of family became less a practical, political consideration than a genealogical obsession, as those of 'ancient blood' sought to prove their descent through many generations, and arrivistes invented theirs. Heraldry was studied as the source of memory for a lineage and as a flamboyant declaration of descent.

The world of kin was open and flexible. Recognition of kin depended upon affection, neighbourhood, cupidity and politics, beyond the simple ties of blood. People could behave as kinsmen should to those who in genealogical terms had little claim upon them, and indigent cousins would look, hopefully, to grand and distant relations for favour. Even for the nobility and gentry, loyalty and pride in name and blood did not transcend the interests of the head of the family and his heir, and the stern recognition of the paramount duty of defending the estate. For upper and lower orders alike, the sense of family that mattered and where the ties of obligation and affection were strongest, ran up, and down, through three generations, from parents to children and grandchildren, and across to nephews, nieces and cousins. The family was defined very narrowly indeed when it came to the transmission of property. Through most of England, except, unusually, in the Weald of Kent, and in the remote uplands and the Scottish Marches, among almost all those with something to pass on, the principle of primogeniture prevailed. Lands and wealth passed to the eldest son, whose right was accepted without question, if not always without resentment. For the landed society of England, wealth was something to be inherited, not created; passed on, not passed around. Generation by generation, the gap between the prosperity of the head of the family and his descendants, and the younger brothers and theirs widened, as the families of younger sons made their gradual social descent. Yet in noble and gentry families younger brothers were usually left some modest annuity and daughters were given a marriage portion; not only through affection, but because it did not accord with the 'worship' of a house for sons to live in penury or daughters to marry beneath them.

The family represented an ideal of permanence which was spiritual as well as secular. Lords were buried in churches near their family seats. Entombed in chantries resplendent with the family arms, with prayers for souls endowed in perpetuity, lords asserted their authority even in death, and the immortality of their family. Heraldic emblems were displayed on tombs, in windows, on vestments, in pavements, as symbols of the undying family, in despite of death and infertility. The emblems of the northern nobility – the saltire of the Nevilles of Raby, the bend azure of the Scropes of Bolton – were emblazoned in local churches. In the late fifteenth century some nobles and gentlemen still chose to lie under effigies of recumbent knights in armour, with a faithful dog at their feet, for they continued to see themselves as a martial order. In Ireland that memorial tradition continued longer, and there, where mourning was so extravagant that there was a proverb 'to weep Irish', lords like Tibbot *na Long* of Mayo in the early seventeenth century had 'weepers' sculpted on their tombs.

Further down the social scale, among the common people of England, lineage may have meant little. For them, the world of kin hardly existed beyond the nuclear family. If they made wills, bequests to kin other than children were rare. Migration undermined the bonds of kinship. On the wild uplands of the borders with Scotland younger sons could stay at home, to run and reive cattle, and kinship ties remained strong. Elsewhere, teenagers apprenticed to relations in towns, or townspeople returning to their home village to help bring in the harvest, might keep alive family relationships. Some left money to bring their families together every year. But those children who left their cottage homes, seldom to return, often lost touch with their relations, and created new families of their own upon marriage. The poor, dispersed in search of work, lacking money to spend on family visits or hospitality, illiterate and unable to write letters home, became cut off. At the bottom of the social heap, the indigent poor could help neither themselves nor their kin in the crises of want and illness and old age. Parish registers testify to the anonymity and loneliness in which they lived and died. Leaving home, the common people moved to villages and towns where the majority of households were not linked by blood or marriage.

*

The family was at the heart of the wider – sometimes much wider – world of the household; a *familia* of another kind. The household, consisting of the family, its servants, dependants and possessions, was the centre of all social, economic and artistic life, and the focus of political allegiance. The conjugal family was universal: for the duke, as for the lowliest water-carrier, it was the same – father, mother and children – except that in the case of a great nobleman, marrying young himself, and to a younger wife, there was time to generate many more children. But the household of the great was quite different in kind. Magnanimous and gregarious, with swarms of servants and dependants to manifest their master's greatness, a magnate's household often numbered the size of a village. Edward, Duke of Buckingham, had 187 in his household in 1503–4, and 225 on his check roll in 1511. In the Earl of Northumberland's household in 1511–12 there were 166 men, women and children; in the Earl of Rutland's in 1539 there were 135. Among the households of the realm, as everywhere else, hierarchy and precedence were observed: the household of a duke must be greater than an earl's, but lesser than the king's. The royal household, the court, was to be 'the mirror of others', in which all lesser households were reflected. In the household of a humble artisan and in the court of the king alike the service of one man to another was the defining, dominant social relationship.

'Faithful service', owed not only to God but to the master, was the cohesive force of early Tudor society. In the unwritten code binding lord and man, service and 'faithfulness' were offered to the lord in expectation of his 'favour'; the patronage and protection which constituted 'good lordship'. Service was a personal relationship in which the servant could be called upon to perform any service which the lord required. Service to a lord, even body service of a menial kind, was 'honourable', imparting trust. Dishonour came only when that trust was broken, as in 1521 at the trial of the Duke of Buckingham for treason when his chancellor betrayed secrets which intimate service had made him privy to. The great lord's household maintained his estate – in the sense both of his landed power and of his 'honour'. His household officers – all the stewards, bailiffs, chamberlains, constables and keepers – duly moved into the aristocratic world of the lord's circle. Lords sometimes remembered more officers and servants in their wills than relatives, for the relationship might be closer, the loyalty greater. The 9th Earl of Northumberland told his son 'that in all my fortunes, good and bad, I have found them [his servants] more reasonable than either wife, brother or friends'. The lord's affinity, the overlapping groups of family, household and estate officers; all his 'well wishers', 'good servants', 'true lovers', who were 'bounden during life', might be a focus of loyalty in the local and national community. Over generations one family might offer faithful service to another.

A great household was no mere domestic establishment, but the unifying centre of the family's following, splendid in peace and armed in war. As he dined in public in his Great Chamber, waited upon by carvers and cupbearers, servers and ushers, sung to by his minstrels, entertained by his players and fools, a great lord at the end of the middle ages dazzled and awed with his magnificence. Beneficence was a mark of honour; avarice a sign of shame. The great household should be open to all, offering hospitality to the prosperous and alms to the poor. At Epiphany 1509 Buckingham feasted at Thornbury, entertaining 519 to dinner and 400 to supper. In Gaelic Ireland, where conditions were too unstable for courts and palaces and pageantry, the lords displayed their greatness through hospitality. The Irish annalists, recording the deaths of Gaelic lords, customarily remembered their hospitality and liberality. In England, lords endowed public works, repairing highways, supporting hospitals and lazar [leper] houses and prisons; their almoners gave alms and 'broken meat' [leftovers] to the expectant poor, all in return for prayers. Although some household accounts record larger sums spent on gambling than on the poor, it was never forgotten that acts of charity were a social and religious duty.

The great household was also a religious community which must work for its own salvation and that of its lord. The domestic chapels of great nobles were served by chaplains, morrow mass priests, family confessors and riding priests (who rode with their lord on his journeys). The daily office, Mass and prayers for the dead marked the household's day; they were a way of inducing order as well as devotion. The Duke of Buckingham ordered in his check roll of 1519 that all household members attend Mass daily, because 'no good governance nor politic rule may be had without service to God as well'. The nobility could use religious festivals and processions to vaunt the extent of their following as well as their piety. When Buckingham visited the tomb of Edward, son of Henry VI, in 1508 he was demonstrating to a doubtful Henry VII his loyalty to the House of Lancaster. Reverence was owed to the 'worship' of a great family itself; to its chivalric past and the immortality that virtuous deeds had conferred on the family arms. The family badge – the Percy crescent or the Stafford swan – was a badge of virtue. It drew loyalty and must be defended, even if that loyalty was often expressed among the nobles' community of honour by acts of violence.

Positions of honour around great lords were taken by the sons of the nobility and gentry who were sent, as young as seven, to another lord's household to be his pages of honour, his 'henchmen'. Since personal service was offered by social equals, a duke's son would be page to a prince. Household officials, chaplains and schoolmasters may have been more important in bringing up a nobleman than his own family. In great households boys learnt not only what it was to be lordly and to 'keep countenance', but also the deference and duty to superiors upon which Tudor society was founded. They learnt what it was to be a gentleman; to possess not only wealth (though that was important) but chivalry, courtliness, generosity and martial honour. The chivalric code, the highest secular ideal, was instilled from an early age to discipline the knightly class by its emphasis on service, honour and loyalty. Chivalry was taught in theory through heraldry, history and romance, and in practice through swordplay, riding, jousting and hunting. The nobility had an obligation to lead in war. Fighting was not at a distance, but hand-to-hand, usually on horseback; mortally dangerous if the noble was skilled, lethal if not.

In England, the custom of sending children away to be trained in another lord's household was prevalent in the early sixteenth century, but dying out by the end. In Ireland, the custom of fostering, where lords committed the upbringing of their very young children to others, endured and created intense and lasting loyalties. The death of two of his foster brothers in 1597 preyed on the mind of the Earl of Kildare. Fostering had political consequences. In 1540 complaints reached the Privy Council that because of fostering 'all our secrets are discovered to the Irishmen', and at the end of the century fostering between the Anglo-Irish and Gaelic Irish was seen as the 'bud of our bane', the cause of English destruction.

In humbler households, too, children came to serve and to be trained. Leaving their family home, seldom to return to it, most children found service in another household and spent their adolescence with a family which was not their own. Servants were employed in agriculture, in trade and crafts, and as domestic helpers, a group distinct from wage labourers, who lived in their own homes. They comprised by far the largest occupational group; perhaps one-third to half of all hired labour in agriculture. Servants, away from their family, exchanged duties to parents for duties to masters and mistresses, and learnt that the world was organized by authority; that masters, like fathers, disciplined them, and taught deference along with a craft. As in the great household, the servant owed duty and obedience; the master care and protection. Servants lived as part of the family, eating and sleeping with them. Although some masters abused their authority, and servants defied it, dying masters often bequeathed the responsibility of looking after widows and children to their servants, and servants might choose to stay on after the master's death. Close ties were formed not only between master and servant but also among those in service together, as servants shared their work, rooms, beds and lives. Service brought stability, yet youthful servants moved on, and since the contract of service was only for a year, could be casual members of the household and community. Although the household was the basic unit of society, it was mutable.

The relationship between an apprentice and his master was closer, more enduring. An apprentice was formally bound by oath and indenture to his master for a term of years; to learn a trade, to live within his household, and to obey him. The master was bound also; to teach and to discipline his charge at this unruly stage of life. A master had a duty to chastise a disobedient apprentice, and a boy who wished to protest against ill-treatment had to prove that he had been beaten more constantly than was considered reasonable. Apprentices were sent into the adult world but were still utterly dependent; with prospects of wealth but with none yet. About 1,250 youths arrived in London every year from all over England in the mid-century, and found a home and initiation into the ways of the great and growing metropolis. In Tudor London two-thirds of all men had served as apprentices from the age of eighteen or so, and usually for terms of seven years. Apprentices formed a large element in London society; a disruptive element if ever they banded together, so curfews for apprentices were always ordered at times of political unrest. Yet they lived under close supervision – for a master governed only one or two apprentices – and learnt what it was to be a master of a trade and a household, a member of a company, and a citizen.

By apprenticeship a youth was initiated into the 'secrets' of a mystery or trade and promised mastership and membership of his craft fellowship in time. The craft guilds – a hierarchy of apprentices, journeymen (wage labourers), householders (or master craftsmen), liverymen and assistants – were enduring institutions in late medieval and early modern towns. Through their craft fellowship a master and mistress and their household found a place in their town. The guilds, whose powers stemmed from the solidarity of their members, claimed the right to regulate the establishment of businesses in the crafts and trades which they controlled, and to settle disputes among members who were, after all, economic competitors. Membership of a guild was, in most towns, the only way to citizenship, the possession of the prized 'freedom' which alone allowed full participation in economic, social and political life. In many towns only a citizen enjoyed urban privileges, including the essential right to engage independently in economic activity, to set up shop as a master craftsman or retailer. In early sixteenth-century Coventry four of every five male householders were free of the city; only they could take part in ceremonial processions or in the Corpus Christi plays. In Norwich and York about half of the male population were citizens; in London three-quarters. The guilds were essential in the ordering and defending of a town. It was through the guilds that marching watches were arrayed at midsummer, when men paraded through the streets in military equipment; and through the guilds that a town showed itself in ceremonial array – as at the entry of a monarch.

The fellowship in the craft was real. Spiritual brotherhood had been the first reason for the existence of the guilds, and in the sixteenth century the first reason still mattered. Guild members processed and worshipped together on the day of their patronal feast and maintained lights in churches. They attended the marriages and funerals of their fellows and the 'drinkings' afterwards: such was the action of a friend, the mark of respect of a colleague, but also the sworn duty of a company member. The duty extended to dead members, whose anniversary masses were attended by their fellows. Charity was given to members who were ill and old. Writing his will, a citizen of any town would describe himself first as citizen, then name his craft and lastly his parish. These were the fellowships which justified and sustained him.

*

Their families dispersed, their own kin distant and incidental, most people looked to other fellowships, other communities, to assume the traditional obligations of kinship. From their neighbours, whom they chose as 'trusty friends' and 'gossips' (*godsibb*), they might find the support and loyalty which kin had once provided in some lost world. Neighbours were chosen as godparents, attended childbirths, baptisms, weddings, sickbeds and deathbeds; celebrated or commiserated at the rites of passage; were witnesses to wills, and trusted to look after widows and orphans. They lent each other implements and money, and acted as guarantors and sworn witnesses before the courts. In the 'play called Corpus Christi', at the trial of Mary and Joseph the summoner calls Mary's neighbours to appear: Malkyn Milkduck, Lucy Liar, Fair Jane, Robin Red, Lettice Littletrust – the familiar world of late medieval neighbourhood. True, it was neighbours who usually brought the charges in the first place, for neighbourly relations often descended into quarrels and recriminations. Neighbours who were offended might – like the Wicked Fairy at the christening – curse. It was for violation of the duties owed by neighbours and in retaliation for some breach of charity that alleged witches performed acts of maleficence, the darkest example of malign neighbourly relations.

Even in the supposed anonymity of a great city neighbourly obligations were taken seriously. In London neighbourhoods loyalties could transcend the divisions between rich and poor and sustain friendships between families who otherwise moved in different social spheres. People remembered poor neighbours in their own parishes in their wills; paupers whom they knew by name, like 'John with the sore arm'. John Stow, London's chronicler, recalled the great summer festivals of the 1530s, of his youth, when wealthy citizens set out tables with food and drink and invited their neighbours to 'be merry with them in great familiarity'. Bonfires were lit; '*bon* fires', according to Stow, because of the 'good amity amongst neighbours' they engendered. But Stow remembered this social unity half a century later with the nostalgia of one who thought it lost and hardly to be recovered.

Neighbourliness and fellowship were Christian ideals; the amity in Christ created by one faith and one communion. In the course of the sixteenth century the fellowship of the neighbourhood was subject to strains which eroded concord. Population increase and subsequent impoverishment undermined the obligations of the rich to the poor, whom they were less and less likely to know personally. Religious divisions fractured the community of faith. Yet the bonds of religious and social obligation were strong and often held people together during this century when divergences in faith and economic exigencies threatened to drive them apart. That 'perfect love and charity' necessary before anyone could receive the sacrament was not forgotten, however hard that amity was to achieve; neighbours might insist upon it, and priests exclude the rancorous and unforgiving until they were reconciled with the community. That community was not only the neighbourhood, but also, more formally, the parish.

England's parishes, more than 8,000 of them, had been formed by 1300, as a result of people's wish to worship together in small congregations close to their priest. This wish remained in the early sixteenth century, and people worshipped in their parishes by custom, by desire and by ecclesiastical sanction. Everyone was necessarily a member of a parish, with attendant duties and rights: duties to attend and maintain the church and to support the priest; and rights to spiritual consolation through the sacraments. Parishioners not only worshipped but celebrated together. At St Margaret Pattens in London there was a bowl used, not for sacred, but for festive occasions: it was inscribed on the outside, 'Of God's hand blessed be he that taketh this cup and drinketh to me,' and on the inside, 'God that sitteth in Trinity, send us peace and unity.' Where there were disputes within a parish they were put into arbitration, or 'daying'. Churchwardens' accounts everywhere tell of the determination of parishioners to beautify their churches; of the church ales, plays and shooting matches organized to finance the continuing rebuilding and adornment. This was a great period of church building; perhaps a sign of devotional vitality, but not necessarily. In Renaissance Rome a high point of building corresponded with a time of spiritual inanition.

In an ideal world mutual concern and charity among fellow parishioners, living and dying, would have been guaranteed. But the world was not ideal, and the community of the parish was formal, compulsory, its boundaries fixed – no longer the voluntary association of fellow Christians it had been at its origin. Seeking closer fellowship, people chose to join religious guilds both within and beyond their parishes. Brothers and sisters in these lay confraternities swore oaths to support their living fellows through friendship and charity, and their dead members through their prayers. Brothers and sisters could be incorporated after death in the guilds' immemorial membership. Sisters in the guilds had – as almost nowhere else – more or less the same status as brothers. Religious guilds existed in their thousands in England, and were still being founded, a vital expression of late medieval religious life. In the early sixteenth century Londoners remembered over eighty guilds in half the parishes of the City in their wills. In Dublin at the same period there were at least eleven religious fraternities flourishing in the City and the county. The guild dedicated to St Anne in the parish of St Audoen, with its own chapel and chaplains, who celebrated daily at St Anne's altar, and six singing-men, was the most important. This guild survived into the seventeenth century, a focus of intense Catholic devotion. In Gaelic Ireland, where the bonds of kinship were so strong, there were no religious guilds, no invented brotherhood.

What marked the confraternities as religious? In which ways were the lay brotherhoods spiritual? All the guilds maintained lights before the image of their patron saint upon their own altars; their members attended mass on their patronal festivals; some supported their own priest. The Christian imperatives of preventing sin and fostering virtue were paramount, and the guilds insisted upon moral probity in commercial relations between the brethren. In their rules the first avowed purpose was to live in charity; in some guilds this ideal was symbolized by the kiss of peace. Their duty was also to offer charity of another kind: the seven works of mercy towards their fellows, especially burial of the dead.

Some sought fraternity in a religious life more intense by far. The monastic way of life, to which all religious orders were in some way assimilated, had been in existence for almost a millennium by the early sixteenth century. Men and women still chose to live as brothers and sisters in communities of witness, dedicated to God's service. At his profession, a monk took vows of lifelong poverty, chastity and obedience to his abbot and his Rule. Regular canons lived by a Rule like monks, but one step less divorced from the rest of the world. The mendicant orders of friars – so called because they were originally meant to live by begging – followed Christ in their preaching and apostolic poverty. The formal commitment of the religious orders to a shared and regulated life forever separated them from both the laity and the secular clergy (priests). They were, above all, celebrants of divine service, and their penances and prayers might inspire the laity living beyond their walls. Their houses also offered alms to the poor and sheltered pilgrims and travellers. In England in 1500 there were perhaps 10,000 monks and 2,000 nuns, living in 900 religious communities. In Ireland, a generation later, there were about 140 monastic foundations and 200 mendicant communities.

Most of these communities had fallen far from the pursuit of Christian perfection which was the ideal of their founders. Few truly religious houses remained. Spiritual corporations had, over the centuries, become economic corporations. The religious houses were an integral part of society not only – or even – because of their penances and prayers, but because of their immense power as landlords. The religious had come to hold more wealth than they could easily control without prejudicing their spiritual life, and a pervasive secularism had entered the cloisters. In Ireland, the hereditary principle often prevailed in the succession to abbacies, in violation of the vow of chastity. The extravagant projects of building and adornment in Irish Cistercian houses cast some doubt upon their austere following of a Rule which insisted upon simplicity, though they suggest vitality of a kind. Great and flaunted wealth attracted envy and detraction. In England, their critics accused the 'monkery' of degeneracy, even of depravity, and suspected that their every vow was travestied and broken. When the testing time came it was a matter of record that many of the religious thought too much of the flesh they should have subdued; that their spiritual aspirations were lost to the claims of the world. For the most part, if they did no good, they at least did little harm, though that was shame enough.

Some in the religious houses did seek Christ and provided an inspiring example to the very end. In the Charterhouses, the monks followed their

Rule of cold austerity, silence, prayer. The Bridgettine foundation at Syon Abbey, established at Isleworth on the Thames in 1415, manifested a spirit of renewal. In England, the Observant Franciscans revitalized the religious life of their order by reinstating the Rule from which it had fallen. There were six houses for Observants in the early sixteenth century. In Ireland, the spirit of reform touched three of the four mendicant orders and the friars' fervour and moral authority gave them a powerful influence among the laity. True, the reform movement in Irish religious orders was partly an assertion of their freedom from being controlled from the English province, and a protest of Gaelic communities against Anglo-Irish ownership, but the spiritual inspiration was plain. That many of the religious orders were exempt from the hierarchical jurisdiction of the Church, and directly under papal authority, came to threaten them.

*

The *Lay Folks' Mass Book* urged each attender at Mass to pray:

> My heart to be in peace and rest,
> And ready to love all manner of men:
> My sib men namely, then
> Neighbours, servants and subjects,
> Friends and foes and foryectes [outcasts].

Loving enemies and outcasts was hardest of all. All the communities of household, religious fraternity, craft fellowship, neighbourhood and parish still left some, perhaps many, excluded. Brotherhood, it has been well said, implies otherhood. Personal disasters and social stresses left many stranded and outcast. For some, the rejection was of choice. Christendom might be spurned not only by infidels, but by those who doubted the faith of their 'even christen' and thought their own faith invalidated theirs. These were the heretics.

The poor are with us always, but at some times more evidently than at others. The Tudor century saw a terrible growth of impoverishment. A huge population rise from the early century; agricultural transformations; and the operation of the land market in favour of the aggrandizing, left many homeless, landless, destitute. Even in what passed for good times there was never enough work to go around; what work there was was seasonal and increasingly badly paid, and the poor were often driven on to the road to look for it. In bad times those who lived on the edge of subsistence were especially vulnerable. Failing harvests drove up prices beyond the ability of the poor to buy, and destitution followed. At times the desperation of the poor cried out. At a dole of bread in Southwark in 1533 there was such a press of people that four men, two women and a boy were crushed to death. Some in their terrible poverty abandoned their children in the doorways of the rich. In the 1550s Londoners remembered foundlings in their wills, and sometimes bequeathed them in turn: 'My little child William, whom I keep of alms, I give as freely as he was given me.'

Time was when the poor had been seen as somehow blessed, as Christ's own image. But when the poor became so many that they confronted the rich on every street corner, covered with sores and begging with menaces, it became harder to see them as beatified. The destitute in towns, especially in London, did not keep a decent distance in ghettoes and out-parishes: rich and poor lived side by side, the rich in great houses on main thoroughfares, the poor in side alleys and lanes behind. A harsher doctrine began to prevail towards charity and the poor, and some recalled St Paul's warning to the Thessalonians: 'If there were any that would not work, that the same should not eat.' There was increasing discrimination, in law and popular attitude, between the 'deserving' and 'undeserving' poor, the 'able-bodied' and the 'impotent'; between those who wished to work but could not, and those who could work but would not. It was a long time before the authorities acknowledged that there was insufficient work to go around. The 'sturdy [and] mighty vagabond' was increasingly seen as a threat to the common-wealth rather than part of it.

A society which sought stability and order, which believed that every man must have a master, found a danger in the increasing number of utterly transient, rootless human flotsam; a danger which lay in their mutability and masterlessness. Parliament had first made masterlessness a crime in the fourteenth century, and by the sixteenth century the vagrant poor could be arrested not because of any action, not because they had committed any crime, but simply for being masterless and adrift from their family, members of no settled household, nor likely to be. Very many of the vagrant poor were young, not only because most of the population was young, but because this time of life was most insecure. Orphans and abandoned children were often left to wander the streets, unmarried servants who became pregnant (often enough by their masters) were cast out of the household, and passed from one parish to the next which did not wish to shelter them. Derelicts gave their last trouble to society by dying in the streets. The authorities feared that there were 'fraternities' of vagabonds, conspiring to cause trouble. Not so; a few vagrants might band together for safety and mutual support, but companies of travellers were rare.

The worst desolation was not poverty or the recourses it led to – begging, prostitution, and crime – but the mental desolation of despair. Suicide was a kind of murder, a felony in criminal law and a desperate sin in the eyes of the Church. Suicides were tried posthumously by a coroner's jury and, if convicted of self-murder, their goods were forfeit and they were denied Christian burial, instead being buried with macabre and profane ceremonies. For these reasons, evidence of suicide must often have been covered up. Yet in May 1532 there were fourteen suicides in London, by hanging or drowning, at the time that a traumatic assault on the liberties of the Church caused Thomas More to resign his office. Thomas More thought often upon suicide, and wrote in one of his last works of the 'very special holy man' tempted by the Devil to imagine that it was God's will that he should destroy himself, and thereby go straight to heaven. But suicide was the ultimate act of religious defiance, a sin for which there could be no penitence, for the sinner would be dead.

Those who committed terrible sins and were impenitent were excommunicated, cast out from the Church and the communion of the faithful. 'First we accurse all them that break the peace of Holy Church'; so went the curse of major excommunication pronounced quarterly by the parish priest. People who were cursed were denied sacramental grace, and the solemnity of the anathema was marked by the ringing of bells and the extinction of candles. In 1535 a curse was pronounced against Thomas Fitzgerald and his adherents for a terrible sin: the murder of John Alen, Archbishop of Dublin. It called on God to strike them with fire and sulphur, hunger, thirst, leprosy, madness.

As ye see these candles lit and the light quenched, so be the said cursed murderers . . . excluded and separated from the light of heaven, the fellowship of angels, and all Christian people, and shall be sent to the low darkness of fiends and damned creatures, among whom everlasting pains doth endure.

And yet, divine forgiveness and salvation at last awaited even the worst sinners, if penitent. The curse ended with the hope that 'Jesu Christ, of His infinite mercy, may call them to the grace of repentance.'

3

Ways to Reform

THE CHALLENGE TO
THE CHURCH

Anyone who wilfully denied cardinal doctrines of the Catholic faith, and persisted in error, might be burnt at the stake as a heretic. This was the punishment for society's worst enemy. People bringing faggots to the heretic's fire were promised forty days of pardon from the other-worldly fires of purgatory. The burnings were terrible, but they were very rare: so they were meant to be, and had been, at least during the century since the penalty of burning for heresy had been instituted in 1401, and after heretics and rebels in Sir John Oldcastle's abortive rising of 1414 had attempted no less than the dispossession of the Church and the capture of the King. As the darkest of sins, heresy threatened to call down the vengeance of God not only on the heretics but also upon the society which harboured them. Long before, in the reign of King John, when England had fallen under papal interdict, it was said that the corn had failed and neither grass nor fruit would grow. If England were ever cut off from Catholic Christendom again because of the will of a king, or if heretics became too many to be cast out, natural disorder would return. In 1532 Sir Thomas More thought that that time had come, and prophesied that God would withdraw His grace and let all run to ruin.

*

There were heretics within the community when Henry VII's reign began, but they were few and, for the most part, hidden. The history of heresy is often inseparable from the history of persecution. Heretical enclaves were discovered only when the authorities sought and found them; the nature of their dissent revealed only in the light of the questions which the persecutors asked. Only the Church, which had been dis-obeyed, could define what was heresy, judge and condemn it. The heretics who were discovered were usually those who scandalized their neighbours and offended against the ethics of the society in which they lived; those who held their heresies in private and lived obscure were likely to remain safe, unknown to the persecutors and to posterity. No single and adamantine code of heretical belief existed in England at the end of the middle ages. There were individual dissidents, with beliefs so deviant that they alone held them. There were also distinct heretical communities of men and women with their own creed, tradition, martyrs and code of behaviour; a sect which recognized itself as marked by special providences. To their enemies they were the Lollards; to themselves, the 'privy' or 'known' men and women; known, that is, to themselves, but, they hoped, not to others, for they kept their faith in secret, hiding from persecution.

Lollardy was first inspired by the ideas and ideals of John Wyclif at the end of the fourteenth century, but the movement was the creation of Wyclif's early disciples as much as of Wyclif himself. Those ideas had been transmuted in the dissemination of them: Wyclif's more subtle teachings upon the theology of the Eucharist were simplified as they were promulgated beyond the Oxford Schools to the wider community, and his more philosophical ideas upon predestination and dominion were gradually diluted. Wyclif's argument that no one – priest or lay-man, king or peasant – whilst in a state of mortal sin had true dominion over anything, either inanimate object or animate nature, had radical implications: the clergy, if not in a state of grace, could lawfully be deprived of their endowments. Wyclif had looked to the Crown and nobility to reform the Church, but the spectacular ambition and failure of the Lollard armies under Sir John Oldcastle in 1414 had cost them any chance of support from the political orders or of conciliation with Church or Crown. Throughout the fifteenth century, the 'known men and women' had sustained their faith in secret, guarding their treasured manuscript copies of the Bible in John Purvey's translation and of Wycliffite texts, but they were leaderless, and without theological guidance to ensure spiritual orthodoxy and regeneration. By the mid fifteenth century the Church was pleased to believe that the heresy had almost disappeared. But it had not. There were sufficient signs of Lollardy's revival by the early sixteenth century for the prelates to begin to hunt for it again, and to find it. They discovered remarkable continuities in the Lollard communities and their beliefs.

Lollardy was a faith practised in households, not in churches. Lollards believed that theirs was the true Church, they God's 'children of salvation', and that the Catholic Church was the Church of Antichrist, the Devil's Church. Usually, they conformed superficially within their communities, often attending their parish churches in order to evade suspicion. Salisbury heretics admitted in 1499 that they received the holy sacrament, not because of their belief in it, but because of 'dread of the people' and of the danger if they did not do 'as other Christian people did'. Yet they saw themselves as set apart from 'other Christians'. Was it true, asked Church officials in 1521, who were in the dark about this closed world, that Lollards only married other Lollards? Sometimes it was. Bound as well by ties of kinship and friendship as by their common faith, the Lollards sustained each other, a fraternity of an heretical kind. Lollard masters took Lollard apprentices and servants; Lollard children were brought up in the faith; Lollard widows remarried other Lollards. Lollard families protected the missionaries who travelled between the communities, and sheltered fugitives from the authorities.

Radical sectaries of the later middle ages were usually of artisan status, and so most Lollards were. In 1523 a disgruntled curate complained, 'These weavers and millers be naughty fellows and heretics many of you.' Yet not all were artisans, nor were they poor. The discovery of Lollards in higher ranks of society made the revival of the heresy the more alarming. In 1514 the Bishop of London's summoner claimed that he could take his master to heretics in London who were each worth a thousand pounds. Fellowship in the faith might transcend the usual barriers between rich and poor. Robert Benet, an illiterate Lollard water-carrier, found shelter during the battle at Blackheath in 1497 at the house of John Barret, a goldsmith of Cheapside and Merchant of the Staple at Calais, one of the richest men in the City. In the Lollard enclave in the Chilterns 'known men' held respected positions within their communities. When the bishops began to look for them once more, the Lollards still congregated where they had always been before: in London, Essex, Kent, Coventry, Bristol, in the Chilterns, and through the Thames Valley from Newbury in Berkshire to Burford in the Cotswolds.

Lollards met together in order to read the scriptures. The Gospels and Epistles of the New Testament, in English, were their inspiration and the fount of their faith. It was the Lollard preoccupation with vernacular scripture which had outlawed the English Bible, not only to them, but to all others, since Archbishop Arundel's Constitutions of 1409. Reading the Bible aloud and evangelizing the Christian message was the purpose of any Lollard assembly, and if some, perhaps most, were illiterate, it hardly mattered, for those who could not read could listen. This was a society used to committing words to memory. Lollards became deeply versed in the texts. Thirteen-year-old Elizabeth Blake, the daughter of a Lollard living by St Anthony's school in London, knew by heart and could recite the Epistles and Gospels. Wyclif's belief in the priesthood of all believers was made reality as they expounded the Word without priests to enlighten them.

Knowledge of scripture was the rule of faith. Their texts sustained their movement. Robert Benet, the poor water-carrier, had already been detected for his heresy in 1496, but in 1504 he sold his looms and shears in order to buy a copy of the Four Evangelists. He could not read it, but kept it safe in his belt, and Thomas Capon, the stationer who sold it to him, taught him its truths. Joan Austy brought a copy of *Wyclif's Wicket* with her when she remarried, as a Lollard dowry. Her first husband had entrusted this treasure to her on his deathbed. The texts were passed around, and read secretly, by night. Possessing them was dangerous. The disciples of Thomas Denys, a Lollard teacher, were forced to watch his burning in 1513, and to throw their books into the fire to burn with him. For the Lollards, as for their spiritual heirs, the puritans, to hear the Word of God was a kind of sacrament. John Whitehorn, rector of Letcombe Basset, who was burnt at Abingdon in 1508 for his heretical ministry, taught that 'whosoever receive devoutly God's Word, he receiveth the very body of Christ'. Asking, did not St John's Gospel begin: 'The word is God, and God is the Word'? he echoed Wyclif's identification of Christ with scripture. John Pykas, a Colchester baker, converted by his Lollard mother, avowed in 1527 that 'God is in the Word and the Word is God'.

A theological chasm opened between committed Lollards and their Catholic neighbours. Lollards thought Catholic devotion was superstition; Catholic veneration, idolatry. What Catholics held holiest, they denied, even derided. For their views on the Mass, above all, Lollards were persecuted, for here many of them were guilty of the gravest heresy of all: they doubted the miracle of transubstantiation. Though Wyclif himself had believed in the Real Presence in the Eucharist, many of his later followers, ignoring or misunderstanding his subtleties, rejected the central mystery. They asked how Christ, one and indivisible, could be at once on earth with mankind and in heaven with His Father; how Our Lord's body could be made by corrupt priests. They maintained that the Eucharist was a memorial, commemorative event; that the bread and wine were only figures of Christ; that priests could not make their Maker. Thomas Denys died for saying that the Eucharist was not 'The very body of Christ, but a commemoration of Christ's passion, and Christ's body in a figure and not the very body'. Denying the sanctity of the Mass themselves, they would impugn its power to others. As he came from Mass at the Grey Friars in 1520, Rivelay, a Londoner, said that he had just seen his Lord God in form of bread and wine over the priest's head. But John Southwick protested that it was only a figure of Christ. Lollards believed that to worship the consecrated Host was idolatry, as was the veneration of images and crucifixes, for the Commandments forbade the making of graven images. The Lollards were the first, but not the last, of English reformers to insist that God did not dwell in temples built with hands.

Lollards despised the crosses which were universally venerated. Why should the cross be worshipped which had brought Christ such suffering? A crucifix carried by a priest to a Lollard's deathbed was spurned as a false god. Lollards would taunt images, and sometimes attack them, challenging them to defend themselves if they could. It was, they thought, not only idolatrous but socially iniquitous to devote time and money to serving saints' images by pilgrimage and other acts of devotion, while the poor, Christ's own image, suffered; true pilgrimage, they believed, was to go barefoot to visit the poor, weak and hungry. The other sort was, at best, folly, and profited only the priests who took the offerings of the deluded faithful. As a woman implored Our Lady to help Joan Sampson in her labour, Joan spat on her and sent her away. Prayer should be directed to God alone, and not to saints, because only God could answer it, and surely the prayer of a good life was more meritorious than the repetition of words, 'lip labour'. Why confess to a priest, when God alone can forgive sin? Views like these put the Lollards outside conventional society.

For every Lollard who died at the stake there were fifty who recanted, but recantation itself left a fearsome stigma, for ostracism awaited those who bore the badge of the abjured heretic, the mark of the faggot. People would pour ashes on a heretic's grave, so that grass should never grow there. So it was at the beginning of the sixteenth century, but not for much longer, for soon a society which had been fundamentally united in religion became divided, and there were too many heretics to be cast out. Lollardy was one of the more coherent heretical creeds in Western Christendom. The Hussites in Bohemia had effected a

Reformation there in the early fifteenth century which was premature, and which remained as a spectre to haunt the imaginations of those in England who feared a similar enormity. Believing that pestilential heresy was on the increase in England, the bishops began looking for it more assiduously, and what they discovered alarmed them. In 1518–21 Bishop Longland's inquisition found over 400 'known' men and women in his great Lincoln diocese. Still Lollards were few. Without political or spiritual leadership, Lollardy offered no prospect of inspiring a national reforming movement; not in England, and certainly not in Wales or Ireland. There had been no new Lollard text written since about 1440. Nevertheless, part of the Lollard creed anticipated the beliefs which made the English Reformation.

The Lollard challenge lay principally in the understanding among some within the Church that Lollard arguments were not always easy to refute; that some of their criticisms were just; that some of their principles were ones which all Christians should acknowledge. John Colet, the reforming Dean of St Paul's, had warned the clergy in 1511 that heretics were not so dangerous to the faith as the evil and wicked lives of priests. Lollards could claim – although it was heresy to do so – that the sacraments were vitiated by the corruption of the clergy. Even the Mass could be portrayed as an invention of priests to beguile the faithful into supporting their indolent, venal lives. This was the true anticlericalism; the anti-sacerdotalism of heresy, which denied the essential place and function of the clergy. Richard Hunne, a wealthy Londoner, mounted a sustained challenge to the clergy and was murdered for it – martyred – or so the Church's critics alleged. Defending a fellow parishioner who abjured the most shocking heresies, he said that her beliefs accorded with the laws of God. He inveighed against priestly power; against prelates 'all things taking and nothing ministering'. But above all, he was charged with reading the Apocalypse, the Epistles and Gospels in English. He defended the right of the laity to read the English Bible. In the prologue of his own Bible was written, 'Poor men and idiots have the truth of Holy scriptures, more than a thousand prelates.' He left a Bible in the church of St Margaret in Bridge Street, for the edification of all who would read it. Yet the desire to have the scripture in English need not have been heretical, and criticism of the Church was far from being simply a negative spirit.

*

There was at the end of the middle ages a pious and fervently orthodox desire among influential laity and clergy for renewal in Christian life. The Church was *semper reformanda*, always in need of reform, but at some times more urgently than at others. Although the papacy itself, preoccupied with war and money, seemed to have forgotten Christ's warning about gaining the whole world and losing the soul, and the Church as an institution seemed mired in worldly concerns, careless of spiritual ones, still there was an impassioned search to rediscover the redemptive presence of Christ within this Church. There were hopes that Renaissance might come in the Church also; that it might move closer to an apostolic ideal. Christianity could be revived by a return *ad fontes* – to the Bible and the Church Fathers. Scripture was rediscovered by applying the new humanist studies of the ancient biblical languages, Hebrew and Greek, to uncover meanings long lost among the distortions and muddles in the Vulgate, St Jerome's fourth-century translation.

The most brilliant exponent of this new spiritual message was Desiderius Erasmus, who captured the imagination of an elite in England and in Europe in the first decades of the sixteenth century. In 1504 he published his *Enchiridion militis Christiani* (*The Handbook of a Christian Soldier*), a manifesto of the new Christianity. Inspired by scripture, especially by the teachings of St Paul, his writings aspired to bring regeneration and collective renewal in Christian life. The ambition was to educate not only those who were educated already, but the simple and unlearned. Every ploughboy at his plough, every woman at her loom, the weaver, the traveller, should know the Epistles of St Paul and the Gospels. The philosophy of Christian humanism bred impatience and scepticism with the pursuit of salvation by ritual observance, or its supposed purchase by good works performed without charity. The *Enchiridion* inveighed against all the distractions from the true 'philosophy of Christ', and this was no mild admonishment. While the poor, Christ's own image, groaned with hunger, 'thou spewest up partridges'; while the supposed Christian lost a thousand pieces of gold in a night's gaming, some wretched girl in her desperation sold her chastity, 'and thus perisheth the soul for whom Christ hath bestowed his life'. True religion lay in righteous conduct, not in fatuous ceremonies. For Erasmus and his followers, all those prayers and penances, fasts and vigils, the mechanical good works of late medieval devotion, made a mockery of Christ's death and of what He had come to do.

Erasmus found kindred spirits in England. Listening to Colet, so he wrote in 1499, was like listening to Plato himself. John Colet came to London from Oxford in 1505, and gave a series of sermons inspired by humanist evangelism. He did not, in the way of the schoolmen, take a discrete text and preach a detailed discourse to prove a particular point of faith; rather he preached 'Gospel history', upon Christ Himself. When he founded St Paul's School, die-hard conservatives feared, so Thomas More wrote, that a crowd of Christians would spring like Greeks from the Trojan horse. A generation of evangelicals did spring from this academy. In his urgency to reform, Colet began to touch upon matters which were politically controversial and seen as doctrinally unsafe. An impassioned poem of the time, 'The Ruin of a Realm', lamented moral decadence: it saw one cause – 'spiritual men undoubtedly/Doth rule the realm brought to misery' – and saw one cleric who stood apart from the self-seeking of the rest. This paragon might have been John Fisher, Bishop of Rochester, the leading theologian and humanist scholar. It might also have been Colet, who warned the clergy against their worldliness, who preached against war just as Henry VIII launched grandiose campaigns, who inveighed against the sin of pride before the magnificent Cardinal Wolsey. And Colet believed that the heretics had something to teach the Church about reform. He read heretical works, and Lollards came to hear him preach. His translation of the paternoster (the Lord's Prayer) into English seemed to confirm suspicions of his orthodoxy, which were all unfounded. A good Catholic should have hoped for renovation within the Church, have deplored its current state, and yearned for a purity which had once existed in an apostolic golden age. Reform was needed, and urgently.

From where would reform come? Perhaps from a General Council of the Church. Erasmus in his *Sileni of Alcibiades* (1515) reminded his readers that although priests, bishops and popes were called 'the Church', they were only its servants. 'The Christian people is the Church.' A century before, General Councils, representing the congregation of the faithful, had challenged unworthy popes, and might do so again. But Councils could become toys of secular rulers. In 1511 Louis XII of France convoked a schismatic Council to force the papal hand, and in turn Julius II, the worldly, warrior pope, responded by calling the Fifth Lateran Council. But these rival Councils, preoccupied with politics, did very little to effect reform, to the despair of Catholic reformers.

Another way to reform would be by education. Education in virtue was the best preparation for civic life. Cicero and classical authors taught the first lesson for the commonwealth: that man is not born for himself, but for the public. A humanist education provided a training in rhetoric, the classical art of eloquence. Christ Himself had been the sublime exponent of this art, the perfect teacher while on earth. Rhetoric was, for the sixteenth century, anything but empty. It had the practical purpose of persuading and providing counsel to those with power in the spiritual and secular realms. Yet, as More's character Hythloday observed, princes might not listen, true counsel might be stifled and flattery prevail.

Satire was a powerful means of persuasion to reform. In the *Julius Exclusus* – anonymous, but written by an Englishman – the irredeemable Julius II arrived at the locked gates of heaven which he could not unlock with the keys to the treasury of the Church. Denied entry by St Peter, he was consigned to hell. In Erasmus's audacious *Praise of Folly*, Folly presented unpalatable truths about the grotesqueries of society and mounted a scathing attack upon the failings of contemporary Christianity; upon monks and theologians; and upon a papacy which was dedicated to war and subversive of law, religion and peace. *Praise of Folly (Moriae Encomium)* was written for More, to More, the title a pun on his name. In 1515 More replied, writing his own satire, *Utopia*. Its rhetorical purpose was to advance reform by contrasting an ideal with the lamentable reality. Readers were invited to judge whether the fool or the friar at Cardinal Morton's table was truly the fool. Yet, if the friar was the fool, he was a dangerous one: 'We have a papal bull by which all who mock at us are excommunicated.' These satires were immensely popular: *Praise of Folly* was reprinted fifteen times before 1517. Yet as the satires passed beyond the humanist audiences for whom they were written, the dangers as well as the exciting possibilities of print became apparent.

The best way to restore religion would be to reveal 'pure Christ' in scripture; scripture freely available and translated according to the best humanist principles. Erasmus translated the entire New Testament from Greek, and published the Greek text in 1516, with a parallel Latin translation. This translation was received with huge optimism by many, but criticized by conservatives who thought that to meddle with the Vulgate at all was doubtful and dangerous. Thomas Cromwell, a London lawyer, took Erasmus's New Testament with him on a journey to Rome in 1517–18, and learnt it by heart. It marked him, and the Reformation in England that he helped to make. A decade later, Stephen Vaughan wrote telling Cromwell, his friend and former master, of his search through London to recover a debt from the evasive Mr Mundy; of how he found him at evensong, not inclined to discuss money. But Vaughan told Mundy that if he wished to serve God he could not do so better than by making restitution. Here was a joke about hypocrisy, but behind it lay the essential humanist belief that true piety lay in right action not conventional obsequies.

In 1516, the year when Erasmus published his New Testament and More his *Utopia*, everything seemed possible. This was a liminal moment. Reformers, within the Church but deeply critical of its practices, still hoped for renewal, through scripture. Christian humanism laid the foundations for all that was to come: while its spirit was essentially orthodox, it prepared the way for a more radical vision. Yet Erasmus's learned translation still left the Bible only for the educated. The term associated with Erasmus, *philosophia Christi* (the philosophy of Christ), suggests the limit of its popular appeal. There came demands that scripture no longer be locked up in Latin, mediated by priests, but available in English to give the faithful an infallible rule whereby to judge the Church and its claims to absolute authority in matters of faith. For William Tyndale, the great reformer and biblical translator, Christians should believe nothing without the authority of God's Word. Erasmus had, in his insistence upon inner conviction rather than outward ritual and his demand that Christians focus their hearts inwardly on grace given by God, prefigured the great debates on faith and salvation which would soon divide the Church. In Wittenberg, Martin Luther was reading Erasmus's New Testament, and in 1517, on All Saints' Eve, he posted his ninety-five theses, and challenged the papacy and the Church.

*

Luther, monk and theologian, had been wrestling with the deepest metaphysical questions concerning the nature of man's will and divine grace, of God's mercy and His justice, and of man's sin and redemption through Christ. As he sought the answer to the quintessential question for every Christian – 'what must one do to be saved?' – between 1514 and 1519 he came gradually to a new understanding. Thinking upon the teaching in St Paul, 'the righteous shall live by faith', he had come close to despair. Who could love a God, he asked, who wished to deal with sinners according to justice? For Luther was convinced that the fallen human race, eternally damned by original sin, could never be free from its dominion. He came to believe that human will, bound and captive to sin, had no capacity to attain righteousness. But he found a 'wonderful new definition of righteousness', whereby 'we are righteous only by the reckoning of a merciful God, through faith in His Word'. Sinners are made righteous – justified – through faith alone, by God's grace freely given and received in a state of unstriving trust in His mercy. God alone moved man to repentance, Luther believed, and faith itself was a divine work. He rejected any belief that salvation is dependent upon any decision of the human will.

In 1520, in a tract entitled *The Liberty of a Christian*, Luther described simply the nature of the relationship between Christ and the sinner:

Christ is full of grace, life, and salvation. The human soul is full of sin, death, and damnation. Now let faith come between them. Sin, death, and damnation will be Christ's. And grace, life, and salvation will be the believer's.

For those Catholics who, like Luther, had despaired, doubting that their own striving, their own works, could ever bring their sinful souls to God, these writings brought profound hope and a joyful certainty of salvation. William Roper, a young lawyer at the Inns of Court, assailed by that spiritual doubt which the Church called scrupulosity, was 'bewitched' by *The Liberty of a Christian*. But for Roper, and for all others led into the strong light of justifying faith, there were consequences destructive of the whole sacramental and penitential system of the Church. 'Then thought he that all the ceremonies and sacraments in Christ's Church were very vain.'

Luther came to believe that sinners cannot expiate their sins. Once he understood that man was justified by faith alone, atonement and satisfaction for sin were irrelevant to his reconciliation with God. 'Good works' – including the obligations of prayer, fasting and alms-giving; the veneration of saints and their images; and penances and pardons – which the Church taught could make satisfaction for sin, if performed in a state of grace, were for Luther and his followers unnecessary for salvation, although they were its consequence. For Luther, if the sinner attains faith, he will be saved without the Church; if he does not, the Church can do nothing to help. As Luther developed his new theology, he came gradually to attack not so much the Church's abuse of its power, but its right to claim any such power in Christian society at all. For him, the reformation of its moral life was far less urgent than a reformation of doctrine. This central conviction that Christians need not, indeed cannot, do anything to merit salvation, only believe, was the inspiration for those converted to the new faith.

'In the beginning was the Word, and the Word was with God and the Word was God.' This text, which opens St John's Gospel, was at the heart of the Reformation. Reading Erasmus's New Testament, Luther became convinced that the Church had compromised Christ's teachings. The Church had never denied that all truths necessary to salvation were contained in scripture, but in arbitrating questions of faith, it appealed not to scripture alone, but to tradition as found in the writings and decrees of the Fathers, Doctors and Councils of the Church. For evangelicals – all those who determined to proclaim the Gospel as glad tidings, and to reform religion according to scriptural precept – this appeal to tradition and hierarchy was the blasphemous usurpation of divine by human authority. They asserted that scripture alone, in its literal sense, was sufficient authority, and that scripture was its own interpreter. Evangelical reformers now distinguished between the canonical books of the Hebrew Old Testament, which were authoritative for establishing doctrine, and those which were apocryphal, outside the Hebrew canon. One such apocryphal book was Maccabees, which contained what was held to be scriptural warrant for the doctrines of purgatory and of the efficacy of prayers and Masses for the dead. Now the evangelicals could claim that purgatory was nowhere in scripture, was the Church's invention, and that, as Henry Brinklow (a London mercer and pampleteer) put it, to pray for souls 'availeth the dead no more than the pissing of a wren helpeth to cause the sea to flow at an extreme ebb'.

In 1521 Luther stood before the Diet of Worms and recounted his discovery of the Gospel, claiming that he stood with the Prophets, the Evangelists, Apostles and Fathers of the Church. Yet soon he stood against the Church, under the ban of pope and emperor. From Worms Bishop Tunstall wrote warning that Luther's tract *On the Babylonian Captivity of the Church* (1520) must be kept out of England. In this work Luther attacked the sacramental system of the Church, reducing the seven sacraments to three – baptism, penance and the Eucharist – and repudiating the sacrifice of the Mass. Soon he would deny that penance was a sacrament. Erasmus now pronounced the malady beyond cure. Luther's works, still in Latin, had reached England by 1519, and were being read by those of influence. In a spectacular ceremony in London on 12 May 1521 the papal anathema was pronounced against

Luther, and the English Church thereby declared its orthodoxy and obedience to the papacy. But on the night after the ceremony an outrage occurred which was ominous: on the papal bull posted on the door of St Paul's was scribbled a mocking rhyme.

In the years following 1521 Lutheranism seemed to present little threat in England. Secular and ecclesiastical authorities rallied in force to the defence of orthodoxy. In July 1521 a defence of the sacraments was published: *Assertio Septem Sacramentorum*. 'It is well known for mine, and I for mine avow it,' Henry VIII told Luther. Henry did write it, or part of it, with the help of a committee of theologians, and a grateful Pope gave the King the title Defender of the Faith. The work gave the clearest sign of Henry's keen theological interest, and of his determination to lead the English Church; but it was also a sign of the capricious lead he would give, for later he disowned the work, and blamed others for making him write what he had so proudly claimed. Thomas More and Bishop Fisher were commissioned by royal command to write against Luther: Fisher wrote a measured and theologically brilliant confutation; More a vituperative onslaught. In his *Responsio ad Lutherum* (1524) More – under the pseudonym Guillelmus Rosseus – parodied Luther's evangelical certainty and spiritual pride:

> 'How do you know that God has seized you?'
> 'Because I am certain . . . that my teaching is from God.'
> 'How do you know that?'
> 'Because I am certain.'
> 'How are you certain?'
> 'Because I know.'
> 'But how do you know?'
> 'Because I am certain.'

True faith was, for evangelicals, an absolute assurance of their acceptability to God. Thomas More, who had witnessed this evangelical certainty when his son-in-law William Roper became one of the first converts to the new faith in England, took Roper as his model for the messenger in the *Dialogue concerning Heresies* (1529). Not content to whisper Luther's teachings in 'hugger mugger', Roper and his fellows must evangelize them. Those in spiritual bondage must be brought the liberating message; the Word, hidden from the faithful for a thousand years, must go forth by whatever means and whatever the risk. (I shall refer to the first generation of English reformers as evangelicals; not

'Protestants', because this was a term invented in a foreign country to describe a particular protest, at Speyer in 1529; nor 'Lutherans', because this suggests a precise confession, and Luther's ideas were soon transmuted in English circumstances. Only reformers of later generations will be called 'Protestant'.) The 'evangelical brethren' or 'Christian brethren', as they called themselves – 'newfangled', 'new-broached brethren', as their enemies called them – were fired and organized to proselytize. Preaching was the way the people would hear the Gospel and, though the risk was acute, they preached urgently and often. The Renaissance art of eloquence would be deployed by evangelicals. Thomas Arthur, 'preaching the true Gospel of Christ' in London in 1527, tearfully made this plea:

If I should suffer persecution for preaching of the Gospel of God, yet there is seven thousand more that shall preach . . . therefore, good people, good people . . . think not you that if these tyrants and persecutors put a man to death . . . that he is an heretic therefore, but rather a martyr.

Thomas More warned good Catholics, complacent in their ancient faith, that the new heretics were few but formidable; as different from them as fire from frost. For him, this was an evangelical conspiracy, and it was true that a few prime movers led a revolutionary movement.

Among whom did the evangelicals make converts to their cause? Who would read the books which the brethren ran such risks to distribute? Luther's ideas spread first among his compatriots, the German merchants, and beyond them to their associates in the English merchant communities, especially in London. Lutheran works were not translated into English until later, but they were read in Latin by the educated. Heretical movements often began with *trahison des clercs*, and so it was in England. The staunchest opponents of the new theology were scholars in the universities, at Oxford and especially at Cambridge, but so also were the most fervent converts. Bishop Longland feared 'the corruption of youth' at Cardinal College, Oxford. Some of the establishment were won over also. The Master of Queens' College, Cambridge, Dr Forman, was the mastermind behind a contraband book trade between London and Oxford, and avowed the quintessential evangelical belief 'that all our salvation came of faith . . . And that if our good works should be the cause of our salvation then, as St Paul saith, Christ died for nought'. Hugh Latimer, who had at first combated the 'new sect' and the 'new learning', and wrote a dissertation against Luther's fellow evangelical

Philipp Melanchthon, was converted at Cambridge by Thomas Bilney, who had himself been won to the new theology by reading St Paul in Erasmus's translation.

But Bilney also held more traditional dissenting views. When a Lollard went to hear Bilney preach at Ipswich – that pilgrimages were folly, that prayers should be addressed to God alone, that prayers to saints impugned the sovereignty of Christ, that St Mary Magdalene was a whore – he heard nothing that he had not heard already in his Lollard conventicles. Among the first enthusiasts for the new heresy were the adherents of an older one, the Lollards. The 'known men' and the 'brethren' had much in common. Both held that Scripture enshrined all religious truth, and that to every layman belonged the right to find that truth. They believed that from the freedom to read the Word followed another: the liberation from priestly authority. When the Lollard Thomas Man asserted that all holy men of his sect were priests he anticipated the Lutheran doctrine of the priesthood of all believers; a personal faith, in which 'every layman is priest'. Pardons, confession, penance, 'purgatory pinfold' – the whole penitential system whereby the clergy held the laity in thrall – could be discarded.

Why abandon an old faith and an old obedience for a new and persecuted doctrine? There were many individual rebellions against the Church and its doctrine; each conversion was private, made in conscience, for reasons now, and perhaps then, unknown to others. But for the Catholic opponents of the 'new learning' the reasons were clear: evangelicals looked for liberty; not only Luther's Christian liberty, but licence – 'carnal', 'parasite' liberty. Catholic writers – of whom More was the most indefatigable – saw the evangelical offer of the certainty of grace, the conviction that the will was bound, as leading people to deny their own responsibility for doing good and avoiding evil. For, as More wrote later in his *Supplication for Souls* (1529), if the passion of Christ sufficed for remission of sin without any 'recompense' or 'pain' on the part of the sinner, then this was encouragement to 'bold courage to sin'. He caricatured the evangelical belief: however sinful, all they had to do was 'cry Him mercy', as a woman would as she stepped on another's train.

Soon those who had adopted a purer form of Lutheranism would be yesterday's men. On the great metaphysical question of the Real Presence in the Eucharist – the central issue in Reformation debates – it would not be the moderate Lutheran position that prevailed. Luther taught that in the Eucharist, after the consecration, the substances both of the Body and Blood of Christ and of the bread and wine co-exist in union with each other: this is consubstantiation. More radical teachings on the Mass, stemming from Strasbourg and Switzerland, and closer to the memorialist, materialist beliefs of the Lollards, were soon spreading. The 'Christian brethren', an advance guard among evangelicals, held the sacramentarian belief that the 'sacrament of the altar after the consecration was neither body nor blood', but remained bread and wine as before. This was the deepest heresy, and one which very few had yet adopted, despite Thomas More's fears. But when More charged William Tyndale with being more radical than Luther concerning confession, purgatory, prayers to saints and honour to images, he was right.

Erasmus's dream that every ploughboy at his plough and every woman at her loom should read the Bible could only be realized in England if it were translated. William Tyndale triumphantly accomplished that task. Exiled from England for fear of persecution, and often in hiding on the Continent, he worked on his English translation. In the prologue to his English New Testament he declared, 'By faith we are saved only', and in the marginal notes the new Christianity was expounded. In the greatest danger, on the run from the bishops' agents, the 'brethren' ran a contraband book trade, smuggling Tyndale's forbidden Testaments and the works of Continental reformers into England. In the Low Countries, France and Germany, English exiles provided inspiration for their fellows at home and writings to sustain the cause. Sure that there was an eager audience waiting for the English Bible, Tyndale and his supporters printed 3,000 copies, maybe more, of his first edition of the New Testament in Worms in 1526. 'Behold the signs of the world be wondrous,' the evangelicals promised.

An underworld of evangelical brethren had emerged under persecution in the 1520s. 'Brethren', 'for so did we not only call one another,' wrote Anthony Delaber, an Oxford undergraduate, 'but were in deed one to the other.' Loyal to each other, and united in their mission, they sheltered and sustained each other, converts bound together lastingly in a common cause. This was a conspiracy to convert. Once their books were in the people's hands, their ideas in their heads, their mission would be fulfilled, the brethren said. The new faith in its heroic early years was a religion of revolutionary aspirations and methods. So dangerous was the mission, because of persecution, that some of the 'brethren' adopted desperate measures and came to be marked by their enemies as rebels as well as heretics. Destroying images, posting bills, singing seditious ballads, spreading forbidden books, hiding those on the run, planning vigilante rescues of their fellows in prison, preaching despite the dangers, they created a protest movement. The bishops, who did not know who and where the evangelicals were, were constantly thwarted and duped. Into Bishop Tunstall's own palace in London the reformers tossed a bill, promising 'There will once come a day'.

Yet, for all their zeal, the 'brethren' were still so few and so beleaguered that the chances of their converting a whole nation might have seemed hopeless to anyone but them. They were winning converts – in London, at the Inns of Court, at the universities, among the old Lollard communities, in towns in East Anglia and the South-East – and the evangelicals were now a fifth column. But their numbers were tiny. The vast majority of the people were devoted to their traditional ways and hostile to the 'new learning', if they had even heard of it. The Word might pass by people who, tied to their work and the land, had no time for it. The 'brethren' were still a church under the cross; persecuted and on the run. Soon there were martyrs. The 'brethren' in exile looked always for the time when they could return; 'when the King's pleasure is that the New Testament in English should go forth'. That that day would come they were certain. In the account book which he was binding for the Pewterers' Company, John Gough wrote on an endpaper the defining evangelical text, Mark 13:31: 'Heaven and earth shall pass away, but my Word will remain for ever.' They seemed to hope against hope.

The new faith needed protection to survive and grow. The Lollards had failed utterly to win over secular rulers to their cause. Humanists looked to Henry VIII as the model of a godly prince, and hoped that he would listen to their aspiration for renewal in the Church. Surely the evangelicals could expect nothing but persecution from the Defender of the Faith and papal champion? Yet in 1536, when a new conception of what was necessary for salvation had invaded England against the wishes of the great majority of its people, the monks of St Albans Abbey looked upon the desolation of their religion and way of life, and asked how it had come about. Their answer was simple, and treasonable: 'The King hath done it on his high power.' Was the King so powerful?

4

Imperium

COURTS AND KINGS

> The bell tower showed me such a sight
> That in my head sticks day and night;
>   There did I learn out of a grate,
> For all favour, glory or might,
> That yet *circa Regna tonat*
> [It thunders around thrones].
>
> Thomas Wyatt, c. 1536

At Christmas 1529 Henry VIII was at Greenwich, designing a royal palace to be built at Whitehall; a palace vast in scale and novel in conception, a display of his magnificence and an emanation of his power. That October, two days after the fall of Cardinal Wolsey, Henry had taken Anne Boleyn to survey York Palace. The seizure of this palace of Wolsey's and the eviction of hundreds of hapless lesser subjects from a whole Westminster suburb made way for Henry's grand design, which was built at great speed and cost. At its centre was the Privy Gallery, where the King would live and rule apart in his privy lodging, his bedchamber and closets. At its west end the Gallery joined the Great Hall, the Great Chamber, and the Presence Chamber, which was dominated by the throne and its canopy. Here Henry's subjects were symbolically – but not actually – in the royal presence. The King himself was guarded and watched behind a series of doors locked by master keys. No one who entered this painted palace and passed through the two great courtyards and three outer chambers and on to the Privy Gallery could doubt the power of this king. On the walls of the chambers hung splendid tapestries, including a series acquired in 1528 of the *Story of David*, the godly king of Zion, with whom this king of England so strongly identified. In the Privy Chamber, the most intimate inner sanctum of royal rule, Hans Holbein would in 1537 paint a great mural in which Henry VIII dominated the foreground, with his father behind. This was a manifesto in art of the power of the Tudor kings. Intended to awe, it did. Yet very few were allowed into the royal presence, the source of all 'favour, glory or might'.

Next to Whitehall on the river, but a world apart, lay Westminster. Westminster was the old palace of medieval kings, built beside the Benedictine Abbey. Here were the law courts of King's Bench, Chancery and Common Pleas; here was the Exchequer. The Lords of Parliament met at Westminster in the White Chamber. This was an official world of laws, precedents, parchment rolls and tallies, ordered by men robed in black. It was not Westminster which Henry VIII inhabited, but the world of the royal court, which had its being wherever the king was. The court was the royal household where the king's servants served him; the scene of public ceremonial and of private life. It was also the centre of policy and of politics.

All power rested in the will and person of the king and was quintessentially personal. Access was all. Courtiers, circling and crowding, constantly in competition, sought always to penetrate the private world of power, to gain access to the king and influence over him. The most private affairs of a king were also inescapably matters of state. Letters tell of 'privy' communications in the inner spaces and private recesses of the court, of whispering at windows. Leaning against a window, his hand over his mouth, Thomas Cromwell explained, disingenuously, to Eustace Chapuys, the ambassador for the Holy Roman Emperor in April 1536 that it was only recently that he had learnt the frailty of human affairs, especially those of the court, 'of which he had before his eyes several examples that might be called *domestic*'. The king never had privacy; he was never alone; he did not sleep alone, nor wake alone, nor dress, eat, bathe, or attend the garderobe alone. Courtiers were always, endlessly, in attendance. When Sir Francis Bryan addressed Sir Thomas Heneage as 'bedfellow', he meant it literally for, as Gentlemen of the Privy Chamber, they slept together at the foot of the royal bed.

The succession of each new monarch brought a new world, for the character of a king determined not only policy but also the style of government, the nature of his court and of those he had about him. A king so secret and distant as Henry VII had sought secrecy and distance at his court also. He devised ways to live and rule apart. Traditionally, the later medieval royal household had been divided into the service side of hall and kitchens, served by ranks of yeomen of the larder and buttery, pastry chefs and scullery boys, presided over by the Lord Steward; and the king's private apartment or chamber, under the Lord Chamberlain. But even the division of the chamber into the Great or Guard Chamber, Presence Chamber and Privy Chamber was not separation enough for Henry VII. In about 1495 he made an institutional change at his court, an innovation little remarked at the time, but of great political conse-quence: he set the Secret or Privy Chamber apart from the others, establishing a frontier for access, and gave it its own tiny staff of grooms and pages. Only they could enter. From this Secret Chamber Henry VII excluded all those whom he did not regard as essential for his service; he especially excluded those who regarded themselves as essential: his nobles. Fearing, and with reason, conspiracy within as well as conspiracy without; wishing to devote himself uninterruptedly to dispatches, accounts and high policy, and to be free of the insidious counsels and tiresome ceremonial which attended his greater subjects, he chose, unusually, to have menial servants instead of lordly pages to perform menial service. So he guarded himself and his secrets. Henry VIII believed that he could keep his own secrets – 'If I thought my cap knew my counsel, I would cast it into the fire and burn it', he said. But he was often deceived and he deceived himself. Kings were prisoners of the courts they made, and Henry VIII created a court in his own image, quite different from his father's.

The accession of a new prince is often welcomed with jubilant expec-tation – especially when the passing of the old prince is a relief – but the joy which greeted the second Henry Tudor in April 1509 was unusual. 'Heaven and earth rejoice ... Our King is not after gold or gems ... but virtue, glory, immortality': such was the promise. Thomas More celebrated the new King's accession as the ending of a tyranny. When he wrote that his new prince had 'a character which deserves to rule' it was true, or partly true. Henry had a powerful, if unoriginal mind; he was educated and cultivated; he had courage, charm, even humour. He was well versed in theology and pious. Qualities of mind and character, his splendid physical presence, and his chivalry seemed to make him the ideal Christian knight, and would have impressed, and maybe capti-vated, even if he had not been king. But he was a king, of commanding will. Thomas More warned, even as the reign began, that unlimited power tended to weaken good minds.

Henry VIII's reign began, as it would end, with a comprehensive deception practised for high political purposes, as a courtier with a

NEW WORLDS, LOST WORLDS

'smiling countenance' concealed the news of the old King's death. This courtier was a Groom of the Privy Chamber, and courtiers colluded with some of Henry VII's councillors to secure the succession and organize a coup. Two days after his father died the new King was being served as though he were still Prince of Wales and Henry VII still alive. On the first day of the new reign, Henry VII's hated councillors Edmund Dudley and Sir Richard Empson were sent to the Tower, to the delight of the people, who saw them as agents of Henry VII's oppression rather than as victims of his son's. (They died traitors' deaths at Tower Hill in August 1510.) Already the ruthlessness of the young King seemed apparent, but it was, and always would be, uncertain how far Henry directed what was done in his name. At one moment he claimed that his dying father had urged him to marry Catherine of Aragon, and so he must obey; at another, he expressed doubts about the propriety of marrying his brother Arthur's widow. He did marry her in June 1509, and they were jointly crowned on Midsummer Day.

The young and chivalrous King – whose accession day was, fittingly, the eve of St George, England's martial patron – sought to be king in the image of the great kings of the English past and to rival foreign princes of far greater kingdoms. At home, he aspired to lead a noble order of chivalry; abroad, to pursue honour. Reading chivalric romance, especially Thomas Malory's *Le Morte d'Arthur*, Henry saw his court as a chivalric fellowship united in a quest for honour and loyal service to their prince. The mottoes of courtiers vaunted their loyalty: 'Loyaulte me oblige', promised Charles Brandon. Henry VII, too, had seen the political necessity of magnificence; had followed Edward IV in emulating the chivalric courtly culture of the dukes of Burgundy; had encouraged his courtiers to joust; had judged their tournaments. But he had been spectator, not participant. Henry VIII was the glittering champion of the tournament. He ran in the tilt-yard, despite all the dangers, and the courtiers with whom he jousted became his closest companions, recipients of his confidence and favour. Valour in the tilt-yard became a way to high military position, to wealth and ennoblement, as Charles Brandon, created Duke of Suffolk, found. Here chivalry and politics met. But chivalric values did not easily accord with the competitiveness of life at this court.

Chivalry was the training for war. Henry's guiding ambition, as his reign began and still as it ended, was to assert the ancient claim to dominion of France, to regain a lost kingdom and a lost throne. War against France was half a chivalric crusade. He determined to emulate Henry V's victories of a century before; his goal was glory before commercial advantage. At his accession Henry was seventeen – not even of age. He was, for a while, governed by his father's councillors, his father's policies. The doves in the Council opposed his plans; the humanists, who had hoped for a pacific king and universal peace, lamented. No matter. The French King Louis XII's support for a schismatic General Council of the Church against the Pope provided the cause for war, and by the end of 1511 Henry, horrified by Louis' rebellion against papal authority, had persuaded his Council that the truce with a perfidious France must be broken, and an invasion prepared. This was his first venture as papal champion, and one which would look strange thereafter.

Henry wanted freedom from an obstructive Council, he wanted freedom from the infinite boredom of administration, and he wanted conquest in France. His liberator, and the mastermind of a policy designed to be glorious in peace and war was Thomas Wolsey, royal almoner from 1509, Bishop of Lincoln, and successively Archbishop of York, Cardinal, Lord Chancellor, and papal legate. In 1513 Wolsey planned Henry's invasion of northern France. The small episcopal city of Thérouanne, and Tournai, a French enclave within the Burgundian-Habsburg Netherlands, were besieged and occupied between July and September. According to Thomas Cromwell, speaking in Parliament a decade later, these were 'ungracious dog-holes'. But any English visitor to the Netherlands was more likely to report that English towns were dog-holes by comparison. For Henry, the importance of capturing these towns lay in their status as part of his dominion as 'King of France'. His standing among European princes was enhanced by this conquest, and by his simultaneous victory in Scotland. In September, the Earl of Surrey inflicted desperate defeat upon the Scots with whom Louis XII of France had concluded a league. The King of Scotland, three bishops, eleven earls, fifteen lords and 10,000 men lay dead in the mud of Flodden Field.

When the old guard among his councillors complained that the new king was too wedded to pleasure and urged that he attend Council meetings more often, Wolsey counselled the contrary. Here, for him, was the way to exceptional favour and power. Wolsey determined, according to his gentleman-usher George Cavendish, to show himself keenest 'to advance the King's only will and pleasure *without any respect to the case*'. From 1514 or so Wolsey came to hold a seemingly

unassailable supremacy in the counsels of the King; he was 'the beginning, middle and end'. He might be challenged, but for fifteen years he
was not overthrown. As long as he could find the means to advance the
King's will and pleasure – whatever it happened to be; Wolsey minded
little – the rest of the Council was almost redundant; its corporate
political role usurped. The Council was still consulted, but only after
Wolsey and the King, in a kind of partnership, had determined policy.
Wolsey would first 'move' Henry towards some idea; the King 'dreamed
of it more and more'; and only then would the Council be informed.
Wolsey's influence seemed supreme, and his household, in its magnificence, looked a rival to the royal court. So completely did he see himself
as *alter rex*, it was alleged, that he would say: 'The King and I would ye
should do thus: the King and I do give you our hearty thanks.' His
pride and splendour were legendary: crosses, pillars and poleaxes, hated
symbols of his authority, were carried before him; earls and lords served
him. But Wolsey was a prince only in the Church, never in the secular
realm. He held authority only so long as he held royal favour, and
he knew how precarious that was. It was the King's will that was
implemented, not Wolsey's. Otherwise Wolsey, whose own aspiration
was for peace in Europe, would not have had to prosecute war. Wolsey's
Anglo-French peace of 1514 was evanescent, for it died with the French
King Louis XII in 1515.

The happy prospect of perpetual peace would have seemed more likely
of achievement had Henry been content to leave England withdrawn
from the Continent. But he was not. Henry's determination, supported
by Wolsey, to play a part in Continental power politics and win international renown, led ineluctably to entanglement in the European war
which always threatened, especially once Francis I had come to the
French throne in 1515. Francis was a king, according to Henry, more
dangerous to Christendom than the Great Turk (with whom, indeed,
Francis, 'the most Christian king', was intermittently allied). Henry's
relations with Francis, whose appetite for glory and whose tastes he
shared (though without the means to emulate them), remained ambivalent through three decades.

Wolsey constantly sought ways to win for England a leading part in
European affairs without recourse to war. In 1516 he schemed with
the Swiss and the Holy Roman Emperor Maximilian against French
domination in North Italy, thinking, like More's Utopians, that if fighting were necessary to secure peace, it were better that others did the

fighting. In 1518 he seemed to achieve his ambition to be seen as arbiter of Europe when, in the Treaty of London, he united all Christendom. It was a precarious peace, and one that England played the leading part in securing. When in 1519 the Habsburg Charles V added the Holy Roman Empire to his estates in the Netherlands and Spain, the configuration of power in Europe shifted: the houses of Habsburg and Valois were more nearly balanced, and their dynastic rivalry grew accordingly. Henry earnestly proclaimed friendship to both these rivals, as the Treaty of London bound him to do, but would become their enemy if either of them broke the peace. England's alliance with either power would give it dominance over the other: her neutrality might guarantee peace.

Henry gained unwonted power in Europe, and a new freedom to allege the ancient claims to France without the likelihood of imminent retaliation. But France could, and did in 1513 and 1521–4, reinstate her 'auld alliance' with Scotland and thereby threaten England on her northern border. The ambivalence of English relations with France was never so apparent as at the Field of the Cloth of Gold in 1520 where the two kings, attended by their courts in all their splendour, met to proclaim their friendship, while all the while the magnificence covered their enmity and the betrayal of the peace which Henry was already negotiating with the Emperor. By May 1522 England was at war with France again, and being urged by her Imperial ally to invade. Henry's freedom to intervene on the Continent was constrained by the perpetual prospect of war on his borders at home. The great lords of Ireland – not only his 'Irish enemies', the Gaelic chiefs like O'Neill and O'Donnell, but also the Anglo-Irish feudatories, such as the Earl of Desmond – intrigued perpetually with England's foreign enemies and, as sovereign princes, from time to time made alliances with the kings of France and Scotland and with the Emperor.

Though Wolsey wanted peace, he countenanced war – despite opposition in the Council – rather than lose England's new-found prominence in European affairs, and, more compellingly, because Henry still hankered after it. In August 1523 a new invasion of France was mounted, English troops were soon within fifty miles of Paris, and Henry believed, mistakenly, that the French crown was within his grasp. In February 1525 that inheritance seemed even closer when Francis I was defeated and captured by Imperial forces at Pavia. At that battle too Richard de la Pole, the White Rose of York, who was the French candidate for the English throne, was killed. Henry urged Charles V to seize the moment and partition France between them, but – to Henry's disappointment and humiliation – Charles held back, and at the end of August 1525 England was at peace with France once more. The Cardinal then helped to create a league against the Emperor, which England sponsored but would not join: another attempt to engineer peace by force. That peace was traumatically broken when in May 1527 Imperial troops sacked Rome, desecrated the Eternal City and took Christ's Vicar into captivity. Wolsey ordered processions and fastings for the Pope's release, but the lack of popular response was telling. The common people 'little mourned for it', wrote Edward Hall, the chronicler. England was a Catholic country, but not a papalist one, and now the resentment which grew, in London particularly, against the Cardinal Legate was transferred from servant to master.

Wolsey ruled outside the court, against the court, from his own great household which became its rival. Around the King his friends and favourites exerted a crucial political influence. To the inner sanctum, his Privy Chamber, Henry had introduced not the nonentities who had served his father, but a new generation of young gentlemen. High-born and high-spirited, they were dashing enough to amuse him, confident enough to be 'homely and familiar' and to play 'light touches with him'. They 'forgot themselves' and the awe-inspiring distinctions of rank which should have set them apart from their monarch. In emulation of Francis I's court, these young gentlemen were elevated in 1518 to *Gentlemen* of the Privy Chamber, a new rank, with new pretensions. Between Wolsey, with his uniquely privileged position as pre-eminent councillor, and the King's arrogant young favourites, a state of hostility – sometimes latent, often open – prevailed. Their battles were always for royal favour, patronage and influence. In 1519 Wolsey succeeded in exiling them to darkest Calais, for a while; in 1526 he purged the Privy Chamber, for a time. Soon they returned, to greater favour than before. As men 'near about the King', they were respected, even feared. They were empowered to represent the King beyond the court. As special messengers embodying the royal will, they were sent to summon or arrest the King's greatest subjects; as diplomats they went on missions to 'decipher' the secrets of 'outward princes' at other courts; they were given high military command against the King's enemies, foreign or domestic; they were entrusted with positions of influence throughout the country as leading members of the Tudor affinity. As royal representatives and royal retainers, they were part of the new world of Renaissance courts and an older one of bastard-feudal affinities.

These men were the nearest to friends that a king could have. Educated, well versed in scripture and the writings of classical antiquity, bound by the chivalric ideal of fidelity, Henry's courtiers thought about the virtue of friendship. One of the first classical works to be translated into English and printed was Cicero's *Of Friendship* (1481). The duties of friends were analogous to the duties of true counsel: telling the truth and constancy; virtues which were at once public and private. Constancy in friendship – or more evidently, its loss and betrayal – was a pervasive theme in the lives and writings of those who served at Henry VIII's court. At the Christmas festivities at Greenwich in 1524 a captain and fifteen gentlemen offered to defend Castle Loyal and its attendant ladies against all comers. Among the defenders were the poet Thomas Wyatt, and with him Francis Bryan, whom Henry called his 'Vicar of Hell', and John Poyntz, both of whom inspired Wyatt's mordant reflections upon the courtier's life. They shared the Renaissance conception of an ideal courtier who told his prince the truth, but their own experience was of the mendacity and malignity of life at court. People were reading Castiglione's *The Courtier* – in April 1530 Edmund Bonner reminded Thomas Cromwell of his promise to lend him *Il Cortegiano* and make him a good Italian – but it was harder to learn its lessons. Flattery – feigned friendship – was the enemy of both friendship and true counsel, and the besetting sin of courts. 'One unhappy thing is in the court', wrote Bryan: many who will doff their cap to you 'gladly would see your head off by the shoulders.' Flattery posed the greatest danger to monarchy, for only honest counsel preserved it from descending towards tyranny. Yet at court plain speaking was rare. Courts always had a dark reputation for intrigue and danger: the collective noun for courtiers was a 'threat'. 'Your ladyship knoweth,' wrote John Husee to Lady Lisle in July 1537, 'the court is full of pride, envy, indignation, and mocking, scorning and derision.' Cardinal Pole, Henry's cousin, asked: 'Who will tell the prince his fault? And if one such be found, where is the prince that will hear him?' The normal way at courts, so Wyatt told his friend Poyntz, was to call the crow a swan, and the lion a coward; to praise flattery as eloquence and cruelty as justice. Many at Henry's court were masters of these silken arts. 'I played the jolly courtier, faith,' Thomas Wriothesley told his friend Wyatt, whom he would betray.

In 1519 Henry declared that 'for our pleasure . . . one we will favour now and another at such time as we shall like'. That fluctuating royal pleasure invited competition. The King boasted that he could tell his good servants from the flatterers, but he deceived himself in this as in much else. With time he grew restless, insecure, capricious and, captive in the court he had created, he could be played upon by the men he had advanced and had constantly about him. The contradictory nature of this king, the unstill centre around whom everything at court turned, had consequences for its life. Any king might be susceptible to persuasion, but Henry became exceptionally so. 'King Henry, according as his counsel was about him, so was he led,' wrote John Foxe, the Church historian and martyrologist, and he had spoken to those who knew. Men and women had always come to the royal household, and still did, to further the interests of their family and kin. The court was not a male preserve, save in its heart, the Privy Chamber, for women of high birth and high ambition came also, seeking more or less the same things: influence, connection and the advancement of their kin. They, too, were drawn into the plots and counter-plots which became characteristic of life there. Family honour and advancement remained at the centre of the competitiveness at court, but where once no principle more abstract than 'good governance' had been adduced, times were changing.

To guide the king was the part of a loyal counsellor, but to challenge the royal will, or to seek to subvert or overrule it, was conspiracy and treason. This was the problem for those in the court who opposed royal policy; they must work by devious means. In such political circumstances faction flourished. In England, as in ancient Rome, faction had malign connotations: the enemies of a group would call it a faction while those within it thought in terms of friendship. What factions sought was the ear of the king and thereby his favour; to persuade him to one course or another, or to give patronage to their clients. They waited for an occasion to insinuate themselves or to oust their rivals. In the personal polity of the court factions, too, were personal. Fleeting, welded together more by promise of mutual service than by unity of principle, they lasted only so long as friendship and common interest lasted.

Away from the court, in the country, there were suspicions that the King was a prisoner of its tiny world. In 1536 the vicar of Eastbourne, walking in his churchyard, declared, 'They that rule about the King make him great banquets and give him sweet wines and make him drunk, and then they bring him bills and he putteth his sign to them.' In these ways his subjects were pleased to explain changes they hated. But they were wrong. This was a king who was determined to rule. Princes cannot err, of course, and Henry's vaunting self-righteousness always led him to blame others for events for which he was responsible, or might have prevented. He knew what he wanted, if not always how to get it, and was seldom thwarted. Although the King was often kept in the dark, and often deceived, the truth could not be kept from him indefinitely, and, once he knew it, he would act. He came to understand well enough that perpetual intrigue surrounded him and that his counsellors and courtiers maligned their rivals. If, and when, he chose, he could protect the vulnerable and those who had been sequestered from his presence. In 1543 he rescued Archbishop Cranmer from the best-laid schemes of Bishop Gardiner, warning Cranmer that, if he were once in prison, his enemies would procure false witnesses against him. But by that time the nature of court politics had been fundamentally transformed.

In November 1527 ambassadors from France had been entertained at court by a Latin play. The dramatis personae included Religion, the Church and Truth, dressed as religious novices; Heresy, False Interpretation and Corruption of Scripture appeared as ladies of Bohemia. Players took the parts of the 'heretic Luther' and his forbidden wife (a former priest, he had married a former nun). The play's main theme was of the Cardinal rescuing the Pope from captivity, saving the Church from falling, and defending orthodoxy from heresy. This was almost the last time that so Catholic an interlude could be played to general approbation, for the new religion had invaded the court and had profoundly changed life there. Now men and women might contend, not for power alone, but for a cause. Also in November a yeoman usher of the court did penance for heresy. But there was now another at court, more influential by far than any yeoman usher, who had been touched by evangelical reform, and whose power over the King was unrivalled: Anne Boleyn.

Anne had returned early in 1522 from long years away at the most glittering courts of Europe, a grand court lady. She arrived at Henry VIII's court to become maid-of-honour to Queen Catherine, and to break hearts. Anne had charm, style and wit, and a will and savagery which made her a match for this king. In her music book, sent to please her, there was an illustration of a falcon pecking at a pomegranate. The falcon was Anne's badge; the pomegranate of Granada, Catherine's. The pomegranate was itself the symbol of a fecundity which had brought

Catherine many children, but no living prince. By Easter 1527 the King was imploring Anne to become his mistress (as her sister Mary had been), but she consented only to be his queen. In an illuminated book of hours Henry scrawled, below an image of Christ as Man of Sorrows:

> I am yours
> Henry R forever.

And Anne replied:

> By daily proof you shall me find
> To be to you both loving and kind.

With evident promise, she wrote this under a picture of Archangel Gabriel announcing to the Virgin that she would bear a son. Neither promise was fulfilled, but from 1527 Anne's influence over the infatuated King seemed secure. Her enemies became the King's enemies; her friends, his friends.

The reign of Henry VIII, like that of Solomon, had begun well. An exquisite portrait miniature drawn by Holbein in about 1534 depicted Henry as Solomon, receiving the homage of the Queen of Sheba, representing the Church of England. Above the throne was the text: 'Blessed be the Lord thy God, who delighted in thee, to set thee upon His throne, to be king elected by the Lord thy God.' Henry delighted to see himself as a godly prince, and to compare himself with Solomon in his justice and wisdom. He forgot that Solomon's reign degenerated, but soon he was reminded, when his own reign did also. Erasmus had written in his *The Education of a Christian Prince*, 'these expressions of a tyrant "Such is my will", "This is my bidding" ... should be far removed from the mind of the prince'. Wolsey remembered kneeling before the King in his Privy Chamber for hours at a time, trying to 'persuade him from his will and appetite', but rather than abandon any part of it Henry 'will put one half of his realm in danger'. This was a king with the power and will to advance his private conscience as a principle to bind not only the bodies but the souls of his subjects, and to set that private conscience against the whole of Christendom.

ROYAL SUPREMACY

Seeking to understand how the great transformation in religion and ecclesiastical authority that was the Reformation could ever have happened, its opponents declared, 'This may well be called a tragedy which began with a marriage.' Throughout the 1520s, the first decade of evangelical reform, Henry VIII had been preoccupied by an intractable problem of conscience, his 'Great Matter'. His desperate need to secure the succession and his consequent desire to rid himself of a queen who could bear him no living sons, became inescapably a theological problem. Henry's marriage to Catherine of Aragon had only been made possible because the Pope had dispensed from the Church's prohibition of a man marrying his brother's widow. As child after child died, Henry began to search for the cause of God's judgement against him, and looking in the Old Testament he seemed to find it: in Leviticus 18:16 and 20:21 – 'Thou shalt not uncover the nakedness of thy brother's wife . . .' and 'If a man shall take his brother's wife . . . they shall be childless.' To Catherine's insistent denial that Arthur had ever uncovered her nakedness Henry never listened. What was needed was for one pope to overrule what another had allowed. Best of all would be to prove that Julius II's dispensation was insufficient in law; Cardinal Wolsey recognized that this was so. But a mere legal solution no longer sufficed. Henry saw that his marriage contravened divine law; it had angered God and affronted his own conscience. He had found the Levitical argument for himself, and would countenance no alternative.

The King stood upon principle: no pope could contradict a biblical command. This was to begin to challenge papal authority. Wolsey urged him against so radical a course, but unavailingly. Divorce was impossible, but Henry now took the first and secret steps to annul his marriage to his queen, secret even from her. On 17 May 1527 Wolsey, as papal legate, set up a clandestine court, summoning the King to answer the charge of living incestuously with Catherine. Then Henry and Wolsey drew back. If they had lost their nerve, it was hardly surprising, because the divorce was difficult in law, and provocative in its challenge to the papacy; diplomatically and politically it seemed impossible, because that May Rome had been sacked by Imperial troops, and the Pope was virtually the prisoner of the Emperor, Catherine's nephew. But at this time Henry assumed – and would never relinquish – the direction of his campaign for an annulment.

Henry's 'scruple of conscience' about his damned marriage was sincere enough, but when he became captivated by Anne Boleyn his desire to rid himself of his first queen became compelling. Anne's influence upon this king, who was so profoundly open to influence, now took a remarkable form. Not the least of the marks of Anne's originality was her commitment to evangelical reform. From her youth spent in France, she was convinced by the Christian humanist imperative to set forth the vernacular Bible, and to return the Church to the true religion. As soon as she held sway over the King she dared to use her influence to advance reform and to protect her friends in the evangelical underworld. Somehow Simon Fish, in exile, knew that if he sent Anne a copy of his anticlerical tract *A Supplication for the Beggars* it would please her: so it did. She sponsored Tyndale's forbidden New Testament, and interceded for those persecuted for its sake. Just at the time when the new faith most needed protection Anne Boleyn was there to offer it. Once reform began to infiltrate and the seemingly adamantine authority of the Church began to be questioned, there could be no going back. All those who blamed religious change upon Anne's enchantment of the King were not wholly wrong.

On 18 June 1529 an extraordinary legatine court opened at Blackfriars in London. Its task was to pass sentence upon the royal marriage. Queen Catherine appeared before the court in person and, before the King and the judges, pleaded that she should not be discarded, dishonoured. Only Rome, she insisted, could determine the legality of her marriage, and to Rome she formally appealed. Bishop Fisher and other leading clerics fiercely championed her cause. The trial was adjourned at the end of July, mired in political and legal wrangling. Now Henry, who had tried to stampede the Pope into judging in his favour, was summoned to Rome, as if he were any ordinary suppliant, to put his case before the Rota, the supreme court of the Roman Church, where the decision was likely to go against him.

By the autumn of 1529 Henry determined upon a more radical policy. Anne had shown him Tyndale's *The Obedience of a Christian Man* (1528), and to a king struggling with a pope and thwarted by a cardinal, Tyndale's argument that the Church had not only nullified God's promises but usurped the magistracy of the prince was appealing. In conversation with the Imperial ambassador in October 1529, Henry announced a startlingly radical credo. Luther was right, Henry said, to attack the vices and corruption of the clergy; and if he had not challenged the sacraments as well, Henry would have defended, not opposed him. The only clerical power over the laity the King now acknowledged was absolution from sin. In 1515 he had already declared, 'The kings of England in time past have never had any superior but God alone.' Henry began to make moves against the Church from which there was no return.

The failure of the legatine court of 1529 to procure an annulment, and the massive indignity of the King's summons to Rome to decide the case had proved the Cardinal's downfall. At last, Wolsey could no longer give the King what he wanted, and royal favour faltered. Wolsey's enemies waited to overthrow him. The noble councillors whom he had for so long displaced and who hated his prelatical pretensions, now circled. In 1527 Wolsey's absence in France had given them the chance to 'deprave' him to the King, but Wolsey survived, and would have survived again, had it not been for the enmity of Anne, whom he called the 'midnight crow'. According to Wolsey's gentleman usher, at dinner, tête-à-tête with the King, she talked of politics: 'Consider what debt and danger the Cardinal hath brought you in with all your subjects.'

'How so, sweetheart?' asked the King.

In October 1529 Wolsey's enemies in the Council prepared charges against him which were specious, but ominous for the whole clergy, for the charge which stuck concerned the exercise of his authority as papal legate. The King was unwilling to sacrifice him, although, as Wolsey saw, he might find it easier to do so than restore Wolsey's confiscated properties or admit that he himself had been wrong. Wolsey was dismissed from the Council and deprived of the office of Lord Chancellor: although the King sent him a ring for comfort, there could be none. In disgrace, Wolsey gave substance to the charges of treason by plotting with the King's enemies; first Francis I of France, then the Emperor. In November 1530 he died on his way south from York, where he had been living for the first time in his hitherto non-resident career as Archbishop. Wolsey's fall left the court and Council more divided than ever; between the Queen's supporters, who saw in her cause both the safety of traditional religion and the assurance of the power of the nobility; and a radical group who countenanced the abandonment of the Roman allegiance and saw the royal divorce as just the beginning of a more dangerous and revolutionary course. In Wolsey's place as Lord Chancellor Henry appointed Thomas More, the author of *Utopia*, the most radical criticism yet of the society he was now to govern. He came determined to stay out of the King's Great Matter, yet he saw what Henry's struggle with Rome portended, and he hoped against hope that confrontation with the English Church could be prevented, and that it was not too late to stop the advance of heresy.

The summoning of Parliament at the end of 1529 offered hopes of reform and redress, but of diverse kinds. There was already in this Parliament a group opposed to the King's purposes, the staunchest defenders of the Queen's cause; a group which ventured perilously close to treason. Thomas More came to reform, seeking new laws against heresy. Others came to reform other abuses: the 'enormities of the clergy'. That common lawyers and citizens of London were so influential in the Commons was the Church's misfortune, for these lawyers had long been jealous of spiritual jurisdiction. Those who wanted reform wanted action, and law, parliamentary statute, was the way to achieve it. Anticlerical feeling was running high and the Church's critics came with a case prepared. Not only was there resentment against clerical exactions and privileges, but also growing fears of the clergy's unfettered powers to summon the laity before their courts and to punish them, acting as both accuser and judge. A Commons' petition demanding reform of the clergy was turned into a series of parliamentary bills demanding the prohibition of the abuses of which the petition complained; such as clerical fees, holding secular office, buying and selling, holding more than one benefice with cure of souls (pluralism), and not being resident in their cures. This was not yet a fundamental assault upon the nature of spiritual authority, but it was regarded darkly by the Church's most prescient defenders. Bishop Fisher compared the Commons to the heretical Hussite Kingdom of Bohemia. Daring to criticize the clergy now incurred the suspicion of heresy, and a campaign began against heretics, who were unprepared to recant, led by a Chancellor and bishops who became more desperate as the heresy spread.

Henry had not directed the anticlerical assault, but he now drew conclusions from it. Through these months it became clear that Catherine's supporters would not move Henry's conscience, but it was still unclear how the annulment would be achieved. But in the autumn of 1530 a way was found. Henry now claimed to be absolute as Emperor and Pope in his own kingdom. The Great Matter could be settled without

Rome, within the realm, and by royal authority. Here was the assertion of the Royal Supremacy over the English Church. In the devising of his caesaro-papal claims, Henry was a student, applying himself diligently to studying the manuscript which contained the – dubious – historical precedents for his Supremacy. Edward Foxe and John Stokesley (who would be rewarded with the bishoprics of Hereford and London) had been compiling evidence to support the King's position, including legal judgements, chronicles, scriptures, and arguments from the Church Fathers and the General Councils of the Church. This was the *Collectanea satis copiosa*. '*Ubi hic?* (Where does this come from?)'; '*Hic est vera* (Here is the truth)', the King wrote in the margins. Henry was now convinced – he needed little convincing – that England had long been, and still was, an empire, within which he had both temporal and spiritual jurisdiction (*regnum* and *sacerdotum*). By October 1530 the King had convinced himself that his imperial authority empowered him to prevent appeals outside his realm. A group of scholars had known the arguments before the King did, indeed had devised them for him, and for some of them solving the Divorce crisis was a way towards reform in religion and society as well as towards transformation of authority within the Church. From the obscurity of his Cambridge college Thomas Cranmer became prominent in the King's counsels from 1531, soon abandoning his conservative humanism for Lutheran evangelicalism. A common lawyer, who had been faithful among Wolsey's faithless servants, was taken into the King's service in the spring of 1530, and into the Council by the end of the year: this was Thomas Cromwell, whose introduction into the counsels of the King was to be of the greatest significance.

Cromwell, possessing a creative intelligence and a vision of a reformed commonwealth, led the King towards policies more radical than he would otherwise have countenanced. Cardinal Pole claimed later that Cromwell had made a pact with Henry, promising to make him the most powerful king yet known in England: royal power would grow at the clergy's expense, and the wealth of the Church would finance reform. This was an unrealistic view: Cromwell was only the King's servant. Yet his influence was profound, for he led the King out of an impasse. Cromwell had learnt the New Testament by heart while on a journey to Rome in 1517: his visit to the papal court and his knowledge of scripture marked him thereafter. Among Cromwell's early friends were leading evangelicals, the advance guard of religious reform in England; men and women whom it was dangerous for him even to know. Cromwell determined to use his new influence to further their cause, which was his own: to advance the Gospel. From 1533 Cromwell and Cranmer worked closely together.

Henry was convinced that England was an empire and he its emperor; but he was anxious, uncertain how to turn this idea into political reality. He could not escape the fear that his subjects might rise in defence of Pope and Queen. Thomas More might still have prevailed over Thomas Cromwell in the battle for the King's conscience, and Queen Catherine had powerful supporters. Many women were outraged by the King's repudiation of her. Unlikely rumours reached the Venetian ambassador in 1531 that thousands of London women had stormed Anne Boleyn's love nest by the Thames and attempted to seize her. The visionary nun Elizabeth Barton, the Holy Maid of Kent, claimed to have had visitations from the Virgin, and prophesied disaster if Henry pursued his adulterous course. In Parliament, Bishop John Fisher was the Queen's unswerving champion. When the first direct assault on the whole Church came in January 1531 – no less than to break the clergy's spirit by bringing a *praemunire* charge against all of them (accusing them of illegally asserting papal jurisdiction in England) – Fisher strengthened their resolve. He won victory from defeat by adding to the clergy's acknowledgement that the King was head of the English Church the vital saving clause: 'so far as the law of Christ allows'; that is, for all those who thought like Fisher, not at all. Fisher called for holy war: by September 1533 he was urging the Emperor to invade England and to depose the King, a crusade which would be as pleasing to God as war against the Turk. England's most learned, austere and saintly bishop had turned traitor. How had it come to this?

Though Henry was still, at the turn of 1532, unprepared to countenance schism, Cromwell had seen a way to achieve Royal Supremacy little by little, and to break with Rome. Parliament would be used to make laws to enshrine Royal Supremacy and national sovereignty, with the assent of the King's subjects, or, at least, the illusion of it. As Parliament met again in January 1532 the antagonism of the Commons towards the clergy was now deliberately revived. On 18 March the Commons submitted to the King a Supplication against the Ordinaries. Most of the Supplication's nine charges were extremely specific, concerning the powers of the Church courts, and the abuses within the system. Old fears of the clergy's powers in heresy trials were heightened as the

Church moved with new severity against people in high places. The King's heart now hardened against his clergy. On Easter Day 1532 at Greenwich William Peto, the head of the Observant Franciscan order in England, warned Henry that 'great and little were murmuring', and that if he married Anne dogs would lick his blood, as once they had licked Ahab's. For a king who identified himself so closely with sage Old Testament monarchs, not tyrants such as Ahab, that sermon may have been decisive. The King's will was made clear to the Speaker of the Lower House; the clergy's answer to the Commons' Supplication must be rejected, and the royal message was minatory: 'We think their answer will smally please you . . .'

On 10 May the King demanded that the Church should renounce all authority to make laws without royal licence. His mood was ominous. Once he had believed, so he told a Commons delegation, that 'the clergy of our realm had been our subjects wholly', but now he understood that 'they be but half our subjects, yea, and scarce our subjects'. On 15 May 1532 the liberty of the English Church was lost. The Submission of the Clergy was subscribed on the following day, and they yielded all authority to make canons without royal permission. A wave of suicides in London was seen as a malign prodigy 'foreboding future evil'. Thomas More resigned as Chancellor: his political battle lost, he claimed now to be resolved to keep silent, never more 'to study nor meddle with any matter of this world'. But in his writings and his secret communications with conservative exiles, he proved still a desperate defender of the Church against heresy. As More yielded the Great Seal, Henry assured him that he would never 'put any man in ruffle or trouble of his conscience', but even if he meant it, the logic of events made this a promise impossible to keep. More's silence marked a conscience opposed to each new move towards Reformation, and was a silence to which all Europe listened.

At the destruction of the royal marriage – as happens at the end of marriages – loyalties among the wider circle of family and friends were bitterly divided. Murder was committed in April 1532 in Westminster sanctuary when rival retinues of the Dukes of Norfolk and Suffolk fought to avenge an insult against Anne, Norfolk's niece, spoken by the King's own sister, the Duchess of Suffolk. Other noblewomen openly supported Catherine and her daughter, including Elizabeth, Duchess of Norfolk (who was estranged from her own husband), Gertrude, Marchioness of Exeter, and Margaret, Countess of Salisbury. Because they were all of the 'royal race', of Yorkist descent and Henry's cousins, their disloyalty was more dangerous. The King, in his sense of self-righteousness and injured innocence, grew bitter and unforgiving. Lord Montague remembered that when Henry 'came to his chamber he would look angrily and fall to fighting'. In the opinion of Lord Thomas Howard, it was this king's 'nature never again to hold in affection any person he had cast from him that formerly he had loved'.

A way out of the Aragon marriage became imperative when in October 1532 Henry took Anne to France in state. This was, at last, their prenuptial honeymoon (their journey home from Dover to Eltham took ten days), and Anne was soon pregnant. The death of Archbishop Warham, a stalwart opponent of the divorce, made way for Cranmer's consecration as Archbishop of Canterbury, and for a marriage ceremony between Henry and Anne at the end of January 1533. They may have married, secretly, already, in mid November upon their return from Calais. This was not a marriage made in heaven. Not for long was Anne 'the most happy'.

There followed, one by one, statutes culminating in the Act of Supremacy in November 1534, which separated the English Church from Catholic Christendom, and surrendered it to a king who, as Supreme Head, claimed even the power to determine doctrine. This was a power which was unprecedented, and which shocked even Luther. The Supremacy was made by Parliament, although the draftsmen of the legislation insisted that Parliament was merely asserting an ineluctable historic truth. The Act in Restraint of Appeals – the first of the revolutionary statutes – was based on the testimony of 'divers and sundry ancient histories and chronicles'. The King's marriage to Anne Boleyn in January 1533, and the birth of Princess Elizabeth that September, necessitated a new succession, and the usurpation of the right of his first-born, Princess Mary. The new laws met opposition in both Lords and Commons. In confession at Syon Abbey Sir George Throckmorton was counselled to oppose to the death the anti-papal legislation, or 'he should stand in a very heavy case at the Day of Judgement'. But there were new and terrifying reasons for compliance.

'It were a strange world as words were made treason,' said Lord Montague. Opponents of the Royal Supremacy could, after the Treason Act of 1534, be executed by this 'law of words'. The Act had made it treasonable to call the King a heretic, a schismatic, a tyrant, an infidel or a usurper. Its first victims were the Holy Maid of Kent and her followers. On the day that they were executed – 20 April – an oath of compliance to the new succession was demanded from the people; the first time that a spiritual instrument of commitment had been used as a political test. Everyone swore, even More's fool swore. But More could not swear. In the Tower he thought on last things and wrote upon the Passion and upon tribulation. From his window he watched the prior and monks of the London Charterhouse leave the Tower for Tyburn and martyrdom, as 'bridegrooms for Christ'. They had refused to swear the Supremacy oath, for they could not deny Christ's trust to St Peter and repudiate the papal primacy. A year later More went to the block, as both traitor to a king and martyr for the universal Church whose unity that king had broken.

*

'What will be the end of this tragedy, God knows,' wrote one friend to another in July 1534. In breaking with Rome, Henry had never meant, he insisted, to follow the 'Lutheran sect' or to 'touch the sacraments'. With the Supremacy, he assumed not only the right, but also the duty before God, to promote true religion. The Act of Supremacy claimed as its purpose the 'increase in virtue in Christ's religion' and the repression of abuses. The Supreme Head would decide which was Christ's religion, which the abuses. From the mid 1530s it pleased Henry to present his Church as balanced between Catholic tradition and evangelical innovation. This was not simply a matter of expediency, but the consequence of the King's insistent, if wayward, theological cogitation. This Church would be at once scriptural and sacramental; it would denounce superstition while holding to devotional traditions; attack idolatry while showing the proper use of images. Successive religious formulations, drawn up after backroom battles between the King and his bishops, and between the bishops themselves, revealed what the Church believed, to the consternation of its clergy and parishioners. As Henry himself became unconvinced by the doctrine of purgatory, doubtful about the sacraments of ordination, extreme unction, confirmation and, finally, confession, traditional religion was undermined. But as the King himself denied the central Lutheran teaching of justification by faith alone, no alternative doctrine of salvation was propounded for his people. The royal intention might have been to hold a 'mean [middle], indifferent, true and virtuous way' between two alternative visions of salvation, but his people were left confused, and he himself was inconstant, manipulable, and unable to control the pace of events.

Preachers were found to exalt the Royal Supremacy. The talents of such evangelicals as Hugh Latimer, Edward Crome, John Bale and Robert Barnes, whose sermons had been anathematized before, were now called upon to denounce the papal usurpation. The preaching campaign against the Pope – now called merely Bishop of Rome – had consequences which the King had not foreseen. The evangelicals, believing that the papal primacy was only a human tradition, believed that other Catholic doctrines were derived from 'men's fantasies' rather than from scripture, the sole rule of faith. Some of the preachers used their new freedom to denounce 'the Bishop of Rome and all his cloisters' as licence to deny also purgatory and the intercessory power of saints. A few even dared to question the nature of the Mass itself. Even so the Supremacy of a king who still protested his Catholic orthodoxy was used to promote evangelical religion.

The impassioned sermons of the 'preachers of novelties' moved those who came to listen: one way or another. Resolute Catholics hated them, fearing their influence. 'These preachers' who took it upon themselves to preach the Gospel 'not truly, but after the new sect, called themselves Children of Christ, but they were Children of the Devil,' protested one outraged vicar. The conservative curate of Harwich complained in 1535 that 'The people nowadays would not believe ... the captains of the Church, but when a newfangled fellow doth come and show them a new story, him they do believe.' Battle lines were drawn in many places between evangelicals and conservative clergy. Reports came to Calais from London late in 1533: 'Many preachers we have here, but they come not from one master; Latimer many blameth, and as many doth allow.' The preachers had introduced 'divisions and seditions among us', never seen before, which threatened universal disorder. 'The Devil reigneth over us now.' Diversity of preaching had sown doubt and disobedience, as well as division. Thomas Starkey warned in the summer of 1536 that 'With the despising of purgatory, the people begin little to regard hell, heaven, or any other felicity to be had in another life.'

Religious divisions were nowhere deeper or more bitter than at court. At the Corpus Christi procession on 15 June 1536, the great celebration of the Mass and affirmation of Christian community, Henry publicly took part. Queen Anne did not come with him, for she was nearly a month dead. He brought his third queen, Jane Seymour, instead. Anne had dared a great deal to become queen, and dared still more once she was queen. With her came her faction. Her lieutenant in the Privy Chamber was her brother, Lord Rochford. The purposes and presence of that faction were most visible in matters of religion. 'Who in the Mass do use to clap their fingers on their lips and say never a word?' a preacher was asked, and his reply was, 'Some great men in court did so' – Anne's friends. Anne determined to advance the Gospel and promote evangelical schemes for the reform of the commonwealth. But she intervened in causes which the King did not support, when for her to intervene at all outraged him. On Passion Sunday, 2 April 1536 John Skip, Anne's almoner, preached a sermon at court which Anne must have countenanced. He told the Old Testament story of King Ahasuerus, persuaded by his evil counsellor Haman to proscribe the Jews against the pleas of the 'good woman' whom the King loved. A court as well versed in scripture as Henry's would have understood the message: Anne was good Queen Esther, trying to prevent the King from listening to the blandishments of Cromwell, who promised him wealth beyond measure; wealth acquired from the Church but not to be spent upon the poor but upon palaces and war. More dangerously, the preacher reminded the court how King Solomon's rule grew degenerate as lust overruled his judgement, just as Henry, who saw himself as Solomon in his wisdom, contemplated taking a third queen.

Having cast off the Roman allegiance, and his first queen, all for Anne (so many believed), Henry tired of her. They danced together in January 1536 at the news of Catherine of Aragon's death, but their mutual delight was short-lived. On 29 January Anne miscarried. She lost not only the prince who might have saved her, but the King also. Anne's enemies at court, who were enemies of her religion too, had discovered in Jane Seymour the perfect candidate for queen for Henry, who never found a wife for himself. They were teaching her a demeanour of self-abnegation and passivity which, after Anne's fierceness, would best please the King. Confronted by this personal betrayal and by the conspiracy of the conservatives against her, Anne fought, but she failed to recruit the most politic of all her co-religionists to her side. At the end of March 1536 Cromwell told the Imperial ambassador that Anne, his erstwhile patron, would like to see his head cut off. His own prospects were grim if Anne survived, but grim also if she did not, for a conservative group at court were now determined to destroy the reforms he had made, and surely him with them. In the most brilliant and deadly stratagem in Tudor court politics, Cromwell plotted to remove Anne and all her allies – despite the religion and ideals for the commonwealth he shared with them – and to do this by allying with the conservatives; but only for a while. Cromwell must devise a way to rescue himself and the achievements for reform while removing Anne and her friends, and permanently. But how? On 30 April a court musician was arrested and tortured, and the tragedy began rapidly to unfold.

Anne was not only the King's consort but also the queen of his court. In the conventions of chivalry and courtly love, the queen must be, by her virtue, most unattainable, most deserving of chaste love and faithful service. But with courtly love might come real love, with all love's malign attendants: jealousy, betrayal, revenge. The game of courtly love had rules, and Anne broke them. Courtly lovers wrote poetry, but Anne mocked Henry's. With her brother, she had joked about the King's prowess, or lack of it, in the royal bed. Unwise certainly, but was it treasonable? More dangerously, she had teased Henry Norris, the Groom of the Stool, about his desire for her: 'You look for dead men's shoes.' To sleep with a queen, if with her consent, was, although remarkably foolhardy, not treason; a queen's adultery was, for it slandered the royal issue. And for a queen and her lovers – for anyone – conspiratorial gossip about the king was treason under the 'law of words'. Looking for a treason which would condemn not only the Queen but all her friends, Cromwell had found it.

After the May Day jousts the Queen and her alleged lovers were taken to the Tower. On 8 May Thomas Wyatt joined his friends there. They might 'make ballads well now', said Queen Anne. Wyatt's own relationship with Anne Boleyn, before her marriage, had been close, too close. In the vision of fugitive love and futile chase which he portrayed in the sonnet 'Whoso list to hunt, I know where is an hind' we may even glimpse what it was like to desire a woman whom the King claimed. Henry was only too willing to be persuaded of the guilt of his queen and his friends. Self-pityingly, he wrote a tragedy about it, claiming that Anne had had a hundred lovers. Probably she had had none but him, but once in the Tower, with false witness brought against her, there was no way but one. On 17 May Viscount Rochford, Henry Norris, Francis Weston, William Brereton and Mark Smeaton went to the block. The following day, the eve of Anne's execution, the candles on Queen Catherine's sepulchre lit spontaneously, so it was said. Wyatt, who watched the Queen and his friends die from his prison chamber in the Bell Tower, wrote their epitaph:

These bloody days have broken my heart;
My lust, my youth did then depart,
    And blind desire of estate;
Who hastes to climb seeks to revert:
    Of truth, *circa Regna tonat* [it thunders around thrones].

Wyatt escaped; so did Sir Francis Bryan, who had been sent for 'upon his allegiance', the ultimate, terrifying demand upon any subject. With the remorseless reciprocity of the politics of Henry's reign, the engineers of Anne's destruction were soon themselves destroyed. Her enemies were charged, not unjustly, with working to restore the Lady Mary to the succession. After long resisting, and to save her friends, Mary acknowledged the invalidity of Queen Catherine's marriage and her own bastardy. The King married Jane Seymour who, on 12 October 1537, produced the longed-for heir, Prince Edward. He was the death of her, for she died, as so many Tudor women did, of 'childbed fever'. The conservatives at court were eclipsed, but lived; though not for long.

Everyone believed that there was one true faith and one Catholic – that is, universal – Church, with a monopoly of spiritual truth, but there was no agreement regarding which Church this should be. The debate 'between Tyndale and me,' More had written, was 'nothing else in effect but to find out which Church is the very Church.' At the Reformation, because of the Reformation, division in religion seemed inevitable, because everyone agreed that anyone not of their Church was against it, and therefore heretic and schismatic. Contention was to be expected, and might even be necessary in a greater cause. Erasmus had once thought that faith and charity would dispel religious difference, but unity came to seem impossible. Latimer counselled his evangelical brethren that where there 'is quietness . . . there is not the truth'. It took an extraordinary determination to reconcile differences between the faiths – like that attributed to Cardinal Pole and like that which More may have discovered at the very end – to see that 'heretics be not in all things heretics'. The break with Rome made reconciliation between the confessional sides more difficult than ever.

*

Violence, even civil war, seemed possible. In Calais, England's last bridgehead in France, its ancient governor, Lord Lisle, was so scared that one sect would rise against another that throughout 1538 he slept in armour. The spectre which haunted Henry and Cromwell as they ventured into the political unknown was of rebellion at home, led by a conservative nobility and clergy, allied with a crusading force sent by the Emperor with papal sanction. Reports came of priests in the confessional – 'the privy chamber of treason' – counselling steadfastness or even resistance. The nobility, with many reasons to resent the expansion of royal power, might move into opposition. In secret interviews with the Imperial ambassador late in 1534, Lords Hussey and Darcy called for the Emperor's aid in 'God's cause', and promised to 'animate' the people of the North to rise and defend the Church. Conspiracy did turn to rebellion, if not in the ways they had intended, and not until changes were made to traditional religion that were worse than any they could yet have imagined.

Cromwell wrote himself a memorandum early in 1536 concerning 'the abomination of religious persons throughout this realm, and a reformation to be devised therein'. In the Cardinal's service, he had helped to dissolve a few religious houses too small or otherwise unworthy to deserve the name, and to apply their wealth to found colleges. The memory had stayed with him. In 1535, as newly-created lay Vicegerent of the King in the new Church, outranking even his evangelical ally, Archbishop Cranmer, he was in a powerful position to effect reform. He instituted a commission to enquire into the wealth and state of the religious houses throughout England. Henry's religious zeal was now directed against the monasteries, which happened to be the richest franchise in his kingdom. The monasteries' defenders believed they understood Cromwell's motives – 'the false flatterer says he will make the King the richest prince in Christendom' – and they compared Henry's assault upon the religious houses to Nebuchadnezzar's destruction of Jerusalem. The commissioners prepared the case for the prosecution; their alleged discovery of 'not seven, but more than 700,000 deadly sins' delighted evangelicals. Even the most charitable witness of religious life in the monasteries would have seen more spiritual torpor than fervour there. In England, as in Ireland, intense religious life was usually the preserve of the reformed orders of friars. Nothing England or Ireland had so far known prepared for the desecration to come.

The Act for the suppression of the lesser monasteries in England (those with an income of less than £200 per annum; 372 houses in England and twenty-seven in Wales) was passed in March 1536.

Communities centuries old and institutionally immortal were under threat. This was not an attack on monasticism in principle, otherwise a quarter would not have been reprieved, nor would the religious have been allowed to transfer to the greater houses. But in the religious houses a mood of desperation prevailed, and a sense of impending disaster; the greater houses, surely, could not escape the fate of the lesser. The testimony of their great defender, Robert Aske, given after he was condemned and had nothing left to lose, is compelling: 'When the abbeys stood the people not only had worldly refreshing in their bodies but spiritual refuge'; without the abbeys, 'The service of God is much minished . . . to the decrease of the Faith and spiritual comfort to man's soul.' The religious, however unworthy their individual lives, stood for an ideal of Christian life, 'of ghostly [spiritual] living'. Their first purpose was to pray, to pray for souls, in a society which believed that prayers availed the dead. 'The abbeys were one of the beauties of this realm', ancient and numinous landmarks, now to be plundered and laid waste.

In the summer of 1536, for the first time, the King used his newly assumed power to define doctrine, and many people believed that the Catholic faith itself was threatened. The Ten Articles of religion of July 1536 were meant to end confusion, but marked instead a long period of uncertainty in the life of the parish. Prayers for the dead were still allowed, but with the proviso that scripture named no such place as purgatory, nor its pains; images of saints remained, but reverence to them was 'only to be done to God, and in His honour'; both veneration of saints and prayers for the dead stood quite apart from things necessary to salvation. Ominously, only three of the sacraments were named. In the North they warned: 'See, friends, now is taken from us four of the seven sacraments, and shortly ye shall lose the other three also, and thus the faith of Holy Church shall utterly be suppressed.' Injunctions to the clergy followed upon the Articles. The conjunction of assaults upon traditional practice revealed the Government at its most destructive. Rumours spread of the impending destruction of parish churches and of treasure given by popular devotion over generations, and when the dissolution of the monasteries began it seemed to prove all the rumours true.

As the parish of Louth in Lincolnshire went in procession on 1 October, following its silver cross, a parishioner shouted: 'Masters, step forth and let us follow the cross this day; God knoweth whether ever we shall follow it hereafter.' Within days 10,000 were in revolt; 'The country rises wholly as they go before them.' The 'dangerest insurrection that hath been seen' followed; a series of rebellions through six northern counties, lasting through the autumn and winter of 1536–7, raising 'all the flower of the North', a force so large that no royal army could have suppressed it if it had come to battle. The Lincolnshire rising was a spontaneous rising of the common people, spurred by their disaffected clergy. But it was inchoate, and soon the disparate elements among the rebels turned against each other.

'Ay, be they up in Lincolnshire?' asked Lord Darcy, who was one of those northern lords who had known that 'it will never mend without we fight for it'. Within a week of the first rising a movement began which was more coherent by far: the Pilgrimage of Grace. Led by Robert Aske, their Grand Captain, who was both visionary and politic, the Pilgrimage united the grievances of a whole society against alien innovations from the South, devised by heretic 'evil counsellors' around the King. The pilgrims' grievances were inevitably economic, social and political, as well as narrowly religious, but only the defence of Holy Church, 'now lame and fast in bounds', could have united so many different groups in this mass demonstration and overlaid it, through long waiting days, with an almost mystical aura.

'God be with them,' said Aske; 'they were pilgrims and had a pilgrimage . . . to go.' This was no less than a crusade. The pilgrims sang as they marched –

> Christ crucified!
> For thy wounds wide
> Us commons guide!
> Which pilgrims be

– and they marched behind the talismanic banners of the five wounds of Christ and of St Cuthbert for protection. Religion sanctified their actions as rebels, and their clergy promised them heaven if they died in that quarrel. True, someone had to invent the oath, compose the songs, contrive the thousands of banners and badges, but that does not negate the pilgrims' faith. True, the people lamented the loss of the religious houses for reasons which were not only spiritual, and feared the intrusion of southern landowners and new ways and the upsetting of their 'old, ancient customs'. Yet the course of the Pilgrimage supports Aske's contention that the suppression of the abbeys was the first cause of the rising. 'Rather than our house of St Agatha should go down, we shall all die,' vowed the people of Richmondshire. The religious were restored by the rebels in sixteen out of fifty-five of the suppressed houses, and there they stayed while the pilgrims held the North. In the aftermath of the rising the King, blaming these 'corrupters of the temporalty [laity]', ordered the monks and friars to be hanged in chains.

The Pilgrimage was never suppressed by a royal army, although large forces marched North under Norfolk, Suffolk and Shrewsbury. The chronicle stories of providential rain which swelled the rivers and prevented battle hid the ignominy that the King was forced to treat with rebels. Henry sent a Gentleman of his Privy Chamber to summon Aske to the royal presence. Aske came south and had 'good words and good countenance' with the King. The rising collapsed because of a paradox within it: that the pilgrims were sworn not only to Holy Church but to their King. Henry was outraged by these protests of obedience, and it was true that the pilgrim oath to defend Holy Church militant might exert a more compelling claim. Lord Darcy, 'Old Tom', faithful servant of the Tudors for nearly fifty years, would not hand over the traitor Aske, to whom he had sworn loyalty, for 'What is a man but his promise?' The pilgrims had a higher loyalty still; they must 'set more by the King of Heaven than by twenty [earthly] kings'.

When the rebels insisted, 'Forward now, or else never,' they were prescient. The rebellion failed, and Holy Church was 'undone'. There were many who regretted not standing with the pilgrims, and though some might warn of another rising – 'Beware the third' – this was the last protest against the assault on the Church and ancient customs which might, just might, have halted the advance of Reformation in England. Later, when people reflected on the deep allegiance to the old Church and wondered why it had not been better defended, they might have remembered the pilgrims. Henry called the Pilgrimage a 'tragedy'; he meant a tragedy for the northern nobility, fallen from high estate. It was a tragedy, too, for those Cumberland widows who cut down the bodies of their dead husbands from the gallows; for the monks who, though often unworthy of the sacrifice made for them, were now cast out; for the religious houses, left open to the sky; for the evangelicals, who had looked for the plunder to be spent upon the commonwealth, not to bloat the coffers of the King and his favourites. Nothing could save the greater monasteries from dissolution and oblivion. Within eight years all the monasteries, nunneries and friaries within England and Wales – though not in Ireland – were put down. The nobility of the North, who persisted in their old allegiance, suffered an eclipse. The people dreaded more radical reform, and were powerless to prevent it. Who would stop the heretics now?

*

The evangelicals, knowing that their time might be short, now moved to bring the Gospel to the people, so that they would never lose it, and to wage war against idolatry and superstition. Ideas which only a while before had been heretical were now enforced as a new orthodoxy, but this was an orthodoxy hard to defend, challenged by zealots who tried to extend the campaign to purify the Church to attack fundamental Catholic doctrine, and also by conservatives who waited and worked for the return of the old ways. Distinctions between true and false worship were always relative. Evangelicals pointed out the inconsistencies in official actions: for Parliament to dissolve the monasteries, while the Church still maintained the doctrine of purgatory was 'uncharitableness and cruelness'. The people must be taught the truth and given certainty. The King might see himself as a purifying Old Testament monarch, but the idols Josiah had destroyed were pagan, not the familiar and sacred images of the Catholic present and past. This king who had boasted himself 'defensor fidei' was now seen as 'destructor fidei'.

In the war against idolatry it was the governing orders who now destroyed the old world of which they had been guardians. Their priority was to inculcate a scriptural faith, but their energies often seemed destructive. An iconoclastic campaign began in 1538 to destroy the idols which led the people to false worship and to confound false miracles with true ones. The most famous and spectacular images were wrested from their shrines and brought to London, a 'jolly muster', to be dishonoured and destroyed. The Rood of Grace of Boxley Abbey, a miraculous crucifix which was believed to speak to its supplicants, was revealed as a puppet, operated by strings. Latimer and Cromwell devised grim iconoclastic carnivals. An ancient prophecy that the image of Dderfel Gadarn, 'the great god of Wales', would set a forest on fire was horribly fulfilled in May 1538: while Latimer preached, the traitor Friar Forest was burned alive with, and by, the image. Such ceremonies were profoundly shocking and subversive: the benefit sought from the miraculous Rood of Grace was no less than the assurance of being in a state of grace; to Dderfel Gadarn was attributed the power to rescue damned souls from hell. And the images failed to respond to the reformers' challenge to defend themselves.

Commissioners were sent round the country to seize 'abused' images, relics and shrines, and record the people's 'fond trust' in them. From Burton-on-Trent they sent St Modwyn, with her red cow and her staff, which women in labour borrowed to ease their pains. At Caversham in Berkshire, they found a piece of the noose which hanged Judas, and an angel with one wing which had brought to Caversham its proudest possession: the spear's head which had pierced Our Saviour's side. Now Caversham lost the mana or spiritual power of that sacred relic, so long in its keeping, and other places lost other treasures. A pathetic tally of the votive offerings found at the shrines was recorded. The cynicism of the commissioners contrasted with the simple devotion of the people, who lost their sacred treasures before they lost their faith in them. In most places the parishioners had looked on, helpless, before the sacrilege; in some, the commissioners moved secretly, by night, for fear of resistance, just as the clandestine, unofficial iconoclasts did. The images of wood and stone could be annihilated, yet the idols in the mind, the imagining of Mary with her child in her arms, which the most fervent and uncompromising reformers would come to condemn, remained. From the Bible the people must learn that God was a spirit, to be worshipped in spirit and truth.

The reformers sought to replace a religion of seeing as believing by a religion of the Word. Tyndale had once promised a learned Catholic that 'If God spare my life . . . I will cause a boy that driveth the plough shall know more of the scripture than thou dost.' In exile, suffering countless setbacks, he had almost completed his translations of both Old and New Testaments when he was betrayed. Yet his martyrdom in Antwerp in October 1536 came only shortly before the first official English Bible was published, mostly in his translation, which marked English religion and the English language thereafter. In 1538 the same Injunctions which outlawed the veneration of relics, ordered an English Bible to be placed in every church. At first the Bibles lay gathering dust, largely unread, and were no compensation for the irrecoverable loss of the painted images and shrines. The people were forcibly deprived not only of numinous artefacts, symbolic of a world unseen, but also of objects of beauty in lives of privation. Religious art was often their only art. Yet even the loss of such treasures was not as traumatic as the shattering of the beliefs they had symbolized. The desecration threatened the end of mediation, propitiation and spiritual solace, in this world and beyond, and very many were left bewildered and bereft. No one watching the destruction, powerless to prevent it, could be oblivious to doctrinal change.

The evangelicals had brought scripture to the people, yet their own downfall was prefigured in their triumph. The reforms in religion were threatened by their divisive consequences. Zealots demanding further reformation moved to commit reckless acts of iconoclasm and to challenge the most sacred mysteries of the Catholic and evangelical faiths alike. Tyndale had warned John Frith, unavailingly but presciently, 'Of the presence of Christ's body in the sacrament, meddle as little as you can; that there appear no division among us.' But there were divisions among the evangelicals, as well as an abyss between them and the Catholics, who grew more resolute in opposition as they saw the extremist tendency in reform. Dissension appeared in every community where the 'new' faith had penetrated, and reports of the trouble reached Cromwell daily from every part of the country; reports which he tried to hide from the King.

Reform could continue no longer once the King knew that ideas more radical than he could countenance, particularly concerning the Mass, were spreading within his Church. At the end of 1538 a repressive proclamation was issued in which the King's hand was visible – not least in the implacability of its penalties. Free discussion of the 'Holy and Blessed Sacrament', and its mysteries by the unlearned was punishable by death and forfeiture. Clergy who married, contrary to their vow, would be deprived. A new wave of persecution began. Henry himself, dressed in the white of theological purity, tried John Lambert, who had been denounced by his fellow reformers, men who held more moderate views than he did upon the nature of Christ's presence in the Eucharist, and who feared that Lambert's radicalism would endanger the whole evangelical cause. Lambert was condemned, and burnt, for beliefs about the Mass which were very close to those which Cranmer would hold himself within a few years. Reform was at a crossroads. Cromwell had determinedly sustained the evangelicals, but he could not protect them, or himself, for much longer. Henry was alarmed by the spread of heresy and sacrilege at home, and by the divisions which the new faith had generated. When he learnt early in 1539 that Calais had become an enclave of 'gospellers' through Cromwell and Cranmer's patronage, his fears were confirmed. Cromwell's conservative opponents, the Duke of Norfolk and Bishop Gardiner, long excluded from court, returned determined to destroy their evangelical enemies and reverse the Reformation.

*

At the end of 1538, at the close of the first phase of its Reformation, England stood alone in Europe, and never in greater danger. The constant warfare between Habsburg and Valois had, until now, ensured that both the French King and the Emperor needed England's amity, but in 1538 the novel prospect of peace between the two enemies threatened to make England, as Thomas Wriothesley put it, 'but a morsel amongst these choppers'. The break with Rome had made the King a heretic and England schismatic and vulnerable to a Catholic crusade. Henry dreaded the imminent threat of a General Council of the Church which would demand the restoration of England to papal obedience. A Catholic League of the Emperor and the Kings of France and Scotland seemed poised to invade and to partition England. Now Henry completed what he had begun: the destruction of the nobility of the White Rose, the surviving Yorkist line in England. There was evidence enough of their treason, under a law which made words treason. After the Pilgrimage of Grace had failed, Lord Montague had said: 'Lord Darcy played the fool; he went about to pluck away the Council. He should first have begun with the head.' Partly in reprisal for Cardinal Pole's papal legation of 1537 to persuade the Catholic powers to crusade against England, Henry moved, lethally, against Pole's family, and Pole himself was lucky to escape the royal agents, Wyatt and Bryan, sent into the courts of Europe to kidnap or even assassinate him.

In the Parliament of 1539 penal legislation against heresy was passed: the Act of Six Articles, 'Gardiner's Gospel'. The intransmutable penalty for denying transubstantiation was death by burning, with no chance given for abjuration. The break with Rome had never been meant to augur the end of persecution, but for six years persecution of evangelicals had been in abeyance. Apart from John Lambert, only Anabaptists, Europe's most radical heretics, had been burnt. Now many evangelicals were fugitive and fearful. Catholics rejoiced at the passage of the 'bloody act', looking for an imminent return of traditional religion, but it did not happen, for the eclipse of the evangelical party at court was not lasting. Some of the gospellers could not be silenced. During Lent in 1540 three leading evangelicals – Barnes, Garrett and Jerome – preached the quintessential message of Christ's saving passion, and called upon the rich to succour the poor. Their defiance was fatal for them, but also for Cromwell because his enemies now used his patronage of radicals to destroy him.

Cromwell had once said, though with a smile, that if the same fate befell him as his predecessors, he would trust to God. That Christian resignation was now tested. His conservative enemies returned to challenge him, exploiting rifts between him and the King. Cromwell's initiative to ally with the Lutheran princes of Germany culminated in a marriage between Henry and Anne of Cleves. Henry married in January 1540, but found his fourth wife repellent. He could, he insisted, 'never in her company be provoked and steered to know her carnally'. There would never be an heir from Anne: 'I like her not.' The events of the spring and summer of 1540 confused those who lived through them. Political fortunes were shifting and the prospects for reform or reaction in religion were unpredictable. Cromwell seemed higher in favour than ever. In April, in addition to his offices as Vicegerent, Chancellor of the Exchequer and Lord Privy Seal, he was created Earl of Essex and made Great Chamberlain, which gave him at last formal mastery of the royal household. By May he sensed a trap closing, and moved against the conservatives, sending Lord Lisle to the Tower for alleged collusion with Pole and Rome. But Cromwell's own arrest followed soon after, and once in the Tower, denied access to the King or trial by his peers, his condemnation was a foregone conclusion. The charges against him were many, accusing him of overweening power, of treason, but overwhelmingly of heresy. Once persuaded – though wrongly – that Cromwell had impugned the Mass, the King allowed his counsellor to be sacrificed. Cromwell went to the block on 28 July, on the same day that Henry married his fifth queen, Catherine Howard: both Cromwell's fall and the marriage were Howard conspiracies. Two days later, in a grotesque demonstration of Henry's 'mean, indifferent' way in religion, the evangelicals Barnes, Garrett and Jerome were burnt, while at the same time three conservatives suffered the death of traitors.

Conservatives now looked for a reaction, and Cromwell's bereft 'factionaries' were fearful for the Gospel. As soon as the coup against Cromwell was completed, a major inquisition for heresy began. Persecution had been the conservatives' first objective. What they discovered horrified them. Cromwell had promised, allegedly, that if he lived another year his party would inculcate evangelical reform irreversibly, so that 'it should not lie in the King's power to resist it'. Persecution failed that summer because the evangelicals who were found were so many and so influential that they could not all be punished: 500 were denounced in London alone. Thomas More, as Lord Chancellor, had once told William Roper:

I pray God ... that some of us, as high as we seem to sit upon the mountains treading heretics under our feet like ants, live not in the day that we gladly would wish to be at a league and composition with them to let them have their churches quietly to themselves, so that they would be content to let us have ours quietly to ourselves.

That day had not come yet, but evangelical ideology and principles had invaded England and infiltrated powerful sections of society. If the new religion were to be extirpated, ways must be found.

Archbishop Cranmer lay low, asking 'Whom shall the King trust hereafter?' Henry thought to rule alone. Cromwell had no successor. Always suspicious, Henry became more so with age and found disloyalty everywhere. Illness and pain made him irascible and unpredictable, and in such circumstances court rivalries flourished. Cromwell's fall, itself made possible because he was outnumbered at the Council board, opened the way for the Council, once again a stronghold of noblemen, to reassert itself as a powerful executive in a way denied to it during Wolsey's and Cromwell's ascendancy. The royal Council had been reconstructed in the aftermath of the crisis engendered by the Pilgrimage of Grace as an institutional Privy Council, a corporate board with a finite membership, including the great office-holders, and with important advisory and executive functions. With Cromwell removed, the new Privy Council could exercise and assert its authority.

Cromwell had left a legacy which transformed the politics of Henry's last years. Into the Privy Chamber itself, as the King's constant attendants, he had introduced his own clients, zealous evangelicals whose determination to advance their faith was only slightly tempered by their knowledge that Henry would hardly countenance it. The royal doctors held untold influence, because the King grew daily more dependent upon them, and they, too, were committed to the new religion. Leading ladies at the English court also had a powerful influence upon the spread of evangelical doctrine. But their faith made all the court evangelicals vulnerable. The conservatives, led by Gardiner and Norfolk, became convinced that the best way to extirpate the new sect was to remove its leaders, permanently: 'Stone dead hath no fellow.' Their own experience had shown that exiled opponents could return. The device of bringing down evangelicals by accusing them of the worst heresies had succeeded against Cromwell, and was used with a vengeance for the remainder of the reign. With time the struggle at court, which became polarized between evangelicals in the Privy Chamber and conservatives in the Privy Council, became ever more bitter with the certainty that the King could not live for ever. But while Henry lived, he ruled, and his obsession at the end of his reign, as at the beginning, was war.

Once again, Henry conceived a grand military enterprise against France, with a secondary campaign against France's ally, Scotland. The renewed war between Habsburg and Valois in July 1541 gave Henry the chance to venture into Europe again. But first, in August 1542, troops were sent north to lay waste the Borders. In November a Scottish army was put to flight at Solway Moss, a catastrophe almost as complete for Scotland as Flodden, for three weeks later James V was dead and Mary, Queen of Scots, only one week old, was on the throne. Endemic feuding beween the Scottish nobility was exacerbated in that 'broken world' as rival groups contended for power and formed bonds to build up alliances and for self-protection. The divisions centred upon which foreign alliance Scotland should make. The faction which fell at James V's death, led by Cardinal Beaton, stood for the old alliance with France, and feared that Scotland would fall to England. The new regent and heir-presumptive, James Hamilton, Earl of Arran, and the Earls of Lennox and Angus led the pro-English party, but with such vacillation that they failed to commit themselves to the Treaty of Greenwich of July 1543 with its proposed union to be created by the marriage of Prince Edward to Mary, Queen of Scots. The punitive English 'Rough Wooing' followed, and the vengeful sack of Edinburgh in May 1544 ended any possibility of friendship between Scotland and England, or indeed of peace.

In England the conservatives had been thwarted. 1541 and 1542 were years of evangelical advance as the King, guided by Archbishop Cranmer, determined to purify his new Church. Moreover, the Howards' queen had disgraced them. For months everyone – except Henry – knew that Catherine was unfaithful. Who would tell him? On All Souls' Day 1541 Cranmer presented him with written testimony of her infidelities, not only before, but during her marriage. Her affairs while queen were fatal to her. The distraught King turned once again to theology, and to war. There was no retreat from reform until 1543, when the new alliance with the Emperor for a common assault on France made Henry anxious to assert his orthodoxy. The Act for the Advancement of the True Religion which, contrary to its name, forbade all dependents and servants, all men under the rank of yeoman, and all women except noble- and gentlewomen from reading the Bible, the foundation of true religion, was a disaster for evangelicals, who saw their cause betrayed. 'Died not Christ as well for craftsmen and poor men as for gentlemen and rich men?', asked Robert Wisdom, a leading preacher. Bishop Gardiner chose Easter 1543 as his moment to 'bend his bow to shoot at some of the head deer', directing his aim at the Privy Chamber. The discovery of a nest of evangelicals in St George's Chapel at Windsor implicated sympathizers at court. At Canterbury, in the little court of the cathedral chapter, there was faction too, and the prebendaries gathered evidence against their archbishop, whom the King, with deliberate irony, called 'the greatest heretic in Kent'. From time to time, and when he chose, Henry moved to protect persecuted courtiers and favourites, and now he saved Cranmer. Though he hated the heresy, he hated too the secret interventions into his own household, and conspiracy in the name of religion. In July 1543 he married again; the triumph of hope over experience. His sixth wife, Catherine Parr, came to reveal evangelical leanings. Holding daily scripture readings in her chamber, she encouraged the younger reforming generation at court.

The invasion of France now preoccupied the King; Scotland, far less a prize, had been, for Henry, an inglorious diversion. In June 1544 a massive English army crossed to Calais, though with little sense of where to go thereafter. Henry determined to campaign himself and arrived in July to lay siege to Boulogne, which fell in September. This was an empty victory for England: her Imperial allies had defected to France, and the overwhelming cost in men and money far outweighed any advantage, save to the King, who was prouder of 'our daughter Boulogne' than he was of his others. English foreign policy was in disarray; campaigns against France and Scotland were financially ruinous, and by the summer of 1545 invasion was threatened from an offensive alliance of France and Scotland which Henry himself had provoked. From August 1545 the glorious commander of English forces in France, Henry Howard, Earl of Surrey, urged the King to further conquest, against all prudence, and against the defeatist advice of the Council to make peace and cede Boulogne.

At court the political atmosphere was tense as partisans for rival stances in religion and foreign policy awaited the outcome of the diplomacy. In the spring of 1546 Henry painfully decided to abandon war and hopes of conquest, and by the summer, England and France were at peace. Surrey had returned from France early in the year, in disgrace, malcontent and vengeful. He began to quarrel with others at a court in which he saw himself as the guardian of chivalry and ancient nobility, stranded in a base world of arrivistes. The dispute between the old nobility and the new men became explicit as rival groups began to vie for control of the regency which must follow the awaited accession of the boy king Edward. The Howards believed that theirs was the strongest claim, and even now, when the King was too ill and bloated to walk – 'moved by engines and art rather than by nature', as Lord Thomas Howard wrote – conspired to provide another Howard royal mistress. But Mary, Duchess of Richmond, Surrey's sister, was too appalled by the prospect to play her inglorious part.

The King's choice of advisers and confidants became even more significant since the group ascendant at his death would hold power in the new reign. The consequences for the losers would be alarming: not only for themselves, but also for the religion for which they stood. The struggles assumed a new ferocity and now centred around the persecution. 'What news in London?' they asked in the country: the news that spring was that a leading preacher, Dr Crome, had been broken by the Privy Council. His confession might implicate the whole network of his evangelical supporters at court, and so might that of Anne Askew, for so many were her friends at court that she might prove the perfect instrument to destroy the evangelicals there. In the Tower she was racked by the Lord Chancellor himself, to force her to name the others of her sect. Which great ladies at court had supported her? Who had sent her money? Through the indiscretions of their wives the husbands might be betrayed. But the conservatives failed in their attempts to bring down the evangelicals in the summer. George Blage, the King's favourite, 'his pig', was condemned for heresy, but Henry protected him. Bishop Gardiner failed in a more desperate ploy: no less than to destroy the Queen by persuading the King that she was a heretic.

At the very end of the reign counsellors and courtiers who had been at odds over foreign policy, religion and place, made common cause to bring down the Howards, the most dangerous pretenders to the regency, even to the throne. The King was more than ever obsessed by the security of the succession. With tremulous hand (his interpolations are marked here in capital letters), he helped to frame the charges against them. 'If a man compassing WITH HIMSELF TO GOVERN THE REALM, DO ACTUALLY GO ABOUT TO RULE THE KING . . . what this importeth?' Henry had looked for a regency for his son which would be strong enough to govern but not strong enough to threaten the throne. Ambition disqualified the Howards. Surrey went to the block on 19 January, ostensibly for the *lèse-majesté* of usurping the royal heraldic arms. Yet his treason was clearest in his poetry, where the shadow of the tyrant looms. Instead of a Supreme Head leading his people in religious truth and virtue, Surrey portrayed a royal throne and an apocalyptic beast, persecuting the innocent:

> I saw a royal throne whereas that Justice should have sit;
>   Instead of whom I saw, with fierce and cruel mood,
>   Where wrong was sat, that bloody beast, that drunk the guiltless blood.

Here was treason. But even at Henry's court some secrets remained secret, and it was not in the manuscripts of Surrey's poetry that his treason was sought and found.

The reign ended as it had begun, with blood, silence and conspiracy. Late in January 1547, as the King lay dying, those around him in the Privy Gallery conspired to overturn the provisions of his will. Henry VIII had the will, but not the power, to rule beyond the grave.

5

Bearing Rule

LORDSHIP

The Earl of Surrey had a proud but dangerous inheritance. He was the son of England's premier noble, the Duke of Norfolk, and grandson of Edward Stafford, Duke of Buckingham, who as heir-general to both Edward III and Henry VI might have rivalled the descent of the Tudors. By aspiration, Surrey was a prince: 'By princely acts thus strave I still to make my fame endure,' he wrote. The servants in his lodgings speculated in 1543 that if anything happened to the King or Prince Edward, Surrey would be king after his father.

'Why, is he a prince?' asked a maid.

'Yea, marry, is he.'

Surrey went to the block for standing too close to the throne. For Fulke Greville, poet, thinker and courtier, looking back from the end of the century upon the nature of Tudor royal power and the constraints upon it, the nobility were meant to stand a 'brave half-pace between a throne and a people'; to restrain the rebellious tendencies of the people on the one hand and the tyrannical impulses of the monarch on the other. Yet there was always the danger that the nobles might use their power over the people to step closer; to conjure the same treason that the angels had in heaven, and 'fall as the angels did, by affecting equality with their maker'. Nobles were the creations of kings, sometimes long past, but the great noble families had political and dynastic traditions of their own which, if threatened, could lead them to defy the Crown; even, in a past which was not forgotten, to unking kings.

Surrey's grandfather the 3rd Duke of Buckingham, magnificent in his wealth, his building, his lands and pretensions, had suffered the heavy lordship of Henry VII and grew to resent any slight, however minor, from that king's son. By 1520 he had 'imagined' the deposition and death of Henry VIII, and was listening to the prophecies of a Carthusian monk that he would succeed to the throne. His plans would come to fruition if 'the lords of the kingdom would show their minds to each other'. Related by blood and marriage throughout the great cousinhood of the English nobility – his brothers-in-law were the Earls of Wiltshire and Northumberland; his sons-in-law the Earls of Surrey and Westmorland, Lords Montague and Abergavenny, and Thomas Fitzgerald, heir to the Earl of Kildare – he thought to turn that alliance to confederacy. Buckingham would be Protector, and Northumberland would rule all England north of the Trent. Links with the Marcher lord Rhys ap Thomas suggested the same kind of alliance between Wales, the Welsh Marches and the North as had threatened Henry IV a century before. Buckingham continued to dream, and to talk, and the suspicions of him grew. In November 1520 he planned to ride with an armed bodyguard three or four hundred strong to his Welsh lordships; from whence, some remembered, his father was to have led his own failed rebellion in 1483. In the spring of 1521 Buckingham was arrested for treason, tried and condemned by his peers, and executed. For all his wealth and power, Buckingham could not raise support: not from his fellow nobles, who condemned him; nor from his tenants, whom he had oppressed. Loyalty to their lord would not persuade Buckingham's tenants to take up arms in support of his private quarrels, especially not against his sovereign. The ambition and fate of Buckingham, and of his grandson Surrey after him, shows both the potential of the nobility for disruption and the real power of the Tudors to contain them.

Who were the nobility? They were very few. Under the first Tudor kings there were only about fifty nobles, and still only about fifty when Elizabeth, the last Tudor, died. In order of rank – and in this society rank was crucial – the nobility were king and prince; and then dukes, marquesses, earls, viscounts, barons – the lay peers who sat in the Upper House of Parliament. Nobility was created by kings, and was inherited. While the French nobility was a nobility of blood, where nobility and the great and jealously guarded judicial and fiscal privileges which accompanied it were inherited by all male children, in England there was only one noble descendant, usually the eldest son. Below the nobility, and far greater in number, came the gentry – knights, esquires and simple gentlemen. In 1524 there may have been about 200 knightly families and four or five thousand lesser esquires and gentlemen. Sir Thomas Smith, anatomist of Elizabethan society, wrote that those 'who can live idly and without manual labour', who could support the 'charge and countenance' of a gentleman, would be taken as one. Contemporaries would have included the greatest gentry among the ranks of the nobility, because they too 'bear the sway in all princely courts and in manner the pillar and stay of all commonweals'. Although this society hated and feared mutability, the children of the nobility would decline into the ranks of the gentry, and the children of gentry rise into the nobility. Gentlemen gained the respect owed to 'men of worship' if they had long ancestry and association with those of noble blood, if they held judicial office, and above all, if they had the land and 'livelihood', the landed income, upon which all power rested.

The nobility were lords of land and they were lords of men. Once lordship of land and of men had been one and the same, but that strictly feudal relationship, whereby holders of fiefs were obliged to provide military service and other payments and services in recognition of vassalage, was by the end of the middle ages lost almost everywhere. In the far north, the 10th Lord Clifford (d. 1523) and his knights still performed the ceremony of homage, but elsewhere, although the personal bond between lords and their gentry clients might have seemed to depend on the tenure of land, a gentleman's dependence on a lord was more often due to his own land lying within the lord's sphere of influence, his 'country'. Although Shakespeare in *Henry IV, Part 1* portrayed the 1st Earl of Northumberland plotting with his noble allies to partition England and Wales, the nobility, even then, never held their land in great concentrations as the French nobility did. Even the 3rd Duke of Buckingham, who was also Earl of Hereford, Stafford and Northampton, Lord of Brecon and Holderness, holding land in all those places worth £6,000 per annum, still did not have an autonomous principality. His lands were scattered, and his authority was fragmented also. Few lords could command the loyalty of a whole region, and where they did, that loyalty was based on things other than land.

The possession of land had always been the foundation of lordly dominion, wealth and honour. Their great lands had given the nobility and gentry an army of tenantry, a *manred*, which the lord could call upon as a personal following for waging war and keeping peace. Behind all authority, public and private, lay the threat of force, but since the coercive power of monarchs was limited not only by the lack of anything like a state police force or standing army, but also by the extreme slowness of communication, they must rely upon those who could readily rally and command men in the localities: the greatest landowners. Lords of manors could call upon the military service of their agricultural tenants, and as manorial lordship weakened, the obligation to turn out might be written into tenant leases. It was the nobility, throughout the middle ages and for centuries to come, who were carriers of royal authority into their own 'countries' and into the shires, and who were the guardians of the interests of their gentry clients. In so hierarchical and deferential a society, it was natural for the gentry to look upwards for leadership and protection. The need and obligation was mutual. The magnate must call upon the military potential of his lesser neighbours, the gentry, if he were to remain a political force in the area in which his lands lay.

The power of the lords had come to lie less in the lands they held than in the number of men they could muster. The affinity – the personal following a lord could command; his dependants, allies, tenants, servants, retainers and kin – was the characteristic social and political bond in the later middle ages and remained so under the Tudor kings. A man offered his service to a lord and received in return his favour and protection; 'good lordship'. All the personal following of a lord wore his badge as the sign of allegiance: the sun in splendour of the House of York, the horse of the Earl of Arundel, or the swan of the Duke of Buckingham. The ties that bound followers might be very close and lifelong, or more tenuous. All the servants in a lord's household, high or low, were sworn to his service and wore his livery. Beyond the household, men with more tenuous ties of service could also be retained.

The leading knights and gentry of the North joined the Percy affinity and served in the Percy household. At the time of his death in 1489 Henry Percy, 4th Earl of Northumberland, was retaining eighty-four lords, knights and esquires, and paying £1,708 yearly in fees and annuities: nearly half of all his revenue. But this was on the Borders, the violent frontier with Scotland, where the two sovereignties met and clashed, and where the rule of law and loyalty to the Tudors were weakest. Elsewhere retainers were not usually paid in return for their services. Through their great estates in Cumberland, Northumberland and Yorkshire the Percys held almost vice-regal powers. For the gentry of the far north the Crown was alien and remote, so their loyalty was due rather to the local lord from whom favour flowed: Percy, Dacre or Clifford. Yet magnate affinities also flourished far closer to London. In 1513 the 13th Earl of Oxford, whose lands lay in Essex and East Anglia, bequeathed annuities worth more than £200 to twelve knights and forty-six other gentlemen.

A great lord naturally had a great retinue: it was a manifestation of power and honour, needed in both peace and war. The nobility were warlords still under the Tudors, with an awesome military potential. Born to a life of chivalry, given the privilege of maintaining armed forces for keeping order, of using violence as the ultimate sanction, the sword was for them still the way of honour. The battle cry, 'thousands for a Percy', was no empty boast, for within the Northern Marches the Earl of Northumberland had 5,000 tenants, and a further 6,200 on his Yorkshire estates. At Kirby Muxloe in Leicestershire in the early 1480s Lord Hastings, the head of a powerful affinity, was building a new castle of brick with gunports in the tower through which to fire cannon, though this fortification could not save him from the ferocity of Richard III. As late as the 1560s the Earl of Leicester was fortifying his castle at Kenilworth and gathering munitions.

Kings had to be able to call upon the nobles' power and know that they would answer the summons. Royal armies were little more than the conjunction of noble bands. In the summer of 1513 an army of more than 30,000 men, including twenty-three peers, their heirs, and retinues, invaded France; an army three times the size of Henry V's at Agincourt. The 4th Earl of Shrewsbury raised 4,437 men of his own and commanded 8,000 others. As lieutenant-general of the vanguard, he led the retinues of the Earl of Derby, Lords Hastings, Fitzwalter and Cobham. The 3rd Duke of Buckingham led 550 men, though without glory, and George Neville, Lord Abergavenny brought a 500-strong retinue which had once been seen as a threat, but which was now needed for royal service. A few months later nine English peers led a victorious army against Scotland.

The noble affinities, based upon fidelity, service and obedience, contributed to the political and social stability which was vital for the preservation of land and 'livelihood'. Yet the pursuit of wealth and 'worship', and the maintenance of family honour, led also to competitiveness, feuds and lawsuits; even to rebellion. In their darker moments the Tudor kings could see in the noble affinities a threat of disorder as well as the promise of support, especially if they ever banded together. 'We might do more . . . when the time should come, what with power and friendship,' promised Sir Geoffrey Pole in 1538, but by then his hopes were illusory and his family doomed. The bands of retainers were a potential threat to order if they were loyal to a disloyal lord. Repeated laws to restrict retaining were passed between the reigns of Richard II and Henry VIII; repeated because they were not obeyed. They were directed against the swaggering routs of idle retainers, who meant trouble and caused alarm, whose links with the lord were tenuous and temporary; not the household officers, retained for life. In 1507 George Neville, Lord Abergavenny was prosecuted for retaining 471 men, all below the rank of esquire. When Lord Montague dreamt of a noble confederacy thirty years later, he lamented Abergavenny's passing, 'for if he were alive he were able to make ten thousand men'.

Most magnates knew that their best hopes for advancement lay through service to the Crown, in its offices. This had always been true, and became more true. Only desperation would drive them to rebellion. Yet when they were excluded from offices to which their rank and ancestry entitled them, they could sabotage royal policies. The Crown's attempts to curb the power of the great families which dominated the Northern Marches and broke their peace through their incessant quarrels, Percys against Dacres and Dacres against Cliffords, brought its own dangers. The 5th Earl of Northumberland, who succeeded to the earldom in 1489, was denied the border wardenries which had become almost a hereditary Percy fief and, in an attempt to divide and rule, Thomas, 3rd Lord Dacre of Gilsland was appointed in his place. That usurpation ignored the strength of the web of alliance and dependence which bound the northern gentry to the great houses. Dacre could never win the trust of the Percy clientele, and consequently he failed to raise troops against Scotland or to enforce March law. While such feuds prevailed – some even in collusion with the border reivers and Scottish border earls, as the Dacres were themselves – lawlessness could not be contained. Meanwhile the Percys, who saw this chaos as proof of their own indispensability, were restored when the King's lieutenant persistently failed to arrest Sir William Lisle, a gentleman turned bandit, who was a Percy client. The 6th Earl eventually became warden late in 1527. Yet the power of the Percys was soon broken, and the family did fall from high estate, undermined not by the Crown, which needed them, but by the actions of Henry Percy, the 6th Earl. The childless Earl made Henry VIII his heir, in the hope that a grateful Tudor dynasty might restore a future generation of his family.

The power of the nobility was personal, in the way that the power of the monarch was personal, and the nobility, like the monarchy, was subject to the vagaries of character and ability which primogeniture produced. So the history of the House of Percy might have been quite different had Sir Thomas or Sir Ingram, not Henry, been heir. In 1538 an observer of the English nobility described character as well as 'power' (that is, manpower) and land: so, 'the Earl of Arundel, aged sixty, a man of great power, little wit and less experience', or 'the Earl of Derby, the greatest of power and land, young, and a child in wisdom and half a fool'. A lord must be able to offer good lordship, and could impose his will only if he could carry his clients and tenants with him. When a lord was weak, untrustworthy or inadequate, the gentry might find it safer to rely upon their friends and neighbours.

The nature of the lords' affinities began to change as the increased economic consequence and social assurance of the gentry made the good lordship of a magnate less vital for the gentry's security and prestige. The most powerful could still draw gentry to their households and service, but lesser lords could hope for little more than a share of the goodwill of the knights and greater esquires who were the leaders of society in any area. Many of the nobility began instead to look to create an affinity from the yeomanry, who probably held land from only one lord and had more reason to be loyal. In 1549 the Earl of Rutland remembered how Thomas Seymour, the Lord Admiral, advised him to cultivate the gentlemen in his 'country', but warned him that they were not to be trusted: rather he should 'make much of' the 'honest and wealthy yeomen as were ringleaders in good towns', sometimes even deigning to dine 'like a good fellow in one of their houses'. He would thereby 'allure all their good wills to go with me, whither I would lead them'.

Noble power and influence in the localities might begin to retreat once the gentry, whose landed power was collectively far greater than that of the nobility, learnt to be more self-reliant and independent. They learnt also to look above the nobility for lordship, to the Crown. The royal affinity grew hugely with the extension of the Crown's estates, and the power of the Tudor kings rested in the knights they retained, whose undivided allegiance they demanded. The king's servants wore badges of allegiance, as nobles' servants did. When in 1519 Sir William Bulmer abandoned Henry VIII's service for Buckingham's, the King raged at him in the Star Chamber: 'he would none of his servants should hang on another man's sleeve'; he could 'maintain' Bulmer as well as the Duke could. Had the Tudor kings substituted alliance with the gentry for royal cooperation with greater nobles? Philip Sidney reportedly told Queen Elizabeth that her father 'found it wisdom by the stronger corporation in number [of the gentry] to keep down the greater in power'.

Some believed that the whole order of nobility was under threat. Welcoming Henry VIII's accession, Thomas More had seen the recovery of the 'ancient rights of nobles', 'long scorned', as symbolic of the restoration of good governance. Yet under Henry VIII some of the greatest noble families were disgraced, eclipsed or destroyed: Courtenay, Stafford, de la Pole, Howard, Percy. The Pilgrims of Grace were sworn to the defence of noble blood, and promised to 'expulse all villein blood and evil counsellors'. They looked to a time when 'nobles did order under His Highness'. All bad governance and threats to the old ways were seen in terms of the subversion of the natural order, of which the unnatural ennoblement of base-born men like Cromwell was a sign. 'These new erected men would leave no noble men alive,' said the Earl of Surrey. Accused of raising new men and ignoring the old nobility who were his natural counsellors, Henry VIII denied being the instigator. 'We do not forget,' he said, how few were the nobles in the Council at his accession: Lord Darcy, he remembered, was only a 'mean born' gentleman 'until promoted by us'. Yet by 1536 Darcy had long forgotten the novelty of his nobility, and he promised Cromwell that even if Cromwell cut off every noble head 'yet shall there one head remain that shall strike off thy head'. A noble coup destroyed Cromwell, and the animus of the old against the new appeared at the Council Chamber as the Duke of Norfolk tore from the new Earl of Essex's neck his George and Garter, the symbol of his pretended nobility. The nobility, like the rest of society, was divided by the Reformation. The cause of reform was associated by its opponents with new men of Machiavellian motives and high ambition, and the cause of the Catholic Church with that of the ancient nobility.

The noble families ruined under Henry VIII had destroyed themselves, guilty of treason and rebellion which no king could countenance. Noble families were subject to the disasters that strike any family, but their decline came also from the penalties for treason: execution and attainder, which brought forfeiture and annihilated the right of inheritance. Contemporaries, thinking upon the cult of Fortuna, knew that those who were raised high might soon, in their pride, be dashed. 'The high mountains are blasted oft,' wrote Wyatt. Yet if the King sometimes found it difficult to rule with the nobility, he could not rule without them. At the end of his reign, as at the beginning, nobles counselled him, and in their regional strongholds they ruled under the Crown: Derby still held sway in Lancashire; Shrewsbury in Derbyshire, Shropshire and Hallamshire;

Arundel in Sussex. But there had been changes. Charles Somerset, created Earl of Worcester, had been given lands to rival and supplant the Duke of Buckingham in the Welsh Marches. The tyranny and corruption of Worcester's son, the 2nd Earl, in collusion with his Herbert henchmen, was one reason for setting up the Council in the Marches of Wales, dominated by English marcher gentry, to bring control. In the south-west John, Lord Russell had received lands, lordships and stewardships to replace the dominion of the Marquess of Exeter. Charles Brandon, raised from the gentry to become Duke of Suffolk, had amassed great estates in Lincolnshire, and the Herberts lorded it in Wiltshire and South Wales. New men – Wriothesley, Audley, Seymour, Dudley, Paget, Rich – had partially succeeded the older peers in the Privy Council and were rewarded with lands, titles and provincial commands.

In 1485 Lord Mountjoy, mortally ill, counselled his sons 'never to take the state of baron upon them, if they may lay it from them, nor desire to be great about princes, for it is dangerous'. Greatness about princes now usually depended precisely upon being 'about them', at court. Power now lay in the influence which could be used to augment clients' interests, rather than in simply defending them. Lords needed to 'labour' and 'sue' for the fees and offices which were in the royal gift, a patronage which increased greatly after the dissolution of the monasteries and chantries. But lords, departing their own 'countries' for court, left much of their household, with its fidelity and service, behind them, and abandoned their localities to look after themselves. This was easier for lords of softer shires than for marcher lords, whose lands were vulnerable to invasion. A border baron like Robert, 4th Lord Ogle never once left his manors in the far north to attend Parliament or state occasions.

In the aftermath of the Pilgrimage of Grace, the Duke of Norfolk advised that the wild borderers could not be controlled by 'mean men', so 'some man of great nobility should have the rule'. Instead Sir Thomas Wharton, a Clifford tenant, was appointed in Clifford's traditional place, and royal authority thereby subverted local order and degree. But the newly risen Whartons – soon Lords Wharton – shared the same attitudes as the lords they had displaced. Over the gatehouse at Wharton Hall in Westmorland in 1559 the first Lord Wharton inscribed his motto: 'Pleasure in acts d'armys'. Marcher society, distant from the court, remained martial and violent. There a different, older kind of lordship lived on. Although brought up at the English court, Garret, 9th Earl of Kildare did not imagine that that world could be transported to the Pale marches. While Wolsey was 'begraced and belorded and crouched and kneeled unto', so Kildare allegedly told him, he himself expected 'small grace with our Irish borderers, except I cut them off by the knees'. Marcher lords still needed to raise their *manred*, to call upon the fidelity of their tenantry. The king might resent delegating such great authority to these still 'overmighty' subjects, but he could not rule half his dominions without them.

SOVEREIGNTY IN IRELAND

Told that the King sent him greetings, Brian O'Connor of Offaly replied with derision: 'What king?' and said that he hoped that within that year, 1528, he would see the king of England without jurisdiction in Ireland. The O'Connors of Offaly, on the border of the Pale, strong in a fastness surrounded by almost impenetrable bog and forest, had extended their lordship over their Gaelic Irish neighbours – the O'Dunnes of Iregan, O'Dempseys of Clanmaliere and MacMorishes of Irry – and imposed tribute. They were a constant threat on the borders of Counties Kildare and Meath, and the Dublin exchequer paid an annual black rent of £40 to save the Pale from their raids. O'Connor was the chief Gaelic ally of the 8th Earl of Kildare, and his son-in-law. Lords like the O'Connors, who had once offered hospitality to thousands and summoned the poets of Ireland to feast, seemed unlikely to submit to the English king. In 1528 O'Connor captured the vice-deputy, Lord Delvin and began the hostilities known as O'Connor's Wars, perhaps in collusion with his Fitzgerald relations. Yet Brian was the last lord of Offaly before the ruin of his family and the plantation of his territory in the mid sixteenth century. The king of England began to make real his claim to rule over the whole of Ireland.

Once Ireland had had sacral kings, invested by sacred rites at hallowed places – like the Hill of Tara, or the Stone of Tullaghoge – in symbolic marriage to the territory and its people. But high kings were later replaced by 'chieftains', 'captains of their nations', whose relationship to the land and people had changed. The essential concept of sovereignty came to lie in the 'name' (the surname), and the lord's personal headship of his own kin. At the inauguration stone, on a hill where chiefs had immemorially been inaugurated, the new chief would be named by the clan name – O'Neill, O'Donnell or Maguire – and proclaimed by those who now consented to his leadership. As he was handed the 'rod of ownership', the new chief entered possession of his lands. It was O'Sullivan Mór, chief vassal of MacCarthy Mór, who placed the white rod in the hand of this paramount chief of Munster. By the sixteenth century all the land rights within a territory were so dependent upon the will of the lord that he held the land as his demesne, the free landowning subjects who inhabited it being regarded as his tenants.

An Irish lordship did not lie in the ownership of a closed and defined territory, but was a complex of rights, tributes and authority. The paramount chiefs had overlordship rather than ownership of a territory. So O'Neill of Tyrone demanded tribute and services from the ecclesiastical tenants of Armagh, although the Church was owner of the estates. In the later middle ages the O'Connor lords of Carbury exerted powers of overlordship over the lesser lords of Sligo – O'Hara of Leyny, the MacDonaghs of Tirerrill and the O'Dowds of Tireragh – but by the end of the fifteenth century the greater lordships of O'Donnell and of the MacWilliam and Clanrickard Burkes struggled for the control of northern Connacht, and ultimately for overlordship of the whole western province. Soon O'Donnell of Tirconnell was ascendant, and imposed a heavy and ruthless military supremacy. He swept through the lordships, burning crops and driving off cattle of those who resisted paying his tribute.

The overlords imposed their own candidates as chiefs of lesser lordships. Where once O'Cahan had been inaugurated by his own *ollamh*, or master of poetry, by the end of the sixteenth century he was installed by O'Neill. Overlordship without ownership rested upon the power of the lords to enforce the submission of lesser lords. In 1539 the O'Connor chief of Sligo was bound to provide military service to O'Donnell, to submit to his 'counsel' in all matters, to hand over control of the castle and town of Sligo, and to assist O'Donnell's officers in levying his tribute and billeting his troops throughout O'Connor's lordship. In this world of Gaelic lordship the custom of buying the protection (*sláinte*) of a lord became prevalent. If any injury were done to the person whom the lord protected, it was as though the injury was done to the lord himself, and fines were exacted. The 9th Earl of Kildare imposed fines of sixty or seventy cows for the breaking of his protection – *slánuigheacht*, 'slantyaght' or sanctuary. By such 'buyings' lesser lords could appeal over the head of their own lord for the protection of a greater. Such lordship rested less on loyalty than on 'fort mayne', the strong hand.

Succession to a lordship was not by simple right of inheritance. A minor or an idiot could never succeed in Gaelic Ireland, where power was not won or held without force. Henry Óg O'Neill succeeded to the chieftaincy of Tyrone in 1493 by murdering his elder brother. The bardic poet who composed his inauguration ode admitted that 'whichever of you has the best right to the land of Ireland, until he adds his might to the right, he may not obtain union with her inheritance'. In Gaelic Ireland, in an attempt to ensure the stability of succession from an anarchy of contenders within the kin group the tanist (*tánaiste*) was nominated and inaugurated at the same time as the chief, as 'the expected one', to succeed automatically upon the chief's death. But the tanist was often usurped by a stronger contender. In some lordships the eldest son did succeed, but this was because he was in a sufficiently strong position to take over unopposed. Families which adopted primogeniture or restricted succession were unlikely to be undermined through generations of disputes; so the Gaelicized Clanrickard Burkes grew powerful while their inveterate enemies in Connacht, the Mayo Burkes, who might allow even a fourth cousin to succeed, were debilitated through the generations. Son succeeded father as MacCarthy Mór through six generations until 1508, but such stability was very rare.

Within the ruling dynasties bitter succession struggles often led to internal wars. Succession might be disputed by rival claimants – leaders of septs within the lineage. One sept would produce a leader and hope for another; the defeated sept, malicious and vengeful, could even ally with the clan's natural enemies. The disputes might continue interminably until the stronger overcame the weaker, or until an overlord imposed his candidate upon a vassal lineage. From the mid fifteenth century a dissident clan of the O'Neills was always hostile to the ruling O'Neill and in alliance with O'Donnell in the north-west of Tyrone. When Henry Óg, usurper and fratricide, made himself O'Neill in 1493 it was with the support of the Sliocht Airt, the sons of Art O'Neill of Omagh. Sub-lordships emerged to rule independently. The chieftaincy of O'Neill of Clandeboye had established itself in the mid fourteenth century and came to rule most of Antrim and Down.

To the Gaelic lord, both the land and the people were his. That confusion between political lordship and landlordship gave the lords great power. Even lesser lords might tax their subject tenants arbitrarily: this was 'cutting upon the country'. English observers condemned a system which seemed to make lords tyrants, and tenants slaves, or worse than slaves, 'for commonly the bond slave is fed by his lord, but here the lord was fed by his bond slave'. The ultimate test of lordship was the ability to levy tribute; to exact dues and to resist the exactions which others might claim from him or extort from his dependants. 'Spend me and defend me' was the ubiquitous proverb of sixteenth-century Ireland, for the compact made between the lord and his people was the offer of protection and justice in return for tributes, heavy in times of peace and seemingly limitless during the perennial wars between lord and lord. Lords could legitimately demand tribute in a bewildering variety of forms in a society where payment was in kind, but there were demands which were seen as tyrannical, 'black'. MacCarthy Mór exacted food for his huntsmen and dogs among the mountains of Desmond in the south-west, and taxed the lowlands for the maintenance of his troops, an exaction called dowgallo, black rent, against which 'all the freeholders cry out . . . as imposed upon them by extortion and strong hand'.

Violence was the sanction which ensured peace in this society, while also undermining it. There was a myth that the Irish left the sword hands of boys unchristened, so that they might give more lethal blows. By the later middle ages the lords no longer summoned their free subjects to take part in military expeditions ('risings out'), but turned instead to hiring mercenary troops: the galloglasses, axemen whose highest loyalty was to their paymasters; and the kerns, the Irish foot soldiers, whose ferocity and hardiness inspired admiration as well as terror. Lords did not arm their peasants, until Shane O'Neill, desperate to increase his fighting force in the 1560s, armed the peasants 'of his country' in Ulster. A lord possessing military power paid for by those subjects whom that same military force could suppress might be little inclined to consult the wishes of his subjects, except those of a few vassals who, like himself, led hired troops. These troops must be fed. When advisers in Westminster and Dublin thought of ways of reforming Gaelic Ireland they uniformly condemned one practice 'invented in hell'. This was 'coyne and livery': the lord's demand of hospitality for his soldiers and servants and their horses, where 'hospitality' might be accounted a euphemism for billeting by intimidation.

Since in Gaelic Ireland a barter economy and subsistence agriculture prevailed, lords could hardly exact taxes in cash to pay their troops. Instead soldiers were billeted upon householders, especially poorer ones, and consumed their wages in kind. O'Neill billeted a standing army, the 'Bonaght of Ulster' upon his vassal chiefs. In this society, which glorified hospitality, every substantial tenant or vassal owed compulsory cuddies (night's suppers) and cosheries (lodging and victuals) to their immediate lord and his retinue. Since the traditional coshering season was in the winter and early spring, when food was scarcest and the provision of feasts most difficult, the lord who could demand this due particularly revealed his strength and rewarded his followers. In 1493 the Abbot of Mellifont complained to the Archbishop of Armagh of the extortion of coyne and livery by 'threats, terrorism, fury'. Here was oppression by lords upon people who were not their tenants, for no public purpose. The principle of taxation by consent hardly existed, save where those who lived in the marches, on the edge of 'the land of war', admitted the need to pay for protection. Many Palesmen were driven to emigrate, to be replaced by Gaelic tenants. An Anglo-Irish tract of Henry VII's reign lamented that 'the most part of all the English tenants had avoided the land'. The extortionate system of coyne and livery, adopted by the Anglo-Irish feudatories as well as the Gaelic lords, was seen to condemn the island to its seemingly endemic lawlessness, as both symptom and cause of its instability.

One observer of the Gaelic polity at the beginning of the sixteenth century thought that he saw an unprecedented stability, and that the Irish chiefs were so successfully keeping their countries in peace that the people could even, unusually, till the fields. Yet while acknowledging the great power of the O'Brien of Toybrien in Clare, of MacCarthy Reagh of Carbery, Cormac Óg MacCarthy of Muskerry, MacCarthy Mór of Desmond and O'Donnell of Tirconnell, he saw their purpose as malign; to protect the people only in order to 'devour them . . . like as the greedy hound delivereth the sheep from the wolf'. Finding oppression rather than protection from their immediate lords, landholders began to look to greater and greater lords in the hope of indemnity and justice. As the sixteenth century began, the paramount chiefs of the great ruling lineages were becoming more dominant still, at the expense of the weaker clans. Many Irish lordships had been undermined in the last part of the fifteenth century. Clan MacMahon had ruled east Breifne in Connacht, but after the death of the tanist in 1469 they were increasingly driven from the chieftaincy of the territory by the incursions of the great local family of O'Reilly, until the last lord of the sept, Sean, was murdered by the son of the ruling O'Reilly in 1534. But the O'Reillys, too, looked for protection from a greater lord; not now from their territorial overlord, O'Neill, but from O'Donnell instead.

The sixteenth-century overlords extended their protection – 'slan-tyaght' – over territories in which they held no land. Since this slantyaght was a protection usually extended by force, in return for tribute, it had to be defended, and defended fiercely, for whenever a chief failed to protect a subject chief against a rival, the victim must then change allegiances, with dangerous political consequences. The paramount chiefs asserted their power by progressing in person or sending a *maor* (collector of dues) into the lands of their vassal chiefs. So, in 1539 O'Connor of Sligo, vassal to O'Donnell, bound himself to go with O'Donnell's *maor* into Lower Connacht to impose his lordship and levy his tribute. The creation of great slantyaght networks, bound by mutual promises of protection in return for tribute and military service, not by territorial ties, marked Gaelic Ireland in the last days of the independent rule of the Gaelic chiefs, and determined its politics. But the greatest overlords were not the Gaelic chiefs, but the great Anglo-Irish feuda-tories, who had adapted Gaelic practices to those of their own society.

No lords held greater power in Ireland than the Fitzgerald earls of Kildare. A score of Irish lords looked to Garret Mór, the 8th Earl, for protection. For the hosting (military expedition) to Knockdoe near Galway in 1504 against Ulick Burke of Clanrickard, Garret Mór brought the lords of Ulster and the midlands who owed him allegiance: members of the O'Neill clan of Tyrone, also of the O'Reillys of east Breifne, the MacMahons of Oriel, the O'Hanlons of south Armagh, the Magennisses of Iveagh, the O'Connors of Offaly, and the O'Farrells of Annely. According to the O'Clerys, historians to the O'Donnells of Tirconnell and known as the Four Masters, this was 'the charge of the royal heroes'. O'Kelly of Hy Many, the Mayo Burkes, MacDermot of Moylurg, O'Connor Roe and Hugh Roe O'Donnell also followed Kildare, together with lords from the Pale, and the victory was his. His and the king of England's, for Kildare was not only the overlord of Gaelic lords, but the royal Lord Deputy, and the expedition to the west had been to assert the authority of Henry VII, as Lord of Ireland. Garret Mór held the office of chief governor for thirty-three years, and his son Garret Óg inherited it in 1513, almost as part of his patrimony.

No lord since the high kings had held such power as Kildare. The 8th and 9th Earls had mastery of much of Ireland through their possession of great lands, their numerous tenantry, their command of soldiers, and their networks of clients, including many Gaelic lords around the Pale and far beyond. The rental book of Kildare in 1518 listed twenty-four

Gaelic chiefs who paid him tribute. The 8th Earl's constant campaigning throughout the island left the lords in no doubt of Kildare power. 'Some sayeth,' it was reported in 1515, that there had never been such peace in 300 years; 'that the Irish enemies was never more adread of the king's Deputy than they be now.' The 8th Earl had exercised seemingly unlimited power in County Kildare, which he administered as a liberty, its officials appointed by him, its law either English or Irish, as the case required. There he imposed coyne and livery, but with the vital difference that it was by consent. The earls of Kildare were the extreme examples of English marcher lords, potentially overmighty and with the closest associations with English enemies in the 'land of war'. But they never doubted that their power and honour rested in their royal office. They neither wanted nor sought the independence of a Gaelic paramount chief. The 9th Earl wrote to Henry VIII, whom he had served in their youth at the English court, protesting an allegiance which, if it ever failed, 'should be the destruction of me and my sequel for ever'.

In 1520 O'Donnell warned that if Henry VIII gave the office of chief governor to Kildare again, he might as well resign the lordship of Ireland to the Fitzgeralds forever. In 1522-4 Piers Butler, 8th Earl of Ormond was made chief governor, but only for a time, because he lacked the military and financial resources to discharge the duties with which he was entrusted, and because a sulking Kildare used his power to obstruct his rival. Ormond's failure and replacement by Kildare in 1524 left a legacy of hostility to disturb the peace of the lordship. The intrigues of Kildare's Fitzgerald kinsman, the 11th Earl of Desmond, with Francis I of France, allowed Ormond to impute treasonable communication with the King's enemies to Kildare also. In 1526 both Ormond and Kildare were summoned to court, leaving Gaelic borderers to raid the Englishry. Two years later Ormond returned to Ireland, but Kildare was detained. Meanwhile, O'Connor of Offaly ran riot, not without Kildare's collusion. That year Kildare came very close to being charged with treason.

Now and throughout the century factional rivalry within Irish politics was closely enmeshed with alignments at court in England. Kildare was restored yet again as chief governor in 1532, partly through the favour of the Duke of Norfolk, who was not only concerned to protect his own Ormond inheritance against the Butlers, but saw in Kildare the best hope of peace in Ireland. But Kildare's rivals, Archbishop Alen of Dublin and the Butlers, were in communication with Thomas Cromwell, who was taking a closer interest in Ireland, an interest that was regarded with the deepest suspicion by Kildare. In September 1533 Kildare was summoned to England once more. His countess went, but he stayed and began marshalling ordnance. Late that year Cromwell's memorandum noted: 'to adhere as many of the great Irish rebels as is possible'; and 'to withstand all other practices that might be practised there', where 'practice' meant conspiracy. In February 1534 Kildare arrived in England, leaving his son, Thomas, Lord Offaly ('Silken Thomas') to rule in his absence. Three months later 'manifold enormities' were proved against Kildare, and a message came to Offaly from his father, telling him to 'play the best or gentlest part' and not to trust the Council. On 11 June 1534 Offaly marched through Dublin to the Council, denounced the King's policies, yielded his sword of office, and signalled Geraldine (Fitzgerald) resistance. Archbishop Alen was murdered, Dublin Castle besieged.

This was rebellion from a feudatory of the Crown, rebellion not from desperation but from overweening confidence. The Geraldines could not believe that any English government could replace their grand networks of alliance and power, nor that any policy could be pursued which they opposed. Presented with moderate proposals for reform, they revolted. This rebellion, like every rebellion in sixteenth-century Ireland thereafter, claimed a religious motive, although no changes in religion had yet been effected there. Lord Thomas began to call up that great 'knot of all the forces of Ireland' which were 'twisted under his girdle': Conor O'Brien of Thomond in Munster, Fitzgerald of Desmond, Conn Bacach O'Neill in Ulster, O'Connor of Offaly. The revolt was a desperate miscalculation. Even the forces of Kildare and his allies could not withstand a Tudor campaign army, and the promised forces from Emperor Charles V never came. Seventy-five of the revolt's leaders were executed. The ascendancy of the Fitzgeralds was shattered, their slantyaght leaderless, their great lands confiscated. This was a disaster not for the Fitzgeralds alone but for all the lords of Ireland, for the destruction of the House of Kildare destroyed also the fragile equilibrium and peace which their supremacy had intermittently assured. As the English governors now stumbled erratically towards alternative ways of ruling the lordship, the Gaelic lords entered new alliances to replace the old, and politics became ever more volatile, until finally a radical estrangement appeared between the two worlds of Englishry and Irishry.

As Henry VIII asserted his imperial authority in England, he thought to extend it to his lordship of Ireland also. A corpus of Reformation legislation was enacted in the Irish Parliament in 1536–7. The King was constituted 'the only Supreme Head in earth of the whole Church of Ireland', and granted spiritual jurisdiction over the Irish religious communities. 1537 saw the dissolution of a few of them. Their own spiritual malaise and morbidity, their virtual ruination and abandonment were reasons for their demise. So, too, was the evidence that some of the religious had, in their support for the Geraldine rebels, revealed their higher loyalty to local lords than to their king. The attainder of Kildare and his adherents, and the confiscation of Geraldine and monastic lands allowed the Crown to boost its revenues and to distribute patronage. Sir Patrick Finglas, the Anglo-Irish Chief Justice of the King's Bench, had proposed a scheme in *c.* 1534 to '*plant* young lords and gents out of England' in dissolved monastic possessions in the turbulent borderlands south of Dublin. His moderate scheme was not implemented, but it was the forerunner of increasingly aggressive proposals for the settlement and plantation of people. Many who pondered how Ireland might be reformed – and who had read their Roman history – came to believe that the establishment of plantations or colonies would have the strategic and moral imperative of advancing English law and custom, and of reminding the Irish lords of their altered obligations in the new Irish Kingdom. With plantation would come a new breed of English in Ireland; migrants not born in Ireland, who came to settle, to plant, and to exploit it – the New English.

The replacement of the pope by the king of England as Head of the Church at first met little resistance. That quiescence was temporary. The Friars Observants ('Friars obstinates') offered a campaign of passive resistance. The final surrender of religious houses in the Crown territories took place between the summer of 1539 and the summer of 1540. This followed an assault in the winter of 1538–9 upon images, shrines, places of pilgrimage and of popular devotion. The annalist of Loch Cé lamented that 'there was not a holy cross, a statue of the Virgin, nor a venerable image within their [the Crown's] jurisdiction that they did not destroy'. An air of apocalyptic foreboding pervaded the Pale. But in the territories of the Gaelic lords – in Munster, Connacht and Ulster – the suppression campaigns did not advance. The friars maintained their traditional ways with impunity, 'using the old popish sort'. Later, the very association of Reformation with the English monarch became an added reason to oppose it. The campaign for suppression coincided with a revolt of Irish lords of unprecedented menace. Their cause could easily be identified with the threat to the old religion, and a Gaelic revolt with political ends could be presented as religious crusade.

The failure of the Geraldine rebellion had left the old system of dynastic alliances in disarray, but not destroyed. The lords were never so fearful, never so individually vulnerable, but their local power was intact, and together they constituted so formidable a force that no Tudor army could easily suppress them. Great Gaelic lords like O'Reilly, O'Neill and O'Donnell could field more horsemen than the king's chief governor. With the old alliances disrupted, the lords were volatile and dangerous as they waited to exploit the opportunities offered by the Geraldine desolation, and made novel alliances with former enemies. They would not easily submit to Tudor overlordship. MacCarthy Reagh defied the Crown: 'What he has won with his sword, he will hold with his sword.' In Ulster, O'Neill and his underlords remained hostile, and the new O'Donnell, Manus, was as extravagant in his claims as in his talents. The septs of Leinster – the O'Connors, O'Mores and Kavanaghs – waited their moment to prey upon the Pale. In Connacht the Mayo Burkes, the O'Connors of Sligo and the O'Malleys held out, still unsubdued. In the western lordship of Thomond in Munster the O'Briens gave sanctuary to Geraldine refugees. A band of Geraldine followers, bound by 'kindred, marriage and fostering', longed 'more to see a Geraldine to triumph than to see God come amongst them'. The hopes of all those 'branded at the heart with a G' rested with Lord Offaly's half-brother, 'Young Gerald'. He had been spirited to the west of Ireland by his aunt, Lady Eleanor MacCarthy who, now married to Manus O'Donnell, hoped to ally the great Gaelic lords of the north with those of Munster and to restore the Geraldines.

Into this unstable world came Lord Leonard Grey, made chief governor in 1536. Through the following three years he campaigned relentlessly against the Irishry, though with forces so mutinous that he feared them more than he did the Irish. As he turned to conciliate where he could not conquer, he was accused of confederacy with the Irish, of restoring the Geraldine band, with himself at its head. His enemies claimed that he held 'secret intelligences' by night with the Irishry; O'Connor of Offaly, the scourge of the Pale, was 'his right hand, and who but he?'; the O'Neill was his godson; O'More's sons were his 'chief darlings'; 'my Lord Deputy is the Earl of Kildare newly born again'. These charges came from the Earl of Ormond and his followers, whose own hopes to inherit the Geraldine ascendancy were thwarted as the governors of the colony feared and guarded against another overmighty lord. Grey became dangerously entangled in the old rivalries as he supported the Butlers' traditional enemies against them. But his strategy of offering protection to those lords who would submit to the Crown, and inflicting retribution on those who would not, might have worked had he been less restless and aggressive.

Now, in retaliation, a novel alliance had formed in this shifting world which was more alarming than any yet. In the late summer of 1539 the War of the Geraldine League broke out. O'Neill and O'Donnell with their Ulster underlords swept down through Louth and Meath, aiming for Tara, where O'Neill intended to be inaugurated high king of Ireland. The Geraldine League confronted the Crown with new dangers: a united Gaelic resistance in the name of the old religion and the papacy, with the prospect of aid from France and Scotland. Friars and priests denounced Henry VIII as 'the most heretic and worst man in the world' and promised the rebels that they would go to heaven if they died in that cause. 'Mortal enemies' – O'Connor of Sligo and O'Donnell; O'Donnell and O'Neill – were now sworn one to another. O'Brien would not make a truce with Ormond, for O'Neill, O'Connor and the O'Tooles were 'his Irishmen whom he intendeth to defend'. The League survived into 1540, despite its defeat at Bellahoe on the Ulster border, and was overcome not by Tudor military power, but by the diplomacy and patronage of Sir Anthony St Leger. Lord Leonard Grey fell in the summer of 1540, a victim of the coup at the English court which brought down Cromwell: St Leger, a client of the Duke of Norfolk, arrived in the autumn to replace him. Young Gerald, 'the traitor boy', fled to France, and Geraldine hopes with him.

Conquest by the English Crown through a policy of grants to great Anglo-Irish lords to enable them to win mastery of the island had, over three centuries, failed; conquest by military occupation must fail through lack of resources; conquest by conciliation was the way now devised. In the Parliament held in Dublin in June 1541 Henry VIII was declared, not Lord, but King of Ireland. This was a constitutional change of the greatest consequence. Ireland now had a king who had never been acclaimed, nor anointed, nor ever bound by coronation oath to uphold the shaky liberties of his Irish subjects. The king of Ireland never existed separately from the king of England, and where the interests of the two kingdoms clashed, it would always be those of the king of England which prevailed. The Irish Parliament and the Irish Privy Council, too, were subordinate to their English counterparts. Ireland was now a kingdom, but it was not an independent sovereign entity. Its own king never visited it; distrusted it; found its ways alien; and denied its autonomy.

Ireland was no longer to be a land of many lordships, but of one. The Act for the Kingly Title provided the statutory basis for the exercise of the King's jurisdiction in the sovereign Gaelic lordships. The King must make his authority real: his religion, his law, his taxes must be imposed. Any resistance would now be rebellion by subjects, rather than opposition from Irish enemies. Distinctions between the King's English subjects in Ireland and his former Irish enemies were dissolved. Now both were subject to the same laws, and under his protection if they obeyed them. St Leger proceeded by negotiation and conciliation in an attempt to win over the Gaelic chiefs and to unite the disparate political communities of Ireland in submission and loyalty to the English Crown. His success in overcoming the Gaelic lords' suspicion of the King's ambitions for the wealth of their territories was, in the circumstances, considerable. Yet the fate of the suppression campaign was instructive. In the Gaelic territories, the dissolution of the religious houses was a matter for negotiation between St Leger and the lords, and here although ownership may have been transferred from ecclesiastical to secular lords, very many of the houses survived, with the religious still in possession.

Under St Leger there began a policy towards the great chiefs of the Irishry which would last the century. They were to submit themselves to the King, surrendering their own sovereign jurisdiction and lands in their territories, their use of the clan name as a title, to be regranted in return feudal title and feudal tenure under letters patent. Gaelic lordship was to be transformed to feudal lordship; the Gaelic tenurial system replaced by an English one. Now the Irish lords were to hold land freely by law, no longer by the sword, with their lands passing, by primogeniture, to their heirs. But the English legislators confused lordship of a territory with its ownership, and granted lands as property to the lord in a way unknown to Irish law and custom. In Gaelic Ireland the land was the sept's not the lord's. The clans were now dispossessed not only of the right to elect and be elected, as primogeniture replaced tanistry, but also of land. No wholesale confiscation followed, but some lords gained at the expense of their underlords. The English hoped that primogeniture would prevail in time, but tanistry was not easy to outlaw. The submission of one lord might not bind his successors, or his sept, for the lord was subordinate to a Gaelic system which had elected him, and septs which had not always remained loyal to a tanist were even less likely to accept a chief dictated by birth alone, or to allow designation of an heir by the lord. Of gravest consequence was Conn O'Neill's choice of Matthew as heir and Baron of Dungannon, instead of his son, Shane, the clan-elected tanist. Matthew had the legitimacy of royal approval, but had no standing among the O'Neills, and was eventually murdered in 1558 in a clash with Shane's supporters. Shane's accession to power in Tyrone and Ulster was seen by the English as usurpation, a dangerous derogation of the new principle of inheritance, which must be protected to save the royal honour. Yet with many lords the policy at first succeeded. One by one, the great Gaelic and Gaelicized lords submitted. They surrendered lands and the name; they promised to ride in hostings against the King's enemies, and in return they would be defended. Resolving to submit to the Crown, they renounced the pope also, seemingly without scruple. That they were delegated jurisdiction over benefices in their territories helped to persuade them. The greater lords – like O'Neill, Clanrickard Burke and O'Brien – swore fealty to the Crown and received earldoms, becoming Earl of Tyrone, Earl of Clanrickard, Earl of Thomond. Lesser lords received lesser titles.

Why did they submit, these lords who had previously ignored or defied the English king? Why did they, who had so recently vowed that 'they will have all or lose all', now surrender? Some succumbed to force, like O'Neill, after devastating rodes (incursions) through Tyrone, and this lord's submission was instructive to all the others. Underlords looked for freedom from the dominance of their overlords, like the MacCarthys of Muskerry, released from MacCarthy Mór. Others, vulnerable and fearing future deprivation, conceded. The lords saw the instability of the old factionalism, feared the militarism of the Lord Deputy and understood how evanescent were the promises of foreign princes. Agreement with the King brought them defence of their property and the possibility of disarmament. The prospect of advancing one heir instead of 'twenty bastards' might appeal, so one jaundiced official thought. Perhaps few believed that their submission was permanent. The obedience of the Gaelic lords was only ever conditional and pragmatic, never the absolute loyalty of the subject. Though Conn O'Neill agreed 'utterly to forsake' the name of O'Neill, believing that he could be at once an Irish noble, the Earl of Tyrone, owing fealty to a king in England, and a Gaelic lord who had once thought of the high kingship, his successors would renounce the earldom and the fealty and long to be O'Neill once more, to go to the stone at Tullaghoge and receive the name. By the late sixteenth century the 'stone' and the 'name' came to be resonant with rebellion. 'The traitor,' Sir Henry Bagenal wrote darkly of Hugh O'Neill in 1595, 'is gone to the stone to receive that name.'

JUSTICE

As Anne Boleyn was taken to the Tower, she asked: 'Shall I die without justice?' Assured that 'the poorest subject the King hath, had justice', she laughed. She was tried before judge and jury, condemned and executed, according to the laws of England. Yet since the jury was packed with men hostile to her and servile to the King, the guilty verdict was inescapable, even though she was, surely, innocent. On a book of hours associated with her, a contemporary wrote beside an illumination of Christ before Caiaphas 'even so will you be accused by false witnesses'. The courtiers who laid odds of ten to one that Anne's brother, Lord Rochford, would be freed, because no evidence was brought against him, lost their bets. The law has always had limitations as an instrument of justice. At the trials of those in high places, political necessity might exert a more compelling claim than impartial justice; and to the poor the law might bring more suffering than benefit. But the cause of injustice in England was not so much imperfect law as the perversions which separated the theory of law from its practice: the corruption and weakness of juries, the partiality of sheriffs and justices of the peace, and even the demands made by kings who were sworn by their coronation oath to uphold the law.

In the Tower in 1541, charged with treason, Sir Thomas Wyatt wrote a defence of himself and a vindication of the laws of England. Under threat of death, he needed to believe that no jury would condemn a man it believed to be innocent. Wyatt insisted that his king forced no man's conscience; 'he will but his laws and his laws with mercy'. He reminded his own judges that when Lord Dacre had been acquitted by his peers in 1534, no royal reprisals had followed. Yet Henry was a king who, as Supreme Head of the Church of England, did force consciences. He chose to pardon Wyatt, but he might as easily not have done.

Laws were believed to be consonant with divine justice, and this king saw himself, and was seen by loyal subjects, as divinely appointed.

Henry came to deny any legal constraints upon his kingship: 'of our absolute power we be above the laws'. For those who feared a Tudor despotism Henry's emendations to the *Bishops' Book*, his formulary of faith of 1537, would have been alarming. The text stating that kings might only coerce and kill subjects according to 'the just order of their laws', the King changed to allow that only 'inferior rulers', the King's agents, were so constrained. There were dangers that the King might use the rule of law without tempering it by conscience or justice. A chief justice of the King's Bench warned that 'sometime *extremum jus* is *summa injuria*'; extreme justice could be extreme injustice. Wolsey counselled the judges to advise the King that a lawful right might not always accord with justice: 'although this be the law, yet this is conscience'. Henry was a king whose instinct was not always to temper the law.

Attainder, public and parliamentary condemnation for treason, was used by Henry VIII, as by his father, as a means of political proscription. It was through Parliament and by statute that Henry extended his legal competence, creating new treasons of frightening latitude, and novel punishments. A convicted poisoner would now be boiled alive (although this penalty was only inflicted once, against the man who tried, and failed, to poison Bishop Fisher); sodomites would be punished by death, as in Levitical law. The Royal Supremacy and the new Treason Act of 1534 had given the King alarming new powers over conscience. Catherine Howard warned her lover never to reveal in confession the things that had 'passed betwixt her and him', for 'surely, the King, being Supreme Head of the Church, should have knowledge of it'. Yet the reign of terror which so many feared did not follow. In the years 1532–40, 883 people of England, Wales and Calais came within the compass of the treason laws. Three hundred and eight of them were executed. Yet, of these, 287 had been in open rebellion against the Crown, undeniably guilty of treason. This was hardly a massacre of the innocents.

One man died who had surely never committed treason: Sir Thomas More. When More refused to swear the oath of succession, and resolved never to 'dispute kings' titles nor popes' titles', he had found, in silence, the perfect defence, for the Treason Act could only punish express denial. To die on the scaffold, if by silence he could avoid it, would be suicide: this was what More meant when he called the act a 'two-edged sword' by which a man put either his body or soul in peril. More kept silent, while no one, especially the King, doubted that More's silence marked his utter disavowal of the King's proceedings. Yet in the Tower, in conversation with Sir Richard Rich, the Solicitor-General, on 12 June 1535, More in lawyerly 'putting of cases' breached his silence upon the Supremacy. So Rich alleged, and it was upon Rich's evidence, which More insisted was perjured, that More was convicted at his trial. On 6 July, the eve of his own saint, Doubting Thomas, More went to the block. The King had desired his death, but the proper legal forms were observed.

Though the new laws terrified, they were kept as a threat which was usually unfulfilled. In England, unlike the rest of Europe, torture was not used as an ordinary part of the legal process. Under the first Tudors, no judges were removed, and very few juries punished. Even packed juries sometimes acquitted. Yet people remembered the fear. Edward VI's councillors denounced 'the cruel and bloody laws' of his father; 'Dracon's laws . . . written in blood'. Bishop Gardiner later claimed that the oaths he had taken under Henry and Edward were 'Herod's oaths'. Henry saw himself rather as Justinian, the lawgiver. Yet the laws of England had never been codified by kings.

The law of England was, and is, composed of three great elements: common law, equity and statute. The common law was created by the custom of the people and the decisions of judges: it was unwritten, enshrined in the collective memory of the common lawyers; it was immemorial, traceable to no original act of foundation, and proved by long experience; it was, so common lawyers claimed, constantly reinterpreted, but always the same. The central common law courts – King's Bench, Common Pleas and Exchequer – sat at Westminster, prototypes for the same courts in Dublin. Tudor common lawyers, defending their law against the competing, and foreign, claims of civil (based on Roman law) and canon (Church) law, thought it not merely the best law in the world, but the oldest. Yet if it was old, it had also failed to adapt: its procedures were antediluvian, its processes in tatters. The work of the King's Bench had been in decline since the mid fifteenth century. Litigants were abandoning the common law to seek justice in the Chancellor's courts of Chancery and Star Chamber, hoping that they would find swifter process and immunity from the corruption of local sessions and assizes.

Equity jurisdiction had developed centuries before when, if the courts of common law had failed to give redress, litigants would petition the king, who set up the Court of Chancery to hear them. The Chancellor became keeper of the royal conscience. The rules applied by Chancery became law, and where there was variance between common law and equity, equity prevailed. Yet there were dangers that judgements in Chancery might be arbitrary, for the Chancellor – whether he was learned in any law or not, whether impartial or partial – had enormous discretionary powers. Unlike the common law, conscience was uncertain. The same complaints of arbitrariness could be made against the jurisdiction of the royal Council, which was also based on principles of equity. So great was the judicial role of the Council under Henry VII and Henry VIII that it developed into an established feature of the legal system (although without statutory foundation). The sessions of Council sitting in Star Chamber became, under Wolsey, those of a regular court. The spectacular rise of Star Chamber was his great achievement, and the consequence of his vaunted confidence that he could provide impartial justice. His ambition was to minister justice indifferently to rich and poor, and more litigants flocked to his courts for remedy than could be satisfied. He intended also to assault the corruption which perverted the legal system, but justice always depended upon the faltering probity of the laymen who operated it.

As a great prelate of the Church, Wolsey held further judicial authority. The Church governed the spiritual lives of the people, and what it could not prevent it punished. The most elaborately codified law – the canon law – and the most complex system of courts in Europe belonged to the Church. Its universal jurisdiction arose from its responsibility for faith and morals. Marriage was at once a sacrament and a relationship involving questions of ecclesiastical discipline; the validity of marriages and the legitimacy of children was decided by the Church. The Church's courts exercised enormous powers of detection and judgement, not least in cases which seemed to pertain only tangentially to the cure of souls. Since the observation of an oath involved the immortal soul, and 'Dame Perjury' led her followers to hell, any promise or contract fortified by oath could be brought to the Church courts for enforcement by excommunication. The Church drew to itself cases – like slander and breach of promise – which the common lawyers thought belonged to them, but handed over to lay justice the duty to impose the worst penalty of all: burning for heresy.

England had a law of great antiquity and continuity, and an established and sophisticated judicial machinery. The system of law and law enforcement ran all the way from the king down to the lowliest villager.

In the country, assize judges went on circuit twice a year, trying criminal cases which were beyond the competence of the Justices of the Peace. The JPs were the keepers of the peace in local communities, commissioned to enquire into felonies and trespasses, to arrest criminals and to try them at their quarter sessions. Although the Tudor institutions of justice bear the same names as their modern counterparts, they are hardly to be judged according to modern standards of the numbers of crimes solved and criminals convicted. The best of legal provisions could be subverted. Trial was by jury – a right enshrined in Magna Carta – and the verdict in every case that turned on an issue of fact belonged not to judges but to the jury. This was meant to ensure fairness, but might not. The sheriff was charged with ensuring that defendants appeared and with empanelling the jury. If the sheriff were corrupt, or intimidated, or if the jury were, then a partial verdict would be brought and there would be not justice, but a travesty of it. In a society of powerful loyalties to kindred, lord or dependants, justice might be partisan. In his *Dialogue between Pole and Lupset* (written between 1529 and 1532), Thomas Starkey wrote 'matters be ended as they be friended'; if the judge were friend to the man whose case he heard 'the matter cannot go amiss'.

Royal justice in the later middle ages ran alongside, without conflict, a private system of justice which was older. The king's law was called upon only where private settlements had failed, and that public law could only operate with private force behind it. Normally lands would be secured, litigation avoided and local peace sustained not by the mechanisms of the law but by the mutual trust upon which social peace depended. It was always the duty and privilege of lords to settle disputes for their followers; not to shelter them from the consequences of their crimes, nor to abet their quarrels, but to pacify them. Magnate councils seem to have spent their time in arbitration and adjudication. The threat that the lord would withdraw his protection if a dependant refused to accept his judgement was a powerful sanction. It was natural that people would rather seek justice from lords whose decisions bound them in other matters, and to whom deference was due, than in alien courts, perhaps in remote capitals. Private settlement was likely to be more expeditious, less expensive and more flexible than the cumbersome process of law. Personal arbitration by powerful lords could provide satisfaction – if not legal victory in court or the security of title, of judgement, of a court verdict – and so bring peace and stability.

Yet lords who held such power in local communities could use it for malign purposes to deflect the law in contempt of justice. In 1502 Sir Robert Plumpton was dispossessed of estates when Sir Richard Empson, Henry VII's councillor, was successful in an action against him. Empson had conspired not only with the Justices of the Peace, but also with the many knights, esquires and yeomen who rode with him to the assizes at Nottingham and York to maintain his cause. Plumpton's own patron, the 5th Earl of Northumberland, was impotent to protect him. That lords defended the interests of their followers in courts – by maintaining suits at law to which they were not party, influencing justices, bribing juries or overaweing the courts – is clear from the repeated legislation against such abuses. The law sought remedy, but remedy lay with the justices and juries who were themselves corrupt or frightened. The more the law was partial, the more people sought powerful protectors. The greatest threat of violence and disorder came not from brawls between common people, which were easily suppressed, but from men of power, with their followings, in their disputes over land and honour. Yet such men usually wanted justice, and played the leading part in providing it. It was in the country that most law was exercised, with the lords in the natural position to judge between parties. But arbitration began to decline, as law developed, as more cases came before the courts, and when the older reliance on the use of private jurisdiction began to be challenged.

There was a plurality of laws in the lands which the Tudors claimed to rule; in England, Wales and Ireland. The royal writ did not run everywhere. On the Marches with Wales and Scotland, and in the border world between the Pale and the Irish Gaelic lordships, royal justice was excluded where legal authority had long ago been granted elsewhere. The great feudatories in Ireland and the Welsh Marcher lords controlled enclaves of private jurisdiction, their local liberties and palatinates. There were also the lay liberties of Tynedale and Redesdale on the Scottish borders. Lords in the Church held liberties too. Outside the walls of Dublin was the liberty of St Sepulchre, under the private jurisdiction of the archbishops of Dublin. The County Palatine of Durham was ruled by its prince-bishop, and at Hexham there was an ecclesiastical liberty controlled by the Archbishop of York. Some places could offer sanctuary – permanent protection – to criminals fleeing there. Into these areas independent of royal justice murderers and thieves fled as into a foreign land. Although in England protective jurisdiction in the hands of laymen had largely disappeared, those held by abbots and bishops remained.

The South had few, but notorious, sanctuaries – for example, within the precincts of Westminster Abbey and St Martin le Grand – but in the North there were many. They remained as a threat to order and a mockery of justice. In 1487 the Westminster sanctuary men gathered to rob the houses of those campaigning with the King against rebels.

Since the thirteenth century relations with Scotland had been regulated on the borders by March laws, an archaic collection of dooms and treaties, scarcely codified; the only Anglo-Scottish law. On days of truce the English Warden of the March and his Scottish counterpart exchanged those who had offended the laws of either kingdom. At the day of truce held in 1541 by Sir Thomas Wharton and Robert Lord Maxwell, the murderers of three Armstrong brothers appeared, still with blood on their faces. Those offending within the English liberties of Tynedale and Redesdale were tried by baronial courts and laws; part equity and part local custom. But the itinerant royal justices at sessions of oyer and terminer, where they were empowered to 'hear and determine', tried offenders too, for in these frontier zones, despaired of as lawless in Newcastle as well as in distant London, it mattered little how culprits were condemned, so long as they were.

On the borders of Wales, within each marcher lordship, the lord had legislative power and virtual judicial omnicompetence. Royal justice did not hold there. Law in the Marches was still governed by Welsh concepts into the fifteenth century and beyond, and these, as in Ireland and Scotland, were radically different from those of England. The distinction between criminal and civil cases, which lies at the heart of English common law, was not yet recognized in Welsh law, nor in Irish or Scottish. There neither manslaughter, nor even wilful homicide, were, strictly speaking, crimes, whereas in England, by the thirteenth century, homicide like other felonies was a crime against the community, to be judged in royal courts: the prerogative to punish belonged to the public prosecutor, and no compensation between wrongdoer and victim could affect this. In England, the kin of the victim could prosecute the murderer but had no further right. Not so in Gaelic Ireland, nor in Wales and Scotland, where it was the kin, whose peace had been broken, and to whom reparation was due, who sought settlement. Injury to the victim – whether deliberate or accidental; little distinction was at first drawn – would never be considered an offence against the whole community until a social conscience more powerful than a kin conscience developed, and this was impossible while a weak executive administered uneven justice. In post-conquest Wales the law of *galanas* – the blood feud and its settlement – lived on. The principle of compensation was fundamental to the justice of the feud, wherever it still operated; in Scotland, Gaelic Ireland, the Northern Marches and Wales, but no longer in England. Justice was not always seen as retributive; what was sought was the return of peace to two warring families by compensating the kin for its loss.

Observing different kinds of justice, which he did not recognize as justice, operating within his imperial jurisdiction, Henry VIII determined that English common law should be extended throughout his dominions. He wrote in 1520 that 'realms without justice be but tyrannies and robberies'. In 1536 independent jurisdictions were dissolved, and the great liberties of the North, even the county palatine of Durham, were opened to royal criminal justice. Four years later sanctuaries, too, were abolished, and all the liberties and franchises of dissolved monasteries were vested in the Crown.

Henry VIII believed that Welsh March laws were 'sinister usages and customs', imposed by marcher lords as yet another aspect of their 'thraldom and tyranny'. In 1536 the power of the Welsh marcher lords was broken. Union between England and Wales was created by statute in 1536 and 1543: constitutional reform of the greatest consequence. The principality of Wales and the marcher lordships were amalgamated into twelve shires, and English county administration was extended to Wales. The new shires and county boroughs were now to elect and send twenty-four members of parliament to Westminster. Every distinction in legal status between the King's subjects in England and Wales was removed. In 1543 it was enacted that English rules of tenure and inheritance must replace Welsh ones. In order to introduce common law into Wales, courts of great sessions – county sessions held twice yearly – were established. The Council in the Marches of Wales, which acted as a Welsh Privy Council and Court of Star Chamber, enforced English law throughout Wales and on the borders with England. In Wales it was clear that the landowners were not so attached to the native culture that they would be unable to accept English law. Not so in Ireland.

For Henry VIII and all Tudor monarchs after him the best hope for the reform of Ireland and of its advance to civility lay in the extension of English common law throughout the island. This would be an uphill task. English kings had once claimed that their law was law throughout Ireland – *una et eadem lex*, one and the same law – and extended its benefits to free-born Irishmen. But by the fifteenth century the English common law operated only in Crown territories, and there uncertainly, and the Irish were usually denied access to it. Without royal judges there could be no royal justice, and none had been sent to Munster or Connacht after 1400. The king's writ did not run in the great liberties of the feudatories, and there, on the marches with the Irishry, either English law or Gaelic law, or a march law which was a hybrid of the two, were used. The 9th Earl of Kildare applied either law as 'he thought most beneficial, as the case did require'. Pragmatism prevailed. As Kildare told Wolsey, those safe in England little knew how necessary it was 'for every noble man in Ireland to hamper his uncivil neighbours at discretion, wherein if they waited for process of law . . . they might hap to lose their own lives and lands without law'.

Gaelic Ireland had its own ancient legal system, the brehon law. One English justice admitted that, although alien to common law principles, it worked: 'divers Irishmen doth keep such laws which they make upon hills in their country . . . without breaking them for any favour or reward'. In Gaelic and Gaelicized Ireland every area had its own official judge, a brehon, from a hereditary lineage of jurists, who heard cases in public, usually upon a hill, and awarded arbitration. They had their immemorial brehon law codes, but Roman law too influenced their judgements. There was no system of public, criminal law, and the principles upon which brehon law was predicated – compensation and kin responsibility – were ones which the English common law opposed. In English law sanctions were applied to the guilty party, not to his kin; to his person, not to his property. In Ireland crimes such as thefts were simple torts, wrongs whereby the injured person acquired a right of action for damages, and resolution came by the payment of compensation.

An ancient system of ransoms and indemnity payments lay at the heart of Irish secular law. Ransoms – *éirics* or *sautes* for murder or manslaughter; *cáin* for theft or felony – were awarded by the brehon, according to what the offence deserved or what the perpetrator could pay. The greater the person wronged, the greater the compensation due. In the 1530s the brehon appointed by Lady Katherine Power ordered a ransom of five marks for stealing a sheep and the same for drawing blood; twenty shillings for drawing a weapon, and a hundred shillings for mutilation. Part of the fine would be paid to the victim's lord. When in 1542 Maguire agreed to become vassal of O'Donnell he ceded half of the blood money for homicide in Fermanagh. According to the legal institution of *comairce* ('comrick'), if anyone under the protection of a lord were violated, the offence would be taken as an offence against the protector himself, and if the protected person offended, the lord must offer satisfaction. An *éiric* was often offered and accepted on behalf of the lord's retainers, for if they were executed the lord and his protection would be dishonoured and the consequence would be feud and local war.

Execution was not customary in late medieval Ireland, unless public outrage were stirred, but lords could impose punishments of death or mutilation. In 1500 Maguire ordered the hanging of Melaghlin Bradach ('the thief') O'Flanagan. There were also the sanctions of exile and casting adrift. A man who was poor, or unable to summon kin or friends to redeem him, could legally be hanged by those whom he had injured. If the defendant refused to pay compensation, the plaintiff could seize his property or that of his kin, under the rule of 'kincogish', the collective responsibility of the kin. It was this private seizure of property, and the cattle raids which ensued, which was particularly condemned by English legislators. But they accepted pragmatically some brehon law principles, such as 'kincogish', in their dealings with the Irishry; the two systems were not always radically estranged in practice. Brehon law began to retreat after 1541, when the king's Irish subjects came under his protection and were subject to his justice.

But the notion of justice, as opposed to law, still seemed remote in some parts of Ireland and for many of its people. A conversation between Captain Docwra, commander of the English garrison in Derry, and Niall Garve O'Donnell at the end of the Tudor century revealed the awesome and arbitrary powers which the last generation of Gaelic lords still claimed:

'The country [of Inishowen] is mine,' saith he [O'Donnell], 'and so is all Tirconnell, and I will use and govern it to my own pleasure . . . Let the Queen do with her rights what she will, Inishowen is mine, and were there but one cow in the country, that cow would I take and use as mine own.'

'And how would you provide for the poor people to live?' said I.

'I care not,' saith he. 'Let a thousand die, I pass not of a pin; and for the people, they are my subjects. I will punish, exact, cut [tax], and hang, if I see occasion, where and whensoever I list.'

THE COMMONS

The common people, or 'commons', the vast majority of the population, were the estate in the Tudor commonwealth who were bound 'only to be ruled, not to rule other'. They were allowed no authority, no voice, and their part was usually as silent spectators to the actions of the great. In his *History of the Reign of King Richard III* More judged that the commons were hardly implicated in that tyranny, for politics were 'king's games, as it were stage plays . . . in which poor men were but lookers on'. Tudor political theory, expressed in homilies, sermons and tracts, constantly invoked a divine order of strict hierarchies where people were set in ranks. Just as God had set 'an order by grace between himself and Angels, and between Angel and Angel, and between Angel and man', so He had ordained distinctions between men and men, which 'God willeth us firmly to keep without any enterprise to the contrary'. So Edmund Dudley explained in his *Tree of Commonwealth*, which he wrote in the Tower in 1510, while imprisoned for treason. As it was in the human body, so it was in the body politic: just as the foot obeyed the head, so must the people obey the king. This was both the divine and natural order and not to be questioned. 'These folk may not grudge nor murmur to live in labour and pain.' Suppose siren voices whispered to the commons that their subservience to the upper orders was unfair – 'Why should they sport and play and you labour and till?' – or against the divine promise – for were not the commons, too, the children of Adam and had not Christ redeemed them 'as dearly as the nobles, with . . . His precious blood'? – they were not to listen. They must remember that God had ordained both rich and poor, and that rich and poor owed reciprocal duties. The rich must provide work and relief; in return the poor owed deference and service.

That there was civil government at all was seen to be the consequence of man's first disobedience and Fall. After that God had set kings over men, as God's ministers, to protect the righteous and punish the wicked. The people were especially unfit to rule, for they could not, unlike the nobility, be educated to virtue. Their ignorance made any presumption to govern, at the least, unfitting – 'a ploughman shall make but a feeble answer to an ambassador' – and could decline to something much worse. For the people to rule was a kind of tyranny – 'the many-headed tyranny' – because they suffered from the same vice of intemperance which afflicted the tyrant. Any form of popular democracy, where government was handed over to the sinful majority, was monstrous, as when the 'foot taketh upon him the part of the head, and commons is become a king'. This was the spectre which haunted Tudor governors, whose fearful imagination metamorphosed the confederacy of a handful of malcontents into the status of rebellion. They had seen in their own times terrifying examples of subversion: the German Peasants' War and the anarchic commune of Münster.

There was a long tradition of popular revolt in England. Tudor chronicles told of the insurrection of 1381, when peasants and townspeople, in their great hour of corporate articulacy, had subverted the social order, denounced their oppressors, and wrought havoc. The fear was always that the commons would rise again. Yet the power of the people was usually latent. The poor would be cast weeping from their homes when land was enclosed, consigned to dereliction without offering resistance. Any use of their strength in numbers was illegitimate; mob rule. Yet, under duress, they might be provoked to action. Insurgency of a greater or lesser kind – whether rebellion against the Crown or revolt against landlords – might have seemed the natural consequence of a political system which allowed the great majority no channel for grievance, in which any appeal for redress was taken as rebellion. What else could they do but rebel? Sometimes the voice of desperation was heard. 'We shall never have good world till we fall together by the ears,' so a Norfolk woman threatened in 1537, 'and with clubs and clouted shoon shall the deed be done.' These were the only weapons of the peasantry, but frightening if wielded by many.

Rebellion took many forms, inspired as it was by myriad motives. Most commons' revolts were local, animated by particular grievances and directed against particular objects and persons, typically against enclosing by venal landlords which threatened commons' rights. Usually, after spontaneous breaking down of fences, the rioters would retreat. The violence was almost always shortlived and soon subdued, for in local trials of strength between landlords and commons there was little contest, especially where the lord moved swiftly to exercise summary justice 'to the terror of others'. Few of these commons' riots aspired to challenge the bonds of 'estate and degree' which bound society in chains of mutual dependence. But a few did. In a May game in Suffolk in 1537 the player acting the part of Husbandry in a play of 'a king how he should rule his realm' said many things against gentlemen which were not in the text; and three years later, in neighbouring Norfolk, a confederacy formed against gentlemen, who bore 'little favour . . . to us poor men'. It would be good, some said, ominously, if there were 'as many gentlemen in Norfolk as there be white bulls'. Such threats were rare, and usually empty, but the East Anglian gentry had cause for alarm, as the events of 1549 would show, and the East Anglian commons had reason for animus against a venal gentry which was unfit to govern. The central authorities were generally little concerned with local riots, for the grievances expressed were not against them. But not all commons' revolts were of a peasantry chafing against local injustice; some were for a cause which was national. These were more dangerous by far.

Suppose the passions of the people of a whole region were roused against the actions of the government? At times, the commons showed allegiances quite contrary to those which the Tudor monarchs required, especially in moments of greatest royal insecurity. At Henry VII's accession loyalty to Richard III and the Yorkists remained strong in the North, and the commons was the element in northern society most persistent in refusal to accept the first Tudor. They followed captains who took names like 'Robin of Redesdale', which were evocative because they had been used before in rebellion against the Crown. London often threatened to declare itself for the Tudors' enemies; a fearful threat, for it was, as John Stow, its greatest chronicler admitted, 'always a mighty arm and instrument to bring any great desire to effect, if it could be brought to a man's devotion'. The 3rd Duke of Buckingham listened to advice to 'win the favour of the commons and he should have rule of all', and when he was executed in 1521 for his treason the universal grief of the Londoners caused the City fathers to set watches. In London a few could raise many, rumour turn to action, and threats to violence. In 1517 two London apprentices had, within hours, mustered hundreds of others to rise on May Day against foreigners: a riot remembered as 'Evil May Day'. Thereafter the apprentices were always distrusted as an unstable element, especially on holidays and their traditional days of misrule.

Although few denied the obligation to support the monarch in times of necessity, the commons might baulk if the royal necessity were not theirs. In Yorkshire in 1489 the commons, led by the pseudonymous captains Master Hobbehirst and Robin Goodfellow, opposed the levying of taxes to fund the King's campaign in distant Brittany. So, too, in Cornwall in 1497 the commons revolted against taxes to finance war in even more remote Scotland, a war, they said, which was 'but a pretence to poll and pill the people'. Fifteen thousand Cornishmen, led by Michael Joseph ('The Smith'; *An Gof* in Cornish), Thomas Flamank, a gentleman, and Lord Audley, marched, largely unopposed, to London. Their demonstration and defiance ended, as others would, in carnage. Ill-armed and ill-led, they were cut to pieces or put to flight at Blackheath.

Poverty drove them to resistance, the commons claimed; a claim hard to gainsay. In Yorkshire in 1513 the commons volunteered their personal services for war, but no money, 'because they have so little of it'. A decade later Henry VIII demanded a tax large enough to finance his ambition to win 'the whole monarchy of Christendom'; a sum, said the Commons in Parliament, 'impossible to be levied'. In 1525 the King called for the Amicable Grant, which was neither amicable nor, as it turned out, a grant. There were 'pitiful curses and weepings' from a commons already undermined by catastrophic harvests, recurrent plague, and a collapse in the wool trade. In Kent many accounted themselves as 'desperates'. In Suffolk there was mutiny. 'Two or three hundred good poor fellows together . . . would have a living' by whatever means, they threatened, and 'he that had the most should have the least peradventure'. Crowds flocked to present their grievances, clamouring like 'geese in corn'. Asked who was their captain, the reply came: 'Forsooth, his name is Poverty, for he and his cousin Necessity hath brought us to this doing.' Claiming poverty exculpated the commons from charges of treasonous rebellion and allowed a king, who was unable to subdue them by force, to concede and to pardon with seeming grace. The perennial dearth and calamity which clouded the world of the peasantry lay behind every popular revolt, yet there were causes for rebellion far more compelling and unifying than poverty alone.

The greatest rebellions of the century were in the name of faith and justice. So it was in the Lincolnshire rising and the Pilgrimage of Grace of 1536. When the assault upon the monasteries gave focus to all the inchoate fears and rumours of heretical innovations imposed by an alien court, of inequitable taxation, of despoliation of churches and transfer of land and disruption of tenure, the whole of northern society was threatened and rallied to the defence of 'its old ancient customs'. A rebel force rallied so large that no royal army could counter it. The commons of the North had initiated the great rising, and much of it was created in their image. The oaths they swore were to 'God, the King and the commons', and the names of the commons and the commonwealth were constantly evoked to strengthen their resolve. In the North-West the commons' leaders were 'simple poor men', whom they called Lord Poverty, Captain Pity and Captain Charity. At the great Pilgrim councils the commons' voice was heard through their own representatives. But they could not act alone. Because they were conservative, because it was their 'old ancient customs' they were determined to restore, they wanted, indeed demanded, the support of their natural superiors; the nobility and gentry. With the accustomed battle cries – 'thousands for a Percy', 'a Dacre, a Dacre' – they called upon their traditional leaders to lead them as before. But this seeming deference took strange forms.

The gentry and nobility assumed the leadership of a movement whose aims they approved but whose means they abhorred: but they were adamant that they were captives of the mutinous commons, victims of the rising not its prime movers. Sir Stephen Hamerton claimed that upon his return from hunting he was warned by women that he must save himself. Surrounded by 300 armed men at Giggleswick, he was told that 'he had ruled them, but they would now rule him', and was compelled to swear the rebel oath. Is his story to be believed? Certainly the King and those around him found it hard to absolve the gentry and to accept their pleas that their servants and tenants would not stand with them. But when the leaders of the army sent against the Pilgrims wrote 'in desperate sort as though the world would be turned upside down' if the King did not accede to the rebel demands, their fears were genuine, the subversion real. The deference of a nobleman's retinue was conditional, and the loyalty of tenants mutable. The force that a nobleman mustered against the Pilgrims could defect to the Pilgrim ranks. In 1553 the commons would marshal successfully to impose their will upon their social leaders and effect a great political and religious transformation. Their actions attested not only to their conviction, but their confidence. In England, wrote the Elizabethan poet Edmund Spenser, 'every man standeth upon himself and buildeth his fortunes upon his own faith and self-assurance'.

Hierarchies and structures of power were extended and diffused throughout society. In their parishes and villages men sought office and authority and a political voice. Yet participation in the public life of a parish was highly circumscribed. Yeomen and wealthier tradesmen monopolized the higher parish offices such as churchwarden; lesser offices, like that of sidesman, went to husbandmen. For the labouring poor there was nothing. Parish office was not only a measure of rank, but conferred real power; the control of land, distribution of poor relief, or moral regulation. Although parish life, centred upon the church, was ideally based upon the values of charity and neighbourhood which should transcend rank and degree, still there were deep divisions between the 'better' or 'chiefest sort' who gave poor relief, and the poorer, 'meaner sort' who received it. The parish leaders came to give alms conditionally. Sometimes they opposed the marriage of poor people, on the uncanonical grounds that they were likely to become a burden on the parish. In 1570 the 'chiefest' of Adlington in Kent were 'sore against' Alice Cheeseman's match, urged her to abandon it, and threatened to expel her from the parish if she defied them. The poor, like her, might be powerless even to marry and to settle in personal security. When Spenser wrote so confidently of the self-assurance of the English commons, he was comparing them to the Irish.

'Now this ye are to understand,' said the character Irenius in Spenser's *View of the Present State of Ireland*, rebellions in Ireland were never 'begun by the common people, but by the Lords and Captains of Countries', whom the people were 'forced to follow'. Not a single peasant rising was known in medieval Ireland. The oppressive system of coyne and livery kept the people poor, submissive and silent. The lords hardly needed to listen to the popular voice. Ruling by the 'strong hand', they knew that the commons dared not challenge them. By the late sixteenth century the lords claimed the right to retain their tenants and denied them the right to leave the land. The English planters and administrators chose to see the Irish peasantry – 'churls', as they called them – as bond slaves. In law, the peasantry may not have been subject to a hereditary condition of unfreedom; in practice, their status and standard of living were so low that it seemed so.

There were people in England and Wales also who were powerless and without justice. This was not only because of their poverty, for even the poorest had legal status and rights. Thieves who stole out of desperation could and did plead necessity in mitigation. Those without justice were the bondmen. Serfdom survived still in England and Wales throughout the sixteenth century, and on those estates where this antediluvian form of tenure persisted, lords had an unfettered right to seize the property of bondmen, to imprison and beat them. The rapacious 3rd Dukes of Buckingham and Norfolk tried to extend serfdom on their estates. Henry VII had in 1507 granted manumission (freedom) to serfs in Merioneth, Caernarvon and Anglesey, but Tudor kings lacked the power or the will to intervene on private estates. By 1549 villeins on the Howards' Norfolk estates were asking, like the German peasants in 1525, for manumission in the name of the Lord of all lords: 'We pray that bondmen shall be made free, for Christ made all men free by his precious blood shedding.'

Within the smallest communities – even the family, especially the family – there were those who held power and those who owed duty. All communities, except nunneries, were patriarchal. Female power and freedom had no place in Tudor views of the social and political order. 'Ye are underlings, underlings, and must be obedient,' so Hugh Latimer explained. That unfreedom was enshrined in the English common law, which distinguished a *femme sole*, a widow or unmarried woman legally of age, from a married woman, or *femme coverte*. Single women could acquire or dispose of property, contract debts, make wills, and engage independently in a craft or trade. Married women could not. But women's social and legal subordination did not mean that a husband's supremacy was always imposed, nor prevent husband and wife from working in partnership to sustain the family and household. Wives were named as executors of their husband's wills and administrators of their estates in full confidence that they would know how to manage them. Women were unlikely to be passive and submissive under an overbearing patriarchy, whatever the theory. Denied a role in the public, political sphere, at any level, their influence might nevertheless be immense. Even the fundamental principle that women should not bear rule was soon breached by two Tudor queens regnant.

6

Rebuilding the Temple

THE REIGNS OF EDWARD VI (1547–53) AND MARY I (1553–8)

The accession of a baby queen, Mary, and a boy king, Edward, to the thrones of Scotland and England offered the chance to solve an ancient problem: how should two alien powers share the same island? This seeming coincidence was taken by England's governors as a sign of divine providence, of God's plan that the heir and heiress should marry and unite their two kingdoms as 'Great Britain'. By the Treaty of Greenwich of 1543, Mary, who had ascended the Scottish throne in 1542, one week old, was promised to marry the young Prince Edward. Yet the Scots saw the advantage as all on England's side. As Sir Adam Otterburn sagely asked, 'If your lad were a lass and our lass were a lad, would you then be so earnest in this matter?' Rather than have an Englishman as king of Scotland, 'our common people and the stones in the street would rise and rebel against it'. The Scots soon broke their treaty, and when they jilted the English a terrible retribution followed. The English 'Rough Wooing' of 1544 and 1545 left the Scottish Lowlands a smoking waste and the Borderers condemned to live wretchedly in the ruins of their countryside. The Scots grew ever more determined to remain free from the 'thraldom of England', while the English still asserted their putative sovereignty, increasingly regarding the Scots not so much as foreign enemies but as domestic rebels. Scotland did not stand alone. While England was at war with Scotland the King of France, Henry II, bound to the 'auld alliance', would never be at peace with England. Both England and Scotland faced long and dangerous minorities of their rulers.

In Scotland, as in England, divisions in religion transformed the nature of politics, as the factions struggling for ascendancy fought also for the advance or the destruction of reform. Henry VIII, having broken papal power in England, sought to subvert it in Scotland too. As Edward Seymour, Earl of Hertford laid waste the Borders, he despoiled the great religious houses also. He met stalwart resistance at Kelso Abbey in September 1545, where twelve monks, with about one hundred supporters, made their last stand. Those who held out in the steeple were slaughtered, and the Abbey was destroyed lest it be used as fortress against the English. The leader of Scottish resistance to English aggression, and the chief French partisan, was David Beaton. As Cardinal, he was leader too of the Catholic cause in Scotland. The death of the Cardinal was devoutly hoped for by his political enemies; not least by Henry VIII, who countenanced the assassination of Beaton as he had once before of Cardinal Pole. In the spring of 1547 Beaton was murdered by a group of Fife lairds. As his desecrated body swung from the castle walls at St Andrews the Catholic people were invited to 'see there their god'. Beaton's assassins and other opponents of the regency of James Hamilton, Earl of Arran held out in St Andrews, with English support, until in July 1547 the French arrived to break the siege. Among those conveyed to France in the galleys was John Knox, who would return to lead the Scottish Reformation. Mary, Queen of Scots was brought up and remained a Catholic. Not so her Tudor cousin and spurned bridegroom.

*

Edward VI was a king not only born but educated to rule. Even Erasmus would have approved so perfect an education for a Christian prince. The celebrated humanists Richard Cox and John Cheke became tutors to the 'godly imp', and from them he learnt not only languages but a profound biblical piety. Other princes received ideal educations and learnt nothing, but here was a prince who prepared himself with great discipline for what he saw as the divine obligation of his kingship. He studied history. Its lessons must be put into practice; so he took notes upon English rule in France in Henry VI's reign. He studied geography. He knew all the ports and havens in England, France and Scotland, and the favourable winds and tides for entering them, for a king needed strategic information. He learnt the names and religion of every magistrate, the better to govern. He studied moral philosophy from Cicero and Aristotle. He studied rhetoric. But above all, he knew the scriptures; at the age of twelve he read twelve chapters daily. Edward's youthful passion was to hear sermons, and as he listened he took notes, especially when the preachers touched upon the duties of kings.

When the preachers urged not only spiritual but moral regeneration,

Edward took heed. He had a commanding sense that true religion must be introduced and the abuses in society redressed. From Bishop Latimer he heard that 'to take away the right of the poor is against the honour of a king', and that kings must show the way to their covetous subjects. Not for him a worldly court like his father's, where courtiers had gambled for Church booty, throwing dice to win Jesus bell tower in St Paul's churchyard, and where courtly – and less courtly – love had flourished. Did not Latimer urge the death penalty for adultery? Edward was intent upon emulating Josiah, the young king of the Old Testament who had destroyed the idols of Baal. To his 'dear and beloved uncle', Edward Seymour, Edward dedicated his own collection of Old Testament texts against the veneration of images. Sometime before 1550 Edward had been won to a 'pious understanding of the doctrine of the Eucharist'; that is, to the evangelical faith.

Here was a king with an iron sense of duty and justice. His own chronicle records with apparent lack of regret the fate of malefactors, even or especially those close to him. Edward had inherited the sovereign will and implacability of his father. Also his suspicion. 'A great noter of things that pertained to princely affairs', Edward ciphered those notes into Greek letters, safe from the prying eyes of his attendants. He had reason for suspicion, for he was anxiously guarded, 'not half a quarter of an hour alone', with no one to trust at his court except his dog. He was guarded against kidnap by those who would use him as the most powerful political pawn, and soon became aware of his own vulnerability. For July 1549 he recorded dispassionately in his chronicle that 'because there was a rumour that I was dead, I passed through London'. Although he was king, he was still, as his reign began, a little boy (aged nine), without the power, even if he had the will, to govern in his minority. The evangelicals had their reasons to urge him to use his regal power before the end of his minority to implement religious change; conservatives, like Bishops Bonner and Gardiner, argued otherwise, denying the legality of such precipitate use of the Royal Supremacy.

*

When Henry VIII was dying, those around him conspired to subvert his plan for the rule of the realm during Edward's minority. The King's death was kept secret, while behind locked doors in the Privy Gallery councillors and courtiers bound each other to overturn the royal provisions for a Regency Council of sixteen equal members. Together, they all agreed – save one – that Edward Seymour, Earl of Hertford, the brother of Henry's third queen and the new king's uncle, should be elevated above them all as Lord Protector, 'thinking it the surest form of government and most fit for that commonwealth'. By doctoring the royal will to reward themselves with lands, offices and titles – gifts unfulfilled in the King's life, but intended by him, so they claimed – the loyalty of some and the silence of others was bought, for a time. These secret moves left a dangerous political legacy. The conspirators always looked for further favours and for a share in the power which they had handed over. 'Remember what you promised me in the gallery at Westminster, before the breath was out of the body of the king that dead is,' William Paget, the prime mover, reminded Hertford. That promise was to listen to Paget's advice above all others', and Hertford soon broke it. He also broke his promise to the others that he would do nothing 'without the advice of us, the rest of the Council'. Within days of Edward's accession Hertford, who was now created Duke of Somerset, had effectively assumed the royal prerogative of forming a Privy Council, and began to call it, and not to call it, at will. The policies of the Protectorate were soon exclusively Somerset's own. When Paget wrote to him offering advice to which Somerset did not listen, he wrote of '*your* matters of policy', '*your* determinations for the year to come', '*your* debt', '*your* navy', '*your* foreign affairs'. Since Somerset had taken the devising of policy to himself, his would be the blame if, and when, it failed.

The precedents for a Protectorate were hardly propitious. No one could forget Richard III. Like the boy king Henry VI, Edward had two feuding uncles. The Protector's brother, Thomas Seymour, was convinced that the Governorship of the King and the Protectorship of the realm should be two different offices and that one of these must be his. The treacherous John Dudley, Lord Lisle, urged Thomas Seymour to bid for the Governorship, and by fomenting the quarrel between the two brothers led them to play into his hands. Over the dead body of Henry VIII, who had in his last days tried to exclude him, Thomas Seymour was admitted to the Council. Failing to gain control of his nephew officially, Seymour sought it by stealth; by suborning members of the Privy Chamber, leaving notes under the carpet for the susceptible Edward, sending him pocket money (which the King gave to Latimer), and urging him to 'bear rule as other kings do'. Possession of the King's person gave the essential resource of power – legitimacy – and over him the two uncles fought. Only the barking of the royal dog which guarded the doors of the Privy Chamber saved the King from kidnap by Thomas Seymour in February 1549, and nothing could save Seymour, who was executed for treason in the following month.

Somerset ruled alone. He was, first and last, a military commander and his guiding obsession was the conquest of Scotland; not, as before, by fire and sword, but by permanent garrisoning. This was a policy with consequences for all his others. As the reign began, England was at peace with France and with Emperor Charles V, and 'in an indifferent concord with the rest of the world (except Rome)'. But war with Scotland also came to mean war with France, for Henry II vowed that he would rather lose his realm than abandon the Scots. When Mary, Queen of Scots left for France in August 1548 to marry the Dauphin, England's primary reason for waging the war was gone. By Christmas 1548 Paget was inviting Somerset to consider 'whether at your first setting forward you took not a wrong way'. The defence of Boulogne and of the Scottish garrisons was dragging England towards catastrophe. Only the most desperate financial expedients could meet the prodigious war expenditure, which ran to £200,000 annually in Scotland alone. The great debasement of the coinage, which had begun in Henry VIII's last years, continued recklessly under Somerset, racking an economy which was suffering enough without such sabotage. Latimer in his Lenten sermon of 1549 spoke of the debased silver coin so reddened with copper that it 'blushed for shame'. Extraordinary inflation followed the currency manipulations. Between 1544 and 1551 prices in London – where food could not be grown, only bought – rose by almost 90 per cent. Observing the suffering and social misery, Somerset never admitted that war expenditure and debasement might be the causes. Debasement could not end until the war did but, having embarked upon the conquest of Scotland, Somerset, the proud victor of the Battle of Pinkie in 1547, could not end the haemorrhage of money and men, nor abandon his policy. Nor could he countenance defeat, except, so he confessed upon the walls of Berwick, in his dreams. He could not even admit the massive military superiority of the French and the folly of being drawn into war with them from August 1549. Unable to blame his own policies, Somerset and those advisers to whom he listened placed the cause of society's ills elsewhere.

Somerset saw himself as the champion of the oppressed, hearing complacently the benisons of the poor: 'There was never man had the hearts of the poor as you have. Oh, the commons pray for you, sir, they say, "God save your life".' Such paternalism may have seemed incompatible with Somerset's military brutality, his cruel arrogance and his startling cupidity. As the soldier who had left the poor in the Borders to live like animals in their ruined homes; as rack-renter, sheep-master and encloser; as the ruler who presided over the Vagrancy Act which imposed slavery upon those who, willingly or not, left their homes, he was ostensibly an unlikely social reformer. Yet to that role he aspired. Here was a man as ambitious of virtue, the badge of nobility, as of riches. And there was more to it. Evangelicals harped upon the compelling Christian imperative to relieve the distress of the poor, 'for those injuries we do unto the poor members of Christ we do unto Him, saith He', and the Protector heard them. Somerset and his redoubtable duchess had long sustained the evangelical cause. In the dark days of 1539, after the repressive Act of Six Articles had inaugurated a new wave of persecution, they had welcomed leading evangelicals to their London house. The Duchess had supported the heretic Anne Askew in Newgate in 1546. Now 'hotlings' returned from exile to kneel at their feet and 'devise commonwealths'. In power, Somerset listened to those who looked for the advent of a Christian commonwealth and told him how to achieve it, especially to those who blamed social distress not upon ruinous wars but upon the greed of landowners, and who laid the sins which were the Government's at the door of the sheep-master.

As prices rose ever higher under the Protectorate, people looked for the cause and were puzzled. How was the dearth to be explained when the harvests between 1547 and 1549 had been so good? What could explain the disparity between the price of grain and other foodstuffs? Surely this was a 'marvellous' dearth, a 'monstrous and portentous' dearth, and man-made, the product of covetousness? Though there was uncertainty whether the raising of rents was the cause or the consequence of inflation, there was no doubt that the rentier gentry prospered while the poor suffered. Did the cause of dearth lie in failures and malpractices of the market? Certainly, the Council issued regulations to control prices; exports were restricted; and compulsory purveyance (the king's right to buy provisions at fixed low prices) to provide goods for the army was abolished. The cause and the remedy came to be sought in the way in which the land was used. The agrarian problems to which solutions must be found were those that had exercised Wolsey and More a generation before: the conversion of land from arable to pasture, the victory of sheep over plough, the eviction of labourers from their cottages, rural depopulation, vagrancy. These problems were not new, but they were now believed to be intractable. Whether arable had, in fact, employed more people than wool production is doubtful. The great rise in population undermined all old certainties. But there is no doubt that most Tudor thinkers blamed economic ills upon the sheep flocks. Who would bother to employ twelve people to keep cows and milk them, to make cheese and take it to market, when one shepherd could make a greater profit? Why raise pigs, poultry and beef when the money lay in sheep? While the rich made such judgements the poor could hardly have a living. Latimer foresaw the day when a pig would cost as much as a pound. Where would remedy be found?

Somerset, with the approval of some of the Council, set up a commission on 1 June 1548 to discover how much land had been turned from tillage to pasture, for 'Christian people' were 'by the greedy covetousness of some men eaten up and devoured of brute beasts'. John Hales, to whom the commission was entrusted, presented their charges to the commissioners as a godly duty, 'as acceptable sacrifice to God as may be', but soon found his commission opposed by the landlords whose excesses the commission was meant to discover and into whose lands and private interests it trespassed. But, in spite of 'the Devil, private profit, self-love, money and such like the Devil's instruments', Somerset insisted that it should go forward. While the gentry thought of the commission as a storm which would pass over, it had raised expectations among the commons which could hardly be fulfilled. Rumours spread that if the commons were not satisfied they would attempt reform themselves. Against the will of the whole Council, Somerset, on his own authority, issued a proclamation in April 1549 enforcing legislation against enclosure, and in July ordered a second enclosure commission, with novel and unconstitutional powers to hear and determine cases. The rest of the Council feared that the commissions were an incitement to riot. So it proved.

*

In the late spring and summer of 1549 there were commons' risings in Somerset, Wiltshire, Hampshire, Lincolnshire, Kent, Essex, Sussex, Devon, Cornwall, Bedfordshire, Rutland, Leicestershire, Northamptonshire, Buckinghamshire, Oxfordshire, Yorkshire and East Anglia. So sudden and so widespread were the revolts that there was uncertainty about how and where they began. Not since 1381 had there been such widespread rebellion. So long were the delays in sending troops against the rebels and so profligate were Somerset's pardons offering redress of grievances, that sinister suspicions of his populism were voiced: 'that you have some greater enterprise in your head that lean so much to the multitude'. But the failure was not the Protector's alone. The gentry, who by their pursuit of self-interest had abdicated their duty to the commons, seemed powerless to act, and 'looked one upon another'. Unable to raise their tenants against the rebels, they fled. The commons seemed to hold their governors to ransom. 'Commons is become a king', appointing terms and conditions to their rulers. 'Grant us this and that, and we will go home,' they were said to demand. Somerset now wrote with patrician horror of 'a plague and a fury among the vilest and worst sort of men', who had all 'conceived a marvellous hate against gentlemen, and take them all as their enemies'.

To the mortification of the evangelical establishment there were revolts both in the name of the 'commonwealth', which the commons had appropriated for themselves, and against it by conservatives determined to halt and to reverse reform. How should the governing orders react? All rebellion was sin. Archbishop Cranmer rebuked the rebels: even if their magistrates were 'very tyrants against the commonwealth', subjects must obey. The risings took many forms, as was likely 'of people without head and rule', and there was little cohesion in motive and organization between the different areas. Some cried 'Pluck down enclosures and parks; some for the commons; others pretend religion'. Most of the riots were pacified easily enough, especially where the local lord acted expeditiously, as the Earl of Arundel did in Sussex, and deference prevailed. By 10 July the Council could assure Lord Russell in the West that everywhere was 'thoroughly quieted', except Buckinghamshire, but even as they wrote thousands of rebels were marching on Norwich. Far distant from each other in motive and action as in place, the rebels in the South-West and East Anglia held out and held out.

When the commons of Attleborough in Norfolk tore down hedges on 20 June it had seemed a spontaneous local protest, little different from many another. Yet at the celebration of the feast of St Thomas the Martyr at Wymondham a fortnight later many came prepared for more concerted action. Finding their leader in Robert Kett, on 10 July thousands marched upon Norwich in a protest against the exploitation and venality of local governors who governed in no interests but their own. Leading figures in the city, including the mayor and perhaps the bishop, colluded with the rebels. Above Norwich on Mousehold Heath a rebel camp was set up, with its own laws, discipline and daily service. The rebels summoned captive gentlemen before a popular tribunal, at the Tree of Reformation, crying either 'a good man', or 'hang him', but this vigilante justice was prevented and a certain decorum prevailed. In the King's name Kett ordered purveyance on a grand scale, seizing tens of thousands of the sheep which had dispossessed them in order to provision a camp 16,000 strong. Four times Kett was offered pardon, and four times he refused it: he denied any offence. The Norfolk men had mounted a grand demonstration, not against central government but in support of it, and they waited in their camp for the Council to fulfil its promises of reform and justice. And they waited. Kett's Mousehold camp was one among many in the summer of 1549. In Kent and Sussex, Norfolk and Suffolk, the 'camp men' 'enkennelled' themselves; new words for new forms of alternative government by the commons, a form of self-assertion by the lower orders which bewildered and alarmed their social superiors. In their camps they dispensed justice themselves.

Kett's rebels held out at Mousehold until the end of August, encouraged by a prophecy that

> The country knaves, Hob, Dick and Hick,
> With clubs and clouted shoon
> Shall fill up Dussindale
> With slaughtered bodies soon.

But, after a bloody confrontation with the Earl of Warwick's troops, the slaughtered bodies which made Dussindale a graveyard were the rebels' own. Later, there were those who regretted the quiescence of the camps, promising that next time they would have not a 'lying camp but a running camp'. In the South-West the rebels had never believed that the government was for them, rather against them, and they had planned not to camp in protest but, as once before in 1497, to march upon London. Their actions were different from those rebels in East Anglia but so was their cause. They, too, harboured resentments against their gentry, but their animus was principally shown against the evangelical gentry in their midst. Religion was the cause which had first driven them to rise, and it was for religion that thousands died from the remote

counties of Devon and Cornwall. The Council had swept away ceremonies and practices which lay at the heart of the traditional religion to
which they were devoted. Their rebellion was a direct challenge to the
evangelical revolution which was beginning.

*

The accession of a new king and the rule of a Council known to contain
evangelicals had occasioned high and urgent hopes of reform among
reforming zealots. Under the new Josiah, they expected the temple of
Baal would be cast down, idolatry overthrown, the primitive Church
restored. Zealots rushed to effect reformation, without government
sanction. This was a time of unprecedented freedom and prosperity for
reformist printers. In evangelical strongholds, down went the roods, the
images of saints; in their places were whitewashed walls, the royal arms
and scriptural messages, including, 'Thou shalt make no graven images,
lest thou worship them'. 'Hot gospellers' preached a crusade against
false worship. For some of the radicals the idolatry of worshipping
images of wood and stone was as nothing compared to the idolatry of
the Mass. Many hoped that the Mass was 'yesterday's bird', and sang
ballads against that 'blasphemous monster' which promised remission
of sins by offering Christ's body and blood: 'Farewell to Mistress Missa'.
But the sacrilege and zealotry of the iconoclasts appalled their Catholic
neighbours, who threatened violence against them. The authorities
insisted that it was not for the people 'of their preposterous zeal' to 'run
before they be sent'.

Yet every move of the Protector's government signalled its intent to
lead the infant Church of England under its juvenile king further towards
reform. The homilies that were ordered to be read in every parish from
July 1547 asserted justification by faith alone, leading Bishop Gardiner
to prefer prison to compliance. The injunctions issued on the same day
intended the 'suppression of idolatry and superstition'. Not only were
images themselves to be destroyed but even the '*memory*' of them was
to be obliterated. Could memories be erased as easily as walls could be
whitewashed? Now praying upon rosaries was forbidden, and no
candles were to be lit before images, but only upon the high altar, before
the sacrament. It was an altercation between a Devon gentleman and an
old woman whom he found praying still upon her rosary which provoked the rising of the parishioners in St Mary Clyst in Devon in June
1549. In December 1547 chantries and religious guilds had finally been

outlawed, not, as under Henry VIII's legislation of 7 December 1545, upon grounds of economic exigency but through religious principle. If purgatory was not a place, if it was not found in scripture, if the dead were beyond the power of prayer, then what need was there for chantries? Yet the institutions were cast away before the belief that had sustained them was lost, and people lamented the loss of spiritual solace. The armies of morrow mass priests, Jesus mass priests and chantry priests, who had played a vital part in the life of the parishes, were now redundant. No one who suffered the trauma of the religious changes could doubt the reforming drive behind them.

It was characteristic of this regime to bring in starker changes under cover of moderation and traditionalism, and then, having offered reform, to attempt to suppress the diversity and licence which that reform had encouraged. So the very first Act of Edward's first Parliament was against revilers of the sacrament of the altar, and for communion to be received by all, laity as well as clergy, in the two kinds, of bread and wine. For lay people to receive the consecrated wine was a radical change. Such a change was likely to encourage the 'human and corrupt curiosity', speculation of the grossest kind, into the nature of Christ's presence in the sacrament, which the first part of that Act condemned. All the while Archbishop Cranmer was working towards presenting the people with a new understanding of the way in which they should worship their God.

Human corruption and mutability had perverted divine service, as it did every creation of man, observed Cranmer. The task he now set himself was to create, by drawing upon the great variety of rites and uses through England and from the Catholic tradition of Western Christendom, a single, uniform liturgy, in English. Following St Paul, Cranmer asked how the people could 'say Amen to that they understand not?' And Cranmer's intent was more ambitious still. The people must be brought to a proper understanding of their relationship with God in the central, most mysterious, sacrament: the Eucharist. Cranmer's private belief had been changing; not always in concert with the official orthodoxy which he, as Archbishop, must uphold. His conservative opponents taunted him for this ambiguity: 'What believe *you*, and how do *you* believe, my lord?' Bishop Bonner asked him. Cranmer would insist at his trial in 1555 that he had only ever held two beliefs regarding the Eucharist. He had moved away from the strict doctrine of transubstantiation during the 1530s and, after 1546, believed in the spiritual presence of Christ in the Eucharist. Now he intended to enshrine that belief in the new Order of Communion which was to be universally imposed from Whitsun 1549. Believing firmly that a propitiatory sacrifice had been offered once, and once only, by Christ on the Cross, Cranmer in his new rite sought to remove any implication that the priest was offering a propitiatory sacrifice of the body and blood of Christ, here really present in the form of bread and wine. The Mass was not now to be understood as a good work to remit the sins of those for whom it was offered, living and dead. Instead of a sacrifice, the Communion was a celebration, according to Gospel precept, 'a perpetual memory of that His precious death until His coming again'; a sacrifice instead of praise and thanksgiving. No one should doubt Christ's presence *in spirit* in the sacrament. To all who believe:

He hath left in those holy mysteries, as a pledge of His love, and a continual remembrance of the same, His own blessed body, and precious blood, for us to feed upon spiritually, to our endless comfort and consolation.

But the loss of the elevation at the sacring (the moment of greatest power and benediction), of the pax, of the sharing of holy bread; the obliteration of the great cycle of feast days dedicated to the celestial army of saints; the use of English instead of Latin; and the clear reforming impulse which lay behind the new rite, made the Book of Common Prayer an abomination to all of conservative mind. How many were of conservative mind is uncertain, but perhaps most of the population were, as Cranmer well knew. That the language of the services was so direct, so beautiful, so perfectly suited to the expression of things mysterious that it would last for centuries, could mean nothing at all to parishioners whom it left bereft and bewildered. In Yorkshire, Robert Parkyn, a conservative priest, angrily lamented the loss of the elevation of the elements, of 'adoration, or reservation in the pyx'. The pyx, containing the blessed sacrament reserved, hanging above the altar, had been the focus of popular eucharistic devotion. To many, the new service was blasphemous and absurd; 'a Yule lark', a 'Christmas game', and in various communities its imposition precipitated revolt. The Western rebels' tone was peremptory and vengeful:

We will have the sacrament hang over the high altar and there to be worshipped as it was wont to be, and they which will not thereto consent we will have them die like heretics against the holy Catholic faith.

Yet their rebellious energies were dissipated by a long and fruitless siege at Exeter, and their rising was brutally put down. Their priestly leaders were hanged in chains from the steeples of their churches. The spirit of revolt may have died in the South-West but not, surely, the spirit of inward resistance to the religious changes. The rising's overthrow could not be credited to the Protector's adept intervention, so his opponents in the Privy Council judged.

*

In the aftermath of the risings 'a most dangerous conspiracy' formed against the Protector. At Hampton Court at the beginning of October 1549, Somerset waited with the King, the Archbishop, a few counsellors, and an army of 'peasants' with pitch forks who had answered the call for a general array. In London the rival lords of the Council, led by the Earl of Warwick, waited with the City fathers. In Andover, Lord Russell and Sir William Herbert waited with the army which had suppressed the Western rebellion, fearing 'an universal calamity and thraldom' and hoping that 'no effusion of blood may follow'. Everyone was waiting to see which side would win the greater support, fearing reprisals against the losers.

War among the nobility, not seen since the Wars of the Roses a century before, seemed likely. On 6 October the London Lords, Somerset's rivals in Council, had ridden armed through the City with liveried bands of retainers. A year before Thomas Seymour had dreamed of raising 10,000 men, had imagined England divided into power blocks of 'noble men to countervail such other noble men', and had boasted of his own 'goodly manred' in the Marches of Wales. Now Somerset's tenants might have rallied to him from his estates in Wiltshire had not Russell and Herbert delayed in Hampshire with their troops to prevent them. At this moment of great insecurity an older world of lordship surfaced.

New forces in politics also now appeared. During the conspiracy to bring down the Protector, popular support was rallied in the name of the new religion. Somerset's cause was proclaimed by those who feared that his downfall would end both patronage for the poor and evangelical reform. Yet his supposed championship of the estate of poverty and of the Gospel might lose him as much support as it gained. Proclamations were issued accusing the Protector's enemies both of conservatism in religion and of oppressive social policies, but such was the confusion that rumours spread too that Somerset would restore the Mass. His ruthlessness in pursuit of power made anything seem possible. Hearing that the Lords sought 'his blood and his death', Somerset moved with the King to Windsor to be better defended. 'Me thinks I am in prison,' wrote Edward. So he was, for possession of his person was the key to power. By 9 October, when London's governors and Russell and Herbert declared for the London Lords, the prospect of civil war was averted. The King was safely handed over. Offered his life, though not his liberty, Somerset surrendered.

Who would rule instead? Behind the conspiracy there lay a group of politicians, conservative in religion, led by Thomas Wriothesley, Earl of Southampton, whom Somerset had ousted in 1547. Originally, the conspirators had planned to make the Lady Mary regent, with or without her collusion. But some evangelicals – among whom John Dudley, Earl of Warwick was one – had moved against Somerset partly to save their cause from his reckless egoism, and they were alarmed by any prospect of a conservative revanche with the Lady Mary as its figurehead. Any alliance between such subtle and deadly politicians as Dudley and Wriothesley would be fraught, and conspiracy did not end with Somerset's fall. Now Wriothesley, allied with the Earl of Arundel, conspired against the evangelicals. They determined that Somerset should die, and with him Warwick, whom they would implicate in Somerset's designs: they were 'traitors both and both worthy to die'. Early in January 1550 Warwick, knowing that his fate and Somerset's were bound together, struck before he was struck down. Laying his hand on his sword, he told Wriothesley: 'My lord, you seek his blood, and he that seeketh his blood would have mine also.' Wriothesley and Arundel were evicted from court.

Warwick's control of the court, his 'great friends around the King', placed there in mid October through Cranmer's influence, allowed him to prevent another conservative coup or any future attempt to abduct the King, and to save himself. Now he moved to purge his erstwhile conservative allies and to add his own supporters to the Council. Since it was safer to have enemies within, and to be vigilant, than to have enemies without, Somerset was allowed to return. Bishop Hooper had preached to Somerset in prison at Christmas 1549, urging him not to seek revenge, but in vain. Somerset's evident ambition to return to the principal place remained one of the gravest dangers to the new regime. Acute social distress was reason enough to fear insurrection, but more alarming still was the knowledge that the loyalty of the poor was to

Somerset, and if they rose again it would be in his name. As 1550 began, a court observer warned that 'by the divisions of the great the mad rage of the idle commoners is much provoked . . . so that this year to come is like to be worse than any was yet'.

*

One who knew John Dudley, Earl of Warwick well said that 'he had such a head that he seldom went about anything but he conceived first three or four purposes beforehand'. Past master of the double-cross and double bluff, he had learnt in the hard school of Henry's last years, but not even he could have foreseen the dangers of alliance with Wriothesley, nor his own subsequent betrayal of Wriothesley and its consequences. Having purged the conservatives in Council and repudiated Mary's regency, Warwick needed new allies and a way to prevent any Catholic resurgence which would threaten him. His new allies would be evangelicals, principally Archbishop Cranmer, whose influence over his royal godson was high. Warwick's source of power was the Council, of which he became Lord President, and the court, which from February 1550 he controlled as Great Master of the Royal Household, staffing the Privy Chamber with his own men, who guarded access and patrolled the precincts. He needed also the support of the King, who became more attached to the evangelical cause and more imperious as he grew older. Soon Warwick advanced evangelical reform with such commitment that he confounded contemporaries.

While the councillors fought for primacy during that winter of 1549 to 1550 the imprisoned Catholic Bishops Bonner and Gardiner had eagerly awaited their release. The reformers despaired, thinking that Christ had abandoned England. But on Christmas Day 1549 orders came for the destruction of all Catholic service books and for the enforcement of the Book of Common Prayer. The Lady Mary, thinking Warwick 'the most unstable man in England' and alarmed by the Council's moves to force her to renounce her religion, sought sanctuary with her Habsburg cousins. In May 1550 she prepared for escape by boat down an Essex creek to the Emperor's waiting ships on the coast. Mary's flight was foiled by a general watch for disorder in Essex. There were watches everywhere that spring, for this government lived in permanent terror of popular disturbance.

Tudor government rested upon consent and popular support, and Warwick's regime possessed neither. A general hostility grew against

Warwick and his followers. By January 1551 it was said that he governed 'absolutely' (which was not true), and that he was 'hated by the commons and more feared than loved by the rest' (which was). The social distress was palpable. As the effects of the debasement of the coinage bit more deeply, inflation compounded the penury caused by the appalling harvests of 1550 and 1551. The annual rate of inflation in London for 1549–51 was 21 per cent. The price of flour doubled, and the size of a halfpenny loaf of bread, the staple diet of the poor, shrank. In February 1551 the governors of St Bartholomew's hospital, seeing that the halfpenny loaf would no longer feed two men at a meal, increased the ration by half. The suffering looked for scapegoats. Though the Council was concerned with social justice, and sent out commissions to ensure the equitable provision of wheat, it won no credit for it. The attempts in the spring and summer to restore the coinage were sadly mismanaged and only brought rumours that the rich were profiting from the misery of the poor and that Warwick, in his greed and pride, was creating his own coinage, bearing the stamp of his own badge, the bear and ragged staff. Spring was the 'stirring time' when the people might rise. In the springs of 1549, 1550, 1552 and 1553 Parliament was dissolved and the lords and gentry were sent back to their localities to keep order. Warwick began to elevate powerful nobles to the Council: not only to secure their support but to keep their 'countries' quiet. These men, chosen as experienced military leaders, were licensed to retain fifty or a hundred horsemen and given strategic defensive commands.

So long as Warwick's regime remained so unpopular, Somerset's restoration to primacy was always looked for. Everyone murmured about it; Warwick dreaded it; but was Somerset working towards it? From the moment of his release he began to gather adherents and they laid plans to raise support in Parliament. Somerset saw his best hopes now in leading the leaderless conservatives. Rumour followed rumour: that Somerset would reverse the Edwardian reforms; that he would free Bishop Gardiner; that the Catholic Earls of Derby and Shrewsbury would raise the North. Rumour turned to reality when Somerset and Arundel conceived a plot to assassinate the Earls of Warwick and Northampton at the St George's Day feast on 23 April. The plot was uncovered, but so uncertain were the times that Warwick could not yet risk arresting his enemies.

The spring and summer of 1551 was a time of grave political instability and economic distress, of portents and prodigies. Most devastating of all was an epidemic of sweating sickness in July, an illness as sudden as it was deadly. Not until October did Warwick arrest Somerset. The treason charges against Somerset were framed, so Warwick confessed later, but Warwick's guilt does not exculpate Somerset, who was not innocent. Arundel's insistence that the plan to arrest Warwick and Northampton intended 'by the passion of God ... no harm to your bodies' was never credible. Somerset was brought before his fellow peers in December 1551 and condemned for felony, though not for treason. He went to the block on 22 January 1552. At Somerset's final fall the Council rewarded themselves with greater lands and grander titles. Warwick created the dukedom of Northumberland upon the confiscated Percy earldom and estates, and took it for himself; he planned the dismemberment of the palatinate bishopric of Durham; he assumed the Border office of Warden General. A territorial power base in the North-East was now his. The new resolution in November 1551 that the King could sign all bills passed under the Signet, for his personal commands, without counter-signature by a member of the Council was a way for Dudley, the new Duke of Northumberland, to use his influence over Edward to increase his own authority. Yet the King, bereft of two uncles, began to claim greater power. 'Many talked that the young King was now to be feared.' The most radical reformation yet in religion began, in part because Edward willed it.

The divine hand was seen to punish a faithless people in the spring of 1551; the faithlessness construed differently by conservatives and evangelicals. Those who lamented the loss of traditional ways of worship blamed the disasters upon heresy. That March Princess Mary defied her half-brother and his religious laws – 'her soul was God's and her faith she would not change' – and marked her defiance by riding to West-minster with a great retinue, each servant wearing a forbidden rosary. Her stand encouraged all those of like mind. But most who held to the old faith held it more covertly. In the first English novel, *Beware the Cat* (1553), Mouseslayer the cat tells of her adventures among flawed humans, of how her blind mistress recovered her lost sight as she gazed sightlessly upon the elevated Host at a secret Mass performed in her chamber by an outlawed priest. So should all cats summon that priest to say Mass for their blind kittens, said the feline councillor Pol-noir. Evangelicals, especially in London, enjoyed the joke, but not the reality, as they witnessed Catholics coming to worship the sacrament, even at St Paul's.

At the trial of the evangelical London preacher John Bradford in 1555, he remembered that 'the doctrine taught in King Edward's days was God's pure religion . . .' 'What religion mean you,' asked the Bishop of Durham, 'in King Edward's days? What year of his reign?' As the leaders of the new Church tried to make real their vision of a truly evangelical Church, they struggled to carry with them a whole people, most of whom were still hostile to it, and at the same time to defend it against their fellow reformers who, by setting their individual and unassailable consciences against the institutional Church, threatened to split English Protestantism. Archbishop Cranmer, with Nicholas Ridley, Bishop of London as his lieutenant, insisted that their evangelical revolution must proceed at a uniform pace, with order and discipline, with the authority of the Crown and the consent of Parliament. More restless spirits, like John Hooper and John Knox, came to see Cranmer's cautious policy of making haste slowly as a betrayal of the evangelical cause. In its theological intent, the Book of Common Prayer of 1549 had been radical: the offering of the eucharistic elements of the bread and wine to God in the Mass, their adoration and reservation, were no longer part of the rite of the English Church. Yet ambiguities remained which allowed priests still to counterfeit the Mass. In June 1550 Bishop Gardiner, Cranmer's adversary through two decades, succeeded in subverting Cranmer's masterpiece by saying that it would not offend his conscience to use the Book, and this because 'touching the truth of the very presence of Christ's body and blood in the sacrament, there was as much spoken in that book as might be desired'.

In the winter and spring of 1551–2 Cranmer advanced a triple programme of reform: the revision of canon law, the formulation of a doctrinal statement, and the rewriting of the Book of Common Prayer to save it from conservative sabotage and evangelical criticism. A new Act of Uniformity passed in April 1552 authorized a substantially revised Prayer Book in which the dramatic shape of the rite was altered in order to mark a break with the Church's tainted past. When the faithful received the elements of the bread and wine in the Lord's Supper they were now directed to think on Christ's sacrifice on the Cross, and the words of administration were profoundly changed: 'Take and eat this in remembrance that Christ died for thee, and feed on him in thy heart by faith, with thanksgiving . . .' Bread was still bread, wine still wine, and Christ's presence was spiritual. This Prayer Book brought to an end any possibility of officially praying for the dead, so destroying in the rite the old sense of communion between the dead and the living. Had all of Cranmer's schemes for reform been implemented, the new Church of England would have had parity with the Reformed Churches of Europe. But Northumberland, who had advanced the evangelical cause, now moved to wreck it.

In the spring of 1553 rumours spread that Edward was dying. There had been rumours before, but this time they were true. The Lady Mary was his heir. The prospect of her accession appalled Edward, who believed that she would restore the tyranny of Rome; it was more alarming still for Northumberland, who expected not only his own overthrow but also retribution. Together they determined to overturn Henry VIII's will and the Succession Act of 1544 and to disinherit Mary and Elizabeth. By a 'device' they perverted the succession; it was now to pass to the male descendants of Henry VIII's younger sister, Mary. But neither Mary's daughter, Frances, Duchess of Suffolk, nor her daughters had borne sons. At the very end of Edward's life, the succession was diverted further to the Duchess's daughter, Lady Jane Grey, who had in May married Northumberland's son, Guildford Dudley. Northumberland was kingmaker. When Edward died on 6 July his death was kept secret while the succession was secured. When a 'marvellous strange monster' was born that summer – girl twins joined at the waist, looking east and west – it seemed to many that this signified the two Queens Jane and Mary proclaimed at Edward's death. Which one would succeed? For any queen to rule was against nature, for women were to be governed, not to govern.

*

On 10 July 1553 Queen Jane was proclaimed in London, as the citizens looked on, grim and silent. The Duke of Northumberland seemed to hold all the resources of power. The Council had signed the letters patent which bestowed the crown on Lady Jane, who was married to his son; he had the dying King's blessing; the Archbishop of Canterbury, the Lord Chancellor, many of the court, the mayor and aldermen of London, and leading judges had, however unwillingly, given assent to Edward's 'device'; he controlled the capital, the Tower, the Great Seal, the navy and many troops. Yet, despite all this, Lady Mary was proclaimed queen in London on 19 July. Mary believed her triumph, the triumph of one excluded from the succession, the clearest sign of divine favour, and that belief marked all her purposes thereafter. What of the secondary causes?

A conciliar conspiracy had put Queen Jane on the throne; a popular rising deprived her of it. The revolt of the common people, usually condemned as the work of the Devil, was here believed to be divinely inspired for the preservation of the right: *Vox populi, vox Dei*, the voice of the people is the voice of God. Northumberland held power, but he lacked legitimacy. He also, crucially and inexplicably for so astute a politician, had allowed Mary her freedom. When warning reached Mary of Edward's imminent death she had fled Hunsdon in Hertfordshire for Kenninghall in Norfolk, where the local strength of her household lay, and then proceeded to Framlingham in Suffolk. The leading gentry and nobility of East Anglia, Buckinghamshire, Oxfordshire and the Thames Valley rallied to Mary. On 14 July Northumberland set out from London to arrest Mary, leaving behind a Council which was sworn to him, but whose loyalty faltered with its courage. The news that reached the councillors in their refuge and stronghold of the Tower terrified them. The people were rising for Mary. It was the 'country folk' who flocked to their 'rightful queen' at Kenninghall, and who protested against Lady Jane's proclamation at Ipswich; mariners mutinied against their captains and tenants refused to rise with their lords for Jane. Both Mary's supporters and Jane's prepared for battle. But by 19 July the Council in London, hearing of the universal desertions to Mary's cause, realized that the game was up. This was the only successful popular rising of the century.

Why did the people rise for Mary? Hatred of Northumberland and old suspicion of his motives were enough to discredit Jane, who was queen only by his 'enticement'. Outrage at the perversion of the true succession and fears of divine punishment against those who were cheating Mary of her right led many to oppose that injustice. But there was another cause. Queen Jane stood for reformed religion. On 12 July conciliar orders had come to sheriffs to gather troops against the bastard Mary who threatened the 'utter subversion of God's holy word'. Northumberland claimed that preservation of true religion was the first reason for altering the succession; 'God's cause ... hath been the original ground.' Mary's defiant attachment to the old faith was common knowledge. In July 1553, as partisans for both queens armed, people were faced with disturbing choices. Did conscience dictate a higher loyalty to a divine than to a secular power, a duty to a Catholic rather than a Protestant queen, and what did prudence direct? It was the Catholic gentry who rallied first to Mary's cause. Evangelicals joined her too, far less enthusiastically, motivated principally by legitimism, and bowing to the divine punishment they deserved for not living according to the Gospel when it had been freely given to them. The consequences for the gospellers should Mary succeed were hardly considered at the time, though even amid the loyalist rejoicings at her proclamation there were other voices which cried in the wilderness. Those consequences soon became clear. Upon hearing the news that the turncoat councillors had proclaimed her, Mary's first act was to order a crucifix to be set up in the chapel at Framlingham.

How should the new queen, triumphant yet precarious, rule? Whom should she trust? Mary was, as she ascended the throne at the age of thirty-seven, without any experience of government and innocent of formal political education, but years of deprivation and despair had taught her the first essential lesson: to trust no one at court. Her father had kept her away from her mother, Catherine of Aragon, and had even, in his fury, tried to have her condemned for treason when she refused, for a time, to submit to the Royal Supremacy and acknowledge her own bastardy. From her mother Mary had inherited her stubbornness, courage and Catholic piety; from her father – it waited to be seen. Like her half-brother Edward and half-sister Elizabeth, Mary had received the best humanist education: they had the intelligence and astuteness to benefit fully from it; whether Mary was similarly gifted was far less certain.

At her accession Mary pardoned her opponents, who were too many to condemn, except Northumberland and his closest adherents. Those whose loyalty had been most doubtful – like Sir William Paget, the 'master of practices', and the Earl of Pembroke – now made the greatest show of it, and returned to the Council, for their experience was needed. Into her household and Council Mary took also those East Anglian nobles and gentry who had brought her to the throne, whose devotion was as conspicuous as their inability to offer her politic advice. So inclusive was her Council that Paget sourly judged the government of England to be 'more like a republic' than a monarchy, but soon business was conducted by an inner circle consisting of Paget, Sir William Petre, Bishops Gardiner, Heath and Thirlby, the Earls of Arundel and Pembroke, the Marquess of Winchester and Sir Robert Rochester. Divisions among the councillors were bitter as they blamed each other for the past, resented the promotion of the loyal over the disloyal, envied each other's influence, and remembered old betrayals. How could Gardiner forget that Pembroke and Petre had interrogated him in prison only three years earlier? And there were seismic divisions over policy.

With the accession of a queen came a transformation in the nature of politics. At court, access to the monarch, in her private apartments, was allowed only to her ladies, whose influence with her was great. The queen's intimates, like Gertrude, Marchioness of Exeter and Susan Clarencius, had been trusted by her since the dark days of the 1530s. Men seeking influence with the queen, and information, now tried to 'fall a-talking' to them. And women, too, besought them: 'remember me', 'forget me not'. The Duchess of Northumberland made a desperate appeal to Lady Paget that she intercede with her husband and with Mistress Clarencius and the Marchioness 'in speaking for my husband's life'. Nothing could save Northumberland, who went to the block on 22 August, but they did their best for her sons. In the most secret conferences with Mary, Susan Clarencius was present, and Simon Renard wondered whether 'she knew the meaning of all this'. Renard, the Imperial ambassador, Mary trusted as 'her second father confessor'. She now looked for counsel where she had always looked before, to her cousin, Emperor Charles V, and would not act without his advice. From Cardinal Pole came uncompromising admonitions. Mary's first wish was to restore the Catholic religion of her childhood, to dismantle the Supremacy with which she was so unwillingly burdened, and to restore England to Rome. Each of her advisers offered different advice about when and how this should be achieved. But above all Mary sought divine guidance. She looked always towards the Holy Sacrament reserved in her chamber, and 'invoked it as her protector, guide and counsellor and still prayed with all her heart that it would come to her help'.

*

The Queen needed an heir, a Catholic heir, so she must marry. For herself, she said, she had embraced chastity, 'had never felt that which was called love', but she knew her duty. Whom to choose? Some urged an English husband, and chose Edward Courtenay, a victim of Henry VIII's rage against the Marquess of Exeter and his family, freed at last from the Tower but personally unstable. Yet how, asked Mary, could a queen marry a subject, and why should she be forced to marry a man because Gardiner had been his friend in prison? She listened now to Charles V. Since the first days of her reign, and before, he had planned for her to marry Prince Philip, his son. This would be Habsburg conquest of England by marriage.

No foreigner had been king of England since William the Conqueror, and 'the very name of stranger was odious', so the opponents of the Spanish marriage insisted. Marriage to a 'stranger' would outrage the people. England would by this marriage be 'marrying everlasting strife and danger from the French', who were already intriguing with the Scots and Irish. Since Philip was Mary's kinsman a papal dispensation was necessary: a prospect so objectionable that it must be kept secret, and secrecy brought its own dangers. Philip might promise to adapt to English ways, but no one would believe him, and the Spanish would be as hated in England as they were in Flanders. But Mary was adamant: she would die if she married Courtenay. She now loved Philip, she confessed, before ever she met him. To Gardiner's objection: 'And what will the people say?' she replied that it was not for him to prefer the people's will to hers. When the Speaker led a deputation from Parliament on 16 November to rehearse arguments against the Spanish marriage 'learnt in the school of the Bishop of Winchester [Gardiner]', she roundly rejected their petition. Gardiner's objections may have represented less a narrow patriotism than a politic way of securing the best terms for the marriage treaty; terms so favourable to England that Philip forswore them three times before witnesses, even while he swore them. The fears that 'heretics' would use the marriage as proof that the restoration of the old religion meant foreign domination, that papal tyranny and Spanish tyranny were all one, would not go away.

Conspirators, assassins and rebels were plotting against the Queen, so Renard warned. At the end of November in a nobleman's house in London, a *salon des refusés* of men once advanced by Edward but now out of favour, plans were laid for spring risings from four quarters of England. The Council got wind of the conspiracy. On 21 January Gardiner confronted Courtenay, whom the conspirators intended to play a part in their schemes, and he told all. The rumours which reached London that day that there was rebellion in Devon were false. Two days later a gentleman of Kent, waiting while his horse was shod, told the farrier that 'the Spaniards were coming into the realm with harness and hand-guns, and would make us Englishmen worse than enemies and viler'. And he urged him: 'If thou beest a good fellow, stir . . . all thy neighbours to rise against these strangers.' Only Kent rose. Under Sir Thomas Wyatt, the son of the late poet, and a coterie of Kentish gentry, rebel forces 3,000 strong marched upon London which, they believed, 'longed sore for their coming'. At Rochester Bridge a band of London Whitecoats sent to attack the rebels defected to their cause, and Wyatt's rebels entered Southwark peaceably. The Queen and the capital were beleaguered, threatened by rebels over the river but even more by the fear of an unknown number of rebel supporters within. Such was the terror that on 31 January Wyatt's partisans in the City were given free passage to join him before London Bridge was cut down. While the Queen's commanders played a waiting game, no one knew whether Wyatt would be resisted. 'By God's mother,' said Sir John Bridges to the Tower watch, 'I fear that there is some traitor abroad that they be suffered all this while.' Mary, showing a bravery and resolution lacking in her advisers, rallied the citizens at the Guildhall. The City's gates remained locked against Wyatt, his rising failed, and the quartered bodies of the rebels were hung from London's walls.

The conspirators had, so it seemed, intended no less than to assassinate Mary, enthrone the Lady Elizabeth, whom they would marry to Courtenay, and restore the evangelical religion. Conspiracies are by nature secret, but none more so than this one, for the rank and file of the rebels never knew the deeper schemes of the leaders. 'You may not so much as name religion,' said Wyatt; 'that will withdraw from us the hearts of many.' Had not Mary been enthroned six months before by a rising which had been, in part, in defence of the old faith? The rebels' declared purpose was to withstand the Spaniards. And yet, Wyatt allegedly admitted, 'we mind only the restitution of God's word'. Mary's judgement that the rebels' quarrel against strangers was 'but a Spanish cloak to cover their pretended purpose against our religion' was partly true. The conspirators were men who were excluded from influence, and thwarted, but they were excluded because they were evangelicals. Rebel actions reveal rebel motives. Wyatt offered freedom to all those who were imprisoned for religion. The prisoners chose to wait upon Providence, as did many others of the new faith who remained loyal to Mary while hating her religion, but later events would suggest that there were some who regretted not joining Wyatt when the chance was offered.

The revolt left an ominous legacy. This was a rebellion with an assassination plot at its heart; tyrannicide in the name of religion. No longer would 'evil counsellors' bear all the blame for a monarch's actions. Mary forgot the loyalty of her evangelical subjects, and concluded that all heresy was sedition; that all sedition came from heretics.

By thinking that all of the new faith were her opponents, she risked making them so. An effusion of rebel blood followed. First to die were Lady Jane Grey and her husband, Lord Guildford Dudley on 12 February; Lady Jane penitent for her unwilling treachery but resolute in her faith. The Queen never lost her suspicions of Elizabeth, whose complicity in the plots was hard to deny but harder to prove. Elizabeth was imprisoned first, ominously, in the Tower, and then kept under house arrest at Woodstock, where she scratched in a window with a diamond:

> Much suspected of me:
> Nothing proved can be.
> > Quoth Elizabeth, prisoner.

In Winchester on 25 July 1554 Gardiner celebrated the marriage of Mary to Philip, which he had been unable to prevent. He now presented himself as Philip's principal English counsellor, but it was Paget, Gardiner's rival, whom Philip most trusted. Where the Spaniards' presence was felt they were as unpopular as had been expected. Not a day passed without some 'knife work' at court between the English and Philip's Spanish entourage. The worst fears of the Spanish coming – that it augured the Inquisition – seemed to be realized that September when Bishop Bonner of London began a quest for heresy through his diocese. The attacks upon the Spanish, opposition to Philip's coronation, and continuing support for Elizabeth were the more bitter for Mary while she hoped against hope for a child. At the end of November 1554 came news of her pregnancy. 'How goeth my daughter's belly forward?' asked the anxious Emperor. But by March 1555 rumours were spreading that the baby was a phantom. As months passed, Mary bore no child, nor ever would. Mary's childlessness was a disaster not just for her, but for the Catholic future.

*

The Mass lay at the heart of the Catholic religion, Mary's religion. Forced for so long to hear Mass in secret herself, her first purpose as queen was to restore it. She wanted freedom for others to attend, not to force anyone: so she said, at first. The purpose of the papal legate, Cardinal Pole, was 'not to compel' but to 'call again': so he said, at first. But the world had changed. Now the Mass, instead of binding Christian society, threatened to divide it. For the gospellers, Christ spoke through His Word, not through a painted image or a white wafer; for them the

Mass was 'the idol of the altar', the papist 'god of bread'. In that spirit they had cast down the altars, the idols had fallen. Each religious side saw the other as sacrilegious, and the dogmatism of each drove the other to obduracy. Peace seemed impossible. The Queen 'felt so strongly on this matter of religion', she said, that 'she was hardly to be moved'.

To strengthen her conviction, there was the popular rejoicing at the restoration of the old faith. London women had rushed to kiss their newly-freed bishop in August 1553 and placed their treasured images in their windows as the Queen first passed through her capital. Out of hiding came all the sequestered votive relics of saints, the nails which had pierced Christ, splinters of the Holy Cross. Processions began again. 'To see it is to be in a new world.' The Latin Mass was sung in many places; not by royal command but spontaneously, 'of the people's devotion'. Not by royal command because the restoration of the Mass awaited the sanction of Parliament, for what Parliament had made only Parliament could unmake. Robert Parkyn, in Yorkshire, reported with approval the restoration of Catholic sacraments and ceremonies in the North in September, but noted the irregularity, and remembered that those of heretical opinions 'spake evil' of it. The legal form of service for the first months of Mary's reign remained the Edwardian Prayer Book. The bravest of the evangelical clergy and their parishioners continued to celebrate according to the new rite, while the conservatives watched and waited.

The Edwardian laws were repealed in October 1553, during the first session of Mary's first Parliament. Nearly a quarter of the Lower House voted against the change: a comfortingly small minority for pessimists expecting worse, but still alarming. The English Church now stood officially as it had in 1547: Catholic but schismatic. The Queen was shackled with the Supremacy of a schismatic Church. Could the English Church be reconciled to the universal Church? The Pope's appointment of Cardinal Pole as his legate in August 1553 signalled his commitment to absolve the errant nation, 'fled forth of Peter's ship'. Pole yearned to return home after twenty years of exile, and could forgive no equivocation or delay. Yet England was not as he had left it. The great lands and treasures of the Church which had been alienated to the laity stood in the way of papal absolution, for this was sacrilege. Pole warned of the divine judgement against Belshazzar, who had profaned the holy vessels of the Temple, but few listened. The despoliation had gone so far: the lands had been sold and sold again, the chalices turned into drinking cups, the vestments into worldly finery, and the new owners (mainly Catholics themselves) were markedly reluctant to cede them. The more politic – including Mary and the Pope – saw that there could be no restoration of papal authority without a dispensation to the possessors; without a bargain. The Pope conceded, to Pole's dismay. On 30 November 1554, amidst tears of joy, Pole solemnly absolved the realm. Finally, after many obstructions and delays, the Royal Supremacy was repealed on 3 January 1555. England was restored to Catholic Christendom.

Yet the old world of religious unity and obedience was broken. The converts to the new faith in the first revolutionary generation of reform had believed that they could transform religion and society. They had failed to create the godly commonwealth they sought – every hill was not yet Zion – but the Catholic doctrines they despised had been profoundly undermined. With each acquiescence to ideas and practices they resented, with every purchase of Church property, however small, every parishioner was gradually compromised, even contaminated, by the new religion, even if not converted to it. The habit of obedience to Rome, often faltering among the ambivalent English, was lost. The chains of prayers which bound the living to the waiting dead in purgatory had been broken; the supplications of the faithful to the saints in heaven for their intercession had been officially denied. If belief in purgatory and in the power to influence the fate of souls there had been lost, if the holy helpers had been forgotten, the consequences of the years of schism would be hard to negate. Traditional forms of Catholic worship – holy bread and holy water, palms on Palm Sunday, processions, creeping to the cross in deepest penitence on Good Friday, the 'burial' of the Host in the Easter sepulchre – might be revived; books could be reprinted and images restored; but could the beliefs which underlay them return?

Pole and the bishops moved to restore the churches preparatory to the proper celebration of the sacraments, and, in their turn, they destroyed. Scriptural texts painted by 'children of iniquity' were whitewashed, for they misled the faithful. Altars, windows and vestments were to be repaired and replaced. Resplendent roods, images of the crucified Saviour, must be erected in every parish – not makeshift paintings but proper sculptures – as a defiant affirmation to image-denying Protestants of the power of images as 'good books for the layman'. The Blessed Sacrament was reserved again in pyxes and tabernacles. Backsliding parishes were fined. Yet so thoroughgoing had been the previous seizure

NEW WORLDS, LOST WORLDS

of treasures from the Catholic past, and so venal the politicians in expropriating them for their own gain rather than for the common-wealth, that there was deep disillusion about the future security of any parish possessions. Enemies of the Marian Church accused its leaders of believing that physical restoration sufficed; 'setting up of six-foot roods' would 'make all cock-sure'. Yet they were mistaken.

Pole had been one of the most challenging reformers of the Catholic Church, and his vision of a regenerate Church in England was still that of an evangelical Catholic reformer. He carried others with him. Pole and the Marian bishops had deeper designs for Catholic reform than the recovery of what was past. They restored only in order to move forward. Pole's insistence was upon scripture, teaching and education, and upon improving the moral standards of the clergy. He had understood that there could be accommodation, charity, between the Catholic and Prot-estant reformers, who shared an evangelical emphasis upon scripture and a disapproval of the excesses of Catholic devotion. The leaders of the Marian Church laid far less stress upon priestly power and divinely ordained papal authority, and upon the cult of the Blessed Virgin and the saints, or pilgrimages, which had sustained Catholics in earlier times. Yet upon the seven sacraments they held firm, and upon the doctrine of transubstantiation, they were adamant. And Catholic writers, sharing a humanist background with evangelical Protestants, founded their understanding upon the literal interpretation of scripture.

Catholic renewal would come by reconciliation and education, they hoped. Their emphasis was upon unity, universalism, consensus and upon the charity within the community which had been so undermined. Without preaching there might be no doctrine, but there had been so much preaching, too much preaching. Pole distrusted the demagoguery of the Protestant evangelists, which he blamed for the breach of charity and for misleading the simple, and did not seek to emulate it. The first Jesuits had come to Ireland in 1542, but Pole was suspicious of these emissaries of the Pope. The religious renewal was entrusted to the parish clergy of England, yet they were often unworthy of their charge. The Marian clergy were tainted by their conformity – however unwilling – under Edward, and neither Catholics nor the gospellers could respect worldling priests who had changed religion with the regime. Lady Jane Grey condemned the mutability of her chaplain, who had seemed a 'lively member of Christ' but proved himself, by conforming, 'the deformed imp of the Devil'. And many others with him. In March 1554 priests, who had been permitted to marry by legislation passed in Edward's reign, were ordered to leave their wives. So they did, some seemingly without a backward glance, moving to serve in other parishes, wifeless but hardly celibate. People taught by their clergy to renounce Rome were now adjured by the same clergy to be obedient to it. Disrespect for the clergy was so manifest that, in the judgement of the Queen's chaplain, priests would fare better 'among the Turks and Saracens' than among heretics who mocked and despised them.

Pole thought that by patient pastoral teaching the schismatic past could be buried and forgotten; that heresy was an aberration which would pass. Yet he had not been in England to experience the evangelism and conversion, and he was wrong. Once the medieval heresy laws had been restored by Mary's third Parliament (12 December 1554–16 January 1555), after strenuous opposition and anxious delay, Pole, the bishops and the lay commissioners began to test the strength of evangelical conviction. What they discovered alarmed and depressed them. Maybe half the population was aged under twenty, and so had never known papal authority, only schism; anyone reaching the age of confirmation after the Edwardian changes had never received the Mass, only Communion according to the Book of Common Prayer. They had known no other religion than the one which they were first adjured, then forced to renounce. Innocent of heresy, for they had never fallen away from the Catholic faith, they might now be condemned for it.

*

As soon as the Mass was restored in December 1553 evangelicals were faced with agonizing choices. To receive was damnable, to 'drink of the whore's cup'; not to receive was to draw the attention of the persecutors, constantly vigilant for heresy. The letters which the evangelicals wrote to their ministers, now exiled or imprisoned, reveal the soul-searching. Could a faithful Christian worship outwardly one way, while believing inwardly another, and remain undefiled? Never. They must remember the endless suffering of the hypocrites in hell's fiery lake. Cranmer reminded Jane Wilkinson, an evangelical laywoman, that Christ had departed Samaria to avoid the malice of the scribes and Pharisees, and advised her to leave 'with speed, lest by your own folly you fall into the persecutors' hands'. She left, but Cranmer determined to stay behind to await trial for treason. Exile for conscience' sake was the only way to worship freely and keep the faith inviolate in Mary's reign, and over

800 left England. This was a 'painful peregrination', for the worldly risks and losses were great, even if the spiritual ones were greater for those who remained. From the Reformed cities of Germany and Switzerland, the exiles sent money and tracts to their brethren, and quarrelled among themselves. They thought always of home and the new Jerusalem they would build if ever they returned.

Evangelicals who could not conform and bear with the times chose to profess the Gospel in secret conventicles, always watched and always in danger. Spies were abroad to report their movements. Under persecution, they met by night in taverns and back rooms, in ships and barges, in the houses of powerful protectors. At the Saracen's Head in Islington, under cover of seeing a play, gospellers celebrated the Protestant Communion. The prospect of attending popish services, especially with neighbours jubilant because the old faith had been restored, was intolerable to them. Conscience prevented many receiving the Mass or participating in Catholic rites and processions. Even when they did attend, evangelicals marked their dissidence and disrespect by looking away at the elevation, keeping their hats on at the sacring, refusing to sing, and rejecting the *pax*, the sign of that peace within the Christian community which was now so manifestly lacking. All these evasions were taken as signs of heresy when the inquisitions began. In such dangerous times, while the 'prince of darkness . . . rageth against God's elect', many known gospellers quailed. In the way of things most chose domestic quiet and the peaceful obscurity of their farms and shops rather than the great sacrifices which resistance to the Marian Church required. In darker moments their leaders despaired: 'not a tenth part' remained constant, lamented John Bradford; the rest becoming 'mangy mongrels', 'popish Protestants' in order to save their skins. Yet Bishop Latimer was certain that though 'the wise men of the world can find shifts to avoid the cross . . . the simple servant of Christ doth look for no other but oppression in the world'. Christ had called the faithful to take up the cross of adversity and follow Him, and he had called some to special glory. These were the martyrs.

On 4 February 1555 John Rogers died at the stake, with heroic fortitude. His was the triumph of hope over fear, of the spirit over the flesh, for which the gospellers longed and which the Marian authorities dreaded. Nearly 300 followed him in the next three years to that point of absolute faith, never doubting the horror of the death, but never doubting God's promise either. Others died for their faith not in the fires, but in prison, chained, wretched, cold and starving. The burnings drew large crowds, some so inured to pain and barbarity that they bought cherries from the Kent fruiterers to eat as they watched. These crowds were divided and partisan. Catholics came to celebrate the deaths of heretics in the flames which prefigured eternal hellfire; the godly came to sing psalms, to offer consolation, to try – not always successfully – to shorten the agonies of the martyrs, and 'to learn the way', for some hoped for the courage to follow.

The martyrs died because Mary, Pole and the bishops believed that heresy must be extirpated lest it 'infect' more; because 'there is no kind of treason to be compared with theirs'. They died because some among the lay governors and the common people, hating their heresy, reported them, knowing the consequences. Above all they died because they would never recant. Their heresy was their adamant denial of the sacrifice of the Mass and of transubstantiation; their refusal to accept Christ's corporeal presence in the sacrament. Each martyr's death was a failure for the persecutors, who wanted them not to die but to be reconciled. Every way to win back the errant was tried: argument, persuasion, torture. The gospellers were examined again and again; adjured to remember their mother's tears, to think of their bereft children. As if they could forget them: 'Bring up my children and yours in the fear of God,' wrote Robert Smith to his wife, for then they would all be sure to meet at last 'in the everlasting kingdom of God, which I go unto'. The regime hoped for recantations, but knew that there was always the danger that some who had recanted, who had 'played Peter' and denied Christ might, like the Apostle, return to Him. When Cranmer, broken by solitude and doubt, recanted not once but six times, the authorities rejoiced, but at the last, at his martyrdom in Oxford in March 1556, he retracted his recantation, and thrust first into the flames the hand that had signed it.

The persecution was a waiting game: to try whether the zeal of the persecutors or the martyrs would fail first. So many were the martyrs' supporters at the burnings that curfews were ordered, and the burnings came to be secret, not public. The persecution would fail if it chose the wrong victims. The Queen had insisted that the people see 'them not to be condemned without just occasion', but the persecutors had hunted down those – like the young – who knew only heresy; or the simple and ignorant who hardly knew what was heresy and what was not. The time was past when Gardiner 'bent his bow to strike down the head deer', the leaders in Church and polity, for now they let the 'arch heretics' go, and left the most important Protestants alone. This moved the 'rude multitude to mutter'. An aversion developed to the persecution, less because of sympathy with the beliefs of the gospellers than because of the way it was conducted. The burnings at Smithfield were halted after June 1558, and the officers went less willingly about their dreadful work.

As Bishop Ridley prepared for martyrdom, he wrote bidding farewell to the citizens of London: 'I do doubt not but that in that great City there be many privy mourners', evangelicals who lamented the religious changes, but had nevertheless conformed. With time, the evangelicals' reconciliation with the Marian Church which they intended to be only outward and temporary, might have become genuine and permanent. Half a century later, Fulke Greville wrote slightingly of 'those cobwebs of reconversion in Queen Mary's days', but he had the advantage of hindsight. Many, perhaps most, in England had never wanted evangelical change, and had rejoiced at the Catholic restoration. People devoutly remembered the Virgin and the saints in their wills, trusting to their intercession. But not all the old ways returned. The belief that the living had a ceaseless duty towards the dead in purgatory was not easily abandoned, nor quickly, but by Mary's reign it had been profoundly undermined. The religious guilds which had linked dead and living brethren and been so enduring a part of religious and community life did not return to many parishes. Fear of future sequestration doubtless dissuaded many, but the reluctance went deeper. There had been changes, and there were signs that the evangelical understanding touched Catholics too. Some insisted, more overtly than before, that the Mass was an essential application of the merits of Christ's Passion: the symbol of that Passion here on earth. Wills written in the last years of Mary's reign reveal a spirit which helps to answer the perplexing question of how Christians of opposed convictions could worship together 'in charity', for some began to make religious bequests and to avow beliefs which juxtaposed the conventions and the spirit of Protestant and Catholic faiths. Awareness that those of the old faith and the new shared a common Saviour urged some peace between them.

Yet Catholics feared for the future. Mary's regime was fatally undermined, not so much by failings in policy, but by disasters beyond human control. The revocation of Pole's legatine commission by a pope who distrusted and disowned him demoralized not only the Cardinal but the Queen. The fall of Calais in January 1558 to the Duke of Guise was a momentous loss. But neither of these setbacks could compare with a devastating mortality crisis. The year 1558–9 experienced by far the worst mortality in the whole period 1541–1871. Mary's own death in November 1558 brought the quietus of the Catholic restoration, at least for a time, because the Lady Elizabeth was her heir.

*

The persecution for religion was conducted against a background of misery and despair; of famine and plague and war. Through the winter of 1555 it had rained as though without end. The harvest failed in the following year, leaving food in short supply and prohibitively expensive. Torrential rains came again in the autumn of 1556 and by the winter the situation was desperate. For want of corn, the poorest ate acorns. Unless wheat were cheaper by Easter, so William Cecil's agent wrote, 'many will die of hunger'. The poor did die 'for hunger in many places' in 1556, but demand for food fell, and for terrible reasons. According to grim natural precedent, dearth was followed by pestilence, and now disease not dearth was the killer. 'Hot burning fevers and other strange diseases' became epidemic. The agency which lay behind such agonies was no longer seen as mere policy, or the greed of a few: this was 'scarcity by the direct plague of God'. This affliction, worse than any known in the lifetime of those who suffered, was seen as divine punishment. The reasons for it only He knew, but Mary's enemies, especially those whose anger was inflamed by exile, discerned them. 'When were ever things so dear in England as in this time of the popish mass?' asked John Ponet, quondam Bishop of Winchester. Compounding the misery was the war with France which England had entered as a consequence of Mary's binding it to Spain, and which brought only huge expense and disgrace. One recourse in a time of such adversity was Christian resignation, but there was another.

In 1554 John Knox had sought the Swiss reformer Heinrich Bullinger's advice on the deeply troubling question: 'Whether obedience is to be rendered to a magistrate who enforces idolatry and condemns true religion?' By 1556 Knox had concluded that it was lawful for a true witness (not only the magistrate but also the people) to punish idolaters with death. There was, for the radicals, no greater idolater than Mary, the Jezebel of England. As they considered the limits of political obedience, other exiles concluded that the faithful, oppressed by a tyrant, an ungodly ruler whom they had brought upon themselves, had not only the right but the duty to resist, to depose. Asking 'Whether it be lawful to depose an evil governor and kill a tyrant?' John Ponet answered that it was. When a ruler 'goes about to betray and make away his country to foreigners' tyrannicide may be justified. Knox argued that the people must 'avoid that monster in nature and disorder amongst men which is the empire and government of a woman'. Mary and her Council had had cause for alarm. But not only was Mary a woman; so was her heir, Elizabeth. The voices of militant Protestantism would fall silent if the new queen proved to be an Old Testament heroine, like Deborah, who inspired the Israelites to defeat their enemy. Their arguments waited to be used if ever the same threats of tyranny and persecution overwhelmed England again, and could be adopted, too, in the wars between religions, by Catholic enemies of a Protestant queen.

7

'Perils many, great and imminent'

THE CHALLENGE OF SECURING PEACE, 1558–70

The reign of Elizabeth I began with a sense of uncertainty and danger which would rarely leave it. The fears which assailed her new subjects at the end of 1558 were shared by many of their European neighbours, for England did not stand alone. 'Invasion of strangers, civil dissensions, the doubtful disposition of the succeeding prince, were cast in every man's conceit as present peril,' wrote John Hayward, an early historian of the reign. Memories of Mary's rule cast a long shadow. People read fearfully the prognostications of Nostradamus for 1559. They chiefly concerned religion: 'There shall be difference of sects, alteration, murmuring against ceremonies, contentions, debate, process, feuds, noise, discord . . .' Anyone in Europe could have been thus prescient, and have applied those prophecies just as well to Scotland, France or the Low Countries, as to England. The world of the spirit and the world of politics were more dangerously entangled, and contention over incompatible doctrines of salvation engendered no less than a state of incipient war in Europe, from which England could only by supreme vigilance remain free.

Elizabeth gained her kingdom without having to fight for it, but never forgot the dangers which had lain in the way. In January 1559, leaving the Tower which once, as a prisoner in Mary's reign, she had thought never to leave except in her coffin, she thanked God for saving her as He had Daniel from the lions' den. By this Old Testament analogy she offered a deliberate promise to all those who waited for a Protestant princess to bring their own deliverance. As even her enemies admitted, Elizabeth had 'powers of enchantment', and as she passed through her capital to her coronation she displayed them. Mary had made no response to the pageants which had greeted her, but Elizabeth promised her new subjects a reign of mutual love and undying royal self-sacrifice. Londoners were jubilant. Just as they cast down the idols in their churches in iconoclastic riots and set up the knave of clubs instead of the reserved sacrament, they prepared to worship the secular cult of a painted queen. But London was not all England.

'Remember old King Henry VIII,' called out a man in the welcoming crowd. Elizabeth smiled. Her people waited to see in which ways she was her father's daughter. The new Queen promised to 'direct all my actions by good advice and counsel'. Would she keep that promise? Her high view of her own regality was soon apparent. 'I am but one body, naturally considered,' so she declared in her accession speech, 'though by [God's] permission a Body Politic to govern'; both a woman and the undying embodiment of the law and symbol of royal power. The 'politic life' of all her subjects rested in the life and authority of one woman. Some, like John Aylmer in 1559, assumed that the rule of a woman was tolerable because, in England, it would not be so much government by the Queen as government in her name, on her behalf. Yet this was to reckon without Elizabeth's vision of her imperial power and her determination to rule. Through more than forty years there would be a contest – sometimes dormant, often undeclared – between prerogative and counsel. The duty of her counsellors was to offer advice; the Queen did not necessarily see it as her duty to follow it. Counsellors were bound to preserve Queen and commonwealth, but the Queen could challenge their opinion of the best course for her people, and sometimes they had to risk upsetting her. In 1567 Elizabeth herself contrasted the authority of the prince with 'pleasing persuasions of common good'. The Queen, unlike her father, was not easily led.

With a new monarch came a new court and Council. Elizabeth swiftly dispatched many of Mary's Council. Even Paget was dispensable. Mary had chosen her bishops too well for them to serve, even to obey, a Protestant queen. Elizabeth's Privy Council was composed, at first, of laymen. A few great magnates, even those of suspect loyalty, stayed, a prince's 'natural counsellors', but her Council was far from baronial. Most were men trained to public life at the universities and Inns of Court. The veterans who remained from her sister's, her brother's, even her father's Councils, had deep political experience and, having had the politic wisdom to bow with every religious wind, they now urged caution. At Elizabeth's right hand from the first days of her reign until his own last days was William Cecil, her Principal Secretary. Evading prosecution for treason in 1549 and 1553, he had kept his head down during Mary's reign, even learning Spanish. Now, impelled not only by a deep sense of duty to the commonwealth but also by a commitment to advance godly religion, he devoted himself to counselling the young Queen, who did not share his providential view of politics.

Elizabeth determined to rule by love rather than by fear. Later, her godson, Sir John Harington, remembered that she used to say that 'her state did require her to command, what she knew her people would willingly do from their own love to her'. (Though he acknowledged also that 'where obedience lacked she left no doubtings whose daughter she was'.) A queen who wished to impose a kind of amorous servitude was reluctant to constrain her subjects' affection by making them pay fully the costs of government; even at war. The consequence would be a system of government undermined by financial expedients and fiscal weaknesses. Elizabeth and Cecil presided over a system of taxation which plunged into a decline which they, through inertia and neglect, did not arrest. The value of parliamentary taxation not only failed to keep up with inflation, because tax assessments remained static as government expenditure grew hugely in real terms; its money value depreciated because of tax evasion. A nationwide complicity among taxpayers to under-assess the value of their lands and goods and a failure in vigilance of local subsidy commissioners and assessors was lamented by Cecil, who was Lord Treasurer from 1572, even while he assessed his own income, unchangingly, at £133 6s 8d; a fraction of his real income of £4,000 per annum. Elsewhere in Europe, rulers were inventing new taxes to pay for war. Elizabeth resisted fiscal innovation, or even proper supervision. Major reform was needed, but the Queen preferred to survive by calculated parsimony, by economies in royal patronage and expenditure at court, and by the sale of royal offices and Crown lands. In these ways she lived in the short term and mortgaged the future.

Elizabeth's own history, her birth as the symbol of her father's great refusal of papal power, her survival of Protestant plots for her and Catholic plots against her, her commanding sense of her imperial monarchy and Royal Supremacy, led her away from Rome. Yet to lead her subjects with her was to risk papal anathema, rebellion at home, war in Ireland, even a French conquest. Whether she would take that risk was the first test of her new reign and one of profound consequence for, if England became Protestant again, she would stand alone against the great Catholic powers of Europe. Elizabeth had vitality, intelligence, a power to overawe and to command. Mary Tudor, lacking all those qualities but driven by devotion to the Church of Rome and to the

Habsburgs, had led unwaveringly where they led. Elizabeth had no such lodestars. Her very ability to perceive the myriad possible consequences of every course of action would often lead her to take none. Her reaction in moments of crisis would often be silent, or not so silent, prevarication and indecision. Her instinctive caution was at times a political virtue, but it frustrated her councillors, who were often overwhelmed by a sense of emergency and of the urgency of action.

In the first months of her reign, however, she took a huge and uncharacteristic gamble. As the reign began, religion must be settled before anything else could be. 'Wary consideration' was necessary, so the Lord Keeper, Sir Nicholas Bacon, declared in his opening speech to the Parliament which must effect a uniform order in religion, for the contrary dangers of 'idolatry, superstition, contempt and irreligion' threatened the commonwealth. Although the Queen's will to recover the Royal Supremacy was always clear, nothing else was. Would she restore the Protestant uniformity of Edward's reign; if so, according to which Prayer Book? Peering into the mysteries of the Queen's own religious preferences provided little guidance. On Christmas Day 1558 she had walked out of the royal chapel when the celebrant, against her commandment, elevated the Host. This was a cause of celebration for watchful Protestants, and of alarm for others. But what kind of Protestant kept a crucifix in her own chapel, against the Second Commandment, as the Queen did? Elizabeth defiantly kept this 'little silver cross of ill-omened origin', to the despair of the reformers, and replaced it even when Patch, her fool, inveigled by courtiers, destroyed it.

The inner counsels of the Queen and her advisers as her first Parliament met remain mysterious, but it seems as though Cecil, whose views were more radical than Elizabeth's, introduced bills to restore the Supremacy and to reintroduce Reformed worship according to the 1552 Book of Common Prayer. If that was Cecil's scheme, the House of Lords, dominated still by Mary's Catholic bishops and by conservative peers, crippled it. By Easter the reformers were suffering torments. Another way was devised. The third bill, which became the Act of Supremacy, named Elizabeth Supreme Governor, not Supreme Head, which placated both those who doubted whether a woman could lead the Church, and all those who believed that that honour was owed to Christ alone. The Act of Uniformity did return Edward's Prayer Book of 1552, little changed. That Prayer Book enshrined Protestant doctrines of faith, grace, works and the sacraments and, if it pleased many, it was anathema to uncompromising Protestants now returning from exile, for whom it made too many concessions to a popish past. And, of course, it horrified good Catholics.

The Act of Uniformity passed in the House of Lords by only three votes. A uniformity in religion for which none of the clergy had voted was imposed upon them. The clergy were bound to use the Book of Common Prayer, and the laity commanded to attend church on Sundays and holy days. Ever severer sanctions were imposed upon those who disobeyed. By law, every man and woman in every parish in England and Wales was to be at prayer, using the same Prayer Book, every Sunday. This was a uniformity easier to order than to impose. Nevertheless, in England this 'Church by law established' became the touchstone of stability; an inclusive Church which brought domestic peace and saved it, for the while, from its own religious wars. Yet England's schism brought other dangers. In the reign of Elizabeth's father, England had stood on the margin of Europe. Henry VIII had indulged his chivalric martial ambitions confident that the Catholic powers, embroiled in their own quarrels, would not retaliate. But through one terrifying year England had faced the prospect of a Catholic league against her. Now twenty years later, as Elizabeth led England away from Rome again and made England the leading Reformed nation, would another Catholic league assail her? Her watchful councillors believed so.

*

European wars were now fought for possession of souls as well as for lands and taxes; the struggle against oppression would be for religious as well as other liberties. The lines were being drawn between a perfervid missionary Calvinism and a newly dogmatic militant Catholicism. The General Council of the Church which had been held in the northern Italian city of Trent sat in its final session between 1561 and 1563. In the courts of Europe the nobility fought not for power alone but for the faith, Catholic or Reformed, and urged radical action in political circumstances in which neutrality grew harder to sustain. This was still a cold war, with all its attendant uncertainties. Protestant fears of a universal Catholic conspiracy grew after the Treaty of Cateau-Cambrésis of April 1559, which brought to an end the long war between the greatest Catholic powers, France and Spain (and, incidentally, gave England peace, but peace without glory, without Calais). This novel amity freed Henry II of France to plan his mission against heresy; not only to suppress the proliferating Calvinist churches in France but also, in time, to wage war against the Calvinists in Scotland, that quasi-French province.

In December 1557 five Scottish magnates had subscribed the first Band of the Lords of the Congregation, a bond – a contract of alliance – and religious covenant 'to strive in our Master's [Christ's] cause, even unto the death' in order to advance the Protestant cause in Scotland, then deadlocked and isolated. The accession of Elizabeth gave hope to Scotland's Protestants, but also ended any toleration for them. In May 1559 the Congregation of Christ Jesus, the religious and political community of Scotland's reformers, led by John Knox, newly returned from exile, promised the French Catholic Regent, Mary of Guise, that the threat to their religion would compel them 'to take the sword of just defence'. Here was a call to arms; incipient revolution. To the Pope, Henry II pledged religious war against the Scottish heretics. In truth, that war was not only against heresy, not only to protect the Stewart dynasty, whose Queen was newly married to the Dauphin of France, but also to pursue Mary Stewart's claim to the throne of England. Was not this a Catholic duty? A French invasion of Scotland threatened the return of 'strangers' to England, this time through the 'postern gate' in the North.

The sudden death of Henry II in July 1559, after a jousting lance pierced one of the eyes with which he had vowed to watch the heretic Anne du Bourg burn, removed the imminent prospect of a Catholic crusade. 'God shows Himself from heaven,' rejoiced John Calvin. Ominously, the dying Henry had commended his son the Dauphin to Philip II: a last request which the so-dutiful King of Spain never forgot and could later use to legitimize his interventions in the chaos of France in the name of religion. The death of Henry opened the way for civil war in France because the accession of the boy King Francis II turned the French court into a snakepit of noble feuds. The rival Catholic Guise faction and the House of Bourbon, patrons of Reformed religion, fought for control of Francis II and his second body, 'the body politic' of France. The dynastic ambitions of the Guises were limitless: claiming direct descent from Charlemagne, the Duke dreamt of the Crown, while his brother, the Cardinal of Lorraine, had designs on the papal throne. Their Catholicism was as fervent as their ambition, and their enemies claimed that these 'thugs of Antichrist' advanced their tyranny not only to capture the King but also to suppress the Reformed Church. In turn, the Catholics accused the French Protestant Huguenots of 'secret practices' and subversion. Since the Huguenots came to justify resistance to an ungodly prince in God's name, and to claim that legitimate resistance must be led by the 'magistrates', the princes of the blood, the accusations were just. The 'captive King' was married to a daughter and niece of the Guises, Mary, Queen of Scots. The royal pair were willing, if hapless, instruments in the Guises' designs. France, England's ancient enemy, became more inimical than ever as the Guises denied Elizabeth's right to the throne and sought to have her declared illegitimate by the papacy. Claiming a third kingdom, the young King and Queen quartered the arms of England with those of France and Scotland.

For Philip of Spain the cause of militant Catholicism was a matter of conscience before expediency. What no one could know in 1559, or later, was how many of the overwhelming resources in men or money of his world empire Philip would invest in the Catholic crusade, which was driven from Madrid and Rome. When Philip left Brussels in his Low Country domains in July 1559 it was for the last time. Thereafter, immured in his palaces around Madrid, he remained the overlord of a Spanish and Catholic empire, ruling, to the simmering resentment of his subject lands, in Castilian interests. Most resentful of all were his subjects in the Low Countries. Down the centuries these provinces had revolted to assert their ancient 'liberties' and privileges. They would be forced to do so again, but now they fought in defence of religious, as well as constitutional, freedoms. In 1559 Philip, adjured by the papacy, sought to impose new bishoprics through the Netherlands, in an attempt to undermine local autonomy and to combat heresy. Soon the Dutch began to sacrifice their blood and their purses in what came to be seen as a war against Catholic tyranny, and their cause would become the rallying point for the Protestants of Europe.

England was acutely vulnerable to any disturbance of the status quo in the Low Countries, for her trade and her safety depended upon those maritime provinces and that Channel seaboard. Economic blockade or even invasion remained fearful prospects. Fear of French control of the Netherlands had preoccupied England for centuries, but it was now Spanish domination which threatened. As Elizabeth's reign began, England and Spain were allies in their war with France. Philip, who had protected Elizabeth from enemies within England during Mary's reign, now protected her from external threats, including a papal interdict against her. Despite Spanish apprehension that England would revert to schism, the greater threat was of French conquest of England through Scotland and, by French control of the North Sea and the Channel, French encirclement and conquest in the Netherlands also. This was the nightmare which haunted Philip for years and which held Protestant England and Catholic Spain, for the while, in an ambivalent friendship.

English politics were often driven by events outside the realm as well as within, but Elizabeth found, in the loyalty of her subjects to causes outside the realm, a grave disloyalty to herself. As the struggle between the faiths came to assume cosmic proportions, the supranational obligations which their religious commitments often commended to her subjects might assert a more powerful claim. Most dangerous of all were the enemies within who might find a higher loyalty to enemies without. Any hostile power would patronize malcontents in a rival kingdom: support of a neighbouring kingdom's rebels might be cheaper and more effective than waging open war. The Queen of England was Queen of Ireland too, but from the first the allegiance of many of her Irish subjects lay elsewhere. In Edward's reign the Gaelic lords, led by O'Neill, had pledged their support to the French King with whom England was at war. 'Their quarrel was the maintenance of religion', the religion of their fathers, so at least they claimed, and in this quarrel 'they were determined either to stand or to die'. Under a Protestant queen they might well be in the vanguard of any Catholic conspiracy. Already in 1564 a papal agent was sent to fish in these troubled waters.

How would Catholics in England and Wales respond to the second break with Rome? Were they, as they repined and daydreamed of a lost world, waiting for better times or were they working for them? To these questions the most gloomy Protestants found stark answers. There began then that perennial fear among English Protestants of Catholic retribution and plot. In 1563 the House of Commons revealed a visceral hatred of a 'faction of heretics' within the realm; 'contentious and malicious papists' who 'lay in wait to advance some title under which they may renew their late unspeakable cruelty'. Memories of Mary's reign were vivid: 'their unkindness and cruelty we have tasted'. Although the Catholic people had, almost universally, unquestioningly answered the question of allegiance in favour of the Queen, not Rome, that commitment would be for a long time unknown, untested. The vision of a Catholic restoration was not fantastic, and the fear was that that restoration would come by force and terror. In a world where the religion of the prince was the religion of the people, the forcible reversal of religion could be accomplished by means only very few could contemplate. 'We see nothing to withstand their [the Catholics'] desire but only your life,' so the Commons prophesied alarmingly to Elizabeth. No one knew better than Elizabeth the peril to the monarch of an heir-presumptive of opposed religion, for that was what she had been under Mary. Now her own putative heir, by closest hereditary right, was the Catholic Mary, Queen of Scots. To her supporters, Mary was the rightful occupant of the English throne and Elizabeth a usurper. From that claim Mary never wavered. Mary's ambitions, Elizabeth's virgin state, and the unresolved succession created a permanent political crisis.

*

For Cecil and others in the Council, whose sense of Catholic conspiracy and threat governed their political thinking, England's security lay in the creation of a united and Protestant British Isles which could stand alone, ready to resist invaders. Divine providence had set the islands apart from the rest of the world by encircling seas, 'a little world by itself'. For God's purpose to be accomplished, England and Scotland must share their island in amity, ending their long wars, and Ireland must be peaceful and Protestant. Lessons had been learnt from Edward's reign, when the vision of an island defined and united by Protestant religion, sharing a language and culture, had been blighted by the aggressive means of its realization.

Cecil's constant study of the maps of the three kingdoms made him painfully aware of England's vulnerability. In Gough's map of Ireland of 1567 the proximity of Kintyre and Ulster was graphically clear; a strategic advantage if England and Scotland were allied, a source of danger if they were not. Ulster was the 'very foster mother' of all rebellions in Ireland and could be used as a bridgehead for invasion. Its coast, and that of Wales and the west of England, lay undefended. England's boundaries and priorities had changed with the loss of Calais which was, though no one knew it, permanent. England's southern border was now the sea. Where once England had a territory within France, now France had an enclave within the British Isles, for Mary of Guise was Regent of Scotland and her daughter, Mary, Queen of Scots, was Queen of France. The Guises looked to extend the power of France and of Rome in Scotland.

In the summer of 1559 the Lords of the Congregation rebelled and appealed in the name of religion to England, Scotland's old enemy, for aid against the French. If the Lords failed, the French army sent to put down their revolt might move south to put Mary Stewart on the English throne. Here was a moment of great danger; it was also a great opportunity, which would not come again, to forge a permanent alliance with Scotland. Both prospects were considered, in Cecil's memoranda to himself and before the Council, in the winter of 1559. By early December Cecil was convinced, and convincing his colleagues, that military intervention on behalf of the rebel Lords was vital. More difficult was to persuade the Queen, who was already averse to grand designs, to a foreign policy predicated upon religion. At first she rejected their advice. Yet faced with the immediacy of the threat, she saw the need for preventive war against France, while never accepting the religious and revolutionary claims of the Lords. In February 1560, in the Treaty of Berwick, England's claim to superiority and sovereignty over Scotland ostensibly forgotten, English aid was offered without strings. As an earnest of their mutual cooperation, it was agreed that the Earl of Argyll would help to reduce Ulster to obedience. The English army, besieging Leith, was defeated, but the English navy successfully blockaded the Firth of Forth and prevented the arrival of French reinforcements. The Treaty of Edinburgh of July 1560 ensured the departure of French troops from Scotland. The 'Auld Alliance' was broken, and the Lords, now governing in Edinburgh, completed the overthrow of the old religion. The remarkable chance for alliance between England and Scotland was disrupted by Mary's refusal to ratify a treaty she knew that she could not keep (she was not always to be so scrupulous), and by her return to Scotland. In August 1561 she came home, as a widow and dowager Queen of France, for her young husband, Francis II, had died the previous December. She returned to divide, not to rule. English hopes lay, for the while, not in a united Reformed Britain, but in a prospect of two cousin Queens reigning in harmony. This suited Elizabeth, who always gave primacy to a foreign policy founded upon dynastic principles.

As the proxy war against France in Scotland ended, Elizabeth and her Council contemplated a further confrontation. The beleaguered Huguenots (the name given, at first pejoratively, to French Calvinists) sought the aid of their fellow Protestants, and offered in return a port to replace Calais, a chance to avenge the defeat of 1558. The argument of the advocates of a 'forward' policy, who worked for the vigorous advancement of Protestantism at home and abroad, was, as it would be throughout Elizabeth's reign, that the safety of the Queen and her realm lay in defending fellow Protestants, for their overthrow would leave England open to her enemies. But Cecil, after his first and successful essay in intervention, now turned defensive, thinking first of the risk of engagement. The Queen, too, was cautious. At a moment of decision, in August 1563, Cecil wrote that she 'sticketh at the matter; one part desire to gain, on the other loath to venture'. But, tempted by the prize of Le Havre, she did venture. It was a costly mistake. Her troops withdrew, bringing the plague home with them. Calais was irretrievably lost.

Elizabeth was confirmed in her distrust of grand ventures in foreign policy. That she had ventured at all owed much to the persuasions of Lord Robert Dudley, the son of the late Duke of Northumberland. He was her friend from childhood, her companion in the Tower in a dark hour, and now her favourite. In November 1562 Dudley was sworn to her Council. Within that Council alignments between those, like Dudley, who urged a forward policy of aid to fellow Protestants, and those, like Cecil, who saw the risk before the opportunity, lasted the reign. Her Council usually worked harmoniously, with a common purpose, but there were differences over means, if not ends. Expressions of friendship might conceal ambivalence; the customary gifts to each other of game might not indicate a love feast. That the hold of Dudley over the unmarried Queen was more than that of councillor, more even than that of favourite, caused alarm.

*

Within days of the opening of her first Parliament the Lower House petitioned the 25-year-old Queen to marry. It had been and was her wish, she told them, never to marry; to remain in 'this kind of life in which I yet live'. If God did incline her 'heart to another kind of life' she would never marry against her subjects' interests: 'therefore put that clear out of your heads'. This reply, gentler and less gnomic than later responses to the same question, was still ambiguous enough for the Commons not to hear what they did not wish to know. She made them a promise that was unwise to make if she could not keep it: if she never married, an heir would be chosen 'in convenient time'. Tellingly, she told them: 'And in the end, this shall be for me sufficient that a marble stone shall declare that a queen having lived such a time lived and died a virgin.' Elizabeth's celebration as the Virgin Queen did not begin then, because no one believed what she told them.

Elizabeth may have been averse to marriage but she was not without suitors. The princes of Europe came to court her during the first years of her reign, and one by one they failed the tests set; two kings, two archdukes, five dukes, two earls, and some lesser mortals. The Queen flaunted her potential husbands, not through vanity (though that too), but as proof of what many doubted: her right to rule. Some of Elizabeth's suitors also courted Mary, Queen of Scots. These suitors were not like princes in a fairy tale: their courtships were unromantic, their persons usually unprepossessing. And in real life queenly beggars could not be choosers. Paget had been prescient: he saw in November 1558 that 'there was no one she could marry, outside the kingdom nor within it'. A foreign marriage meant 'carpet conquest' of England, as in Mary's reign; conquest by gallantry rather than valour, but with the same danger of loss of liberty. Marriage to a subject would bring jealousy among the nobility and small honour to the Queen; for these suitors brought little to the proposed unions except themselves. But marriage, any marriage, gave, at least, the inestimable promise of an heir of the body and averted the prospect of an 'invasion of strangers'.

First to propose to Elizabeth was Philip of Spain in January 1559, before Mary was two months dead. Declaring himself (though not to the Queen) a 'condemned man', he prepared to sacrifice himself in order to convert Elizabeth and to gain the kingdom to God's 'service and faith'. He came too late. Elizabeth rejected Philip's proposal just as the religious legislation made its fraught passage through the Lords, and anyway he had already betrothed himself to a Valois princess. Philip now advanced his preferred plan: for Elizabeth to marry an Austrian Habsburg archduke; it little mattered which one. Archduke Charles pressed his suit from May 1559 through the autumn and into the spring of 1560. Elizabeth did not discourage him. It was not that she thought of marrying him, but she needed Philip to protect her from France and from papal interdict. In September 1559 Duke John of Finland arrived in London to urge the suit of his brother, Eric of Sweden. This courtship cut more ice with London and the court, which benefited from Swedish largesse, than with the Queen. Eric was, at least, Protestant; still Elizabeth refused him.

There were English suitors too: Sir William Pickering, scholar, diplomat and ardent Protestant; and that ancient noble Henry Fitzalan, 12th Earl of Arundel, who had sulked and plotted through more than a decade and now sulked still upon his rejection. But to prosper, all her courtiers had to play the lover. The pretence of being in love with the Queen lay at the heart of Elizabethan politics. The Queen, in turn, employed all those changes of heart and mind, the favours given and withheld, of the mistress as a way to control her courtiers and councillors. Yet if the pretence of love turned to real love there would be trouble. Although their virgin Queen had from the first embraced a virgin state, she soon seemed set to abandon it, and disastrously.

Queens should not marry for love, but there were soon fears that Elizabeth would. Scornful rumours spread at foreign courts that Elizabeth would marry her horse-keeper: Dudley. The Queen was a mighty huntress (she could tell the age of a stag from its droppings), and her Master of the Horse became her constant companion. We may imagine the thrill of the chase and covert embraces in coverts: everyone did then. She could hardly have chosen worse. Dudley's blood was new, and that attainted. He could trace his family for only three generations, so the ancient nobles scoffed, and there was a traitor in every one. Those who had betrayed his father, the Duke of Northumberland, now feared the son's revenge; those who had served him looked for reward. Accomplished in all the arts of the courtier, Dudley was also, according to his enemies, 'a time server and respecter of his own advantages'. There was also the small matter of his being married already: to Amy Robsart, whom Elizabeth had excluded from court. The Queen waited only for her to die to marry Lord Robert, so Philip II heard in the spring of 1559. The crisis in Scotland turned the dutiful Queen's attention to that other body, the body politic, but from the summer of 1560 the romance was more fervent than ever. On 8 September Amy Robsart was discovered dead at the foot of a staircase, her neck broken. Was it suicide? Was it murder? Death by misadventure, the jury found. Others had darker suspicions. Dudley was 'in a dream'. Surely the Queen could not marry him now. Why she chose not to marry Dudley, and perhaps never to marry at all, was a mystery. For a Queen, as for any woman, marriage meant loss of power and freedom. Marriage must bring an end to the incessant courtship at court. Perhaps if she could not marry Dudley, she would not marry anyone. Her love for Dudley and her emotional dependence upon him continued until his death; their intimacy celibate enough but close. She never allowed him far from her side. Through the 1560s she watched the catastrophic, and deadly, romantic entanglements of her cousin of Scotland, and saw the consequences if a queen married for love.

The unresolved succession to the throne caused a pervasive dread, for in the Queen's mortality there lay a natural danger as grave as could be imagined. 'Oh, how wretched are we who cannot tell under what sovereign we are to live,' wrote Bishop Jewel in February 1562. Without a husband or children, without a successor named, the safety of the kingdom and the security of religion was vested in the Queen's own life. Her subjects always remembered that she would die, whereupon 'the realm were as good also to die'; religion would be altered, England would be there for the taking, prey to her enemies, within and without. Unless and until she named her successor, her heir by right of blood was Mary, Queen of Scots, who would be at the heart of any Catholic conspiracy. Reading chronicle histories, her subjects remembered how often in the past usurpation by force of arms had displaced legitimacy and disputed succession had led to civil war. Yet Elizabeth had a horror of naming her successor: this would expose her to the enmity of a rival; it would be to contemplate her 'winding sheet', her 'hearse'.

In January 1562 *The Tragedie of Gorboduc* was played before the Queen. This drama, written by Thomas Sackville and Thomas Norton, was a 'mirror to princes all', warning them to shun the vices in government it portrayed. As Gorboduc, ruler of a mythical 'Britain', abandoned his responsibilities, his realm lay open to invasion and the 'cruel flames' of 'civil fire'. Elizabeth saw enacted the 'tumults' which followed without 'certain limitation in the succession of the Crown'. Councillors were called upon in the play to ensure that the succession would continue in an unbroken course by 'undoubted right'. In Parliament in January 1563, a year after the performance of his play, Norton read the Commons' petition for limitation, or designation, of the succession. The Queen listened to her subjects' pleas for her to marry, or to name her successor, but she, at first politely then less politely, declined to do so.

In December 1562, while the Queen lay sick with smallpox, her councillors and subjects stared into a void. The prospect of a 'guideless realm', as portrayed in *Gorboduc*, seemed imminent. A month later Alexander Nowell, Dean of St Paul's, preached of the dangers which faced England, and defended Parliament's right to counsel and to act. At this moment of great uncertainty and danger, Cecil was forced not only to contemplate but to devise a strategy for governing England without a monarch. In the event of an interregnum, he now proposed, the realm would be governed by a 'Council of Estate' (a Privy Council), endorsed by statute, until Parliament could name a successor. This was the politics of desperation.

Nowell had preached of the dangers of religious war. By the end of 1564 Elizabethan governors were confirmed in their suspicion that most of those who were charged with implementing religious uniformity in the country were themselves at best indifferent, at worst hostile, to the Elizabethan settlement. An enquiry into the religious affiliations of Justices of the Peace revealed that 'scantly a third part was found fully assured to be trusted in the matter of religion'. If so many of its governors remained hostile to the new Church in England, the situation was worse in 'her land' of Ireland, where implementation of the religious settlement, easily passed in the Dublin Parliament in 1560, had scarcely begun.

*

Elizabeth never doubted the difficulties of governing Ireland. In March 1566 she wrote to her chief governor, Sir Henry Sidney, 'You are entered into that realm as a world . . . replenished with ravening beasts.' Yet even as she commended his desire to 'labour thoroughly in reformation thereof', she was reluctant to venture the men and money necessary to effect that reformation. 'You make mention of a very great sum to be expended,' she told Sidney, 'if there be not in the writing some mistaking, as it may be.' Her governors' complaints of her parsimony were perennial. Later, 'Black Tom', 10th Earl of Ormond, told Sir Francis Walsingham, Secretary of State that her service would go 'faster forward' if he could feed soldiers with air, and throw down castles with his breath. The Queen had twice denied him the necessary support, but he would 'sooner be committed a prisoner by the heels than to be thus dealt with again'. It was not only the despair of serving in Ireland against enemies who hid in woods and caves, or the misery of campaigning in midwinter, of living in cabins made of grass and boughs, of commanding mutinous troops against a hostile nobility, which brought Elizabeth's viceroys to despair, but the failure of the Queen to support them, and the whispering campaigns of their enemies at the English court.

The consuming obsession of Thomas Ratcliffe, Lord Fitzwalter, the 3rd Earl of Sussex and chief governor in Ireland between 1556 and 1564, was the destruction of Shane O'Neill. When Shane seized what his father had denied him – leadership of the O'Neills and his rightful place in Tyrone – his disobedience and his assertion of tanistry threatened to subvert English law and government throughout the island.

Conciliation with this Gaelic chief would mean disgrace, Sussex insisted, but Shane's defeat would break the Geraldine alliance and bring the Gaelic rebels of the midlands to order. Sussex's strategy prevailed in the English Council, and in 1560 he returned to Ireland with orders to subdue O'Neill. Three arduous campaigns failed as the elusive O'Neill retreated into his Tyrone fastnesses, and Sussex despaired. Yet it was not Shane O'Neill and military failure in Ireland which broke him but his enemies at court in England. Persuaded by Sussex that there was glory to be gained in Ireland, Robert Dudley determined that it must be his.

Rivalries and reverses at the English court increasingly unbalanced the 'knots and maintenances' which lay at the heart of the political order in Ireland. The great Irish feudatories, with their networks of underlords and Gaelic friends throughout the island, looked to the English chief governors for favour. But these viceroys, needing friends in Ireland, were caught in the great web of alliances themselves, even though they were meant to moderate between the factional rivals, and to be indifferent arbiters and impartial distributors of Crown patronage. Sussex was a steadfast supporter of Thomas Butler, Earl of Ormond, who accompanied him on all his campaigns against O'Neill. Alliance with the Butlers brought alliance with the Clanrickard Burkes of Galway and with their chief Gaelic ally Conor O'Brien, the embattled Earl of Thomond. But to be a friend of the Butlers was, as always, to be the enemy of the Geraldines. Ormond's enemies were Desmond's friends.

The power of the great feudal magnates – Kildare, Desmond, Ormond and Clanrickard – rested still upon their systems of protection and intimidation, and the force that they could muster to sustain them. Great private armies were essential in a world of deterrence and distraint, and no lord could disarm until and unless his rivals did likewise. Coyne and livery flourished as before and kept the people in misery. Fear held underlords in subjection and made tenants pay their rents. The threat of violence usually sufficed, and while the power of the lords was balanced there was no out-and-out war. Elizabeth at first turned a blind eye to the illegalities of her overmightiest Irish subjects, and pardoned even flagrant breaches of the peace, but the 1560s saw a descent into private warfare in Ireland, encouraged by the rivalries at her own court.

While Sussex aligned himself with Ormond, he denied Desmond favour, believing that the Geraldines would gradually be broken as their followers deserted them. So it was that as Desmond's political fortunes declined in the early 1560s, as his underlords withdrew the services they owed him and challenged his authority, he was increasingly driven to collect dues by distraint, and to the violence which led him so consistently into trouble with the Crown. Yet Sussex's vulnerability at court gave hope to the Geraldines. Throughout 1562 and 1563 Sussex's enemies, led by Dudley, sought ways to undermine and discredit him, and still Sussex lacked the victory against Shane O'Neill which might have saved him. Shane had visited the English court in January 1562, and had, wailing and prostrate, submitted himself, but soon he looked to the Pope and Mary, Queen of Scots as his sovereigns. Sussex was recalled in 1564. His successor was Sir Nicholas Arnold, one of Dudley's clients, and, in the way of things in Ireland, Arnold naturally turned to the enemies of his predecessor for support, to Gerald, 11th Earl of Kildare. But the revived favour towards the Geraldines inflamed their feud with the Butlers, with dangerous consequences. In Thomond in the far west there was war among the O'Briens as Desmond and Arnold supported Sir Donnell O'Brien in the bitter succession dispute, and Clanrickard came to the aid of Conor O'Brien, Earl of Thomond. In Munster, the feud between Desmond and Ormond became war. At the ford of Affane early in 1565 the vassal lords and Gaelic allies of the rival earls, bearing their banners, fought a private battle. Hundreds were killed and Desmond was taken Ormond's prisoner. Incensed, the Queen summoned both earls to her presence. Arnold had allowed feudal war and Gaelic rebellion, and he was powerless against Shane O'Neill, whose continued depredations in Tirconnell he had sought to conceal. In 1565 he was replaced by Sir Henry Sidney, Dudley's brother-in-law and client.

Sidney, like Sussex, had larger plans for reforming Ireland than the extinction of Shane O'Neill, but all other schemes – the extension of common law justice, the setting up of presidencies and provincial councils – waited upon O'Neill's submission, and Sidney's reputation would depend on the 'fortunes of the wars' against Shane. Sidney came to Ireland vowing to bring impartial justice, but found impartiality confounded by the factions between the feudatories, 'how indifferently so ever I shall deal'. He was consumed too by an awareness of the intrigues and insinuations of his enemies in England, Sussex and Norfolk, who plotted to discredit him and thereby his patron, Dudley, who had been created Earl of Leicester. The Queen, aware of the feuds, told him in 1565 that she could 'patch' but not 'heal' them. She urged friendship between Sidney and his brother-in-law Sussex, even as there was now friendship at court between the inimical rivals Leicester and Sussex. The Queen's anger against her overmighty feudatories and her Chief Governor's impolitic patronage moved her insistently to intervene. To 'Harry' she wrote an obscure letter – so secret that he must consign it to 'Vulcan's base keeping' (to the flames) – warning him to distinguish 'twixt tried just and false friends'; to reward Ormond, not to favour Desmond. She suspected '*leger de main*', seeing 'the balances held awry'. Still in August 1566 she wrote telling Sidney that he had 'entered into some great mist of darkness in judgement' in his dealings with Desmond. The Queen refused to appoint a president of Munster, which Sidney saw as the way to order; for Sidney's candidate, Sir Warham St Leger, showed, she said, 'an inward preferred friendship' to Desmond. Faction delayed reform in Ireland.

Sidney abandoned Desmond when the Earl, in his insecurity, turned to greater violence to assert his waning power. Sidney despaired, fearing that a new 'great confederacy of the Scot and Shane' portended disaster. Remember Calais, he warned in June 1566. Ireland could be lost also. O'Neill was in communication with Desmond, and under the protection of the Queen of Scots. The Earl of Argyll was now O'Neill's ally, not England's. Shane sought French aid to expel the English from Ireland and to defend the Catholic faith. But the desperate threat he posed to England was ended not by successful campaign, but by his assassination in June 1567, which Sidney had contrived. O'Neill's head was sent to Sidney as a trophy and a warning to others in Ireland who thought to disobey the Queen. Ulster was, for the while, quiet; so were Leinster, Meath and the Pale. Rebellion now came from another quarter. Sidney had warned in September 1566 that rebellion in Desmond's lordship was inevitable. Yet, so the Queen charged him as revolt convulsed Munster in the summer of 1569, his foreseeing it had not prevented it.

Desmond's continued violence had led Elizabeth to order his arrest in April 1567. The seven years of imprisonment which followed brought disaster for the Desmond lordship as his vassals deserted him and his tenants forgot their rents. Desmond's patrimony was despoiled, his authority eclipsed and bankruptcy loomed. Into this void stepped James Fitzmaurice Fitzgerald, appointed captain-general of the Desmond Geraldines in the Earl's absence. His grudges against the English government were as deep as the Earl's, and he found remedies more radical. In the new world of English settlement and government, as fledgling colonies were founded in Munster, men like Fitzmaurice who lived by the sword saw no prospects, only expropriation. Calling upon the old Geraldine allies to protect their country and their inheritance and reverse their humiliating subjection, and summoning the Desmond kerns and galloglasses, he assailed the newly settled English in Munster with great ferocity. Gaelic lords of Munster – O'Sullivan Mór, O'Sullivan Beare and O'Keeffe – joined the rebellion. Donal MacCarthy Mór abandoned his new English title of Clancar and his shallow allegiance. Even their inveterate enemies saw a greater threat from England than from the Geraldines, and by the end of 1569 the brothers of the Earl of Ormond were bound fast to Fitzmaurice. With the Butlers came their allies in the west – Clanrickard and Thomond – to join the confederacy. Ormond, 'my professed foe,' wrote Sidney, 'with whispering, did bitterly backbite me, saying that his brethren were driven by my cruelty to rebel.'

The English threat to the traditional society of Munster was easily and dangerously asociated with a Protestant assault on the old faith. Fitzmaurice presented the rebel cause as no less than a holy war, and in the name of the Catholic faith sought the aid of the Pope and the King of Spain against a heretic queen. The rebels, who had risen to resist English schemes to confiscate and plant in Munster, destroyed the newly planted colony of Sir Warham St Leger and Richard Grenville near Cork. It seemed as though all Munster might be lost. Humphrey Gilbert, a Devon gentleman, appointed Colonel of Munster in October 1569, his first military command, waged a campaign of ruthless devastation and exemplary violence. Irish lords who came to submit were marched through a corridor of severed heads. Gilbert argued, as others did later, for extremity and extension of the prerogative in 'cases of necessity', and urged the Machiavellian doctrine that newly conquered nations would yield not 'for love but rather for fear'.

In 1566 Sidney had seen English rule in Ireland at a crossroads. The Queen might bring the people to the just rule of the common law or she could 'banish them quite'. But if she intended to extirpate O'Neill 'so as there shall never be O'Neill more', and to 'unpeople the soil', she might succeed but, so he advised, she should remember that no Irishman would then feel safe, and that this policy would involve prodigious expense.

*

Early in 1569 Cecil composed a memorandum on the state of the realm, foreseeing great danger: 'perils many, great and imminent'. For a decade the preoccupations of England's Catholic neighbours had saved her, but that security was now threatened as Spain turned away from the Turks in the Mediterranean to look north, and the French Crown seemed set to prevail against the Huguenot rebels. England's fellow Protestants in Europe were 'brought to worldly desperation'. News had travelled of the ominous meeting at Bayonne, on the frontiers of France and Spain, in June 1565 between Philip II's militant councillor Fernando Alvarez de Toledo y Pimentel, 3rd Duke of Alva, and the Regent of France, Catherine de Medici. Alva's intent was extreme: the military extermination of Protestantism. Catherine was more moderate; she could hardly be less so. Since 1567 Alva had been attempting to pacify revolt in the Netherlands by sword and fire; his Council of Troubles persecuted heretics and rebels in their hundreds. The rebel leaders Counts Egmont and Horn, were executed in June 1568, and in July Louis of Nassau's forces were obliterated at Jemmingen. This disaster made Elizabeth listen to those who feared for England's safety 'if the planets keep this course'. In March 1569 the Huguenots lost their Prince, Louis de Condé, at the rout of Jarnac. These successes for the Catholic powers freed them to unite to restore the 'absolute tyranny of Rome'; even to place Mary Stewart on Elizabeth's throne. Against this threat, England, without allies, had little recourse. Yet if England's Protestants were gloomy, they were also resolute. Now was the time for a defensive alliance amongst the beleaguered Protestants of Europe. To sustain the cause of the true religion was not only a matter of duty, but would avert present dangers for England. 'What shall become of us, when the like professors with us shall be utterly destroyed in Flanders and France?' How could England stand by and watch? asked Sir Nicholas Throckmorton. Yet, for Cecil, the encouragement must be politic, secret, and short of war, not least because the Queen was not moved by religious enthusiasm and never wished to aid rebels against other monarchs.

In 1565 Elizabeth had refused to send aid to the Protestant Lord James Stewart, who had raised rebellion against his half-sister, the Queen of Scots. She would, she insisted, never maintain a subject in disobedience to his prince. Yet her own principal rebel, Shane O'Neill, was from 1565 under the protection of the Queen of Scots, whom he intended to proclaim Queen of Ireland. In Scotland Mary's misrule, personal and political, brought chaos and disintegration. Her marriage in July 1565 to Henry, Lord Darnley provoked opponents of her regime and her religion to sign the 'band of the nobility'. In England that September the Council debated military intervention in Scotland. Fear of war in Ireland was one reason to draw back, but England's abandonment of Lord James Stewart's cause alienated the Earl of Argyll whose 'double dealing' sustained Elizabeth's rebels in Ulster. No just cause was found to intervene in Scotland, and an uneasy amity held. In June 1566 the birth of a prince to Mary perpetuated the Stewart claim, while Elizabeth allowed the second session of her second Parliament no hope that the Tudor line would continue. While Elizabeth resolutely remained unmarried, her sister Queen burned to marry the Earl of Bothwell. Darnley stood in the way, but not for long. In February 1567 he was found murdered. Mary, suspected of complicity in the murder, and now married to the alleged murderer (acquitted by a court packed with his followers), was forced to abandon her son and her realm. The fall of the Queen of Scots was, said Sir Walter Mildmay, a 'marvellous tragedy', but it was what befell 'such as live not in the fear of God'.

In May 1568 Mary Stewart fled Scotland, defeated and deposed, and sought refuge in England. She appealed to her fellow sovereign and cousin for aid to restore her to her kingdom. So shocked was Elizabeth by the violence, and by the violation of the right of a sovereign which no subject could challenge, that she was tempted to try and restore Mary unconditionally to her realm and to subdue the rebel lords who had forced the abdication. In the Council, Mary's opponents saw her flight to England as an opportunity to sequester this most dangerous enemy in a safe oblivion. Yet the Queen and her advisers found no answer to the problem posed by the cuckoo royal visitor. So compromised was Mary that Elizabeth could neither aid her nor receive her; neither restore her, nor allow her her freedom. Whether in England or in Scotland or in France, Mary posed a perpetual menace, for she always pressed her claim to the English throne, and sought by any means to free herself from a protection which became captivity. Elizabeth agreed that the charges which had brought Mary to her forced abdication should be tested before a commission of leading English and Scottish nobles, although it was doubtful in law how to proceed against a queen who was subject to none in her own country and not bound by the law of another, nor bound to answer. The commission sat between October and December at York and Westminster. Uncertain whether it could pass judgement upon her, or what would follow if it did, the Scottish regent, the Earl of Moray, hesitated to produce the most damning evidence against Mary; the 'casket letters' – partly forged but partly genuine – which showed her complicity in her lover's plot to murder her husband. The case against her neither proved nor disproved, Mary was disgraced.

The Scottish Queen was now sequestered in the heart of England indefinitely. But she was not forgotten, nor forgetting. Desperate for her release, never wavering in her claim to the English throne, she became practised in conspiracy, finding friends wherever she could. As Queen of Scotland she had not sought to reverse the Reformation, contenting herself with being the only Catholic allowed to hear Mass, but as captive Queen in England she presented herself as 'the fairest daughter of the Pope'. She looked to Spain and France and the papacy for aid, and fatefully to her fellow Catholics in England. In the North, the hearts of the nobility had leapt at news of her arrival. Court and Council were divided between those, like Cecil, who thought she must be shunned, and a larger number who thought that, since Elizabeth had vowed never to marry, they must look to the future. One way to tame Mary was to marry her safely. This was the dynastic solution to Anglo-Scottish relations, which Elizabeth favoured. In 1564 she had even proposed that Mary should marry Leicester. In October 1568, as Thomas Howard, 4th Duke of Norfolk rode out hawking with William Maitland of Lethington, Mary's secretary and the 'Michael Wylie' [Machiavelli] of Scottish politics, they talked of a marriage between Mary and the Duke. This was not treason, or not yet.

After a decade England's fragile friendship with Spain was faltering. The alarm caused by Alva's campaign of blood and iron was heightened by lurid accounts brought by fugitives from his persecution. Both England and Spain now sent each other ambassadors who could only worsen relations between them: an uncompromising Protestant to Madrid, a fervent Catholic to London. In the Spanish Indies the viceroy of Mexico's fleet engaged John Hawkins's privateers, and reports of the disaster and news of English losses came slowly home. In the Narrow Seas, privateers bearing letters of marque from the Huguenot princes and William of Orange marauded freely in the name of holy war. Into stormy weather and this threat of pirates sailed a hapless flotilla of Spanish ships in November 1568, seeking shelter in West Country ports. The ships carried bullion from Genoese bankers to pay Alva's troops. Elizabeth granted her protection to the convoys, but Cecil had other plans: the Queen must take the money herself. In swift retaliation, Alva seized English property and subjects in the Low Countries, and in turn Spaniards in England, including de Spes the ambassador, were arrested and their goods sequestered. Here was a diplomatic crisis which portended worse. Cold war turned tepid.

For this terrifying provocation which had brought England and the greatest power in Europe to the brink of war, Cecil was rightly blamed. He had listened to those who saw a chance to diminish Spain and aid fellow Protestants in their distress, but he took an unwarranted risk. If the spring of 1569 was a turning point for England, so it was for Cecil as his enemies conspired with the aim of overthrowing him. To ambassadors observing the political scene, this was a move by the ancient Catholic nobility against the heretic upstarts who had usurped counsel. They were partly right, and in this contest the year would see great losses for the nobility, and Cecil secure.

Norfolk's plan to marry Mary, Queen of Scots was not treason, but it was conspiracy, for it was secret from the Queen. In his lonely eminence as England's only duke, prince of East Anglia, Norfolk could hardly be greater, but he would not be less. He thought now to be consort to a queen; not because as a Protestant he thought Scotland worth a Mass but, he said, to rescue Mary from some 'papist prince'. With Leicester and Pembroke as brokers for the match, and Mary urging him to protect her, he had by the summer of 1569 gone too far in honour to turn back. Not until September did Elizabeth hear of the proposed marriage from the 'women of the court who', according to William Camden, 'do quickly smell out love-matters', and from the belated confession of Leicester 'with sighs and tears'. She forgave her favourite, but warned Mary to beware lest those on whom she most depended 'hop without heads'. Was it then that Elizabeth wrote her poem?

> The doubt of future foes exiles my present joy . . .
> My rusty sword through rest shall first his edge employ
> To pull their tops that seeks such change or gape for future joy.

As Norfolk's noble allies deserted him he left court without leave; an act of rash defiance. He bolted to the Howard estate in Norfolk, where the gentry rallied to him, and where he was armed and unassailable. But summoned to London, his nerve broke, and he returned and found himself by October where he most dreaded being, the Tower.

Norfolk had believed that he had 'friends enough' if it came to an 'open quarrel' with the Queen. Who were the friends; what the quarrel? The quarrel was in part to settle the unsettled succession. His friends were among the ancient nobility who were determined to restore their lost power and (to them) rightful pre-eminence. Some of these friends – Lord Lumley, the Earls of Arundel and Pembroke – were placed under close arrest. But Norfolk's great hopes lay with the nobility of the North. Mary, too, believed that the great northern lords – the Earls of Northumberland, Westmorland, Derby, Shrewsbury and Cumberland – would rally to her cause, for they were 'of the old religion'. Mary Tudor had restored the titles and lands of Thomas Percy, 7th Earl of Northumberland, but the pre-eminence of the ancient houses of Percy and Neville had been abruptly lost under Elizabeth, who doubted their loyalty. Their ancient blood slighted, their revenues diminished, their rightful offices given to southerners, they waited their time. As Norfolk rode back to London in October 1569, he sent warning to the Earls of Northumberland and Westmorland not to rise. His defection, the news that their friends at court 'fell from them and gave them over', precipitated a rebellion that arose out of desperation and which could only fail.

Forlorn and isolated, the Earls had heeded extreme counsels. They claimed to be rising in the name of the old faith. Northumberland had been reconciled to Rome in 1567, and was convinced that the Queen, as a heretic, had forfeited her dominion. As before in 1536, the rebels marched behind banners of the five wounds of Christ, but no longer behind the banner of St Cuthbert, because the wife of the Calvinist Dean of Durham had burnt that banner which legend had told was indestructible by fire. The rebels destroyed the Book of Common Prayer when they found it in the churches on their route, and set up altars instead of Communion tables, but this was often by the Earls' command, not of their followers' own enthusiasm. The rebels rallying to the Earls may have been inspired as much by traditional deference and, in truth, by offers of money as by traditional faith. In the brutal aftermath of the revolt hundreds of tenants paid with their lives for their loyalty to their lords. Few now would rally to so lost a cause, and most of the nobility and gentry of the North sent troops to the Crown rather than against it. In its failure, the rising swept away the great families: the last Nevilles to perpetual exile as Spanish pensioners; the Percys to confinement in the South; the 3rd Earl of Cumberland to distant voyages or to become a 'carpet knight' of the tournaments. Their lands were confiscated; their clientage leaderless. Though no one knew it, the Borders would never again rise in feudal array.

The rebellion of the northern earls was fateful for all English Catholics. When so few had answered the call to rise for the old faith, it seemed certain that if the Catholic Church were to be restored to England, it would not be by rebellion. Yet the crisis of 1569–70 transformed all those who thought of themselves as Catholics into potential enemies of the realm: traitors within. For a decade the Catholics had been quiescent, and had posed no danger. There had been no persecution, few tests of faith. This queen, who desired no windows into her own soul nor into those of others, expected the passage of time to atrophy the traditional faith. She believed that the Catholic Church militant existed only outside her kingdom, despite the warnings of her counsellors and jeremiads from her House of Commons. If Catholics prayed outwardly in the Church of England (even if praying inwardly against it) there was no secular penalty. Attendance at church, with whatever reservations, was the minimum, minimal, test of obedience to the Supreme Governor, and through the 1560s most Catholics passed it. Without the spiritual leadership of the Marian bishops, who had all, bar one, been deprived of their office, and who remained in prison; without lay leadership until the arrival of Mary, Queen of Scots; without martyrs to stiffen their resolve, most English Catholics conformed, and became thereby schismatic from Rome. Whether they partook of Communion – a heretic rite – is much less certain. If and when they asked the Pope, distant in Rome, whether attendance was permissible for a Catholic, the answer was unequivocal: no matter what the danger, it was not. But most did not ask and chose not to know. For a decade the papacy had been strangely silent. Then in 1570 Pius V issued a bull of momentous consequence. *Regnans in excelsis* declared the heretic Elizabeth to be no queen, and commanded all her Catholic subjects to withdraw their allegiance. Would they now disobey her and call Mary, Queen of Scots their rightful queen?

Memories of the rising of 1569 were a long time fading. An almost atavistic fear grew among English Protestants of Catholic retribution and plot. Sometimes the plots were chimerical, but not the one which 'God by His providence' revealed in 1571. Among a half-world of spies and papal agents, Cecil uncovered a conspiracy orchestrated by Robert Ridolfi, a Florentine banker and papal agent in England. With papal money and Spanish troops and the help of 'friends in England', Mary Stewart was to be placed on the English throne. Letters in cipher had been directed to the great lords '30' and '40'. '40' was the Duke of Norfolk, who had never abandoned his communications with Mary Stewart, nor retreated from his promise of marriage and had sent money to the Marian party in Scotland. Like his father, the Earl of Surrey, and his great-grandfather, the Duke of Buckingham, he had stood too close to the throne and must suffer for it. Tried by his peers for treason, the guilty verdict was inescapable. Norfolk was condemned in January 1572. The Queen, paralysed between her princely duties of clemency and justice, ordered stay after stay of execution, and Norfolk lived on between hope and fear in the Tower. As so often in a personal monarchy, private decisions and indecisions brought public danger. The Queen was bountiful with what was not hers to give: her subjects' safety.

Parliament, summoned so rarely and reluctantly in Elizabeth's reign, was called in May 1572 to meet the emergency which the treason presented. This was an extraordinary meeting, summoned not for money but to provide for the Queen's safety. Both Houses called for 'Justice, justice'. Norfolk was sacrificed to these demands, but his death removed only the lesser danger. Unless and until the 'late Scottish Queen' were tried and condemned, Elizabeth might find her realm conquered and herself deposed. The double objection that as an 'absolute princess' she was subject to no law, and as a 'stranger' not bound by English law, was implacably rejected. Be she kin or no kin, stranger or citizen, justice must be done. She was Elizabeth's 'unnatural sister', and only the 'late Queen', for she was rightfully deposed. The language of politics became the language of religion. Mary was a 'serpent', a 'dragon'; images of Antichrist. There were ardent Protestant spirits in the Commons, but the bleakest warnings came not from radical laymen but from the lord bishops. The Old Testament gave examples enough of God's judgements upon princes who disobeyed His commandments to execute justice upon the wicked. 'Thy life shall be for his life, and thy people for his people.' If Elizabeth did not 'cut off' Mary, they said, she would lose her throne at the hands of God, and He would plague her people.

8

Wars of Religion

CHURCHES MILITANT IN ENGLAND, IRELAND AND EUROPE, 1570–84

England's Protestant godly never doubted that God was continually at work in His creation. Nothing happened in the world unless He willed it, for God was no 'momentary creator', sitting idly in heaven. So John Calvin had taught, and what Calvin and his fellow reformed theologians taught was the inspiration of the religion of most thinking Elizabethan Protestants. By God's providence, His 'secret counsel', He superintended and cherished all His creatures, 'even to a sparrow'. Had not Christ said that every hair on a man's head was numbered? What seemed to the unregenerate understanding to be pure chance was to the eye of faith the secret impulse of God. For the godly, there was no such thing as chance, no possibility of coincidence. To imagine otherwise was to doubt divine omnipotence. Christian believers should find in this never-failing Providence an assurance: certainty that Satan, the enemy, was curbed, and that they were not subject to arbitrary fortune. Helpless before divine grace, believers should submit themselves utterly to God and follow His commandments, knowing that no harm would befall them unless God willed it, and that adversity was sent for a purpose; to chasten, to correct, and to encourage faith. God's ways are not men's ways, His time not their time, and Providence was never calculable. God so often confounded human expectations. 'Victory,' Sir Francis Walsingham wrote to William Cecil (now Lord Burghley) in August 1571, 'is in the hands of God, who many times disposeth the same contrary to man's judgement.' Had not the God of the Israelites given victory to little David over Goliath? In ignorance of God's purposes for them, those of lively faith must exert themselves to do God's work, always seeking guidance through prayer, and subjecting every action to the tutelage of scripture. This was no quiescent faith: God helps those who help themselves.

God's absolute sovereignty over men extended not only through this world but the next. At the heart of Protestant divinity lay the doctrine of double predestination, absolute and immutable. 'Before the foundations of the world were laid', according to the Thirty-nine Articles of 1563, the confession of faith of the Church of England, God had decreed 'to deliver from curse and damnation those whom He had chosen in Christ out of mankind'. All the rest He passed by – so Calvin and all who followed him read in scripture – and these were ordained not to eternal life but, as 'vessels of wrath', to eternal damnation. Despite mankind's natural depravity after the Fall, God of His mercy had saved some, though in justice He might have damned all. Only God knew whom He had elected to salvation and whom He had damned. Once called, the elect believer could stumble but never finally fall from grace. In their studies, and in university lecture halls, learned divines debated the order of the divine decrees, asked whether God foreordained as well as foreknew; compelled men or allowed them freedom to choose. These debates were as old as Christian theology, but were conducted with a new urgency as the century wore on. Although these were questions too abstruse for most – certainly for all those sunk in rustic ignorance, the 'common sort of Christians' – preachers preached upon these great themes, and many read scripture with anxiety as well as devotion, and looked to their preachers as prophets.

To the godly, Christ's kingdom was not of this world. Yet, convinced of their election, they must live their lives in such a way as to vindicate God's choice. They were warned against the presumption of identifying themselves in this world as a band born to predestinate grace. The Bible disclosed that the division between the elect and the reprobate would not be made until the Last Day; until then sheep and goats must graze together. The faith of the godly was an evangelical one: all must be brought to the truth of God's Word and hear His promise, though not all who heard would receive it. That evangelical necessity grew more urgent with the sense that the Last Day approached.

Elizabethan Protestants saw the whole of history as a divinely predestined drama, with themselves living in the last act. They read in the Book of Revelation of the reign of Antichrist, Satan's last and deadliest agent, and saw that calamity would precede Christ's return. Finding prophetic meaning in contemporary events, their sense of apocalyptic crisis grew in the 1570s as they awaited the fulfilment of the struggle between the True Church and its satanic parody, the Church of this world. That conflict had changed little through its long history: the True

Church, which served God, had always been marked by suffering, exile and persecution, since Cain had murdered Abel; the False served Satan in idolatry and sin. That False Church was easily identified with the Roman Church by Elizabethan Protestants, not because every Catholic was outside God's grace, but because the papal Antichrist had perverted doctrine.

God, who elected individuals, might also elect nations. He had chosen Israel as the bearer of His promise. England's godly, like the Dutch, read scripture with patriotic intent, and for them England *was* Israel, London *was* Jerusalem. But there was no place for complacency. As Israel had, England tempted God by its disobedience, unthankfulness and continuing idolatry, and must expect punishment, just as punishment had fallen on Israel. Christ wept now over London, as once over Jerusalem. In John Foxe's *Acts and Monuments of these latter and perilous days touching matters of the Church*, better known as his *Book of Martyrs*, English Protestants read of their own part in the history of the True Church throughout the world, of their part in God's plan, as the end drew close.

England's godly had come to believe that the Queen and her people were living dangerously. When Elizabeth had ascended the throne, a Deborah to Israel, they had been jubilant. Preachers then had promised victory 'to the little ones of the weak flock of Christ against the tyrants of the world'. In 1562 a London crowd had taunted a Catholic priest with '*Dominus vobiscum* [God be with you]', because He was not. A decade later, in the emergency Parliament of 1572, the Speaker told of the miraculous change since God's 'merciful providence' had brought Elizabeth to the throne: instead of war, there was peace; hypocrisy had given place to the Gospel; the persecution was ended; the currency restored. God had 'inclined' the Queen's heart to defend His afflicted Church throughout Europe. But there were many who could not believe that the Gospel was truly planted, or that England's peace and prosperity were any more than delusory. Walsingham had warned Cecil in 1568 that 'there is nothing more dangerous than security'. There were dangers within and without, and the Queen, so one member of Parliament warned the House of Commons in 1572, was oblivious, 'lulled asleep and wrapped in the mantle of her peril'. What sort of peace could England enjoy while her Protestant neighbours in Europe were beleaguered and persecuted? England's godly must consider 'the calamities of other Churches, and the ruins of ours, with the heavy judgements of the

Lord which hang over us', insisted Thomas Cartwright, whose aims for the English Church were revolutionary.

The Church of England no longer suffered persecution, but it was assailed in other ways. The Gospel had been in England for two generations, but it was still in bondage to anti-christian ceremonies. Further reformation was needed. By the 1570s evangelicals had grown disillusioned and impatient, believing that a false sense of security was sapping the Church of its vigour and that the survival of popish remnants was leading to the revival of popery. Which were those remnants? The vestments – the 'conjuring garments' which ministers were still forced to wear, making them look like priests; praying towards the East; private Communion and baptism; holy days dedicated to saints; bowing at the name of Jesus; the churching of women after childbirth; candles; the sign of the cross in baptism; the ring in marriage. All these ceremonies and symbols might have seemed trivial, indifferent, but to the godly they were not, for they were the idolatrous means by which Satan tried perpetually to seduce the faithful.

The contention was not – said John Field, a London minister and most ardent reformer – over 'a cap, a tippet, or a surplice', but for great matters concerning a 'true ministry and regiment of the Church according to the Word'. During the 1560s the controversy between the Church establishment and its more radical opponents had centred on the issue of vestments. These symbols of popery could not be worn by shepherds in the True Church. Why should the godly make concessions to barely reconstructed papists? Yet vestments were enjoined by royal injunction and neither bishops nor, more importantly, the Supreme Governor could compromise. The Queen wrote sternly to Archbishop Parker in January 1565 demanding 'one rule, one form and manner of order'. The vestiarian controversy raised fundamental questions of religious liberty and authority, of private conscience and public order. For Protestant radicals Christian liberty lay in total conformity to God's Word, but that liberty conflicted with obedience to the Lord's anointed. So much was clear by the mid 1560s. London was, as before, the heartland of religious radicalism and crowds gathered to defend defiant ministers and taunt their oppressors. Pulpits were silenced and nonconformists suspended or imprisoned. The Prayer Book itself they judged papistical: it enjoined superstitious ceremonies; it contained prayers that all may be saved, which no Calvinist could admit as true; it constrained the essential preaching function of the clergy whereby the elect were called. Reviling the Prayer Book, some godly congregations ceased using it, in defiance of statute.

Their opponents found new names for these radical spirits: 'unspotted brethren', 'precisians' and, increasingly, 'puritans'. According to John Stow, London's chronicler, they called themselves 'unspotted lambs of the Lord', 'puritans'. But they did not: these were the names of their enemies, the language of sectarianism. Stow himself was a Catholic, who had been under suspicion after the Northern rising. Among such neighbours, understanding would be difficult. These 'hotter sort' of Protestants recognized each other and others recognized them by the intensity of their religious life, the extremity of their spiritual effort.

There could be no concessions, said radicals like John Field, to the crypto-Catholic remnant within the Church: 'If all the world might be gained with a little breach of God's Word, it were not to be done.' If the Church would not reform itself, how would reform come? Reformers looked to Parliament, and found sympathy among some, but no answer. William Strickland, who led the puritan campaign for the reformation of the Prayer Book, was sequestered from the House of Commons and silenced in 1571. Puritans pinned their hopes upon the Parliament of 1572, but a message came from the Queen that the Commons must not 'deal in any matters of religion' unless proposed by the bishops. 'The Lord of Hosts, great in counsel and infinite in thought . . . was the last session shut out of the doors', lamented Peter Wentworth in the Parliament of 1576. In London, John Field and Thomas Wilcox, impatient for reform, wrote *An Admonition to the Parliament* and 'A View of Popish Abuses' in 1572. Intending to show how far the English Church diverged from the True Church, they now advocated not reform, but revolution; 'altogether [to] remove whole Antichrist'. The *Admonition* attacked the whole hierarchy – archbishops, bishops, cathedral clergy: 'that proud generation whose kingdom must down' – because their 'tyrannous lordship cannot stand with Christ's kingdom'. Instead of the old hierarchy, it proposed a system of presbyterian synods and elders in every congregation. An austere form of public prayer would replace the Prayer Book. The 'ancient presbytery of the primitive Church' and Calvin's Geneva were the models for this Church on a hill. A long controversy followed this presbyterian challenge, conducted from the pulpit, in Parliament, through the press and petitions. The University of Cambridge was divided by the controversy: John Whitgift answered and Thomas Cartwright defended. The godly despaired as further reformation was thwarted: this was a sign of the sins of the time, a punishment for a people 'so far from God's blessings'.

Not doctrine, but discipline divided the godly; Protestants, puritans and presbyterians. Yet any division among the godly was dangerous. Protestants must be united if militant Catholics were to be defeated. In France and in the Netherlands persecuted Calvinists understood that imperative, and in 1571 their Churches, in both countries, held national synods which defined doctrine and discipline and, attesting a common faith and consensus, provided an organization to sustain a 'Church under the cross'. They looked to their Protestant brethren abroad for the aid which must save them, and looked first to the leading Protestant nation, England. There the godly 'cause' had captured so many of the establishment, but not, crucially, the Queen.

*

England's peace had been preserved so far not, as Elizabeth liked to think, by policy, but, said the godly, by 'God's special favour'. 'Calamities' had beset the great Catholic powers, but as their troubles ceased to distract them, England had better beware. This was the fear of many Elizabethans. They never forgot the menacing meeting of the Duke of Alva and Catherine de Medici at Bayonne in 1565, believing that a pact had been made there to extirpate the Gospel and advance the power of Rome. Against that threat, the only recourse was the 'common cause of religion' throughout Europe, a Protestant league to defend the faith. The 'defence of His afflicted Church' should prevail over all other considerations in foreign policy; not just through principle but through pragmatism. If Elizabeth allowed the Protestants of France and the Low Countries to be destroyed, then her turn was next. The sea that was England's wall could not protect her. Elizabeth remained unpersuaded by such arguments. While some within her Council urged principle, she preferred to let policy rest upon contingency. Not for her the great cause, the adventure for conscience. For her, the course urged by the ideologues, the forward Protestants – including Leicester, Walsingham, Mildmay and Sir Francis Knollys, Treasurer of the Chamber – offered, through terrifying escalation, a war easy to begin but impossible to end. When the threats on all sides were so great, and defence so difficult, when costs in men and money were incalculable, why seek war when temporizing could deflect it? Elizabeth came to regard the arguments of these forward Protestants at first with indifference, then with cold hostility.

Innately conservative, Elizabeth remained mesmerized by the threat from the ancient enemy, France. Yet the power of France, devastated by three civil wars in a decade, was hard to calculate; it was harder still to know how she would use it, especially when the wars were interrupted in August 1570 by a fragile truce. The leaders of the Huguenot and Catholic factions played upon the hatred between the royal brothers Charles IX and his heir Henry, Duke of Anjou in order to advance rival policies of momentous consequence: intervention in the Netherlands, thereby provoking war with Spain; or amity with Spain and the advance of the Roman faith. 'I will have no other champion [of Catholicism] here but myself,' vowed Charles IX in July 1571, as the Guises prepared Anjou for that role. Yet Charles's equivocation made French politics ever more precarious, for he was himself under the influence of the Huguenot leader, Admiral Coligny. By the end of 1571 the fraternal enmity which even the machinations of their mother, Catherine de Medici, could hardly prevent threatened to turn to fratricide. A foreign war would at least distract the French nobility from the renewed civil war which always threatened so long as no end was found to the long vendetta between the Guises and Coligny except death.

Into this deadly house of Valois Elizabeth looked to marry. From the end of 1570 delicate negotiations had been conducted for the Queen to marry Anjou (the future Henry III). Dynastic alliance promised protection for England; and for Catherine de Medici it offered support in her struggle with the Cardinal of Lorraine for control of the Council and of Anjou himself. This was no dalliance, so Elizabeth insisted: she was 'firmly and fully resolved to marry'. Yet there could be no compromise over religion. Anjou could not 'make shipwreck of conscience' by conforming to Protestant rites, and Elizabeth could not allow Anjou the private Mass which she forbade her subjects. As the marriage negotiations faltered, Walsingham feared that the Guises would work towards the conquest of Ireland and the advancement of Mary, Queen of Scots. By the end of 1571 Anjou had proposed instead that Elizabeth marry his (even) younger brother, the Duke of Alençon. If not a marriage, then Elizabeth looked for a treaty with France.

Alliance with France marked a transformation in England's diplomacy, for her defence had traditionally lain with the Burgundian alliance with the Habsburgs. But now that the Netherlands were in revolt, to whom should England look for allies? No longer to Philip of Spain, who had conceived the 'enterprise of England', the proposed invasion of 1571, as God's 'own cause'. Neither could Elizabeth easily countenance alliance with his rebellious subjects in the Netherlands, for how could one sovereign aid the rebels of another? Elizabeth waited to be persuaded that Spain, so long England's ally, was friend no longer. But her councillors now saw the domination of Spain as the greater threat. At the discovery of the Ridolfi plot in 1571 Walsingham had hoped that 'the proud Spaniard (whom God hath long used as the rod of his wrath) would be cast into the fire'. Alva's army waited just across the Channel, ready to invade. If conscience did not impel the Queen to intervene in the Netherlands, where the battle between liberty and tyranny, true and false religion, was being fought, pragmatism must. Such was the insistent argument of one wing of her Council and of the Prince of Orange. The Netherlands would be the first victim of Spanish tyranny if help did not arrive, and England the next. Disaster for the Dutch would be England's disaster too.

In exile from the Low Countries since the rout of their invasion forces in 1568, William of Orange and his brother Louis of Nassau planned a new campaign against Alva. Only by armed invasion, and with foreign aid, could his tyranny be overthrown. Throughout 1569 the brothers had fought with the Huguenot armies in France, and when peace was made in 1570 they hoped to benefit from the reconciliation and looked to Charles IX as the unlikely champion of the Netherlands' freedom. For the French king the 'enterprise of Flanders' offered the prospect of glory and expansion, and he was persuaded by promises of easy conquest there. In August 1571 Nassau came to the French court and proposed a grand alliance of France, England and the German Protestant princes to rid the Netherlands of Alva's armies. Victorious, they would partition the Low Countries between themselves. Surely, wrote Walsingham, God had raised up Louis as an 'instrument for the advancement of His glory'. There were times, he told Burghley in August, when 'nothing can be more dangerous than *not* to enter wars', when wars 'for safety's sake' were imperative. The enterprise of Flanders waited upon Elizabeth's decision. But Burghley saw only dangers; no solutions. England might gain by conquest in the Netherlands, but thereby lose a kingdom in Ireland, for Ireland was as easy for Spain to seize as it was for England to defend. Any alliance with France, he feared, would be transitory. Surely, he told Elizabeth on 31 August, the remedy of her perils lay 'only in the knowledge of Almighty God'.

France was moving inexorably to war, but whether it would be war against Spain in the Netherlands or civil war no one knew. When in

September Admiral Coligny returned to the French court, where his enemies awaited him, civil war seemed more likely. Walsingham feared that the 'devilish practices' of the Guises would lead to Catholic resurgence and renewed amity between France and Spain. But Coligny urged war against Spain, and Charles was persuaded. In early 1572 a treaty was signed between England and France binding the ancient enemies to mutual defence. But the aggrandizement of France had never been part of Elizabeth's strategy, nor the loss of her faltering friendship with Spain. As the plans for multilateral invasion of the Netherlands went ahead that spring Elizabeth's ambivalence unsettled her supposed allies, who could never be sure of England's action, or inaction.

Nassau had feared that the 'rash enterprise' of extremists would jeopardize his grand strategy. So it proved. The Sea Beggars, a vigilante navy for the Dutch rebels in exile, were expelled from their English haven in March 1572, as too provocative to harbour. In desperation, they fled before the wind to the Zeeland coast where on 1 April they captured the Dutch port of Brille. By giving the rebels a bridgehead, access to the coast and command of the Channel, they changed the course of the revolt. Their action precipitated the invasion 'untimely'. It was now or never, so Orange proclaimed on 14 April. At the end of May Nassau seized Valenciennes and Mons in the south and attempted the capture of the Duke of Alva in his viceregal capital. Events propelled England, Spain and France towards a war which none dared enter or knew how to prevent. Elizabeth and Burghley, who must halt the extension of French or Spanish power in the Low Countries, needed all their guile and judgement now. If Alva could contain the rebels, then England would not intervene; if not, and if the French proved 'too potent neighbours', then Alva could have – secret – assurance of English aid, if Philip would end the oppression of his subjects in the Low Countries. Sir Humphrey Gilbert was sent, supposedly a 'volunteer', to hold Flushing, but Elizabeth's covert aid was not for the Protestant cause, not to protect the Low Countries from tyranny, but to prevent either Alva or the French from controlling the coastline. By midsummer all Holland, save Amsterdam, was in open revolt.

Charles IX was now 'so far forward' that nothing could hide his provocation of Spain, and Coligny was given royal permission to depart for the Netherlands on 25 August. But he never left. In Paris, Coligny and the Huguenot nobility gathered in mid July for a marriage which was intended to unite Navarre and Valois. This ended as a 'massacring marriage'; celebration turned to carnage. The vendetta of the Guises against Coligny was ended by the Admiral's assassination on St Bartholomew's Night, 23 August. In the days which followed, the Huguenot leaders were cut down and thousands upon thousands of Protestants throughout France slaughtered in a spontaneous wave of popular Catholic violence; 'the saints of God led to the shambles', their mutilated corpses thrown in rivers. In Paris, Walsingham and Philip Sidney, the courtier and poet, looked on. Neither they, nor any Protestant in Europe, could remain untouched by the tragedy, and in time Sidney would die for the Protestant cause.

Some sought vengeance against the papists, but most bowed to God's judgement. Did not the godly expect persecution? Cecil told Walsingham: 'I see the Devil is suffered by Almighty God for our sins to be strong.' The English people must call themselves to repentance. In Scotland, the General Assembly of the Kirk ordered a 'public humiliation of them that fear God' to mitigate God's wrath upon them for their sins. Protestants everywhere looked for further violence, and certainly the Pope, who had had a medal struck to celebrate St Bartholomew's Night, would have sanctioned it. In Geneva they awaited catastrophe. In the Netherlands the massacre was a disaster for Orange and his cause, for now Coligny would never come, and through the autumn and winter of 1572 the towns which had declared for Orange suffered Alva's terrible retribution; they were sacked and their inhabitants put to the sword. Orange fled, not now to Germany, but to Holland, vowing to 'make that province my tomb'.

*

There were wars of religion in France, in the Netherlands, in Scotland. Could England escape them? As Elizabethans watched the civil wars in neighbouring states, they regarded with gratitude the peace within their own kingdom, recognized 'that restless care' with which the Queen governed, the love she inspired among her subjects, and the justice she gave. They compared their own benign political institutions with the tyranny and oppression suffered by their neighbours. Yet sometimes they wondered whether those troubles might extend to England. In 1579 Philip Sidney reminded the Queen that her subjects were 'divided into two mighty factions . . . bound upon the never-ending knot of religion', and he feared that one faction might rise against the other.

Walsingham had doubted that there could ever be peace in France while there were so many aspirant kings. There was an aspirant queen in England too, for Mary Stewart still fretted and plotted in captivity in distant Derbyshire and Staffordshire. Yet there was only one Queen at the English court, and Elizabeth, as she entered her fifth decade, was at her most commanding, her royal will most imperative. She saw herself as a Senecan princess: constant, unswayed by shifts of fortune. Her councillors saw her otherwise, regretting her vacillations and that a Stoic princess should have such tantrums. In the perennial battle between will and counsel, they found her dismayingly immovable, and planned concerted campaigns of persuasion to make her act at all. In dark moments they feared that though they failed to move her, others might; that even Elizabeth could fall prey to the corrupt counsel of flatterers, which was the prevailing vice of princes and the slippery slope to tyranny. The forward Protestants, who blamed evil counsel for the slaughter and persecution of the wars of religion, were not always confident that the Queen would listen to advice, or to the right advice; theirs. Peter Wentworth had warned in the House of Commons in 1576 that 'no estate can stand where the prince will not be governed by advice'. 'Always or commonly,' complained Walsingham in 1578, thinking of Elizabeth's counsels, 'the persons that wish best, and the causes that work best are most misliked.'

Yet so much in Elizabethan politics was conducive to stability. Those murderous divisions in Council and court, and among the nobility, which brought assassination, plot and civil war in France and Scotland, were absent from England. There could be no deadly feuds over control of Elizabeth, who jealously guarded her independence. No noble at Elizabeth's court went in fear of his life as Coligny had done in France. In October 1573 the Queen's favourite, Sir Christopher Hatton, was attacked, but the assailant had mistaken his victim, and was anyway demented. The old quarrel between the Earls of Sussex and Leicester could still disrupt the court: on 15 July 1581 'the disaster fallen out yesterday betwixt two great planets' was reported by Sir Thomas Heneage, the Vice-Chamberlain. Yet the earls knew 'their Jupiter, and will obey her majesty'.

The Elizabethan nobility, though jealous of their honour and quick to defend it, and as predatory of power and office as their rank demanded, seemed to have learnt to look no longer to baronial revolt as the way of advancement. The 7th Earl of Northumberland, and the 4th Duke of Norfolk had been sent to the block to teach others that lesson. But the ancient Catholic nobility did not see themselves, nor were they seen by worried Protestant contemporaries, as part of a dissolving feudal order. The new courtly nobility which the Tudors had created and patronized quickly chose to forget the novelty of their elevation, and for some of them their noble independence fitted uneasily with ideals of courtly service. While wars were being fought for great causes many lamented being ruled by a queen whose politic virtues were the female ones of mercy and prudence, but who by her nature lacked martial courage and constancy of fixed purpose. Serving at her court became irksome and intolerable for those, like Philip Sidney, who aspired to active virtue. In 1578–9 Hubert Languet, a peripatetic diplomat serving the Protestant cause, observed to Sidney that life at the Elizabethan court seemed less 'manly' than he had hoped; that the nobility there sought reputation rather by 'affected courtesy' than by those virtues which were 'wholesome to the state'. Leicester chafed under his dependence upon the Queen, who would be goaded into calling him a 'creature of our own', and aspired to the magnificence of a Renaissance prince, glorious in war and peace, extravagant in display and patronage. His ambition was to lead his forces in European war, and he had marshalled armaments in his strongly fortified castle at Kenilworth. Yet he also used Kenilworth to stage elaborate pageants for the Queen, and it was inconceivable that he would use his military power and raise his following – as his father had done before, and his stepson would do later – for his private purposes rather than the Crown's.

There was, from the early 1570s until a palace revolution threatened towards the end of the decade, an unprecedented unity over policy and purpose at court and in the Council. No Catholic voice was heard, and Protestant influence was paramount. Even puritans found patrons in the highest places. The advance of Protestantism at home and abroad was the aspiration of most of the Council, even if there were marked differences over ways and means; Burghley usually aligned himself against Walsingham and Leicester, and the Queen remained distressingly intransigent. Disagreements remained, yet the silken arts of courtiers were used to pretend that friendship which the Queen demanded. Irony replaced invective. The court was the centre of all political life and advancement. To leave it without permission became, as the Duke of Norfolk had discovered, almost treason; and to be exiled from it, worse than disgrace. By keeping the advocates of rival policies around her, Elizabeth contained conflict.

Could there have been a massacre at London as there had been at Paris? The same text – Deuteronomy, Chapter 13 – which had stirred the citizens of Paris to slaughter was cited by the lord bishops at Westminster in 1572: death to those who incited the people of God to false worship. The Bishop of London – who, so he said, was 'always to be pitied', so unruly was his flock – feared that the French treachery would 'reach over unto us', and that the Londoners would be excited to violence by young preachers of more zeal than wisdom. London was the heartland of the radical puritan movement. Here presbyterian ringleaders found patrons and audiences. The religious enthusiasm of the Londoners was a powerful impetus to reform, but it was also a deterrent because of the division it brought. When the episcopal reaction came, as it did again in 1573, repression was most marked in London. But even though London's governors constantly predicted trouble because religious passions were often so inflamed, there was no major religious riot in Elizabethan London; no bodies in the Thames nor blood in the streets because of religion. Government in London worked; diffused as it was through all the parishes, wards, precincts, companies, and households. Those who held divergent beliefs usually managed to worship together, work together and trade together. The wars in the streets were only wars of words.

Yet the 'civil wars of the Church of God' continued. The contention was between 'zeal' and 'policy'; between those of the older generation who remembered how far they had come through persecution and exile, how hard it was to keep what they had; and the younger generation, who saw only the deformity and degeneration of the Church, so distant still from the True Church. The more radical bishops always hoped for better times and further reform, but they were, however uncomfortably, servants of a conservative mistress; commissioners for a Supreme Governor who was resistant to change and terrified of disorder. As the bishops stood in the way of reform, the presbyterians thought that they must go. 'What is your judgement, ought there to be any bishops in the churches of Christians?' they asked. Archbishop Matthew Parker, seen as ageing and antediluvian, despaired. In 1574 puritan satirists argued that seventy archbishops of Canterbury had been enough: 'As Augustine was the first, so Matthew might be the last.'

Puritan satirists? The godly were not usually associated with satire, with fun. Puritan jokes were more often made against them than by them; against their behaviour as sanctimonious, censorious, holier-than-thou, hypocritical. As the godly few sought increasingly to impose their will upon the profane multitude the jokes became more bitter. Since the Fall, when humanity lost the divine likeness, every Christian had fought a lonely battle against sin but, because Protestantism stressed human depravity, that battle must now be fought with greater urgency. The godly led a campaign against the drunkard, the blasphemer and the lecher in order to create a society more conformable to God's Word. From the middle of Elizabeth's reign, as Protestantism won over the establishment, and godly magistrates aligned with godly ministers began to tighten their grip upon many a provincial town, puritanism came to be identified with moral and social repression. The old moral discipline of the ecclesiastical courts the godly thought no discipline at all. What punishment was it for fornicators to be 'turned out of a hot sheet' to stand in the white sheet of penance? Paternalist puritan Justices, driven by scripture and righteous indignation, exercised stern rule in their petty sessions. In 1578 the Justices in Bury St Edmunds drew up a new penal code. Women found guilty of fornication would receive thirty lashes 'well laid on till the blood come'. The Old Testament punishment for adultery was death, and the most extreme godly fundamentalists called for its return. Even licit wedded love, they believed, might derogate from the reverence due to God alone. For a husband to vow 'with my body I thee worship' was to make an idol of his wife, said John Field. Romantic love might even fuse adultery and idolatry. 'Let not my love be called idolatry, nor my beloved as an idol show,' wrote William Shakespeare, playing upon that temptation.

In these ways the godly might be at war with what it was to be human. A chasm opened between the old permissive culture of neighbourliness and good fellowship and the godly code of discipline and restraint. The festivities which had bound the traditional community now began to divide it, for the godly denounced church ales, bridal wakes, morris dancing and maying as 'idle pastimes' and 'belly cheer'. It was on Sunday – the only day free from labour, but also the day consecrated to God – that the carnal and the godly were especially at odds. The people, especially young people, were drawn to 'heathenish rioting', drunken cavorting, and dancing that led to debauchery, while the godly spent their time at sermons and reading scripture. So preachers alleged. In the heroic early days of the Reformation reformers had not been at war with music and drama: far from it. The ballad and the interlude had been the medium of the evangelists' message. Protestant play-wrights then had used bawdy jokes for a godly purpose, and scripture songs and psalms had been sung to ballad metre in alehouse singsongs.

In the mid 1570s all this started to change. Religious songs could no longer be sung to the tune 'Greensleeves'. Sacred and secular music were divorced, and even sacred music viewed with suspicion, its beauty seen as part of the Devil's wiles to seduce people from true worship. The writer of the most sublime Elizabethan choral music was William Byrd, a Catholic. At the beginning of Elizabeth's reign, the old religious drama of the mystery plays had continued, but in the mid 1570s the York, Wakefield and Chester cycles were suppressed, for it was thought idolatrous for a man to play God; and polluting for divine truths to be the toy of human imagination. War was declared against drama just as it was about to enter its most brilliant age. Theatres were banished from London in 1575 as 'seminaries of impiety', 'houses of bawdery'.

Were the godly fighting a losing battle? A trumpet blast would summon a thousand to some 'filthy play', while an hour's tolling of a bell would gather only a hundred to a sermon, so preachers complained. But it was always an uphill struggle to save people from themselves. The godly knew that the greater part of humanity – if not precisely which part – were damned, whatever they did. Scripture showed that Christ's promise of heaven was only for His 'tiny flock'; that strait was the gate, narrow the way, 'and few there be that find it'. The question that exercised them, as a matter of practical divinity, was whether the community of those who made Calvinist beliefs the heart of their lives should make that fellowship real and visible by dividing themselves from a national Church composed mostly of papist changelings and carnal worldlings. It was hard for the godly to contemplate communion with the ungodly, but though despairing of the Church of England they stayed within it. The restraint and the impulse to obedience of England's godly should not be underestimated. England's only massacre for religion in 1572, as France ran with blood, was of a Sussex boy who was shot dead as he sawed down a maypole.

Christian religious metaphors are often of war and battle. As Walter Devereux, 1st Earl of Essex, died an exemplary Christian death, he called out: 'Courage, courage! I am a soldier that must fight under the banner of my saviour Christ.' This Christian soldier died in Ireland, which he had known would be the death of him, where he, like others, had used the unchristian methods of betrayal and massacre.

*

If there were no wars of religion yet in England, could they be averted in Ireland? In 1569 James Fitzmaurice Fitzgerald had risen in the name of the Pope and preached a crusade against the 'Hugnottes'. After his eventual submission in 1573 he fled to France and then to Spain to raise Catholic forces for a new holy war against the heretic Queen in Ireland. The godly, as they sought to beam evangelical light into the 'dark corners' and to make every city Jerusalem, faced no greater challenge than in Ireland, for here the new faith had hardly penetrated. A prudent Elizabeth chose not to unsettle and provoke her fragile polity in Ireland by 'curious inquisition of men's consciences' and determined imposition of religious change. Although the statutes of supremacy and uniformity had established Protestantism as the official state religion in Ireland under the royal governorship of the Church, allegiance was hardly tested, nor was non-conformity punished, even in Dublin and the Pale. When Edmund Campion, newly and dangerously received into the Catholic faith in England, sought refuge, it was to Dublin that he came in 1570, to stay in the houses of James Stanihurst and Sir Christopher Barnewall, leading figures of the Pale.

If there were to be rebellion in the name of religion again, it was likely to be in Ireland. But it was not Catholicism which led Gaelic and Anglo-Irish lords to rebel against Elizabeth in the 1570s, nor ardent Protestantism which drew the English to serve and settle in Ireland in the later sixteenth century, though it was often in the language of the Old Testament that the English governors came to speak of the suppression of Irish rebellions. 'It must be fire and sword and the rod of God's vengeance that must make these stubborn and cankered hearts yield for fear,' wrote Ralph Rokeby, Chief Justice of Connacht, in 1571. Sir Edmund Butler, who had with his brother joined their Geraldine enemies in rebellion in 1569, spoke for many when he said: 'I do not make war against the Queen, but against those that banish Ireland, and mean conquest.' But to 'banish Ireland' was still the purpose only of a very few hardliners.

English governors saw a congruity between their defiance of Spanish oppression in the Netherlands and their crusade for the extension of English law and forms of government in Ireland. Burghley supposedly said, 'The Flemings had not such cause to rebel by the oppression of the Spaniards as it is reported by the Irish people [who were so oppressed by their lords].' Those who supported the Dutch in their just resistance against the tyrant Spain also came to fight in Elizabeth's western kingdom. Sir Humphrey Gilbert, who went, he said, 'with Gideon's faith' to help make the inhabitants of Flushing 'owners of themselves' in 1572, had served in Ireland. But there his war of liberation took a summary, sanguinary form in 1569 when he put down the Munster rebellion with what seemed a terrible finality, and proposed wholesale confiscation and colonization there. Philip Sidney, son of the chief governor Sir Henry Sidney, had watched with despair the loss of liberty on the Continent through the 1570s, but argued for an extension of the royal prerogative in Ireland. In justification, he claimed that there liberty was already lost: 'Under the sun there is not a nation which lives more tyrannously than they do one over the other.' The tyrants were the Irish lords, not the English governors. Neither 'wicked Saracen nor yet cruel Turk' so pillaged the 'poor commons' as did the Irish lords who imposed their arbitrary rule. When Edmund Spenser, secretary to the Lord Deputy in 1581, wrote allegorically in his prophetic epic *The Faerie Queene* of the evil force to be conquered in Ireland by the Christian knight Artegall and his iron page Talus, it was Grantorto, the tyrant. Contemporary annotations associated Grantorto, the model of injustice, with members of the Geraldine Desmond family. English claims to own and rule were stronger where the Irish had forfeited theirs, so it came to be argued. Yet although the English saw themselves as liberators they were rarely seen as such by those they came to liberate.

When they thought about the nature of Irish society, with its 'wild shamrock manners' (as John Derricke, the pamphleteer, called them), the English were bewildered. Hopes remained that exotic Gaelic customs would disappear with the extension of English law and 'civility'. The ending of the 'savage life', wrote Rowland White (an Anglo-Irish merchant and proponent of reform) to William Cecil in 1569, 'shall enforce men to civility'. The reformers still believed, in the 1570s, that the Irish people could be won to English ways and that conciliation would be more effective than coercion. Sir William Garrard, the Lord Chancellor, arriving in Ireland in 1576, was clear that the sword was limited as an instrument of civility. 'Can the sword teach them [the "English degenerates"] to speak English, to use English apparel, to restrain them from Irish exactions and extortions?' It could not: 'It is the rod of justice that must scour out these blots.' Of course, a judge would believe that the common law must be the instrument of reform, and to deny that justice was a way to reform was like denying the virtue of education. Justices did go on assize; commissions were sent forth from the Dublin Council into distant regions; statutes were published. Sir Henry Sidney had been Lord Justice before his first period as chief governor (1565–71), and his commitment to judicial reform marked his office. He presided over extended assizes in 1565, travelling with judges in Leinster and conducting sittings in Munster. Yet many of those charged with governing Ireland came to despair that justice could effect reform, and were pessimistic of finding impartial juries in Irish society. If justice failed to bring order, overawe local lords and extirpate the 'savage life', then a military presence must be extended and law must follow the sword. It was less certain whether that military force should take the form of garrisoning or a campaign army.

The superiority of the English system of law was usually evident only to the English. English bewilderment about Ireland turned to disillusion as, through the 1570s, the Irish lords became not more 'civil' but more rebellious. In most of Ireland the people observed the 'old religion' still, followed local lords, and spoke the Irish language. The complexity of Irish society made it difficult to impose uniform regulations. Everything about Gaelic Ireland seemed to the English archaic, anarchic and conditional. This was, so they heard, a land of werewolves and blood oaths, where poets could rhyme a man to death and men would starve themselves to death at the doors of their enemies. The Gaelic lords had promised fealty to the English sovereign and taken feudal titles but, as they moved as freely in and out of these agreements as they did with those they had with each other, hopes that this would ensure their loyalty faded. Conn O'Neill had become the 1st Earl of Tyrone, but within a confused generation tanistry was reasserted, and after the murder of Shane O'Neill, Turlough Luineach was chosen as *the* O'Neill and inaugurated with what Sir Henry Sidney called 'brutish ceremonies'. The first Earls of Clancar, Clanrickard, and Thomond renounced their English titles in protest against the actions of the English governors and, as signal of their revolt, the Earl of Clanrickard's sons – the *Mac an Iarlas* – discarded their English dress and threw it in the Shannon. Even family allegiances might be temporary and opportunistic in Gaelic Ireland. Fosterage could create stronger bonds than kinship, and the practice of 'naming' children – affiliating the offspring of temporary liaisons to their fathers – created mighty alliances. Marriage, too, might be impermanent; an alliance broken, like others, when it no longer suited. Women chiefs could be as redoubtable as the men. Grania O'Malley, the pirate queen of the west, chose her own husband, 'Richard in Iron' Burke of Mayo, and, said Sir Henry Sidney, 'was as well by sea as by land more than

Mrs Mate with him'. To the English the Irish came to seem hardly Christian, sunk in papistry and paganism.

But these exotic, transient ways, condemned by the English governors, had the power to seduce. 'Lord, how quickly doth that country alter men's natures,' wrote Spenser. For those who thought like Spenser, the Anglo-Irish lords of the original conquest had, long before, become 'degenerate', fallen from their race. By fostering and marrying the Irish, speaking their language, using brehon law, they had, as the proverb went, 'grown as Gaelic as O'Hanlon's breeches'. Yet the Anglo-Irish community maintained a long tradition of loyalty and obedience to England which was not easily ended. The Anglo-Irish were neither purged from government nor alienated from its policies in the first decades of Elizabeth's rule, and there had been no radical estrangement between the English born in Ireland and the new generation of planters and soldier-settlers who arrived from England. But a difference of interest and attitude between the Anglo-Irish and the new settlers became clearer. In September 1577 Sir Nicholas Malby, President of Connacht wrote of the 'division among us Council', between 'we of the English' and those of 'this country birth'. By the 1580s a sense grew among the Anglo-Irish community of their dispossession and alienation.

As their way of life was threatened, those with a double loyalty – to England and to Ireland – might be forced to choose between the two. Between 1560 and 1580 all the greatest Anglo-Irish lords – Desmond, Ormond, Kildare and Clanrickard – either rebelled themselves or were in collusion with rebels. As they moved towards rebellion again in 1574, the 15th Earl of Desmond and his Countess adopted forbidden Gaelic dress and reinstated brehon law. The 11th Earl of Kildare, half-English leader of the Geraldines, had been brought up in exile in Italian Renaissance courts. 'A perfect horseman', he had become Master of the Horse to Cosimo de' Medici. As a loyal defender of Mary during Wyatt's rebellion in 1554, he had been restored to his great lands and title, and entrusted with the defence of the Pale. Yet he still spoke Irish and used coyne and livery. He was accused of dealing with James Fitzmaurice Fitzgerald in 1569, and in the early 1570s he shored up his newly restored power in Leinster by suspicious alliances with the unruly O'Byrnes, O'Mores and O'Connors. On his new fireplace at Kilkea he inscribed the ancient war cry of the Geraldines, 'Cromaboo'.

Mystified by the Irish, the English began to resort to primitive ethnology to explain what they came to see as irredeemable barbarism.

Although mostly sceptical about their own foundation myths, the English chose to be credulous about fantastic mythic Irish origins and to believe that Irish savagery stemmed from their ancient Scythian ancestry. The claim that Ireland was part of Britain's Arthurian empire before the Anglo-Norman conquest and the now embarrassing papal grant gave Arthur's Tudor descendants the right to complete the conquest. To many charged with governing Ireland, the Irish were a 'savage nation': they were 'wild beasts' to be 'herded', 'hunted', and 'tamed'; colts to be 'bitted', 'bridled', 'broken'. A proposal in 1570 to establish a university for the 'reformation of the barbarism of this rude people' foundered, like so many Elizabethan schemes in Ireland, until Trinity College, Dublin was established in 1591. Some came to adopt a pessimistic determinism, seeing the whole nation as unregenerate and recognizing that barbarism did not easily fade under the influence of civility. Even Sir Henry Sidney, twice chief governor (1565–71 and 1575–8), and the one who understood the Irish best, as he left Ireland for the last time allegedly boarded his ship reciting Psalm 114: 'When Israel departed out of Egypt and the House of Jacob from a barbarous people.'

'There lies some mystery in this universal rebellious disposition,' lamented Lord Deputy Fitzwilliam in 1572. That most of the island was still peaceful was little consolation to English governors charged with quelling the unrest which seemed endemic. The 'universal rebellion' of Munster, Ulster and Connacht of 1569–72 threatened to recur in the spring of 1574. Yet the causes of Irish turbulence were no mystery; they lay in the increasing ambivalence and contradictory nature of English policy in the last third of the century. The Queen and her advisers still spoke of reform by peaceful means, of the advance of law and civility and of the freedoms of her Irish subjects, yet reform was often undermined not only by Irish rebellion, but by the very governors charged with implementing it. As each chief governor in turn was betrayed by rivals at court and in Ireland, they betrayed the strategy of reform by failing to be thoroughly committed to it. The instructions that came from the cautious and impecunious Queen were often erratic and contradictory, as events not only in Ireland but in Europe forced her to vary her commitment.

In July 1574 Elizabeth wrote to Walter Devereux, 1st Earl of Essex, then in Ireland: 'You allure that rude and barbarous nation to civility rather by discreet handling than by force and shedding of blood.' Yet Essex was countenancing widespread expropriation and colonization.

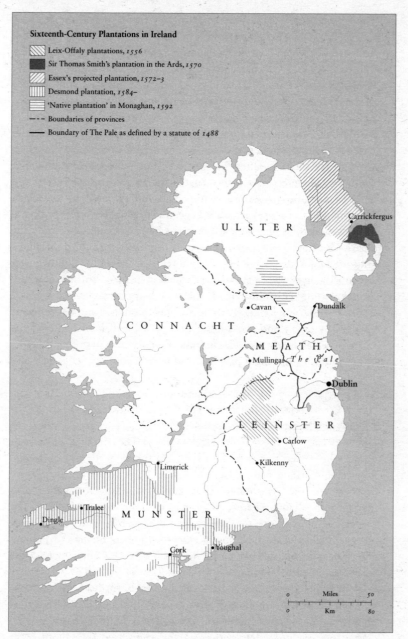

Sixteenth-Century Plantations in Ireland

Leix-Offaly plantations, *1556*

Sir Thomas Smith's plantation in the Ards, *1570*

Essex's projected plantation, *1572–3*

Desmond plantation, *1584–*

'Native plantation' in Monaghan, *1592*

- - - Boundaries of provinces

—— Boundary of The Pale as defined by a statute of *1488*

ULSTER

Carrickfergus

CONNACHT

•Cavan

•Dundalk

MEATH

•Mullingar *The Pale*

•Dublin

LEINSTER

•Carlow

•Kilkenny

•Limerick

•Tralee

•Dingle

MUNSTER

•Cork

•Youghal

| 0 | Miles | 50 |
| 0 | Km | 80 |

There had been desultory projects of plantation during the reign of Queen Mary. In Leix and Offaly in Leinster uneasy garrisons had been established at Philipstown and Maryborough; citadels of English influence around which stalked the displaced and hostile O'Byrnes, O'Mores and O'Connors, waging intermittent guerrilla war. Adventurers with greater ambitions came to Ireland under Elizabeth, seeking easy gain, and were countenanced by a government which saw private plantations as a cheap solution to the perennial problem of how to order Ireland without prodigious expense. The arrival of Sir Peter Carew in 1568 to lay claim to lands lost since the first conquest of the twelfth century engendered fears of the general dispossession of the Irishry, not least because this chancer's venture was not opposed by the Chief Governor. In 1569 Sir Warham St Leger and other adventurers projected a plantation for south-west Munster which was predicated upon the clearance of the native population as though they were all proclaimed traitors; which they were not, or not yet. This failed, and in Munster expropriation by the English led to rebellion in 1569–71. Lord Deputy Sidney was driven from Ireland, and if he had ever supported colonization, he did so no longer. Parliament's posthumous attainder of Shane O'Neill in 1569, and the confiscation of O'Neill lands, offered the chance for the 'enterprise of Ulster'; the establishment of private schemes to colonize this turbulent province and to drive out the Scots once and for all.

With the 'enterprise of Ulster' and the royal grant of the Ards and South Clandeboye to Sir Thomas Smith and his son in 1571, and of the Glynns and North Clandeboye to the Earl of Essex in 1573, all the lords of Ulster were threatened with expropriation. The colonists' promise to those who joined their venture of a 'land that floweth with milk and honey', but which was 'waste', 'desolate' and 'uninhabited', did not impress the Irish who inhabited it, and who now resisted their own part in the colonial scheme, which was to become the colonized. The 'enterprise' forced not only the Gaelic underlords, who had recently sought English protection from the depredations of Shane O'Neill, but also independent lords like Sir Brian MacPhelim O'Neill of Clandeboye and O'Donnell of Tirconnell, into a 'knot to rebel', and as before they looked to the O'Neill, now Turlough Luineach, for leadership. Gaelic unity in Ulster was – ominously – restored. Within a month of his arrival in August 1573 Essex had learnt not to trust the Irish. Essex was no speculator, but a feudal overlord; his services, said the Queen, were 'grounded not upon gain, but upon honour and argument of true nobility'. But in this world of cattle raids, flooded fords, broken promises and guerrilla attacks, his project failed. Betrayed at home – by his wife and 'back friends' at court – his finances in ruins, and denied the highest office in Ireland which might have saved his honour, he despaired. He had vowed never to 'imbrue his hands with more blood' than necessity required, but his methods turned sanguinary. In November 1574 he invited Brian MacPhelim, his family and followers to a feast which ended in their slaughter. At Rathlin Island the next summer Essex found a final solution to the Scottish presence: to massacre the MacDonnells. His vengeful troops hunted down survivors in cliffs and caves. For his 'rare constancy' and 'true temperance' the Queen thanked him.

Returning to Ireland at the end of 1575, as chief governor for the second time, Sir Henry Sidney moved to placate the Anglo-Irish and Gaelic lords of Munster; he also made a truce with Turlough Luineach in Ulster, and took the submissions of the rebellious Burkes and O'Connors. If Sidney had ever been optimistic about assimilating Ireland to English ways, he was not now. He pursued, with relentless energy and some impetuousity, policies which veered between conciliation and coercion. Bound by an impossible promise to the Queen that he would make the government of Ireland pay for itself, and undermined still by enemies at court, he needed immediate results. For him, provincial presidencies and councils were the way of providing an alternative to the exclusive military powers of the great lords, whose maintenance of private armies supported by coyne and livery was the source of perennial instability and oppression; and also a means of providing justice in distant regions, distinct from brehon law and the private jurisdictions of Desmond and Ormond. The presidents were to be military men, provided with the armed force to prevent violence in their provinces, as well as being charged with the maintenance of justice. That the first presidencies had, in the way of reform attempts in Ireland, mutated from their original purpose when, in the face of rebellion, Gilbert in Munster had ruled not by common law but the law of the sword, and Fitton in Connacht had not ruled at all, did not deter him. In 1576 Sir Nicholas Malby became President in Connacht.

The new presidencies of the later 1570s were to be financed by composition; a scheme whereby the old military exactions demanded by the Gaelic and Gaelicized lords and the 'cess' (levy) exacted by the English garrisons would be surrendered and replaced by an annual rent charge based on land. The defence of the territory would no longer rest with the lords alone, but with them in alliance with the presidents and their forces, to whom lesser landowners could now look for protection. There would be a certainty – both military and financial – in the new system which was lacking in the old. In a great perambulation through-out Ireland in 1575–6 Sidney negotiated composition agreements with many of the great lords, even in restless Connacht, and was assured of their obedience. But peace talks in Ireland did not generally last. Rumours spread of Sidney's rapacity; rumours that he had, said the Queen, taken 'our whole land to farm'. There was widespread discontent and a general call to resistance. The *Mac an Iarlas*, fearing the ruin of the Clanrickard lordship, and hating the English even more than they hated each other, rebelled again in 1576. In the following year the hitherto loyal Palesmen refused the cess – the imposition to pay for the Queen's unlovely soldiers in Ireland – as a burden they would no longer carry, and they would not countenance composition. This crisis provoked Sidney's second recall.

Rebellion threatened again, but now when it came it was in the guise of holy war. Sidney had warned the Queen that most of the Irish were 'Papists . . . body and soul'; and 'Romish' not only in religion, for they looked for a prince of 'their own superstition'. In July 1579 James Fitzmaurice Fitzgerald returned, leading an expeditionary force from Catholic Europe, and raised the papal banner in the far west. He promised to deliver Ireland from the excommunicate 'she-tyrant', Eliza-beth. Those who joined him might have had motives less elevated. The Geraldine swordsmen, humiliated by the pacific new world of composition which was intended to turn military retainers into hus-bandmen, rallied. In August 1579 John of Desmond murdered an English official and precipitated the House of Desmond into a revolt which its tormented head, the Earl of Desmond had little choice but to lead. A war between loyal and disloyal Munster lords ensued, with Ormond, Desmond's old enemy, leading the Crown's forces. The following sum-mer a Catholic confederacy formed in the Pale, led by James Eustace, Viscount Baltinglas, a nobleman of the Pale. In the name of the Pope, he called upon the leaders of Anglo-Irish society to join his 'holy enterprise' and to 'take the sword' against the unnatural and unjust supremacy of the Queen. The sons of some leading Pale families joined his cause, and paid with their lives, yet most of the Pale community was, although loyal to Rome, loyal to the Queen also, and did not rise. But the discovery that even a Dublin alderman had been involved in the conspiracy led to alarm that religious dissidence might turn to open defence of Catholicism, and to a new and minatory atmosphere. The rebellion offered the chance for the Gaelic septs of Leinster to prey upon the Pale, and in August the new, and as yet unwary, chief governor, Lord Grey de Wilton was ignominiously defeated by Fiach MacHugh O'Byrne at Glenmalure Pass in the Wicklow Mountains. In Ulster, Turlough Luineach was always ready to menace the English.

The Desmond rebellion destroyed the House of Desmond, disgraced the Earl of Kildare, alienated Ormond from the Crown, and devastated Munster. The English strategy had been to 'prey, burn, spoil and destroy', and it had worked. In the early 1580s Munster was truly waste and ready for colonization. The rebel remnant, wasted by famine, crept out of woods and glens; 'anatomies of death; they spake like ghosts crying out of their graves'. This was the approving description of Edmund Spenser, the prophet poet. The papal garrison at the Fort of Gold at Smerwick in the far west of Kerry was massacred in November 1580, its appeals to the laws of nations and the customs of war unheard. One great Elizabethan poet and courtier, Walter Ralegh, was executioner; another, Spenser, was recorder. Poetry was for camps as well as courts. According to Lord Deputy Grey, who ordered the garrison to be cut down, the Irish 'addiction' to 'treachery and breach of fidelity' was due to their Catholic religion which 'dispenses' with oaths from 'advantage'.

A harder spirit entered English policy. Sir Nicholas Malby warned that if the Queen did not 'use her sword more sharply, she will lose both sword and realm'. All private quarrels in Ireland, so he told Leicester in August 1580, were now converted into 'a general matter of religion'. The Irish might now make Catholicism the symbol of national identity and turn Ireland into a battleground of the Counter-Reformation. Ominously, the new battle cry of the rebels was '*Papa abo* [The pope above]'. What had not begun as a war of religion might become so at last. If the Pope could send an invading army into Ireland, might he send one into England too?

*

Catholics had in the 'days of darkness' at the beginning of Elizabeth's reign been quiescent and acquiescent. Their hierarchy overthrown, their churches usurped and their faith outlawed, most had responded by continuing to attend their parish churches as the law demanded, and as no Catholic authority yet insistently forbade. Most Catholics found ways of retaining both their hearts' allegiance to Rome and their obedience to their sovereign; still performing their public duty, sitting on the magistrates' bench and in their accustomed pew in church. Those who took the understandable path of least resistance and celebrated according to the rites of the Book of Common Prayer while longing for the Latin ones still thought of themselves as Catholics. Yet for the more uncompromising, they were not; they were schismatics, lost souls. This form of surrender would turn them from half-hearted 'Catholics' into half-hearted 'Protestants', and would lead to the loss of the old faith in their children's generation. All Catholics, a great part of the English population, hoped that the Protestant ascendancy was temporary, and that they would not forever be banished in their own land. Many shared a vision that the Church, invincible through history, would be restored. A few began to think that better times would come not by waiting but by working. The lives of would-be loyal and peaceful Catholics could not remain untouched by the increasing militancy of Catholicism at home and abroad. Nicholas Sanders, the most virulent of the polemicists in exile, wrote of the Church on earth arrayed as an army under its papal captain, and he himself sailed as papal emissary to the Fort of Gold in Ireland. A state of warfare between the Churches came to be acknowledged.

The papal bull *Regnans in excelsis* (February 1570) and its consequences in England had made confrontation more likely. When the Pope demanded that Elizabeth's Catholic subjects withdraw their allegiance he had created a fateful link between loyalty to Rome and disloyalty to the Queen. Stark choices faced Catholics once it became harder to maintain that their conforming attendance at church was other than schism and sin. In the shadow of the Northern rebellion of 1569, the leaders of every shire had been charged to declare their assent to Prayer Book services and to take Communion. Some in conscience could not. Open refusal to attend church was recusancy, and the refusing Catholics, the recusants, were subject to increasing penalties. In 1571 a House of Commons full of vengeful Protestants – the first Parliament to exclude admitted Catholics by the administration of an oath which they could not in conscience swear – extended the treason laws to include all those who imported papal bulls or sacred Catholic objects, who reconciled others to Rome or who were reconciled themselves. Priests were the agents of reconciliation. Some among the Catholic clergy who had remained in their parishes since Mary's reign had been urging the spiritual duty of withdrawal from heretic services, envisaging a separated Catholic community; some, of more agile conscience and with a just fear of the consequences of refusal, had said Prayer Book services in public and sung Mass in private. For many Catholics any crisis of conscience might have been passing, as long as sympathetic clergy continued to celebrate something that looked like the Mass, and while 'papist' midwives assisted childbirth with Latin invocations and illegal baptisms. But from 1574 these efforts to sustain the Catholic faithful were inspired by priests of another kind.

Almost a thousand years after St Augustine's mission to England another mission was launched. By the mid 1570s the young exiles at William Allen's English College at Douai in Flanders (founded in 1568) were studying the Jesuit spiritual exercises along with doctrine, and in 1574 the first seminary-educated missionary priest arrived in England. The mission of the seminary priests was less to convert than to rescue conforming Catholics from schism: to be pastors in the spiritual wilderness. They came to insist that recusancy was the spiritual duty of every Catholic, and to sustain them, illegally and secretly, for as long as was necessary. Although Catholic polemic was uncompromising, priests, faced with human weakness and troubled times, might temporize. The missionary priests did not invent the idea of a separated recusant Catholic community, but their arrival made that prospect more likely.

Without priests as agents of sacramental grace, Catholics could hardly be Catholics. But the arrival of the seminary priests brought not only new hope but new danger. Reconciling the faithful to Rome was treason; abetting it was scarcely less so. Priests were fugitive and needed shelter, so Catholic gentry who protested sincerely their loyalty to the Queen found themselves sheltering outlawed priests in their households, for to protect a priest was a duty hard for any Catholic to refuse when the faith depended upon it. Priests disguised as lay stewards, servants, teachers and soldiers, moved from house to house saying Mass, always in danger of betrayal and detection. In 1577 Richard Grenville, the Protestant Sheriff of Cornwall, arrived at the house of a Catholic neighbour, Francis Tregian, whom he disliked for more than religion, and found Tregian's steward in the garden wearing a forbidden *Agnus Dei*. This was Cuthbert Mayne, a Douai priest. Priests, if caught, were faced with a single choice: apostasy or death. Martyrdom was the risk they knowingly took at ordination. In the English College at Rome scholars read chapters from their martyrologies at dinner, telling of the saints executed at Tyburn. Mayne was hanged, drawn and quartered in 1577, the first of more than 200 Catholics martyred during Elizabeth's reign.

The Catholic mission was spiritual. Yet the priests, as emissaries of the Pope who had used his deposing power against the Queen, were enemy agents and traitors. Elizabeth and her Council knew that the overwhelming majority of her recusant Catholic subjects were, as they themselves insisted, loyal, anxious for a quiet life, obedient to the Queen in everything save church attendance, obedient to the Pope only in spiritual matters: what they could never know, until the test came, was precisely which Catholics were loyal and which might not be. Until and unless they knew, all Catholics were under suspicion; an enemy within. Until the late 1570s Catholics were treated with a remarkable latitude: 'By a merciful connivance [they] enjoyed their own service of God in their private houses', wrote the historian William Camden. The Queen remained reluctant for violence to be offered to consciences.

The arrival of the first English mission sent by the Society of Jesus, under Edmund Campion and Robert Persons, the Pope's 'white boys', in June 1580 changed things. But how could two Jesuits, however brilliant and compelling, threaten so entrenched a Protestant establishment? There was no doubting their power to inspire. Campion vowed that the Jesuits would persevere in their mission 'while we have a man left to enjoy your Tyburn, or to be racked with your torments, or consumed with your prisons. The expense is reckoned, the enterprise is begun.' Campion's audacity in travelling through England, celebrating the sacraments and writing controversial tracts, intensified the search for him. In July 1581 he was arrested, and in the Tower he disputed with his opponents. On 1 December he went to Tyburn. But the Jesuits had been sent to England as leaders of a special mission, not as martyrs; to keep the faith alive, not to die for it. To do their job, they must live. Hence the Jesuits' need for worldliness and their development of the art of casuistry – the answering of interrogators' questions subtly enough to escape and thereby to continue to catechize and to celebrate.

The arrival of the Jesuit mission coincided with a crisis for the godly. By the later 1570s England's Protestants feared that all their gains were illusory. English Catholics were, after twenty years, not retreating but resurgent. They were protected by friends in the highest places, and Masses were celebrated even in the heart of London. Early in 1575 there

were rumours that Philip II would persuade Elizabeth to allow four
Jesuits to preach in England; an advance guard of militant Tridentine
Catholicism, the faith redefined and strengthened by the Council of
Trent. Catholics, and especially the Jesuits, were believed to have wiles
to win over even the wary. Spenser's tale of the easy seduction of the
kid (the simple, faithful Christian) by the guileful (papist) fox in his
Shepherd's Calendar was written in 1579, a dark period for England's
godly, when some feared that even the Queen might succumb to flattering
Catholic counsels.

*

In 1577 John Dee, the mathematician, magician and theorist of empire,
had in his *General and Rare Memorials pertaining to the Perfect Art of
Navigation* illustrated the Queen at the helm of the imperial ship Europa.
His hope was that she would seize the chance to establish a Protestant
British empire. Yet if Elizabeth was the pilot, no one was sure which
course she had set. In hope also, the godly lauded Elizabeth as 'the
woman clothed with the Sun' from the Book of Revelation, but it was
evident that she did not share the evangelical enthusiasms of her advisers;
indeed she grew violently impatient with them. In 1578 a puritan divine
saw the deaths of the godly bishops Pilkington, Jewel and Parkhurst as
signs portending the end of the world, and, ominously, with each new
appointment to the episcopal bench – Aylmer, Freke, Piers, Young,
Whitgift (especially Whitgift) – the Supreme Governor signalled reaction. The elevation of Edmund Grindal, a fervent reformer and former
exile, to the see of Canterbury in December 1575 had soon come to
seem aberrant. Elizabeth, always likely to see the disruptive rather than
the evangelical possibilities of preaching, thought that three or four
preachers sufficed for a shire. This was held to be dereliction in a godly
Queen, and the lack of evangelical progress in her reign was, so Grindal
told her, 'lamentable'.

The war between reaction and further reform came soon, when battle
was joined over the issue of 'prophesyings' – self-help groups among
local clergy for the exegesis of scripture. These had caused excitement
in the shires, revealing the chasm between the godly and the rest, as
radical clergy, excluded from the Church, dared to discuss matters
political as well as divine, and lay people listened. After disquieting
reports in the summer of 1576, Elizabeth determined to end them.
Charged to violate his evangelical principles, Grindal responded with a

challenge to the Queen from which his victory could be only moral: he must choose, so he told her, 'rather to offend your earthly majesty than to offend against the heavenly majesty of God'. In May 1577 he was suspended and sequestered, never to be restored. The Queen willed no less than the deprivation of her archbishop. Should her will prevail, so the puritan Sir Francis Knollys warned, then 'up starts the pride and practice of the papists'; 'King Richard the second's men' (the archetypal flatterers of the tyrant) 'will flock into court apace'. The disgrace of Grindal was cause and consequence of a bitter and growing rift at Elizabeth's court.

England's godly saw terrible dangers at home and abroad as international Catholicism grew more menacing. While lamenting the paucity of England's support for the common cause of religion, they acknowledged that she had done enough to fear retribution. They saw Spain's seeming friendship as treachery: the Queen was seduced by 'Spanish compliments' while their 'secret practices' ripened. In a world devoted to horses, the dangers of 'unbridled' Spanish power were explained in equestrian metaphor: 'The Spanish jennet champs on her cakebread snaffle.' In France, Henry III had succeeded Charles IX in 1574. Guided variously by his mother Catherine de Medici ('the Jezebel of her age', according to Philip Sidney), the Guises, and Philip II, he supported the drive to extirpate the Protestant Church. Scotland, always a potential passage to England's destruction, had been safe through most of the 1570s under the regency of James Douglas, Earl of Morton, but in the spring of 1578 he was overthrown. Whether Scotland's future lay with Protestant England or Catholic France lay once more in the balance. Still in custody, Mary, Queen of Scots dreamt of marriage to Don John of Austria, the brilliant victor of the sea battle of Lepanto against the Turks, and from 1576 Governor-General of the Netherlands.

The Netherlands remained the focus of the hopes and fears of the Protestants of England and Europe. Holland and Zeeland had pursued their revolutionary course under the leadership of William of Orange, but by the autumn of 1575 the cause was in great danger. Attempts to bring peace between Spain and the rebel provinces had failed, and now, without aid, the Netherlands would be prey to France or Spain. Only the Queen failed to see the gravity of the threat or the greatness of the chance; a chance which would not come again, said the prescient. The Netherlands' danger was England's danger; their defence, England's defence, so insisted Orange and the Queen's advisers, as they looked on the growing power of Spain. But Elizabeth always baulked at openly aiding her Spanish ally's rebels and at spending money she did not have. In 1575 she proscribed Orange and his supporters. It was said she 'meaneth not to be a dealer'. In January 1576, in a fury of indecision, she boxed the ears of her gentlewomen and locked herself in her Privy Chamber away from the clamour of her councillors. Always preferring diplomacy to war, she sent ambassadors instead of the men and money needed.

Yet the course of the revolt changed in 1576 just when Spanish victory in Zeeland seemed certain. A reign of terror by mutinous, murderous Spanish troops, demanding 'Gelt, gelt' from a bankrupt Spain, created an uneasy alliance between the rebel provinces of the north and the loyalists of the south, a union made formal by the Pacification of Ghent in November 1576, which followed the apocalyptic Spanish fury when the troops laid waste Antwerp and massacred thousands. The States General, composed of mostly reluctant revolutionaries, convened itself and became the central organ of government of a united Netherlands. In January 1577 Don John of Austria signed the Perpetual Edict of Peace with the States, which was intended to restore the old religion throughout the Netherlands. William of Orange never consented to it, and Don John kept it, not perpetually but only for six months. There could be neither unity nor peace where Reformed religion and Catholicism could not coexist.

Orange, born great and with greatness thrust upon him, was recognized as the *pater patriae*, now leader of patriots not desperadoes. Between themselves, Elizabeth's advisers compared his Stoic constancy with the irresolution of their Queen, a failing they thought intrinsic to her 'womanly' nature. Her endless 'stays and resolutions', her uncertainty – 'sometimes so, sometimes no' – vitiated her actions and their counsel and led them to weary despair. By the late summer of 1577 her leading councillors, even cautious, circuitous Burghley, united in insisting that she intervene in the Netherlands and keep Orange 'in heart and life'. In St Paul's – London's talking shop as well as cathedral – all 'honest men' urged aid to the Dutch. At last the Queen was persuaded to send an expeditionary force under Leicester. She gave her promise. And she broke it. In January 1578 Don John, ignoring the paper peace, routed the States' army. It was a desperate moment for the cause. Surely the Queen would not leave the Dutch 'in the briars'. She would. She did. As before, she chose the security of mediation, of delay, of doing nothing, or almost nothing, to action. When she did send troops they were under the command of Duke John Casimir of the Palatinate (in what was, for Leicester, the unworthy stead of himself). Elizabeth's betrayal drove Orange to do as he had warned; to ally in August 1578 with the French in the dubious person of Francis, Duke of Anjou (formerly Duke of Alençon). Early in 1579, with the Protestant Union of Utrecht in January (which committed the rebel provinces to fight for total victory against Spain) and the Catholic Union of Arras in May (which recognized the full authority of Philip II), the Netherlands were divided; divided forever, when England's aid might, just might, have kept them united.

At this despairing moment, with 'all the world' her enemies at once, something surprising was going on in that uncertain centre of policy which was the royal mind. Determining to be the Virgin Queen no longer, Elizabeth chose the worst suitor in Europe; the faithless, feckless Duke of Anjou, his reputation as blemished as his pock-marked face. The Catholic heir-presumptive to the French throne, half the Queen's age – she was forty-five – was nowhere trusted; not in France, not in England. Slowly it dawned on Elizabeth's councillors that this suit, which had been so repellent to her in 1572, was by 1578 no dalliance. Hers was the policy; hers the pursuit. Supported by Burghley and Sussex, she saw only the advantages: marriage to Anjou was a way of ending England's diplomatic isolation and present danger, a means of asserting control over France by diplomacy and of finding protection against an increasingly aggressive, aggrandizing Spain. Elizabeth believed that she could use Anjou to contain Spanish reconquest in the Netherlands, while also preventing him from annexing them for France, or for himself. She might even ensure the succession by bearing an heir. Diplomatic imperatives gave way to emotional ones as she committed herself to this courtship, which would be her last. Early in 1579 the court watched in horror Elizabeth's romantic raptures with Simier, Anjou's agent, 'Monsieur's chief darling'. In August Anjou, the original 'frog he would a-wooing go', arrived in unprepossessing person.

The marriage proposal divided the court and Council, and threatened to divide the politically aware among the nation. Many saw only danger in the marriage to a 'stranger, a born enemy'. While Elizabeth lived, English interests would be subordinate to French; she would be drawn not into a Protestant but a Catholic league. Should she die – which was only too likely if, at her age, she did conceive a child – the Catholic Anjou might share the English throne with Mary Stewart. Once king of

France, Anjou would rule England through a viceroy as a French province. This marriage, so the godly feared, must be 'the overthrow of religion'. Memories of the persecution which followed Mary Tudor's marriage to Philip of Spain and of the 'massacring marriage' at Paris haunted Protestant minds. The prospect of the match was not quite unspeakable, for some dared speak out. For his pamphlet *The Discovery of a Gaping Gulf wherein England is like to be swallowed*, John Stubbs had his right hand cut off before a silent, horrified, crowd. Philip Sidney wrote warning Elizabeth against marriage to a stranger. Behind Sidney's quarrel that month with the malignant 17th Earl of Oxford, ostensibly over precedence on the tennis court, there lay more than wounded pride and personal loathing, for Sidney spoke for the forward Protestants to whom the Queen would not listen, and Oxford was part of the 'faction then reigning' of Catholic and crypto-Catholic noble malcontents, who told her what she wished to hear. The brilliant and unquiet Lord Henry Howard now dared to joke of his favour at court in the sacred terms of 'the chosen' and 'reprobation'. That autumn Elizabeth thought of introducing four Catholics into the Council. Leicester had seen the hopes of the 'papists' rising; they were 'upon their tiptoes', never in such 'jollity' since Queen Mary's days.

The marriage proposal revealed the distance between Elizabeth and her Council. Leicester, who had most to lose by the match, had remarried secretly in 1578. When Elizabeth discovered this from his enemies she banished him in fury. The Queen could justly protest that the Council, having always urged her to marry, were now thwarting her when she at last acceded. Without their support she could not act, and by the end of 1579 she tearfully bowed to this new exigency. She understood the extent of her power, the force of her will, but now learnt their limits. She had resisted the image of Protestant champion which her godly people wished upon her, but dared not tarnish it by so unpopular a marriage.

The fiction of negotiations for the marriage was not yet abandoned. In October 1580 Alexander Farnese, Prince of Parma, the brilliant successor to Don John as Governor-General of the Spanish Netherlands, contemptuously described Elizabeth's proceedings as 'the weaving of Penelope'. She undid every night what was done the day before; and all with no conclusion, save to weary her councillors, and lose the trust of anyone who dealt with her. Yet the need for alliance with a great power was now compelling. England and the rest of Europe watched impotently as Philip annexed the Portuguese throne. 'How idly we watch our neighbours' fires,' lamented Philip Sidney. In Scotland, the 'postern gate' was open once again to England's enemies, for the powerful and personal hold of the Guise emissary Esmé Stewart, Sieur d'Aubigny, over the young King James VI augured the renewal of the reactionary Catholic 'auld alliance'. In the face of these threats, the Anjou match began to find support even among its inveterate enemies as the only way to security. In the summer of 1581 Walsingham was sent to Paris with an impossible task: to secure an offensive-defensive league against Spain, but to avoid the marriage which would alone secure it. The French fear was that without the marriage Elizabeth would 'slip the collar' and leave France to fight Spain with herself as spectator. Henry III could be persuaded neither of their common danger nor of Elizabeth's good faith. As the negotiations failed, Walsingham dared to tell her that there was not a councillor who did not wish himself in the 'farthest part of Ethiopia'.

The Protestant nightmare of a militant Catholic league of 'mighty potentates that have bent themselves against God' did not go away. How could it when Parma seemed set to reconquer the Netherlands for Spain and for Rome? Yet English Protestants in the 1580s looked to the enemy within. The 'cold-starved papists' had been disappointed in their hopes of royal favour at the time of the Anjou match, but they might find salvation elsewhere. Catholics claimed that their religion was no treason. 'We travelled only for souls; we touched neither state nor policy,' insisted Campion at Tyburn. But his fellow Jesuit, Persons, turned to more sinister methods. In Paris in May 1582, Persons conspired with the Duke of Guise, the papal nuncio, Mary Stewart's ambassador and William Allen to plan an 'enterprise' – the invasion of England through Scotland. Accepting that the assassination of Elizabeth was the logical preliminary to the accession of Mary, Queen of Scots, Persons had begun to work towards it. That plan was aborted when in the Ruthven Raid of August 1582 the Earls of Gowrie and Mar kidnapped James VI in order to rescue him from the malign influence of Esmé Stewart, and Stewart retreated to France. Another 'practice' was conceived. In November 1583 Francis Throckmorton, a Catholic gentleman from Warwickshire was betrayed and arrested. Papers discovered in his study, and confessions extracted upon the rack, provided evidence of a treasonable conspiracy for invasion. Lists of English Catholic sympathizers were uncovered, among them the Earls of Northumberland and

Arundel and the malcontent Lord Henry Howard, who was a pensioner of the King of Spain. The plots were revealed in time by a surveillance network of spies and agents controlled by Walsingham. Men who had once been Catholics themselves knew best how to watch, infiltrate and suborn. Walsingham's turned men stalked the conspirators, but they could not know them all. To kill a queen only needed one assassin, one accurate dagger or bullet.

The assassination of William of Orange in July 1584 dismayed not only the Dutch. The consciousness of the Queen's mortality, the sense of the frailty of the thread on which her subjects' safety hung, were rarely spoken of publicly, but never forgotten. During the Anjou crisis, Leicester's nephew, Sir Philip Sidney, dared to write in his *Old Arcadia*, under cover of pastoral convention, of the Queen's death and its consequences. Surely Elizabeth would never marry now, never bear a child: she was the last of her line. In France, after the death of Anjou in June 1584, mourned only by Elizabeth and by his mother, war over the succession threatened, because the heir to the throne was now the Protestant Henry of Navarre. In England in the autumn of 1584 thousands of the political nation, of the Protestant nation, foreseeing disaster, swore to a Bond of Association. Binding themselves as 'one firm and loyal society', they vowed to defend the Queen and, should she be killed, to put to death the person for whose sake she had been murdered; Mary Stewart. This was vigilante justice, the politics of fear and vengeance, and showed the dark side of the passions aroused by religious division. Elizabeth and England were now left alone to face Spain at the zenith of its power.

9

The Enterprise of England

NEW WORLD VENTURES AND
THE COMING OF WAR WITH SPAIN
IN THE 1580S

'Let sea-discoverers to new worlds have gone'
John Donne, 'The Good Morrow'

In the spring of 1578, a time of despair for forward Protestants, when the Queen broke her promise to the Dutch and abandoned the cause, Philip Sidney told his friends that he was 'meditating some Indian project': a voyage to America. Wearied of 'in servile court remaining', of the flattery and whispers behind the arras, of waiting for royal favour that never came, and haunted by the dishonour of a long peace, Sidney longed to join the discoverers and colonizers who dreamt of finding in the New World the freedom and fortune that the Old denied them. The voyages were both cause and consequence of worsening relations between England and Spain, whose King aspired, wrote Sidney's friend Fulke Greville, to write '*Yo el Rey* [I, the King]' across a map of the whole western world.

England's claim to territory in the New World was old before it was exploited. Henry VII had sponsored John Cabot's voyage and discovery of Newfoundland in 1497, but Spain and Portugal had stolen a march. When Philip II annexed the Portuguese throne and its empire in 1580–83 he became master in the eastern hemisphere as well as the west. His monopolistic and Catholic imperial vision seemed boundless. Spain's immense aggrandizement had come to depend upon her oppression and exploitation of New World territories, and upon the misery of their inhabitants, which became legendary. In the 1570s the English began to envisage an empire of their own, to rival that of Spain. Some had a vision of a British empire as rich in virtue as in commerce; pacific and Protestant. John Dee, the Queen's celestial mathematician, sought to persuade her to make good her claim to a British empire overseas, inherited from King Arthur and from Prince Madog, the Welsh prince who had allegedly discovered America. Elizabeth, of course, rebutted the papal donation of the New World to Catholic Spain and Portugal. Was not 'the use of the sea and air . . . common to all?' she asked. She promised to plant English colonies in lands still uninhabited by Europeans.

The world was all before them, much of it still unknown. Cosmographers, geographers, philosophers and 'painful travellers', observing the movements of the oceans, postulated the existence of a North-West Passage between Asia and America, which they called the Strait of Anian. This would be the way to China and Cathay, to the wealth of the East. More intriguing still was the vast undiscovered southern continent included on their maps by Mercator and Ortelius – *Terra Australis Incognita* – which was believed to contain Marco Polo's kingdom of Locach and fabulous riches. Now travellers must venture in order to prove the theories of the cosmographers. 'Any man of our country, that will give the attempt, may with small danger pass to Cathay,' past the island of America, wrote Sir Humphrey Gilbert optimistically in 1576.

Storms and perils, shipwrecks, freezing cold and burning heat, and mountainous seas tested the voyagers. Psalm 107 told of men who went down to the sea in ships to discover the wonders of the deep, and the sailors did find wonders: sea unicorns and monsters, mountains of 'unmerciful ice', siren voices and ghostly fires. Novel diseases afflicted them, among them the calenture, the fever which lured overboard the sailors who, in their delirium, believed blue seas to be green fields. On dry land there were more wonders: man-eating alligators and anthropophagi (man-eating men). Sailing into unknown waters, running short of food and water, the travellers never knew whether it would be even more terrifying to sail on than to turn back. Parties left behind as colonists might never be seen again; their disappearance, like that of those left on Roanoke Island in 1587, mysterious and ominous. Shipwrecked mariners, like John Drake on the coast of Brazil, might be enslaved by Indians, or worse. To chart all the miseries of his 'sorrowful voyage' to San Juan de Ulúa in Mexico of 1567, wrote John Hawkins, would need a chronicler as patient as the recorder of the 'lives and deaths of the martyrs'. Safe at home, Elizabethans avidly read the travellers' tales. The stories were embellished to promote investment in the voyages, yet the bravery and reckless optimism of the adventurers reach down the centuries.

Between 1576 and 1578 Martin Frobisher led three expeditions to find the North-West Passage. Sailing through freezing fog, past floating

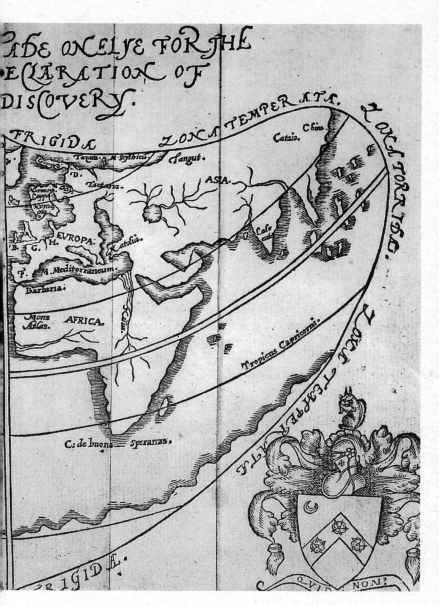

mountains and islands of ice, he claimed what is now called Baffin Island, a place so remote that the only name the Queen could find for it was *Meta Incognita*, the unknown boundary. The discovery of an Eskimo with apparently Tartar features seemed to prove the existence of the passage but, misled by delusory inlets and blocked by ice, these travellers could never find it. They found instead rocks which sparkled in the sun. A gold rush followed, sponsored by wild speculation at home, but that rock proved as heartbreaking and elusive as the North-West Passage itself: it was fool's gold.

In 1582 Richard Hakluyt, the great propagandist of plantation, dedicated a tract to Philip Sidney urging the colonization of 'those blessed countries from the point of Florida northward', still 'unplanted by Christians'. Blaming 'a preposterous desire of seeking gain rather than God's glory' for England's failure to found an empire, he promised that profits would follow 'if we first seek the kingdom of God'. The predatory English privateers who plied their barbarous slave trade between West Africa and the Spanish Indies in the 1560s and 1570s seemed indistinguishable from pirates. Yet religious zeal mingled with cupidity in many of the raiders in the New World. Francis Drake, most brilliant and daring of all English seafarers, who sailed around the world between 1577 and 1580, plundering Spanish treasure as he went, carried Foxe's *Acts and Monuments* with him (with the woodcuts coloured in), and was mortally affronted to find himself described by Philip II as a *corsario*, pirate. For him, every attack upon Spanish possessions was an assault upon Rome; every discovery, for the glory of the Queen and God. But the glory was also his own. On the coast of what may have been California in 1579 he accepted sovereignty for Elizabeth of a territory he called New Albion, and was himself crowned by the Indians, who honoured him 'by the name of Hioh'. The original purpose of Drake's voyage was shrouded in secrecy, but seeking the Pacific approach to the Strait of Anian, he discovered no *Terra Australis Incognita* where he had believed it would be.

Out of sight of land, captains might choose to be traders, pirates or explorers, or each in turn. Who could bind them once at sea? In the tiny world of a ship, captains held monarchical, even tyrannical, powers, if they could prevent their crew from mutiny. So Edward Fenton, sent in 1582 with the Queen's commission on the first trading expedition to the Far East, soon abandoned his mercantile purpose as he listened to a pirate crew who longed for Spanish prizes. 'We could not do God better service than to spoil the Spaniard,' insisted the ship's surgeon on the *Galleon Leicester*. Fenton planned to emulate, even to surpass, Drake, and to set up a colony in Brazil, or on the island of St Helena, with himself as king. Divided counsels and Fenton's indecision undermined the voyage. Should they, against royal command, sail west through the Magellan Strait, which was guarded by a Spanish fleet, to plunder in Peru, or sail eastwards by the Cape of Good Hope to the Moluccas? As mutiny threatened, the fleet's chaplains preached in vain upon Christian charity: that no man could serve two masters. Even on this troubled voyage the watchword was religious: the challenge in the dark was 'If God be with us'; the response, 'Who shall be against us?'

Inspired by Drake's triumph, most Elizabethan promoters and travellers looked westwards. Abandoning the frozen wastes of *Meta Incognita*, they turned their aspirations to the balmier shores of eastern North America; not only to explore but to live and lord it there. In 1578 Elizabeth granted to Sir Humphrey Gilbert for six years the right to discover and plant 'such remote, heathen and barbarous lands' as were still in no other 'Christian prince's' possession. She forbade any aggression against a prince at peace with England. Gilbert's New World schemes had hitherto been directed towards assaults upon Spanish fishing fleets around Newfoundland and piracy in the Caribbean and West Indies; his colonial ventures aimed at dispossession of the Irish in Munster. Now he dreamed not only of the North-West Passage, but of an empire in the West, with himself as overlord. Gilbert's mentor was the magus John Dee, whose arcane vision of a British empire he shared. But Gilbert shared too the ruthless European dream of Indians exchanging a king's ransom for glass beads, and proposed to set poor children to work to make such 'trifles'. Mr Ashley, a playing-card maker who had manufactured beads 'and other devices' for Gilbert's venture in 1582, was hoping for the day when a letter posted in London on May Day would reach China before the following midsummer.

Gilbert gained almost unlimited powers over unlimited territory and peoples yet undiscovered by Europeans. Held by homage to the Queen, these lands would be governed by him; his the right to grant tenures and make laws. Still in England, Gilbert sold a vast paper empire of twenty million acres which he had never seen. It was not until June 1583 that Gilbert sailed for Newfoundland and for 'Norumbega', the future New England. At St John's, he claimed Newfoundland for the Queen, cutting a turf as an archaic symbol of possession, and establishing law and religion according to English practice. What kind of colony he would have created in Norumbega cannot be known, for he never arrived. Like his half-brother Ralegh, like Sidney and Dee, Gilbert practised the 'starry science' of alchemy and, finding ore, his saturnine imagination became 'wholly fixed on the Newfoundland'. He left, promising to return, but disasters followed his little fleet. The *Delight* went down with all hands, and with the charts and ore still containing their secrets. Refusing to abandon his 'little company' with whom he had 'passed so many storms and perils', Gilbert was lost at sea. Last seen upon the foundering *Squirrel*, calmly reading, he called out: 'We are as near to heaven by sea as by land.' Perhaps he was drawing comfort from Cicero's Stoicism, but perhaps the book was More's *Utopia*, for this was Hythloday's aphorism, and *Utopia* had lessons for colonists.

The Americas offered to those who ventured the prospect of a 'golden world', like that of the first Creation before the Fall, when an uncorrupted earth brought forth its fruits without human labour, and when mankind lived 'void of all guile and treason'. Such was the country which Sir Walter Ralegh's agents claimed to discover in 1584 in Wingandacoa, which they renamed Virginia, after their Queen who was virgin too. In this earthly paradise the land smelt 'sweetly . . . as if we had been in the midst of some delicate garden'. Yet these English conquistadors sailed also in search of gold of another kind. The New World promised endless wealth, there for the taking; not beyond the dreams of avarice for men of fevered imaginations and unbounded optimism. Here, so they told prospective investors, was soil so fertile that a day's labour in planting would provide food for a year. All the commodities of southern Europe and of the East – oils, flax, frankincense, fruit, sugar – awaited the planters. There were drugs too, including tobacco, which Thomas Harriot – as fatally for himself as for millions thereafter – thought a health-giving herb. This cornucopia had the not inestimable advantage of being possessed by 'savages' who did not know how to exploit what they had. When Ralegh went in person to the New World in 1595 he found in Guiana a land which 'hath yet her maidenhead'. Yet to discover might be to despoil, and suspicion and venality entered this new Eden with the discoverers.

English claims to lands in the New World rested upon their being uninhabited by any Christian prince (not that this would stop them preying upon Christian neighbours from their new lands), but there were 'natural inhabitants' and local princes whose relationship to the colonists needed urgently to be addressed. Thomas Harriot represented the Indians of Virginia as natural theologians, virtuous pagans who, like More's Utopians, believed in many gods but 'one only chief and great god' and in the immortality of the soul, and were already moving towards 'civility and the embracing of true religion'. The aims of the colonists were threefold: to advance true religion among pagan peoples (advertised as the first purpose, when it was usually not), to trade and cultivate, and to conquer. Without conquest there could be neither colonization nor conversion. The first promoters urged that the colonists proceed against the Indians with 'all humanity and courtesy and much forbearing of revenge', for only through amity could trade and settlement prosper. Among the Indians, the settlers planned to live as gentlemen (even if they were not): never to work with their hands, but to live upon Indian labour. But soon came the recognition that they might need to act with 'extremity' in order to conquer, fortify and colonize; that the Indians might not want to cede what was theirs.

How to bring the Indians into subjection and to 'civility'? The dilemma and the argument were familiar from much nearer home; from Ireland, where the 'wild Irish' were increasingly treated as 'savage' and 'pagan', rather than as an ancient Christian civilization, and where some English governors urged that reform and civility must be imposed by force. Of course, the Irish were not pagan, but Catholic; they were subjects of the English Queen, who was also Queen of Ireland, and subject to her laws; and some of the most rebellious and intransigent of her Irish subjects were now not Gaelic but Anglo-Irish; not easily seen as Indians. Yet in Sierra Leone Edward Fenton, who had served with the 1st Earl of Essex in Ulster, found similarities between African native peoples and the Irish, saying, 'This is thoroughly Irish, for thus the Irish are wont to do.' Sir Henry Sidney had compared certain Gaelic clans to cannibals. The debate about Indian and Irish 'civility' was familiar to the colonists and projectors because so many of them – Drake, Gilbert, Grenville, Frobisher, Ralegh, Lane, Harriot, Philip Sidney – were of the Protestant New English who had visited or served in Ireland. Philip Sidney, who was partner in a secret and fantastic scheme to sequester parts of Munster and planned to be baron of Kerry, had purchased three million acres of 'Norumbega' from Gilbert, which neither of them ever saw. Those who had been promoters of schemes to colonize Ireland turned to much wider lands and wilder peoples.

A strange mixture of the quest for virtue in action and a ruthless acquisitiveness marked the lives of the Elizabethan adventurers. The New World offered many freedoms. To those, like Ralegh, Harriot and Gilbert, whose speculation was theological and scientific as well as financial, America was 'a fruitful womb of innovation'. The most enthusiastic projectors for Gilbert's colony were members of the recusant Catholic gentry, seeking escape from the ruinous penalties which awaited them in England for practising their religion. Walsingham encouraged their migration. For the landless and insecure in England, not least for younger sons, there was the prospect of wealth. The lands in the colonies were free from the debt and entail which trammelled landowners in the Old World. In the New World the colonists could live with little recourse to the governor and less to England. On this frontier, without restraint or supervision, with no laws of war, they could test themselves. Ralegh and his friends planned to prey upon the Spanish empire from their colony. America was a 'place of hazard' where furious spirits miscast for the long peace in England might win fame and honour. But that long peace was about to end.

In September 1585 Sidney at last attempted his escape to the New World. He rode to Plymouth to join Drake's voyage to the West Indies, without royal permission: a 'desperate course', judged his father-in-law, Walsingham. On the very eve of sailing, he was ordered back by the Queen's peremptory command. Drake could not countenance a divided command, nor could Elizabeth allow Sidney's disobedience. But with her 'thunder' came her 'grace'. Sidney was appointed Governor of Flushing in the Netherlands, and offered the chance for action in the Protestant cause for which he had yearned. For on 4 September, the day before Drake sailed, Elizabeth's help at last came to save the Dutch in their extremity, in the form of 4,000 troops. Her commission to the predatory Drake to sail along the Spanish Main and her protection of the Low Countries precipitated what she had so long avoided: war with Spain.

*

At the end of 1584 Elizabeth's councillors had confronted an alarming paradox: the only way to secure lasting peace for England might be by waging war. Since the previous summer England had stood alone in Europe. Burghley starkly expressed the danger of that unchosen isolation: 'No help but her own, and that but half a help', since the loyalty of so many Catholics was still suspected to lie with the Scottish Queen and with Rome. Despite her old horror of French encirclement, Elizabeth had sought an offensive and defensive alliance with Henry III to challenge the 'overgreatness' of the King of Spain, and proposed their joint government of the Low Countries. That planned alliance had failed and the Duke of Anjou's dismal rule as elected sovereign of the Netherlands (1581–3) had ended with his abdication. In July 1581 the Act of Abjuration deposed Philip II, and a Dutch republic was created. By the spring of 1583 the state of the rebel provinces was desperate, and Orange's strategy of religious peace, whereby local authorities should tolerate freedom of worship, lay in ruins. Anjou had left the Netherlands that June, unlamented, and Orange abandoned Brabant in the south for Holland which would become, as he had predicted, his tomb. In July 1584 an assassin earned a Spanish bounty by cutting down the *pater patriae*.

The demoralized, mesmerized towns of Flanders and Brabant capitulated, one by one, before the serpentine diplomacy and strategic genius of the Prince of Parma, Governor-General of the Netherlands. Parma, who seemed to retain in his head a plan of all the waterways and terrain of the Low Countries, forced the towns' surrender by distant blockade, by treachery from within, and by the silver bullets of bribes, as often as by military assault. By the end of 1584 only Brussels, Mechelen and Antwerp still resisted: the revolt in the south seemed doomed. Fearful of falling into Spanish hands, the Dutch prepared to throw themselves into French. 'He who would escape Charybdis falls into Scylla,' remarked Sir Edward Stafford, English ambassador to Paris. At the end of 1584 the rebel states offered sovereignty to Henry III, who refused it. France was entering a new and dangerous phase of her own civil war. The death of the Duke of Anjou left the Protestant Bourbon leader, Henry of Navarre, heir to the French throne. The militant Catholic League, first formed in 1576, was now revived under Guise leadership; it was sworn to resist the succession of a heretic, by *main forte* if necessary, and to defend Holy Church. From the late summer of 1584 the Guise lords rallied their noble clienteles in the provinces of the north and east of France and at the end of the year Philip II promised aid to the Leaguer army. If the League won, the French Channel shore, where the League was strongest, would lie open to Spain. Would France become Spain's client? The English watched events over the Channel with mounting alarm.

Once again, England's help was the last hope of the rebel Dutch.

Would Elizabeth at last allow the cause to die? Her councillors, in conference at the end of 1584, debated two momentous questions: should England protect the United Provinces; if not, how should she defend herself against Philip II's 'malice and forces', which would surely turn against her once he had subdued Holland and Zeeland? There could be no 'quiet neighbourhood' with a victorious, vengeful Spain. Better to wage war abroad, and with allies, than to encounter the power of Spain at home, undermined by enemies within: this was the argument of Sir Walter Mildmay and the interventionists. Against this strategy were presented the arguments which had always persuaded Elizabeth before: to aid the rebels was against 'honour and conscience'; they were a 'popular state without a head', against nature; and the cost of the war would be as great as it was incalculable, and her subjects might resist paying for it. The interventionist argument at last prevailed. As Burghley concluded, it was safer to enter the war now to prevent Philip from attaining the 'full height of his designs and conquests', which would be irresistible and leave Elizabeth and England helpless before his 'insatiable malice, which is most terrible to be thought of but most miserable to suffer'. Recognizing this as a time of great danger, Elizabeth's Protestant nobility and gentry bound themselves in the Bond of Association.

In August 1585, in the Treaty of Nonsuch, Elizabeth and the Dutch made formal their mutually reluctant recognition that they were the only allies for each other. To offer protection to the Dutch was to invite retribution, and the Queen who had tried to risk nothing now risked everything. 'She took the diadem from her head and adventured it upon the doubtful chance of war,' said the King of Sweden. All her provocation (despite her prevarication) – the seizure of Alva's pay-ships, the 'volunteers' sent in 1572, the secret loans, the knighting of Drake after his circumnavigation and seizure of Spanish treasure – led at last to her grudging adoption of the cause. Philip II's past hostile actions were alleged in formal justification of Elizabeth's protection of the Netherlands. Yet even as English help came, it came too late; too late to save Antwerp which, blockaded and starved, finally surrendered to Parma three days before the treaty was signed. The great metropolis, once the heart of the revolt, became a Spanish bastion. Could Antwerp have been relieved? Many thought so, and did not easily forgive Elizabeth. Although she sent help, the Queen's objectives had never changed and were not those of the Dutch. Fearing French encirclement, her hope was still merely to restore ancient liberties of the Netherlands under Spanish sovereignty, even though the Dutch had finally and formally forsworn it in the Act of Abjuration of 1581. Elizabeth always drew back from their last demand, for her to rule. It was one thing to accept the sovereignty of New Albion; quite another to become queen of the rebel Dutch. Some around her had other ideas.

Her great magnifico, the Earl of Leicester, was sent to the Netherlands as the Queen's Lieutenant-General. He arrived in December 1585, attended by the flower of English chivalry, many of them fired with enthusiasm for the Protestant cause. Leicester sought 'as much authority as the Prince of Orange' had, but he shared rather the arrogance and ineptitude of Anjou than Orange's personal authority. Nevertheless, for a while his arrival strengthened the faltering resolve of the Dutch. He was awaited as 'the Messiah', so Philip Sidney told him. In the midst of the euphoria, Leicester was offered the governor-generalship of the United Provinces. Unknown to the Queen, and against her express command, he accepted it, thereby giving the impression that the Queen herself had assumed sovereignty, with Leicester acting as her viceroy. In January 1586 he was installed as 'absolute governor'. Elizabeth's fury once she discovered this, her 'storms' and 'great oaths', made her counsellors run for cover. Leicester saw himself as a Renaissance prince, but to the Queen he was her 'creature'. Her fear, as a queen and as a woman, had always been that her greatest male subjects would conspire to overrule her. Now they had.

Leicester had not acted alone. There had been a conspiracy in the Privy Council. Surely this had been the 'plot for the establishing of some well-settled government' in the Netherlands about which Walsingham's agents had conferred with some of the 'best-affected patriots'. Leicester's 'friends' protested loyalty to him, while distancing themselves from him. His brother advised exile to the 'furthest part of Christendom'. Not until the end of March did the Queen call Leicester her 'sweet Robin' again, wrote Ralegh, whom Leicester suspected of traducing him. Elizabeth's anger was partly stirred by rumours of an alternative court in the Low Countries, with the Countess of Leicester queening it there, but more by the knowledge that she had been deceived by her councillors; that she had been the last to know of an act which made her 'infamous'. The forward Protestants had been moved to desperate measures to protect a cause which Elizabeth had never truly supported.

As he had left for the Low Countries, Leicester suspected that Burghley would exploit his absence to further the peace. Rumours spread that the Queen was preparing to deal with Parma, to renege upon the cause even as her troops risked their lives for it. 1586 saw a series of dismal military failures. Parma's constancy and strategy brought gain after gain for Spain, while Leicester's complaining and inaction led to reverses for the allies. Not that everything was Leicester's fault. His arrival had precipitated a constitutional and political crisis in the infant Dutch republic. His function uncertain, his instructions contradictory, his bedraggled army without provisions (except from his own resources), his queen dealing behind his back, Leicester could hardly have succeeded.

Haunted by 'danger, want and disgrace', Philip Sidney wrote to Walsingham at the end of March that 'if her Majesty were the fountain, I would fear . . . that we should wax dry'. But she was not. For Sidney, the conflict in the Netherlands was part of a cosmic struggle: 'I see the great work indeed in hand against the abusers of the world.' In that struggle, the 'wise and constant man' must play his part truly, trusting to 'man's power' and never despairing of 'God's work'. Outside Axel in August Sidney urged on his troops to holy war and, amidst a series of English reverses, his 'camisado' (night attack) there was a rare success. Yet without pay, mutiny and defeat threatened. At a raid outside Zutphen on 22 September Sidney received the wound that would kill him. His contemporaries knew what they had lost. Ralegh, who had been jealous of him in life, wrote:

> Back to the camp, by thee that day was brought,
> First thine own death, and, after, thy long fame,
> Tears to the soldiers, the proud Castilian's shame,
> Virtue expressed, and honour truly taught.

A riderless horse was led in the Accession Day tilts that year, caparisoned in mourning black. Even as Sidney had left for the Netherlands, he had already doubted that victory against Spain could be won there, for Parma's advance seemed inexorable. He had dreamt of greater action on a wider stage, wanting England 'to carry war into the bowels of Spain', either on the Spanish mainland, or into the heart of her empire.

*

The Queen's motto was '*Semper eadem* [Always the same]', and she had tried to live by it. Elizabethan politics had seemed to be frozen. No answer was found to the perennial questions: what was to be done about the succession? and about the haunting menace of the Queen of Scots? Elizabeth's other motto was '*Video et taceo* [I see and keep silent]'. She had known her own mind, even as she watched and waited, and had been shrewd in her caution. Yet her councillors increasingly doubted her powers of judgement. Walsingham wrote to Leicester in May 1586 of the Queen 'whom I do find daily more and more unapt to embrace any matter of weight'. They despaired of her failure to listen to them, her refusal to allow open debate in Council, and her willingness to take advice 'underhand'.

War must transform the nature of politics. Elizabeth's personal emblem of the rusty sword for a peaceful reign was no longer appropriate; nor was her way of governing. Politic inaction, delay and prevarication might serve for peace; but not for war, where deep strategy, quick reactions and instant decisions were necessary. Her councillors might risk her fury again by taking decisions for her, as they had done when Leicester accepted the sovereignty of the Netherlands. And a wider band of her subjects too might seize the initiative. In 1584 thousands had, in the Bond of Association, sworn to prosecute to the death anyone who attempted anything against the Queen. The Act for the Queen's Safety (1584–5) had moderated that arbitrary, vigilante justice and instituted legal process, but the 'fellowship and society' of the Bond remained bound by oath to act if the Queen's life were threatened. In 1586 another conspiracy was discovered.

In the secret world of Catholic exiles, spies, seminary priests and young idealists won to the Catholic cause at the universities and the Inns of Court, the dream remained of freeing the captive Queen of Scots and placing her on the English throne. At Whitsun 1586 John Ballard, alias Captain Fortescue, a 'silken priest in soldier's habit', revealed a conspiracy to Anthony Babington, a young gentleman of Lincoln's Inn. A massive invasion of England was planned for that summer, supported by the great Catholic powers. There would never be a better time, since English chivalry was away fighting in Flanders. To Babington's objection that English Catholics would not rise while the Queen lived, Ballard replied that she would not live long; plans were laid for her assassination. But some of Mary Stewart's agents were Walsingham's agents also. Among the Catholic idealists, prepared for martyrdom, Walsingham had insinuated the most cynical of *agents provocateurs*, men who would act for the highest bidder. For Walsingham, 'knowledge is never too dear'. He was accused later of laying a trap for Mary. In reality – if that is a term properly applied to the deluded Queen – she had needed no luring.

Early in July Babington wrote to the Queen of Scots telling her of the proposed conspiracy and of the 'six noble gentlemen' ready for the 'tragical execution'. This was a request for her assent, and she gave it. Every letter from Mary to her friends, and from her friends to her, was hidden in a beer barrel delivered weekly to Mary's prison at Chartley, the Earl of Essex's house in Staffordshire, and every letter was intercepted, copied and passed to Walsingham. By 17 July he had in his hands Mary's own reply to Babington: the proof of her complicity, the evidence of her treason. Babington and his accomplices were hunted down, arraigned and condemned. Elizabeth was known for clemency, but these conspirators could not be spared. In the Tower, one of the conspirators, Chidiock Tichborne, wrote an elegy:

> I sought my death, and found it in my womb.
> I looked for life, and saw it was a shade.
> I trod the earth and knew it was my tomb.
> And now I die, and now I am but made.
> The glass is full, and now the glass is run.
> And now I live, and now my life is done.

The full penalty for treason was exacted upon the conspirators: to be hanged, cut down from the gallows while they still lived, and dismembered before their own eyes. Babington watched the agonies of his fellows, until his turn came.

On the copy of the letter which told of Mary's treason, Walsingham's agent had sketched three lines – ⌐ – death to anyone who intercepted the letter, and, surely, for the Queen of Scots. Mary was tried before a commission of councillors and peers at Fotheringhay Castle in mid October, and the verdict of guilt was given. Could she be allowed to live? As before, in 1572, an extraordinary Parliament was summoned: not to make laws nor to grant subsidies but to advise upon the fate of Mary Stewart. Lords and Commons demonstrated their unanimity in speech after speech, and on 12 November the two Houses presented a joint petition calling for her death. Speaker Puckering insisted that mercy towards Mary was cruelty to her subjects: 'to spare her, is to spill us'. His speech contained a not-so-veiled threat. Had not thousands of Elizabeth's subjects sworn before God 'to pursue to death . . . such as she is by just sentence now found to be'? Either they must now act against Mary, against the law, or allow her to live, against their oaths and to the peril of their souls. On 24 November Elizabeth replied, but her answer gave no answer; she asked them to 'take in good part my answer answerless'.

Would Elizabeth succumb to the cruelty of pity? Sentence had been proclaimed against Mary on 4 December, the warrant for her execution drawn up and signed, but not dispatched, and still not dispatched. Elizabeth would not be seen to kill her sister Queen. 'We princes, I tell you, are set on stages in the sight and view of the world duly observed.' Emissaries came from Scotland and France to intercede for Mary's life. Elizabeth saw Mary's death in her dreams, so she told her Secretary of State, William Davison, but she could not bear the guilt of it. Would no one ease her of her burden? Would not Paulet, Mary's gaoler, fulfil the oath he had taken when he joined the Bond of Association and 'shorten the life of that queen', she asked? No, he would not. Since Elizabeth declined to act, her councillors must act for her. On 6 February Beale, clerk to the Privy Council, delivered Elizabeth's warrant to Fotheringhay, and on 8 February the axe fell. Mary met her death with a resolution that Elizabeth had lacked in allowing it, 'glad that the end of all her sorrows were so near'. Refusing the Protestant prayers offered, Mary prayed God to forgive her enemies as she forgave them, asked for His blessing upon Elizabeth, and besought all the saints to pray her Saviour to receive her. She died a Catholic.

Elizabeth received the news of Mary's death in a frenzy of guilt and grief. Estranging herself from the Council which had deceived her, she denied access to Burghley and sent Davison to the Tower. That Lent a court preacher dared to rebuke the Queen for her false pity and unthankfulness; for being a failing Deborah for Israel. Spenser, subtlest of poets, revealed in The Faerie Queene the agonized ambiguity of a queen torn between mercy and justice as, in transparent allegory, Mercilla appears, but only appears, to spare Duessa. Mary's death removed the menace of a queen-in-waiting within England, but brought new danger. With the succession still unsettled, the old questions of religion and allegiance were laid bare. English Protestants could now support the succession of James VI of Scotland, the Protestant king of a Protestant country, but to English Catholics he was a heretic and intolerable as king. Philip of Spain had been planning an invasion to place Mary upon the throne: hers was the right and she was a Catholic who would restore

England to Rome. Now that Mary was dead, would Philip, who had once been king-consort of England and was heir to its throne by descent in the Lancastrian line from Edward III, claim the throne again not only by conquest but by right?

*

Philip had never wanted war with England. He had given half-hearted help to Guise's proposed 'enterprise of England' in 1583, but was not yet planning his own. When Pope Sixtus V adjured him in the summer of 1585 to undertake some glorious enterprise for the faith, Philip was reluctant. All Elizabeth's provocation invited retaliation, but for that a mere punitive expedition to Ireland might have sufficed. Then Philip changed his mind: he determined instead upon a great crusade to restore the faith to England. Drake's voyage around the world had raised the spectre of constant English raids against the Spanish empire. In the spring of 1586 the Pope agreed that once Mary, Queen of Scots was on the English throne, Philip could choose her successor. That the succession would pass to his own dynasty – not to himself, but to his daughter, the Infanta Isabella – Philip kept secret. Through 1586 preparations were made for a great Armada. The felling of so many trees, the storing of provisions, the levying of thousands of men throughout Italy and Iberia, could not be hidden. A great fleet would sail, but where and against whom? That spring the talk among soldiers in the Netherlands was of the invasion of England. Others thought the Armada was intended for a final assault upon Holland and Zeeland. Speculation was universal, but only Philip and his most senior commanders knew the strategy, and Philip's mind kept changing. In the summer of 1586 he had sent a message to Parma, for Parma's eyes alone, that he would command an expeditionary force from the Netherlands to join the Armada for a combined invasion of England through Kent. This was a grand plan which left much unplanned.

Philip had bought powder and shot and biscuit. He had also bought the English ambassador in Paris. Sir Edward Stafford, feuding with Walsingham and Leicester and now looking to the rising sun, the next monarch, made his own the fourth generation of traitors in his family. Early in 1587 he promised Don Bernadino de Mendoza, the Spanish ambassador to London until 1584, and subsequently in Paris, that not a single warship would be equipped in England without Spain's knowledge. That April he revealed the most secret of plans: the Queen's instructions to Drake to sail to Spain and destroy all the Spanish shipping and property he could; to 'singe the King of Spain's beard'. But his information arrived just too late to prevent Drake's spectacular raid on 19 April. In January 1588 Stafford sent news to England that the Armada was abandoned; in April that it sailed for Algiers; in June that it was bound for the Indies, and then that it had been diverted back to Spain: all false, all treason, at a time of consummate danger for England. At the end of May the great Armada sailed from Lisbon, under the reluctant command of the Duke of Medina Sidonia. A fleet of 130 ships, with 18,000 soldiers and 7,000 sailors, left La Coruña in July 1588 – the greatest fleet ever seen – and still no one in England knew its exact destination or purpose.

On 19 July the Armada was sighted off the Scilly Isles. The Lord Admiral, Charles Howard, Lord Howard of Effingham led the Queen's fleet out of Plymouth harbour, and the next day it saw the Armada sailing slowly up the Channel under full sail in its awesome crescent formation; its galleons, with their high turrets, like floating wooden castles. On the 21st the Lord Admiral sent the *Disdain* to bear his challenge to the Spanish admiral. His flagship, *Ark Royal* exchanged broadsides with the Levant squadron, while Drake in the *Revenge*, Hawkins in the *Victory*, and Frobisher in the *Triumph* assailed the Armada's 'rearguard' commanded by Vice-Admiral Recalde. The English ships were smaller than the Spanish, but they were faster, more weatherly and, crucially, they had seized the advantage of the wind. Through the terrifying days ahead the English evaded the Spanish tactics of grappling and boarding, and were fleet enough to keep the distance they chose and to use their superior guns.

In deciding to let the Armada pass and to pursue it up the Channel, the English commanders had taken a terrible risk. They could never break its grim formation, and the Armada sailed on towards the Calais Roads and its rendezvous with Parma. Parma had an assault force of 17,000 men, including some of the best fighting men in Europe, yet he had already lost confidence in the enterprise, and wished to halt it. Medina Sidonia anchored off Calais on the 27th, waiting to escort Parma's invading transports to Kent. What he could not have known was that Parma was helpless to help, blocked by the Dutch flyboats which controlled the banks and shoals of the Flanders coast. As the Spanish waited for the meeting that never came, there appeared out of the dark of the night of the 28th blazing fireships, borne upon the wind

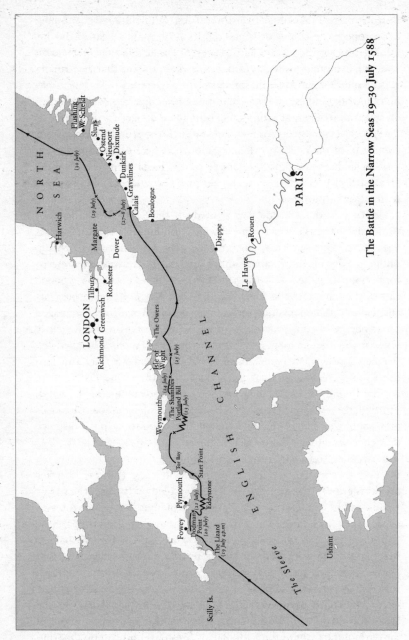

The Battle in the Narrow Seas 19–30 July 1588

towards them. In horror that these were 'hell burners', explosive as well as incendiary, the Armada scattered. It re-formed, and engaged the English fleet the next day. The sea battle off Gravelines was fiercer even than that at Lepanto, so Spaniards remembered, but that had been a great Spanish victory and this was not.

The Armada sailed north before the wind, with the English in pursuit. Driven to leeward by wind and current, it was within minutes of grounding on the Zeeland sands, to be saved only by the providential backing of the wind. Still the Spanish commanders planned to re-engage, but the Armada fled on northwards, driven by storms, making for Scotland and, by the longest route, for home. Shortage of water forced the Spaniards to throw their horses into the sea where, later, a Dutch merchantman came upon them swimming, swimming. Philip had collected charts of the English coast, but there were none for the lethal west coast of Ireland. Spanish wrecks lie still in the waters off Kerry, Donegal and Sligo. There was little comfort for those Spaniards driven ashore in Ireland by shipwreck or famine. The Irish, wrote Sir George Carew, stood 'agaze until the game be played'. Only a few chiefs, like O'Rourke and Mac-Clancy in Leitrim, dared offer shelter. Others, fearful of retribution, handed over hundreds of Spaniards for summary execution by English officers. On Clare Island the O'Malleys murdered survivors from Don Pedro de Mendoza's ship for their gold. By sword or sea, Spaniards died in their thousands in Ireland. Since the Spanish were allies of the Irish against England, they could be given no quarter by Ireland's English rulers. At the height of the scare the English-born councillors in Dublin added a secret postscript to a dispatch, 'signed only by us of the English': in their terror that not only Gaelic Ulster but the Pale would rise with the Spanish, they called for 2,000 men.

Perhaps half of the great fleet returned to Spain by mid October; the ships battered, as many as 9,000 men lost, and the remnant starving, thirsty, even dying. So much had gone wrong in the preparation for this invasion: too few seamen, too little food and water, and, crucially, the failed embarkation of Parma's troops. Yet England had lain open. The fortifications of the south coast were pathetically inadequate; the land forces there 'artificers and clowns [craftsmen and peasants]' who knew nothing of war. Raw, untrained, unprovisioned levies, under the command of Leicester, so unsuccessful a commander, gathered at Tilbury in Essex for the defence of London. After the Armada had fled north, but before fears of its return had subsided, Elizabeth came in glorious person to the camp to rally her troops: 'I myself will take up arms, I myself will be your general, judge and rewarder of every one of your virtues in the field.' So magnificent, so gallant, and yet so useless if the Spaniards had landed, as planned, in Kent. The English fleet had been too short of food and shot to pursue the Armada north. Against nature, the Lord Admiral ate beans (which were peasants' food) and his mariners drank their urine.

In the Tower, where he languished for his suspected complicity in Catholic 'practices', Philip Howard, Earl of Arundel had composed a prayer and had a Mass of the Holy Ghost said for the 'happy success' of the Armada. This was treason, and unavailing. Parma had feared early in 1586 that 'God will soon weary of working miracles for us'. Now it seemed He had. Both English and Spanish saw God's hand in every victory and defeat. Drake rejoiced that God had sent 'this proud enemy of His truth by storm and tempest', and certainly most of the providential winds had blown to England's advantage. Many were complacent. Armada medals were struck, parodying Caesar's boast: 'It came, it saw, it fled'. But many saw instead what had been lost. 'Our parsimony at home,' wrote Captain Henry White, 'hath bereaved us of the famousest victory that ever our nation had at sea.' Elizabeth had been unable to raise money: at home, because of a trade recession; abroad, because no one thought the English could win. Lack of provisions had left the victory inconclusive, and the Armada defeated only for a while. Walsingham, perennially pessimistic, lamented, 'So our half-doing doth breed dishonour and leaves the disease uncured.' Elizabeth now seemed set to hazard her kingdom by disarming, yet few doubted, either in Spain or England, that another Armada would sail. And when it did, God might not again send England the victory. The Armada was, for England's godly, not merely an enterprise by the national enemy, but an emissary from the papal Antichrist; only one event in the inevitable apocalyptic confrontation.

10

The Theatre of God's Judgements

ELIZABETHAN WORLD VIEWS

An incendiary rumour persisted in Essex through the 1580s and 1590s, of the arrival of an avenging army of vagrants, led by the King of Spain and the long-exiled Earl of Westmorland, to free the poor of England. This was the delusion of despair. In the 1590s the suffering and privation of the poor was worse than anyone could remember. In their distress, would they seek remedy? Hearing the news that wheat was on sale at nine shillings a bushel at Bicester market in the autumn of 1596 – three times the price of earlier in the decade – a man asked, 'Then what shall poor men do?'

'Rather than they would be starved, they would rise,' came the reply.

The Elizabethan governing orders looked on the poor, usually so passive and deferential, with mounting alarm.

The years of peace before 1585 had been years of prosperity; 'the mother of riches . . . the father of many children', so William Lambarde, the Kentish antiquarian and JP, described them. The population of England had expanded at a startling rate: perhaps by 1 per cent every year between 1576 and 1586, and by as much as 35 per cent during Elizabeth's reign – from 3.3 million in 1571 to 4.15 million in 1603. The growth of London had been more spectacular still. In 1548 perhaps as many as 60,000 people lived within the walls of the City and in its precincts north and south of the river; by Elizabeth's death the population of the growing metropolis, extending beyond its ancient walls, may have been as many as 200,000. Migrants swarmed to the City, and there, in the crowded alleys, the mortality rate continually exceeded the birth rate. The poor did not come to London in order to die, but that was very often the consequence.

All these mouths had to be fed, an exigency which presented new opportunities and new dangers. There were many gentry and yeomen farmers who rose to the challenge, producing surplus food for sale in the markets, and farming more intensively and more cost-effectively. They bought up smaller farms, engrossing the subsistence holdings of their poorer neighbours into their own more economically efficient holdings. As the population grew, they exploited the increased supply of labour by cutting wages; as competition for land increased and the law of supply and demand drove up rents, they outbid those who were struggling. The enclosure of open fields under tillage or of common pasture land was the most infamous device adopted by rationalizing landlords to wipe out customary rights. In many areas enclosure had taken place long ago, but in others aggressive landlords continued to enclose, and each new enclosure was more bitterly resented by those it deprived. As important as the real map of enclosure was the map in the minds of those it threatened. The economic advantage of enclosure – for the enclosers – was overshadowed by its social and moral costs. Preachers like William Harrison of Radwinter in Essex saw enclosure as the unbridled pursuit of self-interest, and as unregenerate use of divinely given resources.

The beneficiaries of the agricultural changes grew rich, built new and grander houses, had their portraits painted, and in their new-found wealth and confidence sent their sons to the universities and Inns of Court. Certainly there were rack-renting landlords who mercilessly evicted their tenants as leases expired, who extended their game parks by taking in the miserable half-yardlands upon which their neighbours subsisted, and who let acre upon acre to absentee graziers, but the great agricultural transformation of the later sixteenth century was caused far less by a conspiracy of agrarian capitalists than by the extraordinary population pressure. Economic growth and agricultural advance were gained at a terrible cost. Families were left landless and homeless when their subsistence holdings were no longer viable; they could not afford to pay their rents or the entry fines which came due when land changed hands by sale or inheritance, and were forced deeper and deeper into debt to buy food and seed corn until compelled to sell holdings which they would never recover. Wages were driven down because of the labour surplus, and many could hardly keep their families, however long or hard they worked, even if there were work to be had. Gleaning and gathering firewood were vital to the lives of the poor, and the poor's assertion of, to them, customary rights sometimes led to disputes when landowners denied those rights. As indigent families were driven from their holdings, and the caste of landless rural wage labourers and cottagers grew, there grew also an estrangement between the yeomen and the poorer sort. The impersonal forces of the market had tragic personal consequences.

The lives of the greater part of the population, in town and countryside, were always precarious, resting as they did upon the health of the main breadwinner in each family; but for all poor people the difference between survival and privation depended upon the quality of the harvest. In good years, the poor's own land might allow them to subsist, their wages suffice to buy the grain to make the bread that was the staple of their diet; if not wheat then rye, if not rye, then barley or oats. The poor might weather one year's bad harvest, but not if another followed, and then another. For the first thirty years of Elizabeth's reign the harvests had sufficed, but in 1586 the harvest failed. In 1594-7 unrelenting rain and unseasonable cold destroyed four successive harvests. For the poor, with no savings, with nothing but their labour to sell, the seismic impact of harvest failure upon the grain markets was a disaster. The failed harvest of 1594 caused grain prices to leap: in Cambridgeshire, Nottinghamshire and Oxfordshire they were double those of the previous year. In the harvest year 1595-6 prices rose further, and they reached a peak, unprecedented in the century, in the terrible year 1596-7, when there was famine: the last, so far, in English history.

Death followed dearth. The parish registers attest to communities burying their dead rather than celebrating baptisms and marriages. In many areas of England – in rural villages and hamlets, particularly in the North and West, and in the poorest quarters of the cities – bad harvests led to high mortality. Death from starvation alone was rare, but in some places it was the killer. In July 1597 Robert Cecil received a warning from County Durham that the people flocking into plague-stricken Newcastle had not eaten bread for twenty days. When three Dutch grain ships came into the harbour the desperation was temporarily relieved, but in September and October Newcastle Corporation paid for paupers' burials for twenty-five 'poor folks who died for want in the streets'. Malnutrition reduces resistance to disease, so the poor succumbed more easily to dysentery and tuberculosis and to epidemics like typhus. In their desperation, the starving ate the inedible, which brought enteric disease – the 'bloody flux' – which hastened their demise. The epidemics were most devastating in the winter and spring when the shortage of food was most acute. Many stages of suffering preceded a slow death from privation and neglect.

There were attempts to relieve the poor. The Privy Council, recognizing the extremity of the misery and fearing its social and political consequences, intervened during the dearth to regulate the grain market; many town councils organized public granaries from which grain, flour and bread were sold at subsidized prices; they imported grain. Still the poor suffered agonies, especially in the North and West, where in 1595–7 the mechanisms of poor relief seem to have broken down under the scale of the disaster. A flood of migrants came in search of food to towns which could hardly feed their own citizens. Vagrants took to the road, seeking work, or begging. Some stole rather than starve, and then were hanged for it. As hardship increased in the second half of the 1590s, so did indictment for crime, especially for offences against property – larceny, burglary, robbery – and assize judges made exemplary use of the death penalty. In Devon in 1598 seventy-four people were sentenced to death. When the numbers of migrants, squatters, day labourers, petty thieves and social derelicts increased, the charity which was the basis of neighbourliness came under severe strain. No one could remember such misery. In 1598 the vicar of Wendlebury in Oxfordshire wrote in his diary: 'This was a sorrowful time for the poor of the land. God grant that such a dearth and famine may never be seen again.'

More dreaded and dreadful even than famine was the bubonic plague. If not technically endemic, plague was recurrent in Tudor England. Plague was catastrophic not only to the families who were left bereaved and perhaps indigent, but to the whole community. Work stopped, trade was paralysed, the people impoverished. Worse still, the life of the community was traumatized as people faced a grim dilemma: should plague victims, in charity, be helped or, in prudence, be shunned? Should one flee contagion or wait upon providence?

Plague was mainly a disease of the poor, especially in cities. In towns, there might be a chance of relieving the starving, but there was no way of preventing infection spreading through the overcrowded alleys and tenements. In 1579 nearly one third of the people of Norwich died of plague. London, most populous and most crowded, was most persistently afflicted. In 1563 more than 20,000 died in the City and liberties, nearly a quarter of the people; in 1593 nearly 18,000 died; in 1603, 30,000. In 1563 the mortality had been highest in the heart of the City, but by the end of the century the plague struck hardest in the crammed parishes just outside the City gates: Cripplegate, Aldgate, Bishopsgate. In 1603 in Yorkshire Lady Hoby heard that the plague was so virulent in London that the living were counted rather than the dead. 'Lord grant,' she wrote in her diary, 'that these judgements may cause England with speed to turn to the Lord.'

Since the whole Creation was a monument to God's providence, every natural event was taken to be a manifestation of His omnipotent will. More awe-inspiring than the harmonies of nature – the seasons in their due order, the fruitfulness of the earth, the stars in the firmament – were the disruptions of the normal, benign patterns of nature. Divine admonitions lay behind natural portents: God was telling His people something. Illustrated pamphlets describing storms, earthquakes and monstrous births were anxiously and avidly read. Changes in the heavens or in the weather were ominous. In 1593, when pestilence struck London, 'Saturn was passing through the uttermost parts of Cancer and the beginning of Leo', as in 1563, another plague year, wrote Camden. The conjunction of Saturn and Jupiter in 1583 was taken to bode ill. Yet the theatre of nature was an object of wonder, not to be searched into, so it was taught.

Francis Bacon, whose aim was to revolutionize the scientific study of nature, famously told his uncle, Lord Burghley, in 1592, 'I have taken all knowledge to be my province.' Yet in the same year he wrote that God had recently sent plague – 'but with a very gentle hand' – to teach the curious who dared seek its natural cause to ascribe it only to His mercy. To bow with becoming submission to the first, divine cause was a pious necessity. The danger lay, so clerics taught, in confusing first and second causes, and in imagining that to understand the natural world was to penetrate divine mysteries. The cosmos was not subject to rational interpretation, for divine providence could work independently of the natural order. Could human reason ever have predicted that God would destroy his Creation in the Flood? Only scripture held the key to nature.

So far as human reason could observe and understand it, God ordered nature according to regular laws. But plague was haphazard: it struck one town, not another; usually declined in the winter, but not always; was seemingly irresistible, yet some survived. This very unpredictability proved its providential origin. In the case of bubonic plague, its second cause was believed to be the conjunction of stars which drew pestilent vapours from the earth, creating a miasma. (That God was working through the fleas which infested the black rat, *rattus rattus*, was still unknown.) The corruption which was the origin of plague was understood to be moral before it was physical. So in 1603 Thomas Dekker described plague in London: 'Death (like a Spanish Leaguer or rather like stalking Tamberlane) hath pitched his tents ... in the sinfully polluted suburbs.' God sent plague, as he sent any other form of natural calamity, against sin. That malign natural sequence – the summers which were not summers, the unrelenting rain of the 1590s – was necessarily explained in the same way. 'He is blind,' preached George Abbott in December 1596, 'who now beholdeth not, that God is angry with us.' The cause of a disaster afflicting a whole community was to be found in the sin of the whole people and their ingratitude in not accepting revealed truth. The punishment came from the one to whom ingratitude was shown: God Himself.

*

For the calamities which struck individuals – lingering illness, the death of a child, the sickening and loss of animals, cows yielding blood instead of milk, the mysterious failure of butter to set – people increasingly found an explanation not directly in divine providence (though nothing happened without divine permission) but in the malign and occult force of witchcraft. Satan, lord of this world, was believed to have agents at work, with mysterious, diabolical power to do harm, *maleficium*. Like idolatry, witchcraft was a sin against the first table of Commandments. Belief in the power of witches was very old, but the persecution of alleged witches was an obsession of the later sixteenth century, when the injunction in Exodus – 'Thou shalt not suffer a witch to live' – was taken literally. The conviction that witchcraft was a reality offered an explanation for unexpected personal catastrophe, and witch-hunting offered the remedy. Acts of 1542, 1563 and 1604 (the last not repealed until 1736) first made witchcraft a statutory offence and provided the mechanism for the trial and punishment of witchcraft as a crime. George Gifford, a preacher in Essex, the county where most witches were sought and found, wrote that the common people were convinced that 'if there were no witches, there should be no such plagues'. If witches were hunted down and cast out, so it was believed, acts of harm would cease. The Devil could be defeated in the courts by hanging his human agents.

In pursuit of this simple remedy there was a great rise in witchcraft prosecution, which reached its peak in the last decades of Elizabeth's reign. At the home circuit of the assizes, covering the counties of Essex,

Hertfordshire, Kent, Surrey and Sussex, there were 109 indictments in the 1570s, 166 in the 1580s, and 128 in the 1590s; thereafter the level fell until the middle of the next century. Between 1570 and 1609, 64 of 263 accused witches were executed; 53 of those 64 were convicted in Essex. At the Essex assizes witchcraft cases formed 13 per cent of all criminal business in the 1580s. Why the obsession was so strong in Essex, where social and economic conditions were not so different from its neighbouring counties, remains unexplained. Ninety per cent of all alleged witches in England were women; their crime, *maleficium* – causing harm.

The horror of the witch-hunt, and the social breakdown and mental torment which lay behind it, should never be forgotten. Women – for it was prevailingly women – who were poor, old, ill-favoured, unprotected, were accused of crimes against their neighbours: the only evidence against them the fact of the misfortune, a conviction of their old malevolence, their possession of a 'familiar' – often a cat – which was believed to be a diabolic spirit, and some bodily blemish which could be construed as a witch's mark. Then as now, a cat fed out of a saucer and cosseted in a wool-lined basket might have been the only comfort of an elderly poor woman; but then it might have been taken as a sign of demonic covenant. For those who wished to find witches, and evidence of their guilt, there were ways enough.

The alleged witch was invariably someone known to the accuser, whom the person harmed had once offended; she was an unquiet spirit within the community, perhaps a scold. In a patriarchal society, these poor old women were often living outside the conventional hierarchies of family and household, without father, brother or son to validate or protect them. It was a perversion of power structures for women to seek power at all, let alone diabolic power. If there was a pattern to the accusation of maleficence it was that the alleged witch had gone to the house of her victim, typically someone richer than herself, and asked for aid – for food, for drink, for alms, for a loan – which was refused. The witch may have been affronted or teased, perhaps by having her geese driven away or even a bough covering a muddy patch by her door removed. So she would have her revenge. Sent away empty-handed and slighted, the witch would curse her uncharitable neighbours, from the master of the household to the piglet in the sty. In the weeks and months which followed the malediction, a misfortune would occur, and the victim would remember being 'forespoken', think of the beggar's curse, and know whom to blame. The Surrey mother whose child fell from her arms into a fire in April 1567 and died from burns that September, without medicines to heal or opiates to relieve pain, had long months of torment in which to brood upon the witchcraft which she blamed for the accident.

The persecution of a witch in its midst usually had the sanction of the whole village. At a time when economic change brought a growing estrangement between the social orders within a community, and as rural poverty increased, the old woman in search of alms was transformed from a worthy recipient of charity to a threat to the stability of the village. This was a period of some confusion and moral ambivalence in the treatment of poverty. The duty of charity to the deserving poor was urgently invoked as their plight became more apparent, but the growing estate of the landless and derelict was regarded with alarm. The old institutions of the Church and manor were failing, while the new institution of the poor law was not yet established. As charity came to be demanded, it might be less freely bestowed; as poor relief was ordered, it might be less readily handed out. The clash between resentment and duty brought an ambivalence which led richer neighbours to turn away beggars and then to feel guilt about their lack of charity. In Ireland, where social conditions were quite different, there was no witch-hunt.

The social context of the witch craze was the divided village; its intellectual and emotional origin was the intense belief in the immanence and power of the Devil. Villagers became convinced that living among them, in altogether familiar surroundings, there was someone in touch with perverted spiritual presences from the lower world. Witchcraft was just one part of the eternal, cosmic struggle between God and Satan, between good and evil, between salvation and damnation. Alongside the popular preoccupation with the witch's power to do harm by occult means was the theologians' belief that witchcraft involved a pact with the Devil. William Perkins, Elizabethan England's pre-eminent divine, urged the execution of all witches; not because of the harm they caused, but because they depended upon Satan as their god. Although the diabolical covenant was not mentioned in the statutes of 1542 and 1563, and English witches were generally accused of maleficence rather than the heresy of a demonic pact, some of those accused of witchcraft declared a terrible allegiance. In 1566 Elizabeth Francis confessed that every time her cat (ominously called Satan) performed some sinister service for her, she rewarded him with a drop of her blood. Mother Samuel, one of the three witches of Warboys in Huntingdonshire tried in 1593, confessed that she had forsaken her Maker and given her soul to the Devil. Even where the alleged witch had explicitly invoked the name of Jesus, as Elizabeth Lewys of Waltham in Essex did in 1563, saying, 'Christ, Christ, my Christ, if thou be a saviour come down and avenge me of my enemies', she was still accused; for it was not God but Satan who executed curses.

The Devil, the Prince of Darkness, was believed to have lost none of his ancient wisdom, none of the pride which had brought war in heaven, none of his power to tempt people to sin and despair. Once one of God's angels, Satan knew all the secrets of the natural world and the hearts of men. He could counterfeit human or animal shape and appear at will. God allowed Satan to operate as agent of His justice. 'Prince and god of this world,' so John Knox acknowledged him, Satan was also lord of hell, presiding eternally over the torments of the damned. Satan's powers were undiminished, yet the sinful Christian was left with fewer tangible aids to combat him. The incantations, charms and blessings of salt, water and wax which the Catholic Church had given to the laity to banish the Devil and his demons were outlawed by the Protestant Church. The ceremonies and prayers in the liturgy to exorcize the Devil, anointing and making the sign of the cross to ward off evil, were shunned as idolatry and superstition. In their place, the Christian was left with faith, the scriptures, repentance, fasting and prayer: a powerful armament certainly, but the battle was a lonely one. Penance was now not a sacrament but an individual wrestling with conscience. The Devil became more threatening than ever, even to the strongest mind.

*

One of the devils on stage at the Belsavage playhouse in 1588–9 was not an actor. That imagined demon appeared during a performance of Christopher Marlowe's *Tragical History of Doctor Faustus*, a play upon a dangerous subject. The audience discovered Doctor Faustus, a Renaissance scholar, in his study at Wittenberg, ranging discontentedly among his books, dismissing each of his studies in turn: logic, physic, law, 'Divinity, adieu!' ''Tis magic, magic that hath ravished' Faustus. He declared that:

> These metaphysics of magicians
> And necromantic books are heavenly . . .
> A sound magician is a mighty God.

'That famous art' of the magician would give Faustus power 'on earth as Jove is in the sky', so the Evil Angel promised him. But the magician's art was a 'damned art'; damned, so William Perkins preached, because the magician aspired 'to search out such things as God would have kept secret'. It was for eating from the forbidden Tree of Knowledge that Adam lost Paradise. Curiosity, man's first disobedience, brought the Fall and would bring the fall of Faustus.

Faustus was a Renaissance magus, a magician. Renaissance magicians aspired to regain the understanding of nature and the divine revelation once granted to Adam. They believed that Adam's knowledge had been transmitted through a succession of *prisci theologi*, pre-Christian yet divinely inspired teachers of ancient wisdom: from Moses to the legendary Hermes Trismegistus, who represented Egyptian wisdom, to Zoroaster, representing Chaldean wisdom, to Plato, Orpheus and Pythagoras. From Hermetic writings Renaissance thinkers learnt that through mystical regeneration man's dominion over nature, lost at the Fall, could be recovered; that man might manipulate and compel nature for sublime purposes. The aim was to reach God Himself through contemplation of nature and of the sympathies uniting the universe; the great series of analogies and correspondences operating through all creation. The final aspiration was to rise from the mutable, physical world to the divine, super-celestial sphere, there to commune with God and learn the hidden laws of the universe. A way to unlock cosmic powers was by the magic of the cabbala, the permutation of the sacred Hebrew alphabet.

This magical, occult, cabbalistic knowledge was given to very, very few. In England, Dr John Dee, Elizabeth's celestial mathematician, was unique in his fantastic, polymathic learning, and in the intensity of his speculations, but he and his philosophy had influence in the highest political and intellectual circles, and his library was an academy for the most questing intellects. On his deathbed, Sir Philip Sidney, who knew both Dee and Giordano Bruno, the Italian cosmographer, philosopher and spy, had asked what was the opinion of the *prisci theologi* regarding the immortality of the soul. Dee, in a spirit of intense piety, was known to have used ceremonial magic to communicate with angels in order to come closer to the divine. The first conference between Dee and Archangel Uriel was recorded in 1581:

> DEE: Are there any more beside you?
> URIEL: Michael and Raphael. But Michael is the leader in our works.

Sir Humphrey Gilbert, the colonizer, was taught the science of navigation by Dee. He, too, communicated with spirits in another world, through the medium of a scryer (seer). Adam told him: 'Go clean in apparel; and be good to the poor; and leave swearing . . . then nothing shalt thou lack.' Such magical manipulation could be used for good or evil, but was condemned as necromancy. Supernatural power could emanate only from two sources, from God or Satan, and secret knowledge was soon construed as diabolic practice. The audience watching *Doctor Faustus* were uneasily aware of the dangers of his arcane enquiries and drawn into his conjurings.

Faustus, seeking to be 'great emperor of the world' through his occult power, drew the magician's circle around him and dared to conjure a spirit from hell. Enter Mephistopheles: not because Faustus has summoned him, but because devils appear to those who blasphemously 'pray devoutly to the prince of hell'. 'So Faustus hath', for 'this word "damnation" terrifies not him': or not yet. Faustus, who had already 'incurred eternal death/By desp'rate thoughts against Jove's deity', offered Lucifer his soul in return for twenty-four years of living 'in all voluptuousness' and for command of Mephistopheles' service:

> To give me whatsoever I shall ask,
> To tell me whatsoever I demand.

Still Faustus might have abjured magic but, despairing of God's love, he turned to magical dominion as a perverted substitute. Swearing a solemn covenant bequeathing his soul to Lucifer, he signed it with his blood. '*Consummatum est* [It is finished],' he declared, in blasphemous imitation of Christ's last words upon the Cross. But for Faustus this was not the end, only the beginning.

Faustus's first question to Mephistopheles, once the pact was made, was one which haunted him and his audience. 'Tell me, where is the place that men call hell?'

Came Mephistopheles' chilling reply: 'Where we are is hell/And where hell is must we ever be.'

Faustus never heeded Mephistopheles' first warning of the anguish of separation from God and could not believe it now: 'Come, I think hell's a fable.'

'Ay, think so still, till experience change thy mind.'

Experience would, for Faustus learned through twenty-four years' 'journey through the world and air' that led everywhere and nowhere except back to Wittenberg, that hell is both a real place and in the mind. For a time 'sweet pleasure' conquered 'deep despair' as he heard blind Homer sing, disported with 'fairest courtesans' and saw a vision of Helen of Troy, heralded in surpassing poetry:

> Was this the face that launched a thousand ships
> And burnt the topless towers of Ilium?
> Sweet Helen, make me immortal with a kiss.

But that delusive Helen was a demon, who exchanged a kiss for his soul; the ultimate demonic pact.

Faustus had pledged his soul in order to learn the forbidden secrets of the universe. Mounted upon 'Olympus' top', 'seated in a chariot burning bright' drawn by dragons, he had 'gone to prove cosmography'. Faustus and the audience before whom his tragedy was played lived during a period of astronomical revolution. The old certainties of the geocentric Ptolemaic universe had been broken by the discoveries and theories of Copernicus and Bruno. The revelation that the cosmos was infinite, that the sun was at the centre and that the earth revolved around it, that there were unseen stars with an incalculable influence, and that there were worlds beyond worlds beyond this one was profoundly shocking: too mysterious, thought John Dee, for lesser minds to know. Giordano Bruno's lectures on Copernican cosmology at Oxford in 1583 had been halted, though whether because of his exposition of a revolutionary system in a die-hard university or whether because of his extensive plagiarism was hard to tell.

It was chastening to discover that the earth was a planet like any other, subject to the same laws of motion; alarming to see the heavens lose their perfection as they were observed to be subject to corruption and change. How was it possible for a 'new' star to appear, as people believed one did in 1577? From the leads of Ralegh's Durham House in London, Thomas Harriot turned his telescope – the first in England – on the skies and, like Galileo, found blemishes on celestial bodies: spots on the sun, craters on the moon. Such astronomical discoveries undermined the fundamental distinction between things sublunar and things celestial, and even the subordination of the earth to heavenly bodies. So Faustus's questions to Mephistopheles about the nature of the cosmos took the audience where the most sceptical and questioning minds of the time were at debate; to the dangerous limits of legitimate and forbidden knowledge; to the baffling confrontation between the Ptolemaic and Copernican systems.

'Tell me,' asked Faustus, 'are there many heavens above the moon?' The questions Faustus asked did not directly concern the contested doctrine of heliocentricity, but they touched upon a central inadequacy of the Ptolemaic system; its failure to account for the unequal motion of the planets. Mephistopheles, who was bound to tell Faustus anything he asked, told him nothing he did not know already. 'But tell me,' Faustus asked impatiently, 'hath every sphere a dominion? ... Tell me who made the world . . . Sweet Mephistopheles, tell me.'

Mephistopheles refused: 'Move me not, for I will not tell thee'; to do so would be 'against our kingdom'.

Faustus, the divinity scholar, had asked a blasphemous question, for every schoolboy knew that God made heaven and earth in six days; *ex nihilo*, from nothing. Yet some had begun to challenge even that. 'Well, I am answered,' said Faustus, understanding that his quest for forbidden knowledge was futile and that he had sold his soul for nothing. How many in the audience wondered, with Faustus, whether the orthodox cosmology of the age was a deception and shared his resentment that the truth was hidden? And if doubts about the physical universe disquieted them, the play raised questions about the moral universe more disturbing still.

Faustus must pay the price for his absolute defiance of heaven. Eternity haunted him: 'O, no end is limited to damned souls.' Yet when he thought of heaven, he began to repent and wondered whether paradise was forever lost. The few and feeble forces for good in the play promised grace if he called for mercy, and Faustus was intermittently convinced:

> Be I a devil, yet God may pity me;
> Ay, God will pity me if I repent.

If. But it was not in the nature of devils to repent. Faustus's heart was hardened, his will in bondage to evil; he could not will himself to repent:

> I do repent, and yet I do despair.
> Hell strives with grace for conquest in my breast.

Faustus chose evil. It was God who, in justice, hardened the hearts of those whom He rejected; who, in His mercy, saved some but not all. On the edge of the abyss Faustus was, with divine irony, vouchsafed a beatific vision of forgiveness through the blood of Christ: 'See, see where Christ's blood streams in the firmament!' Half a drop would have saved Faustus's soul, but he received instead 'the heavy wrath of God'. Faustus's fall was just; the play, with its stern view of salvation, strictly orthodox in doctrine. Yet Faustus, in his alienation and despair, was left with little help. This was no simple morality play, but a work terrifying in its intensity and daring which hinted at a dangerous questioning.

*

Drama is not life; Faustus was not Marlowe; yet Marlowe courted catastrophe and went to the bad with some of the mocking bravura of Faustus. He created a just God in drama whom he scorned in life, so it was alleged. In an age when homosexual acts were punishable by death, Marlowe portrayed the doomed love and desire between Edward II and his 'sweet favourite' Gaveston. Once a Catholic, in 1587 Marlowe went as a double agent in Walsingham's secret service to spy upon English Catholic exiles in Rheims. The blasphemy alleged against him was extreme; that he jested at scripture; was an atheist; willed people 'not to be afeard of bugbears and hobgoblins', and espoused a Machiavellian conception of religion – that it was a device to keep the populace in awe. These allegations came from Thomas Kyd, author of *The Spanish Tragedy*, with whom Marlowe shared a chamber, and from the spies with whom Marlowe consorted. In May 1593 Marlowe was killed in a Deptford tavern during a brawl supposedly over the bill. In the shadows, behind these allegations and Marlowe's death, there lay the feud at court between Sir Walter Ralegh and the 2nd Earl of Essex.

Marlowe and Ralegh are forever connected poetically. To Marlowe's exquisite, pagan plea of the 'Passionate Shepherd to his Love':

> Come live with me, and be my love,
> And we will all the pleasures prove,
> That valleys, groves, hills and fields,
> Woods, or steepy mountain yields

Ralegh replied, with intimations of mortality and mutability:

> If all the world and love were young,
> And truth in every shepherd's tongue,
> These pretty pleasures might me move,
> To live with thee and be thy love.

The two men were associated in their religion too, or alleged lack of it. Robert Persons, the Jesuit, accused Ralegh in 1592 of keeping a 'school of atheism' where young gentlemen scorned scripture. Perhaps it was at this supposed 'school' that Marlowe had 'read the atheist lecture to Sir Walter Ralegh and others'. If Marlowe were found guilty of atheism, then Ralegh would be suspect also. If Thomas Harriot's alleged – though unlikely – heresy regarding the resurrection of the body could be proved, then the beliefs of his master, Ralegh, would be impugned. Ralegh's dangerous reputation for atheism persisted, though all his sayings and writings disproved it.

On a portrait said to be of Marlowe in Corpus Christi College, Cambridge is a motto; that kind of dark, esoteric message beloved of Elizabethan intellectuals: '*Quod me nutrit me destruit* [That which nourishes me destroys me]'. What was it that both nourished and destroyed: love, ambition, knowledge? In the way of late Elizabethan portraiture the uninitiated onlooker was not meant to understand, but surely the sitter followed too many dangerous trains of thought. That kind of portrait, of the young man darkly attired, with folded arms and arcane motto, was the classic portrayal of the melancholic. Melancholy, imported from Italy – like the rapier, the epic, the sonnet, the madrigal, fashionable black, homoeroticism, atheism and Machiavellianism – was the humour associated with the imagination, with genius, and the stance adopted by the young Elizabethan aesthete. Melancholy was in part a mannerism, but also in the 1580s and 1590s a political statement. The melancholic was a malcontent. His (for the malcontent was male) talents unused, his ambition thwarted, his time wasted, he was forced to look on as his rivals seized the rewards rightly (he thought) his. So Sir Robert Sidney, passed over for honour and office like his brother Sir Philip, spent the 1590s in semi-exile in Flushing, the 'grave' of his youth and fortune, and wrote wintry, tenebrous poems, full of images of violence and imprisonment.

These were years of political disillusion for the younger generation of the Elizabethan nobility. Allured to court, there to wait – for favour and reward which did not come, for something to happen – in their disappointment and frustration, they turned to the courses of spectacular dissipation that having too much money and all the time in the world allowed. All those vices against which puritan divines and prudent fathers warned they made their own: gambling, duelling, illicit love. They played deeper, gambled for higher and higher stakes, threw down challenges on the slightest pretexts, were more openly 'grateful to ladies', or so it seemed. The prodigal extravagance of a few dazzled the whole court, for these few happened to be leading nobles – the Earls of Essex, Southampton, Rutland, Oxford – who happened also to have been the wards of Lord Burghley (who lived on to see his avuncular counsel flouted). So it was that as the Four Horsemen of the Apocalypse – war, famine, pestilence and death – rode in what the preachers called England's last days: as the poor starved; and foundlings were abandoned at Christ's Hospital, their names – Orphan Stonegarden, William Cloister – their only patrimony and a sign of their wretched provenance, a few gilded beneficiaries of an increasingly corrupt system spent recklessly. In 1597, the year of greatest desperation for the poor, one courtier lavished £2,000 on his mistress, and Mrs Ratcliffe, a maid of honour to the Queen, appeared at court in a dress of cloth of silver costing £180.

An Essex labourer who was asked 'What can poor men do against rich men?' had answered: 'What can rich men do against poor men if poor men rise and hold together?' His answer was rhetorical, for the poor did not rise, save for a few grain riots. Discontent was manifest, but did not turn to rebellion. A rising was planned in Oxfordshire in 1596, intending the assassination of plutocratic local landlords rather than the usual attacks upon property, but it was stillborn. It failed to rally support, for the poor had grievance but not energy enough to rise, and did not know their own strength. Yet the Elizabethan ruling orders began to fear that the poor would learn to know their strength, and use it. Some saw upon how fragile and illusory a structure the political order rested. In the Parliament of 1593 Fulke Greville warned that 'if the feet knew their strength as we know their oppression, they would not bear as they do', and urged, radically enough, that the parliamentary subsidy be collected only from those who could afford to pay it. Only the enervation of poverty, the habits of obedience and the arts of power held the poor in order. The cause of poverty was never one for which the nobility, to whom the poor traditionally looked for leadership, would rise. The rebellion, when it came, was that of turbulent nobles. Like the barons ranged against the upstarts in medieval England, of whom they read in epic poetry and saw portrayed in the history plays of Shakespeare and Marlowe, they raged against the monarch as she raised new men, denied them what they saw as their rights, and impugned their honour.

11

Court and Camp

Predicting the Queen's death was treason. Yet secretly, in 1596 (when she was sixty-three), Thomas Harriot cast Elizabeth's horoscope and gave the date of her expiry as 1617. Her subjects, awaiting a new reign with apprehensive impatience, both hoped and feared that she would live so long. They behaved as though the Queen must survive; but they knew that she could not live for ever, and were deeply uneasy about who and what would follow. Under a declining prince political morality declined also. Elizabeth was the last of her line, with no dynastic interest, no personal stake in the future; she lived as she had always done, in the short term, content with survival. Yet while she lived, she ruled, her will imperative still. Knowing the constant speculation upon her mortality, she would say wryly that she was *mortua non sepulta*, dead but not buried. She presented herself, and was presented, as changeless, beyond time. There were no mirrors at court to reflect the Queen's decay, and portraits of her were censored to hide time's ravages. Only the image of the 'mask of youth' was circulated, as a memento to her adoring subjects. An amorous servitude was demanded by the Queen, who pretended that her subjects' love and duty was their choice rather than her compulsion. Her courtiers, required to worship her this side idolatry, and beyond, played upon that devotion. When Ralegh showed the chieftains of Guiana the Queen's portrait, he quickly took it away again, he wrote, lest by adoring her they be guilty of idolatry. The cult of the Virgin Queen of England usurped the veneration of the Virgin Queen of Heaven: Elizabeth's own birthday was celebrated instead of the feast of the Nativity of the Virgin Mary. So the Catholics claimed, and Protestant denials rang weakly.

Elizabeth had always had her favourites about her, jealously demanding their utter dependance, their constant presence. There had been Leicester, whose death in September 1588 had been a profound

blow to her (though, to some others, no less a blessing than the Armada's defeat); there had been Hatton, who died in 1591. These men had been content to share her favour; she content to have one watch over the other. But there came a successor who would not be willing to share pre-eminence, who fought for sole favour, and the consequent battles split the court. This was Robert Devereux, 2nd Earl of Essex. His nobility was of blood, but also of the *megalopsychia* of Aristotle's *Nicomachean Ethics*, the high-mindedness or proper pride of the superior soul, whose greatness of mind was equalled by his courage. Essex aspired to the active virtue which, cultivated by learning, was to be devoted to the service of prince and commonwealth. His most brilliant rival was Sir Walter Ralegh; the quintessential Renaissance man: scholar, explorer, poet, alchemist and soldier. The Queen had raised him high, and he lived 'very gallant', but Ralegh was from a Devon gentry family. 'I know what he has been and what he is,' sneered Essex, secure in his ancient lineage.

When Ralegh wrote, 'Twelve years entire I wasted in this war,' the war was between the favourites, for the Queen's favour, and it began in the late 1580s. They fought at first by sonnet and portrait. In 1588 Ralegh was portrayed dressed in the black and white of constancy and purity, the queen's colours; in his ear, a pearl, her jewel. On his right was his own motto, '*Amor et virtute* [Love and by virtue]'; above it, a crescent moon. The moon symbolized Ralegh's devotion to Cynthia, the moon goddess, timeless lady of the seas, waxing and waning but always the same: the Queen herself. The cult of Cynthia was the personal cult of Ralegh, the self-styled Shepherd of the Ocean, but soon became the cult of the whole nation. At about the same time, a portrait of another young man was painted. Leaning melancholy against a tree of constancy, embowered in eglantine, the Queen's flower, he too was dressed in black and white. The motto – '*Dat poenas laudata fides* [My praised faith causes my suffering]' – associated him with Pompey, the military commander and darling of the citizens of Rome. The young man was almost certainly Essex, the incandescent favourite; the portrait a private declaration of his painful devotion. The story of his relations with the Queen was already one of quarrels and reconciliations, provocations and forgiveness, for he presumed upon his great favour with her. His identification with Pompey was portentous. Francis Bacon, Essex's intimate, warned him, unavailingly, that an incited popularity and a dependence on military honour were the wings of Icarus which would draw him fatally close to the sun.

'I know that God hath a great work to work by me,' Essex told Anthony Bacon, his secretary, in 1596. That great work was not to flatter an ageing queen, although that seemed to be his fate, but to carry war into Spain for England's honour, and his own. Essex could not easily play the favourite, yet it was by devout attendance on the Queen, and endless persuasion, that military command was won. Philip Sidney had bequeathed his sword, his chivalry and his hopes to Essex, and in 1590 Essex came with his followers to the tiltyard, arrayed in mourning black for Sidney, 'whose successor he in love and arms had ever vowed to be'. To the Queen's displeasure, Essex married Sidney's widow. The great design of the old advocates of militant Protestantism – Walsingham, Leicester, Knollys, Mildmay and Sidney – for a coalition against the forces of militant Catholicism lived on in Essex, who believed that peace could come only by resolute war. Against that view stood, perennially, the Queen and Burghley, 'old Saturnus', whose influence was now greater than ever, as he monopolized the offices of Lord Treasurer, Master of the Court of Wards and acting Secretary of State. Elizabeth was always averse to the grand design; reluctant that religion should dictate national policy. The Queen's temperament, her lack of impulse to martial greatness and empire, and her just assessment of her poverty always inclined her to arm for defence rather than to make war. But Essex was contemptuous of those who, lacking honour, sought peace abroad. For the Queen's sake, he said truly, he would have counted 'danger a sport, death a feast'.

The repulse of the 'invincible Armada' was not the end but the beginning of England's outright war with Spain. For Spain, war became not a matter of retaliatory raids but of revenge and of total conquest in England, France and the Netherlands. Events moved Elizabeth to that offensive war from which she naturally recoiled. In 1589 the Armada lay temporarily helpless in Spanish harbours, unmanned and unseaworthy, while urgent preparations were made to restore it. Now was the chance to send a force into 'the bowels of Spain'. Remarkably, Elizabeth took it. In April 1589 an English Armada sailed; with 19,000 soldiers and 4,000 sailors, it was scarcely less formidable than Spain's. Its purpose was to destroy Spanish ships, to place Dom Antonio on the throne of Portugal, and to seize the Islands – the Azores – in order to prey upon Spanish commerce.

Divided counsels and conflicting purposes wrecked this 'enterprise of Portugal' even as it sailed, for this was less a royal armada than a massive privateering venture; the commanders, Drake and Norris, were adventurers before they were admirals. The first aim of the Queen – the destruction of the fleet in order to prevent another invasion – was not theirs. They dreamt of prizes and the sack of Lisbon. Sea and land forces were deployed on an uncoordinated attack upon Lisbon, but the Portuguese people failed to rise for Dom Antonio. The enterprise was a disaster for the Queen, but a greater one for more than half of her forces, who deserted or died. Elizabeth was confirmed in her opposition to the great venture for martial glory. Not so Essex. Escaping court as the enterprise began, defying the Queen's absolute command to stay, Essex (not being Master of the Horse for nothing) rode 220 miles in a day and a half to join the expedition at Plymouth. Into the gates of Lisbon he stuck his pike: a promise that he would return.

*

England had so far avoided the civil wars which racked France and the Netherlands. France was a 'theatre of misery' where anxious observers in England watched religious fervour metamorphose into revolution and saw the extreme courses which attended the extinction of a dynasty. The Catholic League, reconstituted in 1584 to restore 'holy Church' and prevent the accession of the Protestant heir, had moved to purge the eastern provinces of Huguenots. In Paris, the leading Leaguers, the Sixteen, organized thousands of militants into neighbourhood cells and planned similar networks throughout France. Knowing that Henry III lacked ardour in the Catholic cause, the Sixteen planned a coup against him, and in May 1588 the citizens took to the barricades and drove out their king. The Duke of Guise was master of Paris. At the end of the year Henry, on the point of losing his kingdom, successfully ordered the assassination of the Duke and the Cardinal of Guise and was denounced as a new Herod by the Paris preachers. The League moved to more desperate courses, sanctioned neither by law nor precedent but by religious mission, and repudiated their duty of allegiance to a King who had violated his sacred trust. The Sixteen ruled Paris by terror, and established a revolutionary commune. Henry III was driven into an unholy alliance with his heir, the Protestant Henry of Navarre, and in April 1589 Valois and Bourbon armies advanced against the League. The alliance did not last long, for in July Henry III, the last of the Valois, was assassinated. Reports reached England of the anguished piety, the spectacular torchlit processions, the extreme penitential fervour which attended this period of political crisis.

France became 'the stage of Christendom wherein all nations seek to play their tragical parts'. So Sir Henry Unton said in Parliament in 1593. Philip II had bound himself to prevent Henry of Navarre ever ascending the French throne. Now, in September 1589, a reluctant Prince of Parma was ordered to lead the Army of Flanders to aid the League. Here were new alignments in Europe's wars of religion. The war in the Netherlands was reduced to a defensive holding operation, just when the many victories and long attrition seemed at last to be leading to Spanish victory. Only a rump of the Spanish army was left behind to face Dutch forces, supported by English auxiliaries, who grew confident under their brilliant commander Maurice of Nassau. English aims in the Netherlands had not changed: Dutch liberties must be defended, but Dutch independence was not to be fought for, because an independent Netherlands could never withstand an aggressive France. As always, England's safety lay in a balance of the two great powers: she needed a restored France to counter a militant Spain.

Philip's move from the 'enterprise of England' to the 'enterprise of France' in 1589 was only a temporary reprieve for England. As Parma's army marched towards the French border, England's danger grew, for if the French Channel coast fell to Spain the Spanish Armada's task would be easy. The power of the Catholic League stretched from Lorraine in the east to Brittany in the west: a proximate threat to England, which had known invasion from Normandy before. Elizabeth had offered a loan in 1587 to fund Henry of Navarre's German mercenary levy, and could not now avoid sending aid and money; not only to protect Henry's right and to save France from Spanish domination but also to save England. In September 1589 Lord Willoughby crossed to France with 4,000 troops as auxiliaries. Without them Henry could hardly keep the field, yet he could not provide for them. Unpaid, unfed, consumed by disease, the English troops suffered a terrible attrition. Henry, beleaguered and indigent, controlling only half of France, with his camp as his court, could hardly drive the League from the north. His prime objective lay elsewhere. Paris was in the hands of the Sixteen, and the King must capture his capital before he could win his kingdom. In 1590 he laid siege to Paris; unavailingly, for in September Parma and his army arrived to relieve it.

Normandy became the focus of international politics: it was the heartland of militant Catholicism. In 1591 Elizabeth sent two expeditionary forces: one to Brittany, one to Normandy. A great effusion of English manpower and money followed: 20,000 men sent and £370,000 spent between 1589 and 1595. All to little purpose. Henry's strategies and exigencies were never Elizabeth's. He could not be induced to keep his promises, to arrive on time, or to give full support to English forces he regarded as his mere auxiliaries. Henry, for his part, told Elizabeth that she 'made war good cheap against so great an enemy', looking on while he did her fighting for her. Yet the war seemed costly enough to her war-weary commanders, forced to decisions which they knew would be ill received at home, and to their ragged and broken armies drifting purposelessly through the devastated French countryside. As Henry IV tired of endless campaigning and faced the prospect of failure, rumours reached England in April 1593 that he was preparing to 'make that metamorphosis': to abjure his Protestantism. In July 1593 he attended Mass at St Denis: the price of Paris. Elizabeth was distraught, pained by his apostasy, and fearful that he would ally with Spain and repudiate his great debt to her. She sought the consolations of philosophy and translated the Stoic Boethius.

War in France had been unsuccessful and inglorious. Yet it had seemed a great chivalric moment to England's martial nobility, who saw themselves as born to command but were still untested. Essex wrote to Elizabeth, pleading for command: while the armies campaigned there, Normandy was the 'great school of our age'. Resistant to the Crown's attempts to domesticate and pacify them, emulating their glittering commander, Essex's 'gallants' vied with each other in acts of chivalry, skirmished in 'bravadoes' which were usually futile, sometimes – as for Essex's brother, Walter – fatal. Elizabeth, warning Henry IV of Essex's recklessness, advised that he would need the bridle rather than the spur. Outside Rouen, Essex challenged the Duke of Villars, Governor of Le Havre, to single combat. The Queen, unimpressed, accused him of venturing 'like the forlorn hope' that went first into battle.

In 1592 Essex returned from command in Normandy to court and learnt bitter lessons: that military honour went unrewarded and was little regarded; that his whispering adversaries had undermined him in his absence; that, in Elizabethan politics, the pen was mightier than the sword. Burghley intended to hand over his power and offices to his immensely able son, Robert Cecil. In 1592 it was alleged that Burghley deliberately suppressed the ancient nobility, and it soon became commonplace to say that the Cecils promoted only 'base, pen clerks'. The contrast between the splendid Essex and the hunch-backed Cecil personified the Renaissance antithesis between chivalry and bureaucracy. As Cecil determined to assume his father's monopoly, so Essex set himself to prevent him. He pressed for a part as Privy Councillor as well as favourite. Determined to command the knowledge that would allow him to direct events, Essex began to appoint a secretariat of brilliant men, worthy of the most educated of English nobles, to procure intelligence of foreign affairs and 'practices'. In February 1593 Essex was at last sworn Privy Councillor.

One of Essex's rivals was removed, for a time. In the summer of 1592 Elizabeth discovered that Ralegh had secretly married Bess Throckmorton, a Lady of the Bedchamber, so defiling one of her vestals, and violating the inner sanctum of her court with all its secrets. Ralegh was banished, and the Earl's friends rejoiced that he had chased him out of court and into Ireland.

*

In May 1593, exiled from favour, Ralegh wrote despairingly to Robert Cecil, 'We are so busied and dandled in these French wars, which are endless, as we forget the defence next the heart': the danger from Ireland, which was almost a matter of home defence, to which everything else, even national solvency, must yield precedence. That spring Ralegh had warned of the acute danger of a new 'Irish combination', but like 'the Trojan soothsayer' he was not believed. The Queen had already spent a fortune in Ireland, he complained; she might have bought a better kingdom cheaper; yet its security was less assured than ever. Now Spain, by arming the Irish, had raised up 'troops of beggars on our backs'. Ralegh's letter exposed, too, the deepening disillusion and division among Ireland's governors. A great chance had been lost in the 1580s, Ralegh believed, when Ireland 'lay bare to the sword'.

In 1580 Sir Henry Sidney, advising Lord Grey of Wilton, his successor as chief governor, had alluded to a crisis in counsel in Ireland: should English governors temporize, or aspire 'to a perfect reformation of that accursed country'? Grey had chosen the second course in Munster and the Pale; one of brutal repression. Impelled by what he saw as moral and political necessity, Grey could show no pity and give no pardons to the Irish who were addicted, he thought, to 'treachery and breach of fidelity'. There, compassion was delusive. To the hardliners, Grey had shown what could be done to bring 'perfect reformation' by famine and the sword, but those who held still to an ideal of reform by diplomacy and persuasion saw the limitations to repression, the failure to exploit short-term devastation for any long-term political gain. Grey had left under a cloud in 1582. He was replaced two years later by Sir John Perrot, past President of Munster, who had plied the Council with ambitious schemes through the 1570s, and came with all the zeal of a reforming governor. He aimed to bring a final settlement to Munster and to establish extensive plantations there; he planned to drive the Scots from the north-east, where Turlough Luineach O'Neill and his wife, the Lady of Kintyre, were seeking to create a 'new Scotland', and finally to pacify Ulster for, as always, if Ulster were settled so might all Ireland be. He saw an assault upon tanistry as a way of ending the seemingly endless succession disputes and the consequent militarization of the Gaelic lordships. More ambitious still was his scheme, inherited from Sidney, to negotiate and complete throughout Ireland a general 'composition' or agreement to commute 'cess' (a range of impositions), in order to give the government a regular income and a local militia.

Perrot began a tour of the country in 1584 – the first of his annual perambulations into the heart of Gaelic Ireland – and marched into Antrim in August to hunt down the Scots. That autumn he persuaded the Ulster lords to accept commutation of their traditional claims over their people for a fixed rental income to be collected by an English resident army which would exact from the country more than the lords' own forces had done. Having enforced the commutation, the army would be withdrawn, and smaller forces left to collect the sums agreed upon for the lord. Yet when Elizabeth vetoed Perrot's contingent scheme for a series of forts, she undermined his policy. There was no way of compelling the lords, who now used the composition troops, who still 'cut upon the country', in their private wars. Most of Ulster was soon divided into three lieutenancies, granted to Sir Henry Bagenal, Turlough Luineach O'Neill, and Hugh O'Neill, Baron of Dungannon. Fierce and inveterate jealousy burned among these three men, and for the two O'Neills no English lieutenancy could transcend the overlordship in Ulster they claimed already and disputed between themselves.

Perrot's determination to undermine the social and political structure of the Gaelic lordships had been evident even in his inaugural address, when he had promised to end the oppression of 'churls'. At the end of 1584 his plan to extinguish tanistry by subdividing the lordships began in East Breifne, the lordship of the O'Reillys. With the division of the lordship among four heads of the main lineages, tanistry was in abeyance there. But in Mayo, Perrot's move in 1586 to partition the Lower MacWilliamship between six competitors drove the Burkes and their following septs into recurrent revolt. 'They would have a MacWilliam,' they vowed, 'or else they would go into Spain for one.'

Perrot continued his assault on the Gaelic lordships by extending that policy whereby the lords submitted and surrendered their lands to the Crown, to be regranted them by letters patent or indenture. By the end of his governorship, the only great lords who had not made agreements were O'Donnell, O'Cahan and O'Rourke. Yet the lords' submissions were often fleeting; the agreements a way of usurping rights and claiming lands throughout the lordship which had never been theirs. And if they lacked the will to honour the agreements, they also often lacked the power. The allegiance and rents they offered the Crown were given in return for protection against their Gaelic overlords. So the O'Connor chief of Sligo expected the Queen to defend him against O'Donnell of Tirconnell. When that defence failed, the lord found himself subject both to the Queen and to O'Donnell, bound to pay tribute to each, and ultimately to choose between them.

So many of Perrot's policies were only declaratory, formal, fragile; the rents were not paid, the agreements not honoured. In Ulster, his plans to restructure the Gaelic lordships fell into disarray. The greater the attempt to reform, the greater the failure. His many critics in Dublin and London were turned into enemies, not only by his authoritarian and abrasive style but also by the collapse of his policies. The possibility of reform by anything other than military repression came to be doubted by many of those who were charged with governing Ireland. Hopes for the extension of English law and civility were disappointed when the Irish consistently refused to recognize what was, to the English, the ineluctable superiority of English law and processes. The programme of the reformers began to give way to the more ruthless schemes of the hardliners. It also gave way before the new imperatives of an English government at war with Spain and fearful of an invasion from the east, not recognizing yet the likely prospect of one from the west. In 1586 Elizabeth ordered Perrot to desist from policies involving expense. Perrot should have lived under Henry VIII, Walsingham told him sympathetically, for then 'princes were resolute to persist in honourable attempts'. When Perrot was recalled early in 1588 he left Ireland peaceful. That peace was deceptive.

Munster was quiet: with the quiet that came of exhaustion and despair. Devastated and depopulated after the savage suppression of the Desmond rebellion in 1583, it lay open to the colonization which some saw as the remedy to the Irish problem and a way of bringing regeneration and order out of chaos. To 'plant' was to cultivate both land and manners. In December 1585 a scheme was drawn up for the plantation of Munster. Lands were to be divided into units of regular size – seignories (a name resonant with lordly aspirations) of 12,000 acres – and granted to Englishmen who would 'undertake' to inhabit them with English – *not Irish* – settlers. Ralegh, the planter of Virginia, had little to do with planning the Munster plantation, but moved with courtierly assurance to claim three-and-a-half seignories, when the limit for any undertaker was one. From 1587 he held 40,000 acres of the best land in Counties Cork and Waterford, and in 1588–9 he was Mayor of Youghal.

Edmund Spenser's poem *Colin Clout's Come Home Again*, addressed from his house at Kilcolman, County Cork, celebrated the encounter of two poetical shepherds; Colin Clout, who was Spenser himself, and the Shepherd of the Ocean, Ralegh. 'He pip'd, I sung; and when he sung I piped.' Colin lamented his banishment 'into that waste where I was quite forgot', yet when he was 'come home again', home was Ireland, not England. Exile from 'Cynthia's land' was painful, for in England, unlike Munster, there was 'no grisly famine, nor no raging sword'. Yet life in the wild offered freedoms. In Ireland, Spenser pined not only for England, but also for the lost time when the Protestant circle, of which he was part, aspired to save the soul of Europe. It was in Ireland that he wrote his prophetic, apocalyptic, allegorical epic, *The Faerie Queene*. And in Munster Spenser wrote another work: not a chivalric epic – far from it – but a manifesto for the New English, a work of utter disillusion and cold brutality: *A View of the Present State of Ireland* (written by 1596, but censored and not published until 1633). A sinister and desolating life on the frontier of English rule, circled by the dispossessed and hostile Irish and Anglo-Irish, made Spenser contemplate radical solutions; to answer the threat of rebellion with starvation, garrisons and total subjection.

Ireland was abandoned to pragmatists, planters and freebooters. Perrot's successor, Sir William Fitzwilliam, an old Ireland hand, came as chief governor again in 1588. With no ideals, no commitment to any group or policy, he was mainly concerned to protect himself against

Perrot's sniping from London and to sweeten the bitterness of his service with bribes from the Irish. His hope of ensuring peace by doing nothing, by leaving well – or not so well – alone, was his delusion and Ireland's great misfortune. Fitzwilliam's ineffectual rule unleashed the provincial governors, whose ambitions and energies Perrot had tried to curb. In Connacht, Sir Richard Bingham, commissioned in the summer of 1584 to execute martial law, had fallen to that duty with a vengeance. In 1586 he 'hunted' the rebellious Mayo Burkes 'from bush to bush and hill to hill' and slaughtered their Scots mercenary forces in their hundreds at Ardnaree. Bingham began to renegotiate the first composition agreements, increasing his own exactions, denying the claims of some lords, and revising the freedoms granted and settlements made with others, most notably O'Rourke. Bingham's violence and extra-legal methods alarmed his masters as well as the Irish. Fitzwilliam reserved for him the ultimate Tudor insult: 'atheist'. In December 1589 Bingham was cleared of charges of misgovernment by a Dublin court and set loose to prosecute the Burkes and their followers whose renewed revolt against Bingham's regime had spread through Mayo, Sligo and Leitrim. Thereafter Bingham consolidated his military control over Connacht, and through a network of military offices granted to his brothers, cousins and friends, lived like an arbitrary Gaelic lord himself.

The shiring of Ireland – begun by Sir Henry Sidney and completed, in name, under Perrot – had brought all the familiar officials of English local government: sheriffs, bailiffs and constables. But they came with quite different incentives and rules than the stalwarts of the English shires. 'These Seneschals, Sheriffs and others, that should have been the reformers . . . became the only deformers,' wrote Barnaby Rich, a New English soldier of fortune. In Sligo, the exactions of O'Connor of Sligo and O'Donnell were ended, for the while, in 1588 when O'Connor of Sligo's estate was forfeited to the Crown and Hugh Roe O'Donnell, who had been kidnapped by Perrot, fretted in Dublin Castle, but the people now bore the burden of Captain George Bingham's 'cutting' upon the country, his extortion of money by torture. Sheriffs toured their new shires with large retinues, demanding food, lodging and the 'black rent' formerly extracted by the Irish lords. At the end of the 1580s a northern assize circuit brought royal justice to Ulster, its judgements to be enforced by Sir Henry Bagenal, who, said Hugh O'Neill, sought to rule like a 'little king'. For the Irish, the extension of English law seemed to bring servitude, not justice.

Fitzwilliam had not come to reform. Yet as a consequence of his actions, which they saw as arbitrary and self-seeking, the Gaelic lords began to fear for the survival of their power, lands and customs. In Oriel, the MacMahon lordship in southern Ulster, Fitzwilliam's prescriptions were so radical, so exemplary that every Gaelic lord was fearful thereafter. In 1587 MacMahon had surrendered his lands in order to free himself from the overlordship of Hugh O'Neill, the Earl of Tyrone, but on MacMahon's death in August 1589 the sept repudiated English sovereignty and, with Tyrone's support, elected a new MacMahon according to Gaelic custom. The heir according to English law, Hugh Roe MacMahon, was arrested by Fitzwilliam and charged with treason. MacMahon's real offence, said the Irish, was not paying Fitzwilliam the bribe he had promised. The Queen urged caution, for MacMahon had committed only 'such march offences as are ever ordinarily committed in that realm', but unavailingly. The trial of MacMahon was of dubious legality, his execution arbitrary, and what followed was a fundamental assault upon the tenurial structure of Gaelic society. The lordship was divided between seven lords, and the land distributed among a new caste of freeholders. The Earl of Tyrone saw this as an attack upon his own supremacy over his dependent lords. The Gaelic lords also understood that they must honour their agreements with the Crown or face retaliation. There began then a 'heart burning' among them as they wondered whose turn it would be next.

It was Sir Brian O'Rourke's. O'Rourke rebelled, and his lordship of West Breifne, now the county of Leitrim, was invaded and occupied by Bingham in the spring of 1590. Taking refuge in Tirconnell, and then in Scotland where he went to recruit mercenaries, O'Rourke was handed over by James VI and delivered into England in April 1591. O'Rourke was tried for the treason of denying the Queen's sovereignty and for aiding her enemies, the shipwrecked Spaniards from the Armada. His trial was held in England – although his treasons were committed in Ireland, which had laws of its own to try him – for the judgement was that he was subject to the Queen against whom the treason was committed. His death by hanging at Tyburn in October 1591 was ominous for all those Gaelic lords who did not recognize themselves as subjects.

The great and growing power of Hugh O'Neill stood in the way of the reform of Ulster and of Ireland. The amphibious O'Neill, fostered among the New English of the Pale, trained in English arms and manners, with friends in the highest places in London and Dublin, was Baron of Dungannon and, from 1585, Earl of Tyrone. But he was also, since 1579, tanist of the O'Neills, and aspired to be *the* O'Neill, Prince of Ulster. He presented himself as defender of the English Pale, pacifier of Ulster against Turlough Luineach and the MacShanes, and as cast aside by English freebooting officials, his services unrewarded. But his way of making promises which he did not keep, his deluding charm and his deep dissimulation were long recognized by the English government, and his loyalty was suspect. It had failed to curb his power while there was a chance; between 1588 and 1591, while the MacShanes were strong and Tyrone was in trouble. By 1592 it was too late.

The long power struggle among the O'Neills which had convulsed the lordship of Tyrone was ending, and the underlords were passing from the control of Turlough Luineach to that of Hugh O'Neill. By 1592–3 he had extended his power at the expense of the less successful branches of his family and assumed full control of the lordship. By marriage and by fosterage, Hugh O'Neill was bound to most of the lordships of Ulster: Hugh Maguire of Fermanagh and Hugh Roe O'Donnell were his sons-in-law. Sir Henry Bagenal became his reluctant, inimical, brother-in-law, when O'Neill eloped with Bagenal's sister, Mabel. Since the kidnapping of O'Donnell in 1587 had been a way of containing O'Neill, his escape from Dublin Castle at the end of 1591 and flight to Tirconnell was a politically momentous as well as a heroic moment. Hugh Roe O'Donnell returned, burning with indignation against English incursions, to awe and regenerate his ravaged lordship. In February 1592 he expelled Captain Willis from Donegal Priory. In May he was inaugurated as the O'Donnell, chief of his clan. The two great lordships of the north, Tyrone and Tirconnell, their long succession disputes over and their traditional rivalries resolved, were now in dangerous alliance.

When, in the spring of 1593, Maguire's country was invaded by Captain Willis, who was attempting to establish himself as sheriff of Fermanagh, the Maguires revolted. The Maguire bard Eochaidh Ó Heóghusa (O'Hussey) had celebrated Hugh Maguire as the saviour who would wash Ireland in English blood and return it to peace and prosperity: 'Hugh is the land that protecteth Fermanagh.' In May 1593 Maguire's forces entered Sligo and Brian MacArt MacBaron invaded South Clandeboye in the far east of Ulster. Maguire was O'Neill's son-in-law, MacBaron his nephew; neither had acted without his knowledge or direction. Their revolt followed the gathering of a synod of Catholic bishops in Tirconnell at the end of 1592. This 'Irish combination' looked beyond Ireland to Spain, and called upon Philip II's assistance to save Ireland and the Church. No help came, yet. O'Neill's name was missing from the appeal, but behind it lay his secret collusion. His underlords had sworn an oath before him to aid the Spanish invaders. O'Neill had unleashed his dependants against his rivals, Bingham and Bagenal, to prove his paramountcy, and that Ulster could not be governed without him.

Not trusting him but testing him, the Dublin Council commissioned O'Neill in the summer of 1593 to disperse the forces of Maguire and bring him to obedience. That autumn O'Neill and Bagenal, as wary allies, campaigned against Maguire and defeated him at the Battle of Erne Ford. O'Neill's wounds in the battle he alleged as proof of his loyalty, but spies told of his secret meetings with the confederates O'Donnell and Maguire. In February 1594 Marshal Bagenal wrote that O'Neill 'doth not in any way covertly proceed', but used his son, brothers and nephews 'as open instruments of his wicked designments'. O'Neill's refusal to comply with royal orders early that year to obtain the submission of O'Donnell marked the beginning of his open progress from compliance to obstruction to treason. Through 1594–5 the Ulster lords moved towards war; a war which O'Neill directed as undeclared head of the confederacy. O'Neill's dependants fought his battles for him, and the Dublin officials failed to arrest him when they had the chance. At the Battle of the Ford of the Biscuits (so called because the English abandoned their supplies) on the River Arny in July 1594 George Bingham's forces were routed by Maguire and Cormac MacBaron O'Neill, Hugh O'Neill's brother. Sir William Russell arrived as the new chief governor; one of the most useless of the century. Beyond O'Neill's deep resentment of English officials' intervention in Ulster, he had personal grievances: he claimed that he was unregarded and unrewarded; that while Bagenal and Fitzwilliam were 'befriended at court' (by Burghley), his own supporters, Walsingham and Leicester, were gone. (He did not mention a 'friendship' with Essex which would prove fateful.) The undeclared war became general when Leinster rebels made a compact with the northern lords. At Clontibret in Monaghan in June 1595 O'Neill finally fought not with the government forces, but against them. Ten days later he was declared a traitor.

The Ulster lords had first rebelled for private causes: to defend their lands and lordships from English incursions; and to prevent Fermanagh, Tirconnell and Tyrone from going the way of Monaghan. But in January 1596 they made a demand that so appalled Lord Deputy Russell that he suppressed it, keeping it secret even from the Council: they demanded freedom of religion, liberty of conscience. The Queen had always chosen to believe that in Ireland Catholics, loyal to Rome, might nevertheless also be accounted loyal subjects to her, and had determined not to punish allegiance to Rome. But in September 1595 a joint letter from O'Neill and O'Donnell to Philip II had been intercepted. In it they asked for aid to re-establish the Catholic religion and promised him a kingdom. As they declared religious war, the Queen regretted her policy of not forcing consciences in Ireland.

*

In England, this queen who had never wished to search consciences, and who had had the wisdom to wait for her subjects to recognize that in religion, as in everything else, she knew what was best for them, grew impatient and was angered by their presumption towards God and her. It was not only the Papists whom she came to reprove as 'dangerous to a kingly rule', but the more uncompromising spirits among the Protestants, the puritans who grew 'overbold with God Almighty', and thought that their private exposition of scripture allowed them to judge a 'prince's government'. As they continued to press for further reformation, they impugned her royal supremacy. Civil and ecclesiastical government were twin functions of the state, and to claim a right to disobey one implied a right to disobey the other. Determined to confront rather than conciliate what she called Protestant 'newfangledness', the Queen increasingly chose councillors and churchmen who shared her views.

John Whitgift had come to the see of Canterbury in 1583, on the death of the disgraced Grindal, with high views of his authority and a determination instantly to restore uniformity of liturgical observance. In this he challenged all those godly puritan ministers who had preached the Word but used the Prayer Book only in part, if at all. In November 1583 Whitgift ordered all clergy to subscribe to articles to which no puritan, no 'precisian' could, in conscience, consent. These men might allow the royal supremacy, as charged, but never that the Prayer Book contained nothing 'contrary to the word of God', nor could they bind themselves to use it, for it still contained all those 'popish' remnants which they found anathema – bowing at the name of Jesus, the language of priesthood, the sign of the Cross in baptism, the ring in marriage, saints' days. Failure to subscribe meant suspension, even deprivation, and banishment from the evangelical duty which had made them take up the prophetic ministry in the first place. Three or four hundred ministers could not subscribe. Whitgift's assault closed the ranks of all those who demanded further reformation, who had been in some disarray, and confirmed many in their conviction that the office of bishop was anti-christian. Extremists, inspired to militancy, threatened to break the ostensible peace of the Church. Their refusal to subscribe, so they insisted, was not a fastidious scruple about things indifferent, but concerned 'great and weighty causes of God's kingdom'. To allow that the Prayer Book was concordant with the Word, that nothing in it needed changing, would only confirm the popish majority in their ignorance and error; while to stand against it was in itself a form of edification. Faced with the extent of schism, even Whitgift faltered, and he allowed subscription with reservation. Casuistry was a puritan as well as a Catholic art. From 1584 the most resolute non-conformists were marked men. The authorities knew who and where they were: they were the leaders of what had become a puritan movement.

Within the wider community of the godly, the majority were moderates, who longed for further reformation but either would not challenge authority to win it or believed that the True Church was unattainable in the corruption of this world. Without the establishment of a learned preaching ministry of 'diligent barkers against the Romish wolf' no reform would come, and the demand for a true preaching ministry was at the heart of the puritan quest for a reformed Church and society. A moderate puritan campaign began to win a hearing for their cause; in Parliament, in Convocation (the assembly of the clergy), in the Privy Council, even from the Queen, who they still believed must listen. But within Elizabethan puritanism was a group, no less than revolutionary, which was prepared to 'tarry for the magistrate' only for a time. These were the presbyterians, who wished to erect the 'only discipline and government of Jesus Christ', to establish a hierarchy of presbyteries – 'conferences', 'exercises' or 'classes' where like-minded clergy would meet – and provincial synods, and to have a Church ruled, seemingly democratically, by pastors, elders, doctors and deacons. In their reformed Church neither the royal Supreme Governor nor the bishops would have any part or power. In the Parliaments of 1584–5 and

1586–7 presbyterians introduced the most radical of bills, proposing to erect a godly discipline and bring in the Genevan service book as official liturgy. This presbyterian platform threatened not only the established Church but also the campaign of moderate puritans for a preaching ministry. It failed. The presbyterians were accused of anarchy: there was nothing anarchic about their discipline nor the ordered lives of their godly community, but their subversion of royal authority and their constitutional challenge were undoubted. While Elizabeth claimed that her authority in Church and state was God-given, in the Commons some asserted that Church government was subject to common law, statute and Parliament. In July 1590 the Queen wrote to James VI, warning him that his kingdom and hers were being infiltrated by a 'sect of perilous consequence', 'such as would have no kings but a presbytery'.

The presbyterians' attempt to erect their system of church government by statute had failed. They moved then to convert the Church of England by stealth, outside and against the law. 'It is the multitude and people that must bring the discipline to pass which we desire,' avowed John Field, their undaunted leader. The plan through the 1580s was to establish a church within the Church, 'presbytery within episcopacy'. Presbyterians proceeded secretly in order to allay the suspicion of schism. In every county where there were radical ministers in any number, conferences were held, all in touch with headquarters, the London conference. Yet Elizabethan puritanism was a spirit more pragmatic and inclusive by far than presbyterianism. Moderate puritans were not concerned principally with church government but with the establishment of a preaching ministry. Even in the Dedham *classis*, whose activities are best known, many felt that the discipline was not the essential, apodictic, mark of the Church.

Preaching was. The moderates feared that the mission of the 'diligent barkers against the Romish wolf', never more urgent, would be put in hazard by the presbyterian hardliners. In a spirit of compromise, puritans in most places had adapted the organization and liturgy of the Church of England to their own reformed purposes: churchwardens and sidesmen metamorphosed into elders and deacons; the Prayer Book was suitably 'mangled', and its 'anti-christian' elements excluded, so that it could form the basis of a worship in which the Word took precedence over sacraments. Listening to epic sermons, following their preachers from text to text in their Geneva Bibles, singing psalms, and conforming their lives to Christ's prescriptions, most puritans hoped to worship truly while still remaining within the fellowship of the Church of England, within its formal communion and the social community of the parish. Their hope, if not their expectation, was that they could transform the Church from within, as the godly leaven in the unregenerate lump, and that their neighbours, too, would turn to the Lord. A few set their children apart from the less than godly rest by giving them emphatically Christian names: Fear-God, Zealous, Perseverance. John Penry, for whom the Church increasingly bore the mark of the Beast, called his daughter, born in hiding in Scotland, Safety. There was no general will to call out a gathered Church of the godly few from out of the profane multitude. It was a religious duty not to separate. But some took a dangerous path away from the established Church. Reading in scripture of a new Jerusalem, 'they thought they were themselves that new Jerusalem,' wrote Richard Hooker, the most brilliant critic of the sectaries.

The failing presbyterian campaign was harmed by friends as well as enemies. From October 1588 a series of pamphlets appeared from a secret press; the name of the pseudonymous author expressed their subversive purpose – Martin Marprelate. These were satirical master-pieces, ridiculing not only the bishops' pomposity and pretensions, but also their essential function. Whitgift was the 'pope of Lambeth', betrayer of the Reformation. The bishops weighed in to reply. Bishop Cooper's ponderous response ('a horse may carry it if he be not too weak', wrote Martin) was promptly answered with *Hay [Have you] any work for Cooper*. Dr Richard Bancroft, the Lord Chancellor's chaplain, preached a menacing sermon in February 1589, when the new Parliament met, attacking puritans as 'false prophets', and asserting a high view of episcopal authority. Martin was never discovered, but his publishers were, and he fell silent in the summer of 1589. The search for Martin uncovered the secret networks of the *classes*, the prototype of synodical government. The Ecclesiastical Commissioners (or Court of High Commission) investigated the presbyterian leaders and called upon them to swear the self-incriminating *ex officio* oath, by which they were forced to answer their interrogators in full. This was a civil law procedure; against the principles of common law. Here was the English Inquisition at work, protested the godly. Why should the Queen's loyal Protestant subjects be persecuted, they asked, when the danger from Jesuits and papists was so much greater?

Speaking in Parliament in March 1587, Lord Chancellor Hatton had drawn ominous comparisons 'betwixt the Pope and the puritans'; both were the Queen's insidious enemies, equally dangerous to her and her laws, subversive of property as well as of religion. Marprelate had accused Whitgift, 'your Canterburiness', of favouring papists and recusants over puritans. The puritans lamented the penal laws against them, and the sermons which charged them with being friends to anarchy and which coupled them with Jesuits and recusants. In 1593 a Government bill introduced to increase the penalties against Catholic recusants to virtual expropriation was extended to include puritan recusants, the sectaries. The House was aghast. 'Men not guilty' would be endangered, warned Ralegh. When on 6 April Whitgift, fearing the defeat of the bill in the Commons, rushed forward the hanging of two sectaries, Henry Barrow and John Greenwood, the Commons' alarm about the 'lawless' proceedings of the bishops seemed proven. The new commission in London which sought out puritan sectaries and 'popish malefactors' marked the new mood of repression. Spies and priest-takers were at work. At the end of May 1593 Christopher Marlowe, whose own allegedly anarchic religious views were under investigation, was murdered. Among his companions was Robert Poley, a government informer. When Ben Jonson, who as a Catholic was no stranger to the world of spies and priest-takers, wrote a poem 'inviting a friend to supper', he promised an evening of unshadowed friendship, safe from named informers:

> And we will have no Poley, or Parrot by;
> Nor shall our cups make any guilty men.

This was no easy time to set the claims of the conscience against the laws of the state; to decide whether to obey God's laws or man's. At this moment, when disagreements over religion were 'at their highest float', Richard Hooker published the first four books of the *Laws of Ecclesiastical Polity*, his masterly apologia for the Church of England, and his polemical manifesto for its reform. He adumbrated the degenerative dangers of puritan pluralism and schism, and advocated an ordered world in which membership of the Church of England and the commonwealth would be reciprocal. But that compromise church, moored between Rome and Geneva, which was the ideal of the Elizabethan establishment, was still scorned by both confessional sides. Job Throckmorton – Martin Marprelate's alter ego? – had complained in Parliament in 1587 that 'obedience to the law of man is the whole sum of religion in this age', and a form of irreligion.

At about the time that the harshest penalties were being imposed on nonconformists, John Donne wrote his disloyal, radical *Satire 3*. 'Seek true religion. O where?' His speaker in the satire was unconvinced by all the reasons for choosing Catholicism, Calvinism, conformity or separatism. Truth must be found by 'mind's endeavours' – tough thinking – for the consequence of the wrong choice was not human punishment but divine. The seeker disparaged the civil penalties which awaited the doubter and nonconformist:

> men do not stand
> In so ill case here, that God hath with his hand
> Signed kings blank-charters to kill whom they hate

Donne had had his own searing experience of religious repression. In May 1593 a young man was arrested in the rooms of Donne's brother Henry, on suspicion of being a Catholic priest. Faced with torture, Henry Donne betrayed him. The priest was executed, and Henry Donne died that summer in a plague-infested prison. John Donne, now under the surveillance of priest-takers, betrayed the Catholic Church of his father, and made the soul-destroying choice that the seeker in his satire condemned:

> Fool and wretch, wilt thou let thy soul be tied
> To man's laws by which she shall not be tried
> At the last day?

Some did refuse to conform, risking 'man's laws'. Sir Thomas Tresham built a triangular lodge on his Northamptonshire estate in 1593: a profession of his Catholic faith in stone. It was an Elizabethan conceit, an allegory of the Trinity and of the Mass. Around the frieze ran an inscription of 33 letters: '*Quis separabit nos a charitate Christi*? [Who will separate us from the love of Christ]' Who indeed? The government certainly tried to separate Tresham from his Catholic allegiance. Rome was still the enemy, the Pope was still the 'Man of Sin', and fear of Catholic subversion had never gone away. The spiritual mission to regenerate Catholicism in England was set to continue indefinitely so long as the persecution intended the faith's oblivion. 'The weapons of our warfare' were solely spiritual, insisted Robert Southwell, the Jesuit: 'Our prisons preach, our punishments convert, our dead quarters and bones confound your heresy.' But after 1584 the leaders of the mission, Persons and Allen, turned to writing radical theories of resistance. English Catholics did not listen to their call to arms when the Armada came, and leading Catholic gentry petitioned the Queen to be allowed to fight for her against the Pope. They wanted the faith restored, but not by invading Spaniards and 'the Pope's bridge of wood made on the seas'. Yet suspicions remained that they might choose differently next time.

Catholics insistently refuted the charges made in proclamations that they were 'unnatural subjects'; fugitives, rebels and traitors. Yet with every invasion scare, every shift in European politics, the danger for all Catholics grew. Every quiescent Catholic was affected by the militancy of a very few. Successive legislation had made priests traitors, and the lay Catholics who knowingly aided them felons. Catholic loyalty was always suspect while the priests worked secretly and unseen. Isolated and hunted, in the midst of Protestant communities, the tiny band of Catholic priests, Jesuits and seminarians took extraordinary risks to say Mass, to preach and to return people to the Catholic fold. The Catholic community lived in a state of siege, keeping the faith whether a priest came or not. But when a priest did arrive in their neighbourhood, the local laity must feed him, shelter him undetected, often in concealed priest-holes, and then speed him on his way. When Robert Southwell left for the mission in 1586, he was already under observation. Stationed in London, often sheltered there by the Countess of Arundel, Southwell received priests whose missions led them to the capital. At the end of 1588 he was sent on a missionary tour. Sometimes he called in disguise upon Protestant sheriffs who, seeing his elegant clothes and aristocratic retinue, welcomed him with sumptuous banquets. Secretly, he ministered to hidden Catholics in their households. But by February 1592 Henry Garnet, Southwell's superior, feared that there was nowhere left for him to hide. In June Southwell travelled from Fleet Street to celebrate Mass at the Bellamys' house at Uxenden in Middlesex, and there he was betrayed by his host's sister. Three years of solitary confinement and torture followed until his martyrdom in February 1595.

Since the priests were sent as missionaries, not as martyrs, they must stay alive and at large and learn to survive among heretics who hated them, and whose heresy they hated. Manuals offered answers to 'cases of conscience'. What should a Catholic do when, while among heretics, his companions began to sing psalms, or wanted to take him to church with them? If, while travelling, a priest was questioned about his destination or his religion, should he avoid the question or was he bound to tell the truth? To the last, Allen and Persons answered that he was bound never to deny his faith, but needed not to confess it if it meant endangering his life. How to avoid telling the truth without lying? They were taught ways of misleading an unjust interrogator while not breaking the absolute prohibition on lying. At his trial, Robert Southwell admitted advising a woman that, if asked upon oath whether she had seen a priest, she could answer 'no' by keeping in her mind the meaning that she did not see him with the intention of betraying him. Most dangerous of all was the 'bloody question' which demanded which side a Catholic would take in the event of a papal invasion.

Catholic resistance centred upon the symbolic act of not going to church, of never intending to go. This was to show the world what it was to be Catholic. Attendance at heretic rites was sinful. Yet adherence to Rome was a very costly choice. There was what Bishop Aylmer called 'pecuniary pain'; the monthly recusancy fines of £20 for richer Catholics, who grew steadily poorer. Some suffered long imprisonment; what Sir Thomas Tresham called 'the furnace of our many years' adversity'. Nonconforming Catholics were excluded from Parliament, from office holding, and from university education. After 1593 they could not travel more than five miles from their homes without a licence. And beyond these mortifying disabilities there was their sense of alienation, isolation and terror.

The priests, recognizing human frailty and that absolute recusancy and separation might even damage the Catholic cause if it led to expropriation and oblivion, condoned concession and compromise. They allowed Catholics to attend Protestant services with the heretics; to wait upon England's eventual return to Rome. 'Just fear', the necessity to save a family from ruin, could justify occasional conformity. In compassion, the leaders of the mission, with assurance from Pope Clement VIII, allowed that conforming Catholics could be easily absolved from what was still a sin. From as early as 1582 these conforming Catholics were abusively known as 'church papists'. Church papistry seemed then an almost irresistible way out, although the vision of a truly restored Church was based upon the official fiction of undeviating recusancy. Faced with the prospect of imprisonment and impoverishment, Catholics moved from recusancy to church papistry, and back again. Men attended church from time to time, often leaving their recusant wives at home; or they came to church but did not receive Communion, or only rarely. And while conforming for 'fashion sake', they promised themselves that they would make satisfaction; that they would live in one faith and die in another. In the North and West those of Catholic sympathies inclined to recusancy, but in the Midlands and South nominal conformity predominated.

Church papistry might be particularly necessary for those families upon whom many others depended: the nobility and gentry. The Catholic leaders recognized that any movement needed the protection of the great, who must keep their positions of honour so that after the death of Elizabeth they could forward the faith. Many of the Elizabethan titled nobility and members of their families were Catholic or crypto-Catholic. Special dispensation was granted to noblemen and women to attend upon the Queen when she went to church. Viscount Montague kept a Catholic household, managed by his saintly wife, but still attended upon the Queen. But for a few, conformity was agony. Philip Howard, Earl of Arundel, reconverted to his faith by Campion's public disputations of doctrine in the Tower in September 1581, paced around Westminster Abbey during services or found excuses for staying away, until finally he could conform no longer. He was captured while escaping to exile.

The survival of the faith under persecution owed much to the protection of Catholic congregations by the nobility and gentry. The old ways of deference would incline a tenant to follow the faith of his lord, and that deference might be strengthened if the lord defended that faith. The great Catholic households could provide an alternative to the parish. Although the processions and festivals which had been so vital a part of the old religion were lost, within great households the celebration of the major Catholic feasts could be subsumed within the annual cycle of hospitality. The priest could be a guest among others, or live in the house disguised as a tutor or steward. Church papists could worship within the parish for the sake of legality, but receive Catholic rites within the household for the sake of religion. The whole household could be endangered if one disaffected servant revealed to the authorities the Catholic ways followed within it. Yet many Catholics *were* still the authorities. They saw no conflict between devotion to Rome and devotion to the Queen, and insisted upon their duty to serve her by upholding civil law and order. In Lancashire, Cheshire and Sussex, even a generation after the purges of the 1560s, church papistry persisted within the commissions of the peace and the town corporations. The vice-president of the Council in the Marches of Wales was the occasional conformist Sir John Throckmorton. Many local gentry were, as JPs, unenthusiastic persecutors of Catholic neighbours, to whom they were bound by ties of kinship and friendship. Philip Sidney found the prospect of collecting recusancy fines repugnant.

The presbyterian movement had, by the early 1590s, been shattered, but the zeal of the godly community had not. And Catholicism had been broken as a political force, but survived as a living faith. Protestantism and Catholicism became more divided over the great issues of faith: grace, free will, sin, predestination, justification, scripture, sacraments and the authority of the Church. And there were now ominous divisions among Protestants themselves. Through the 1570s and 1580s disputes among the godly had centred upon the debate about the system of church government, not about doctrine, for within the English Church Calvinism was ascendant. Calvinism had entered its dogmatic phase, as the systematizers of Calvin's ideas – the most brilliant of whom was William Perkins – advanced views on predestination which were still more uncompromising than Calvin's. Perkins taught that God had divided mankind unconditionally into the elect and the reprobate, even before the Fall of Adam, and denied that grace was universal. Yet some within the Church began to question these central doctrines as too deterministic and to assert that election and reprobation were *conditional*. They believed that Christ had died for all, and that saving grace was offered to all (if not granted to all); they impugned the Calvinist doctrine of Christian assurance. In the mid 1590s the foundations and consensuality of Elizabethan Protestantism were assaulted, and dangerous crypto-papist doctrines came to threaten the peace of the Church.

Presbyterians and Catholics alike knew that there would be no advance for their causes while the Queen lived, and they awaited her death as a day of judgement. Robert Southwell wrote that England was 'so full of makebates and factions' that the prospective 'civil mutinies' were worse than any enemy invasion. As the question of the succession grew more urgent, some Catholic exiles, including Persons, combined to write a work of radical resistance theory. The *Conference about the Next Succession* (1595) argued that, while hereditary monarchy was the best principle of government, neither monarchy nor the principle of succession were inviolable. The monarch who broke the coronation oath and covenant with the people was a tyrant and might be deposed by the people, who could also alter the course of succession. The work was dedicated to the figure in Elizabethan politics to whom aspirant groups – Catholic or puritan – foreign heads of state, soldiers, writers and the people now turned: the Earl of Essex.

*

Early in November 1595 the Queen showed a copy of the treasonable *Conference about the Next Succession* to Essex, who believed its dedication to be a design by his enemies to harm him. He left court, looking pale. That night the court gates were locked; the Lord Chamberlain kept the keys and the Comptroller of the Household patrolled with torches. Essex burnt private letters. Such precautions had not been taken since the days of the Queen's father and brother. The mood of intense disquiet had been occasioned by fears of Spanish invasion, by alarm about the succession, and by the 'deadly unkindness' between Essex and Burghley. Ralegh, recently returned from his quest for El Dorado in Guiana, had also left court, but was expected to return, because his friends there were 'many and great'. Within days, as the Queen visited Essex and restored him to greater favour than ever, calm returned to the court. The intense alarm, the 'deadly unkindness', the reconciliations, were the pattern of politics for the later 1590s, and Essex, the turbulent favourite, was at the heart of all the discord.

Essex's ambitions lay as yet within the limits of duty and service. He had promised Elizabeth in 1592 that the 'two poles of your Privy Chamber shall be the poles of my sphere'. As acknowledged favourite, he was privileged and protected, the complacent recipient of almost half of the grants which an increasingly penurious and parsimonious queen had to give. Essex would admit no rival, but neither could he easily play the favourite. His confidant Francis Bacon urged him to 'win the Queen', counselling 'obsequiousness and observance'. But Essex insisted upon 'authority' and 'necessity', upon asserting his will against hers. For him, male dominance must overcome female indecision: 'She doth not contradict confidently,' he noticed during one battle of wills in 1594, 'which they that know the minds of women say is a sign of yielding.' When 'by violent courses' Essex got his own way, he would ask Bacon: 'Now Sir, whose principles be true?' But there were dangers that Essex, in his repeated tests of the Queen's devotion, would go too far; that his presumption would lead to a fatal alienation.

For Essex, friendship, like everything else, was a matter of honour.

He pursued a quest for offices for his friends and clients with no less recklessness than any of his other campaigns. From 1593 he made violent efforts to win first the Attorney-Generalship, and then the Solicitor-Generalship for Francis Bacon, even though his siege was bound to fail because in that year Bacon had opposed the royal interest in Parliament. His campaign to secure, in turn, the offices of Lord Chamberlain, Warden of the Cinque Ports and Vice Chamberlain for Sir Robert Sidney, marooned in Flushing, were also unsuccessful. Like his brother, the late, lamented Sir Philip, Robert was distrusted by the Queen, and his enemies had reported to Elizabeth his amorous pursuit of her maids of honour. But refusal of the Earl's friends was refusal of the Earl himself.

Essex had been, from February 1593, Privy Councillor as well as favourite. Here, too, he was in a party of one: the youngest and noblest on the Council board, almost the only military commander among administrators and politicians, and the possessor of unrivalled foreign intelligence. He held overwhelming advantages, especially in time of war, but his presence caused tensions. In the Council, the inner circle of power, the private sway of a favourite over the Queen was resented, though not easily resisted. The Cecils, particularly, accepted the Earl as a colleague with outward cordiality, even though his public and private ambitions were so antipathetic to their own. They confronted him over patronage, grants and offices, but also over policy. While the war in France lasted, the sense of national danger muted their competition; not so thereafter.

There were deep divisions: not over whether there should be war, but over how and where it should be fought. For Burghley, as Lord Treasurer, the war was a lamentable necessity and should be merely defensive. For him, the great danger lay close to home, in Ireland. For Essex, once the Spanish forces had withdrawn from France and the English had followed, early in 1595, there could be only one strategy: war must be taken to Spain and pursued to the bitter end. The war would be won by assaulting the Spanish mainland and establishing a permanent base there in order to sever Spain from her overseas empire and the streams of American silver which sustained Spanish power. Essex's public and private ambitions were one: in war he would command. He did not count the cost: Burghley, knowing how wide the gulf between income and expenditure was, counted every penny. Here was the cause of the 'deadly unkindness' between them.

The Queen knew well the antagonisms within her Council. There were those who said that she promoted them. An anonymous contemporary wrote that 'her course hath been to feed the factious affections of persons of high quality', so that 'all depending on her favour' for advancement 'might thereby make her own direction more absolute'. He thought that her policy of having Leicester watch over Walsingham, and Walsingham watch over Leicester, and Hatton watch over both, had given her control earlier in her reign. She still tried, so Sir Robert Sidney's agent reported to him in 1596, to 'use her wisdom in balancing the weights', but her favourite upset the old patterns and was not to be counterbalanced. She was wary of granting any office to an enemy of Essex, lest she drive him to outbursts which she could not control, but nor would she be held to ransom by her favourite's fury. In 1594 she offered a warning with her promise: 'Look to thyself, good Essex, and be wise to help thyself, without giving thy enemies advantage; and my hand shall be readier to help thee than any other.'

In 1595 the Queen was persuaded to renew her attack on Spanish power: a measure of the weight of Essex's advocacy, but also of the alarm occasioned by a Spanish raid on Cornwall in July and by rumours of a new Armada. Drake and Norris sailed that summer on what would be their last voyage. Their original purpose was to capture and hold the isthmus of Panama, the route for Peruvian silver, but the proposal of the 'active sort' ('You may guess whom,' wrote one court observer) to send the fleet instead to attack the coast of Spain subverted the venture. Burghley and Elizabeth were slow to believe the intelligence of a new Armada, but when they did, and after despairing delays, a fleet sailed in June 1596 to Cadiz. Essex was Lord General of the Army; Lord Howard of Effingham was Lord Admiral: a shared command. Yet the commanders pursued their rivalries even in the midst of a naval engagement which prefigured 'Hell itself', as sailors leapt from burning ships to drown. Ralegh thrust his *Warspite* into the leading position, so that 'none should outstart me again'; Essex brought his *Due Repulse* alongside. In the *Rainbow*, Francis Vere, Marshal of the Army, fastened a rope to the *Warspite* in order to draw up equal, and Ralegh cut it. Cadiz was captured and sacked. A spectacular victory, but one which brought more glory than gold, and the commanders, in their jealousy, would share neither. As in 1589, the Queen's aim had been to destroy the Spanish fleet in its harbours, and Essex's had been different. Contravening instructions and beyond recall, he demanded to hold Cadiz as an English base. He was overruled by the other commanders during their council of war, but his new disobedience increased suspicions of him.

The Cadiz voyage, and the jealousies and witch-hunts which followed it, brought open divisions into high politics. Once again Essex returned to find, as he saw it, conspiracy at court. The Queen, in her anger, had broken her promise to Essex and made Robert Cecil Principal Secretary, and the navy commanders now impugned Essex's honour as commander of the army by accusing his followers of concealing booty. First among these critics was his old rival Ralegh, who was now returning to royal favour and allied with the Cecils. The disputes between the sea and land officers over the division of the spoils were epitomized in the renewed feud between Ralegh and Essex. Each vied to present himself as the victor of Cadiz, a publicity war so incendiary that their accounts were suppressed. But in this competition, Essex won. Devereux, according to the contemporary anagram, was *Vere dux* (true leader), and he was now accompanied around London by a horde of military officers, the hero of the London crowds. Here was the Pompey of the portrait miniature.

In the aftermath of Cadiz, Bacon wrote a remarkably blunt letter of advice to Essex. The image Essex presented, especially to the Queen, whose favour was all, was dangerous: 'A man of nature not to be ruled . . . of an estate not grounded to his greatness; of a popular reputation; of a military dependance.' Bacon explained how a favourite should behave and of what he should beware. Instead of avoiding emulating Leicester and Hatton, he must take them as patterns and pay court to the Queen. It would be politic to abandon some people, projects and manners in order to please her. He must, above all, let his military honour 'be a sleeping honour a while'. So, instead of seeking great military office, he should aspire to be Lord Privy Seal: it 'fits a favourite to carry her Majesty's image in seal'. To allay the suspicions that his popular following had aroused, he should always speak against 'popular causes'. Above all, he should give way to some other favourite. Essex was, that autumn, in a mood to listen, if not to act upon this advice. Now devout, newly faithful to his wife and magnanimous, his attentions were all turned towards that 'great work' which God intended for him, and he was devising grand strategy for the war with Spain.

Philip II acted to avenge the disaster of Cadiz. But the Armada which sailed in October 1596 was caught on a lee shore in the Bay of Biscay's storms, and wrecked off Finisterre: another Armada scattered by a Protestant wind rather than by prescient English defences. It would not be the last to sail, but it might be the last to be blown off course. At court that threat raised all the old disputes and hesitations: whether there should be an army as well as a navy sent, and who should command. The semblance of accord in the tiltyard and Presence Chamber masked a growing polarization in politics. Essex withdrew to melancholy retreat. Elizabeth threatened to 'break him of his will and pull down his great heart'; but her intervention to subdue her court and impose her will was followed in March 1597 by an unexpected suspension of hostilities, a truce between Essex and Cecil, mediated by Ralegh. Together, they believed that they could master the Queen, share out royal offices among themselves and lay plans for the next venture against Spain. Faced with such a united front, Elizabeth lost the political initiative. Ralegh became Captain of the Guard; Essex, Master of the Ordnance (Bacon's advice quite forgotten). On 18 April they dined together to mark an alliance which could only be temporary.

Against Spain, the only defence was now offence. After furious hesitation, the Queen was brought to agree. In May she gave Essex sole command, by land and by sea; his chance for his great work. The daring, original strategy which Essex had devised the previous autumn – to station an army of disciplined troops in key Spanish ports to create a double blockade – was not to be attempted. His first order was to destroy the Armada now moored at El Ferrol near La Coruña; the second, to intercept the treasure fleet from the Indies. But cast back by storms, forced by the expense caused by long delay to dismiss most of his land forces, Essex never engaged the Spanish fleet. Setting sail for the Azores – the Islands – Essex cruised aimlessly, and the treasure fleet slipped past. By 11 August, Cecil reported wryly that 'the fleet at Ferrol will not be burnt . . . the Islands cannot be taken . . . their weak watery hopes do but faintly nourish that noble earl's comfort'. The only success – the capture of the island of Faial in the Azores – was Ralegh's: a mutinous triumph, according to the Earl, undertaken without his orders. Poems of John Donne, who went on the Islands Voyage, testified to the disastrous weather which broke the expedition: the terror of the storm – 'like shot, not feared till felt' – and the despair of the calm – 'Heaven laughs to see us languish thus'. Bad judgement had compounded bad luck. While Essex was engaged upon those 'idle wanderings upon the sea' which he had condemned in others, England lay open to invasion. Since he had been given a free hand, the greater the disaster of the Islands Voyage, the greater his dishonour.

Essex returned to find, as usual, that his rivals had prospered in his absence. Melancholy and retreat again followed upon dishonour, and Essex refused to attend the new Parliament. At the end of 1597 the Queen placated her favourite and quieted the court by creating him Earl Marshal, head of the community of honour. Essex began searching for precedents for the Earl Marshalship and for the Constableship, a dormant medieval office. According to medieval precedent and contemporary political thought, the Constable could arrest the monarch. The drift of Essex's thinking was ominous. Essex had seen, in France, the powers of the great nobility when political life descended into violence and chaos. If the Queen died, and his favour and protection died with her, he would need support. Who but he should be the power behind the throne in the next reign? In 1598 George Chapman dedicated the first part of his translation of Homer's *Iliad* to Essex, 'most true Achilles', and urged him not to allow the 'peasant-common polities of the world' to distract him from 'godlike pursuit of Eternity'.

News from court was often of 'tribes', 'parties', 'factions', 'friends' and 'enemies'. Essex, in his singularity, had divided the court, but not into equal groups. On the one side was his own party, composed of disaffected young nobles and military men; on the other, the Cecils, Ralegh, and the political establishment. Essex spoke the language of friendship, learnt from the worlds of chivalry and of ancient Rome. Friendship meant private devotion, the camaraderie of honour and arms, but also the public connection of clientage. At court, everyone intermittently pretended friendship to everyone else; that was the 'ordinary infection of court', wrote Fulke Greville. Essex and Cecil and Ralegh still avowed amity and still cooperated. When Cecil went in embassy to France in the spring of 1598, Essex promised to guard his interests. But Essex came to understand friendship to himself in exclusive terms; 'either his only, or friend to Mr Cecil, and his enemy'. Those who were not with him were against him. Bacon remembered that a 'great officer at court', hearing one of Essex's partisans talk about his 'friends and enemies', said 'I know but one friend and enemy that my Lord hath, and that one friend is the Queen and that one enemy is himself'. In the end Bacon and the Earl's other friends would have to choose between friendship to Essex and loyalty to the Queen.

Essex's extreme behaviour now challenged even the Queen's loyalty. When Cecil's embassy to France failed to dissuade Henry IV from making a separate treaty of peace with Spain, the Cecils argued in Council that England too must make peace and leave the Dutch at last to face Philip II alone. For Essex, peace was dishonourable. Burghley, with only weeks to live, silently pointed out to Essex a verse in his psalter: 'Men of blood shall not live out half their days.' That July, during a quarrel, Essex turned his back on the Queen. She boxed his ears; he put his hand on his sword. Affronted, he asked, 'Cannot princes err? Can they not wrong their subjects? Is an earthly power or authority infinite?' He would not, he said, have taken so great an indignity at her father's hands. Nor would Henry VIII have forgiven treason, but Elizabeth forgave Essex, perhaps for the last time. Now in self-exile from court, what was left for him?

In Ireland, there was, by 1598, a threat to Elizabeth's sovereignty and England's security so desperate that, said Essex, only a noble of great honour and estate, with the respect of the army, who had been a general – that is, Essex himself – could be sent. But even as Essex was given the command, and the grand title of Lord Lieutenant, he was appalled by the prospect. His father had died in Ireland. The Queen, he told Greville, planned 'to ease her rebels in Ireland by breaking my heart'. And he thought on death. On Ash Wednesday 1599 Lancelot Andrewes preached before the Queen on the text of Deuteronomy 23:9, 'When thou goest out with the host against thine enemies, keep thee then from all wickedness.' He had a warning for Essex: 'War is no matter of sport.'

*

Rebellion in Ulster and Connacht had turned into war throughout Ireland. Rebellion in Ireland had been called 'universal' before, but this time it was. What had begun as a revolt against the depredations of English officials and Lord Deputy Fitzwilliam's encroachments became a struggle for freedom from English sovereignty. The submission of the Gaelic lords to the Crown had only been conditional: once their submission threatened the extinction of their lordships by breaking the military power which upheld them and by making their dependants freeholders, they turned to defence. Defence of lordship and private interest was transformed – for reasons of strategy as well as faith – into a self-styled crusade; first for liberty of conscience, and then for the formal re-establishment of the Catholic religion. In June 1595 Hugh O'Neill, the Earl of Tyrone, was proclaimed traitor, but now he did not admit himself to be a subject. That September he was inaugurated as the O'Neill at the Stone of Tullaghoge. The Earl of Tyrone, the Queen's feudatory, might be traitor, but not the O'Neill, Prince of Ulster. Some thought that he aimed to be king of Ireland: perhaps, but it was in September 1595 that O'Neill and O'Donnell wrote to Philip II, asking for aid, 'now or never', and promised him a kingdom.

O'Neill and O'Donnell offered to be vassals of the King of Spain, but they were also princes themselves. The Gaelic lords remembered that their ancestors had been provincial kings of Ireland. The drawing together of an Irish confederacy to defend Gaelic lordship now greatly extended the power of the overlords. As Earl of Tyrone, O'Neill had acted, or pretended to act, as the Queen's lieutenant, arbitrating between Ulster underlords and redressing grievances. The Crown and the traditional overlords contended for control of the underlords, *uirríthe* – 'our urriaghs', said the Queen. Now, at war, the great lords of Ulster and Connacht demanded hostages, bonnaght (mercenaries), tribute and 'risings out' (military service) from their underlords as pledges of their dependency, and they obeyed. Cormac MacBaron O'Neill wrote to Philip II in 1596 that 'all the Irish obey O'Neill as the sails obey the wind'. The devotion was of love, he said; but the taking of hostages and the capture of herds as pledges, and the offers to the lords of 'buyings' (the payment of protection money to gain respite from predatory soldiers), suggest otherwise. The lordship of Sligo was 'awed' by O'Donnell. The power to establish *uirríthe* in dependent lordships was the test of overlordship. At Christmas 1595 O'Donnell ordered that the 'royal rath' (fort and residence) of the O'Donnells be surrounded by rings of troops, and exercised his right as overlord of Connacht to arbitrate in the Burke succession dispute. He inaugurated his ally Tibbot Fitzwater Kittagh as the Lower MacWilliam. Soon O'Neill was intervening in succession disputes within lordships, not only in Ulster but throughout Ireland, deposing one lord, establishing another: the sign of his paramountcy. Elizabeth might write scornfully of O'Neill as a 'base, bush kern' but, acknowledging his hold over his followers, she also called him their 'golden calf'.

The English scorned the sovereign claims of O'Neill and O'Donnell, their protestations of ancient liberties and the integrity of Gaelic law and custom, and were especially contemptuous of their newly discovered quest for liberty of conscience. They, too, could present the Irish war as one of liberation, and pose as the champions of the common people of Ireland against lords who rebelled in no interests but their own, and who ruled as 'absolute tyrants'. The common people of Ireland, knowing 'no other king but their landlord, dare not but be ready to rise out with them' in any rebellion, wrote Barnaby Rich in 1599. Spenser said the same. The way to pacify Ireland, according to the English reformers, was to establish freehold tenure, which would release the people from fear of eviction. In 1594 Captain Dawtrey had told the Queen that Irish lords did not distinguish between '*Meum* and *tuum* [mine and yours] and will have all that their sword can keep'. The extension of common law would protect the people from the arbitrary justice of the lords; protect the weak from the strong.

The more violent and oppressive practices of the nobility in England had been curbed. Now the way to stability in Ireland was thought to be by subduing the Gaelic lords and those Anglo-Irish lords who still aspired to rule independent palatinates. When Shakespeare's audiences watched *Henry IV, Part 1*, first performed at some time between August 1596 and February 1598 as the Irish war entered a critical phase, did they see in Glendower's revolt something of Tyrone's resistance? When they saw Hotspur, reeking with blood on the battlefield, confront the 'perfumed popinjay' sent from a court like their own, were they reminded of the martial ethos of the late medieval nobility, who valued honour more than life? As they thought of that lost warrior code, did they think of the man in whom it was revived, sent in 1599 against the rebellious Irish lords: Essex?

Early in August 1598 Cecil wrote to Sir Geoffrey Fenton, Secretary of State for Ireland, instructing him to arrange for O'Neill's assassination. 'We have always in Ireland given head money for the killing of rebels,' acknowledged Ralegh, who was wise in the ways of Ireland. Unfortunately for England, the practice failed. After a brilliant victory by O'Neill, O'Donnell and Maguire over Marshal Bagenal at the Battle of the Yellow Ford on the Blackwater River on 14 August 1598 Elizabeth had all but lost Ireland. Ulster was under O'Neill's control; Connacht under O'Donnell's. The perennially dissident lords of Leinster had, in 1596, made common cause with the confederates. In July 1596 the northern lords wrote urging all the 'Irishry', especially the 'gentlemen of Munster', to 'make war with us'. Soon they did. Early in October 1598 O'Neill sent a raiding party from Leinster into Munster and within days the province was in revolt. Munster's dispossessed took a terrible revenge upon the English settlers. The anonymous author of a pamphlet whose title chillingly expressed its purpose – *A Supplication of the Blood of the English most lamentably murdered in Ireland, crying out of the earth for revenge* – asked 'Why were the rocks and walls painted with the blood and brains of children?' and answered simply, 'Because we *and they* were English.'

The Anglo-Irish lords of Munster – the Fitzthomases, the Knights of Kerry and Glin, the White Knight, the Barons of Lixnaw and Cahir, Viscount Mountgarret and Lord Roche – led the revolt or, at the least, did not prevent the slaughter. Two of the Gaelic MacCarthy septs, old enemies of the Desmonds, had held back. The character Irenius in Spenser's *View of the Present State of Ireland* (1596) had said that the Anglo-Irish were 'more malicious to the English than the very Irish themselves'. The warnings of Anglo-Irish degeneracy now seemed horribly prescient. Spenser himself was driven from Ireland, his castle of Kilcolman razed. The Geraldine affinity, leaderless after the death of the 15th Earl of Desmond in 1583, found their new leader in the illegitimate claimant, James Fitzthomas, whom O'Neill created Earl of Desmond. But only kings had the authority to create earls, and Fitzthomas was called disparagingly *súgán*, the 'straw-rope' earl: one false earl created by another, said the English. In many lordships, the malcontents looked to O'Neill to raise them against their rivals, and O'Neill promised to promote those who supported him and to depose those who would not.

The New English were hated because they took the land of the Irish and because they were English, but also because they were Protestants and therefore heretics. If the author of the *Supplication* spoke for them all, the New English saw the Irish, among whom they lived, as reprobate; '*their* God for whom they fight' was 'mortal', 'sleeping', 'feeble'; the settlers' own, omnipotent, but punishing them for condoning popery. At a meeting of confederate Munster lords at Cahir in November, the papal legate preached hellfire to those who acknowledged Elizabeth as queen. The rebels prayed for the confusion of England's Queen, who was no longer Ireland's. If Elizabeth wanted the crown of Ireland, she must fight for it. All that remained for her was to begin a second conquest.

Essex landed in Ireland in April 1599 to lead an army of 16,000 foot and 1,300 cavalry. His command of so great an army, the amplitude of the commission granted to him, the alacrity of the swordsmen and volunteers to serve with him, seemed to cause as much alarm among those at home who feared his wayward ambition as among the Irish rebels. His greatness was now seen to depend as much on the Queen's fear as on her love of him. With every parley, truce and pardon through

1595, 1596 and 1597, the rebels had mustered and armed and trained.
O'Neill now led against the English the same troops who had fought for
them. As Essex arrived, the confederate army was divided into two
commands: in Ulster, under O'Neill, were all the O'Neill underlords –
MacMahon, Magennis, O'Quinn and O'Hanlon – a force of 6,000; in
Connacht, under O'Donnell, were Maguire, O'Rourke and the Mac-
William – a force of 4,000. For all the English superiority in numbers,
Essex still feared that, as he wrote, the plaster would hardly cover the
wound. Already by the end of April he had been persuaded to abandon
his first purpose, the only strategy that could bring success: an expedition
against O'Neill in Ulster. 'All was nothing without that, and nothing
was too much for that,' the Queen had written.

Instead of the journey into Ulster, he distracted himself and exhausted
his troops through May and June by diversionary 'petty undertakings'
against the rebels in Munster and Leinster. Phelim MacFeagh O'Byrne,
'the wolf of the mountain', inflicted a humiliating defeat upon English
forces in Wicklow on 29 May. The Queen received reports of Essex's
campaign with dismay: his only success, the capture of Cahir Castle
from 'beggarly rogues', was a worthless feat; she was paying £1,000 a
day for the Earl to go in progress. The strategy of O'Neill, ensconced in
his Ulster sanctuary, guarded by defensible passes, provisioned by his
great herds and sustained by money from Spain, was to make the English
hunt him. The English 'gallants', epitomized by the Earl of Southampton
whom, to the Queen's fury, Essex made General of the Horse, longed
for cavalry charges, which the Irish always avoided. By a policy of
defence and interminable delay, O'Neill intended to bring down upon
the English 'the three furies, Penury, Sickness and Famine', break them
by exhaustion and despair, and terrify them in a waiting game. Essex,
who had condemned 'idle wanderings' and longed to take the war into
Spain, would not take the war into Ulster. Reports came to his enemies
in England that all his actions were 'to small purpose'.

Essex had always thought his Irish expedition foredoomed: 'I am like
to be a martyr in Ireland for the Queen.' Exile from court exposed him
to his enemies, who 'now in the dark give me wound upon wound'. He
named names: Lord Cobham and Ralegh. 'I am defeated in England,'
he wrote bitterly on 1 July; sent to Ireland with armour only for his
front, he was wounded in the back, and 'to the heart'. How could
successful war be waged by a disgraced commander? But his failure in
Ireland was his own; a failure of strategy and morale. By the time he

was stiffened to take his 'northern journey' against O'Neill, only a remnant of his great army remained. News of the disaster inflicted by O'Donnell upon Sir Conyers Clifford, President of Connacht in the Curlews Mountains, Roscommon on 5 August persuaded the 'little army' left to Essex of the inevitability of defeat. The Irish among the troops went over to the rebels 'by herds', the others lay sick. 'These base clowns,' wrote Essex, must be taught to fight again. On 21 August the Council of War in Dublin wrote to England that the remaining army of only 3,500 men would be 'far overmatched' if it met the rebel army of the north.

A week later Essex set forth against O'Neill. Their armies never fought. Instead, O'Neill came to the ford at Bellaclinthe on the Ulster border, gravely submissive, waded up to his horse's belly in the river, and there he and Essex parleyed, alone and unoverheard. They agreed a truce. To Elizabeth, that truce was as illusory as it was dishonourable: 'To trust this traitor upon oath is to trust a devil upon his religion.' What they said was their secret. But there were soon fears that the English Lord Lieutenant and the Irish 'arch traitor' had promised each other kingdoms. Essex admitted to his intimates that O'Neill incited him 'to stand for himself and he [O'Neill] would join with him'. Suspicions of Essex grew. Why the secrecy of their meeting? Why had Essex not fought O'Neill? The Queen came to believe that he had other things on his mind in Ireland than to serve her, and she forbade his return. Before leaving Dublin for Ulster, Essex had rehearsed a desperate scheme to his friends: he was resolved to go to England, and to go defended against his enemies. He would take an army with him, land in Milford Haven, and march to London to capture the court. They dissuaded him from taking an army to England – an act of aggression which would be an 'irrecoverable blot' – but not from returning. Riding hard, Essex reached the court by 28 September. The mud-stained favourite encountered the haggard, unbedizened queen in her bedchamber. 'By God's Son,' swore Elizabeth, 'I am no queen; that *man* is above me.'

From that night Essex was detained, at the Queen's interminable, procrastinating pleasure. Since his offence was still only disobedience and dishonour to the Queen, there were no formal charges against him. He grew ill as the Queen's glacial hostility continued. At Christmas 1599 John Donne wrote that 'my lord of Essex and his train are no more missed here than the angels which were cast down from heaven nor . . . likelier to return'. In February Lord Mountjoy was sent to Ireland as the new Lord Deputy, Essex's unwilling successor. The Council urged the Queen to release Essex, ladies at court pleaded for clemency, his popular following proclaimed his innocence. In May Essex wrote reminding the Queen of her message that she meant to chastise, not ruin him, but after a semi-public trial in June, Essex was removed from all his offices, save Master of the Horse. The desolate Queen took great walks about her park in Greenwich. Among Essex's friends, hopes remained; Elizabeth, unlike her father, had been forgiving towards errant nobles, and even though she mortified him, she had advanced none of Essex's adversaries. But her refusal at the end of October to renew his monopoly for sweet wines he took as the sign of her vindictiveness, of his irredeemable oblivion and dishonour. He listened now to his secretary, his sister and his steward, who harped upon his loss of honour and his imminent recourse to the alms basket.

Essex was now an earl without place or income; a patron without patronage; a commander without an army. Even retreat into books and scholarship, which had often appealed to him, had its dangers. His reading in John Hayward's *Life and Reign of Henry IV* of the ancient nobility rising to free the kingdom from Richard II's upstart favourites was soon seen as sedition. According to Ben Jonson, Essex was the 'AB' who had written the lapidary preface to Sir Henry Savile's translation of Tacitus, the Roman historian, in 1591. In Tacitus Essex found a world of vicious courts, of 'privy whisperings', dissimulation, spies, informers, and barely contained violence. Essex grew convinced of the menace of his enemies; he believed that they set spies in his household, suborned witnesses against him, forged his handwriting, and plotted against his life. (It was true that his letters had been stolen, his handwriting forged.) He was convinced too of the utter devotion of his friends, who would venture their lives for him.

Driven to desperation, Essex and his friends sought a way out. Essex spurned flight and exile. Early in 1600 Lord Deputy Mountjoy had offered his services to the King of Scots, even support from the army in Ireland, to aid James against his enemies in England, who were also the Earl's, and to establish his succession. Essex himself had been in communication with James since 1598. James, wary after endless noble conspiracy in Scotland, held back. Mountjoy, whom Essex implored again to send an army from Ireland – or at least a letter complaining of misgovernment which Essex could present to the Queen – enjoined patience. It was too late. Essex now turned to open treason. Emissaries were sent to O'Neill asking him to fulfil his promise that 'if the Earl of Essex would be ruled by him, he would make him the greatest man in England'. At the end of 1600 Essex House in the Strand was the resort of diverse groups: discontented swordsmen, and citizens who came to hear sermons. On 3 February 1601 at Southampton's lodgings at Drury House, Essex's friends met to consider three plans of action: should they seize the court, the Tower or the City? The plan decided upon was to surprise the court and arrest Ralegh, Captain of the Guard, so that Essex could prostrate himself before the Queen and demand the removal of his adversaries. Instead, Essex's summons before the Council precipitated revolt.

On 8 February – a Sunday, shockingly, blasphemously – after the sermon at Paul's Cross, bewildered Londoners came upon Essex, leading a band of noble followers and their retinues, crying, 'Murder, murder, God save the Queen.' As he marched from Essex House through Ludgate, and through the City, the Earl shouted that his life was endangered, and the realm sold to the Spaniard. Like Wyatt before him in 1554, he believed that the citizens would rally to the patriotic cause, but beyond that he thought, from his old popularity there, that they were 'at his devotion'. None joined him. Essex retreated by river to Essex House, and there, after a siege, he was taken. Quixotic apprentices planned to raise 5,000 to rescue him from the Tower and entreat the Queen's favour. Too late. Essex never saw the Queen again, never pleaded for mercy; and there could be none. At Tower Hill on Ash Wednesday, 25 February 1601, he went to the block while his old enemy, Ralegh, as Captain of the Guard, watched. A month later Elizabeth wrote to Essex's dying friend Lord Willoughby, one of the last 'men of service', how it 'appeareth now by one's example more bound than all or any other's, how little faith there was in Israel'.

Essex's revolt was perhaps the last time that turbulent nobles took up arms to demand their – to them – rightful place as counsellors; the last time that English lords expected a popular following to rise for their private quarrels. Essex and his friends were torn between two worlds: a lost world of 'overmighty subjects', bound by friendship in arms, with unimpeded power in their local communities and the military support of a loyal tenantry; and the real world of service at court and dependency upon the crown. Of the first world they dreamt; to the second they belonged. Essex's father might have vaunted his fifty-six heraldic quarterings, but his earldom was a Tudor creation. The 2nd Earl of Essex lorded it in South Wales and the Marches in the 1590s, and planned to invade at Milford Haven as the Tudor pretender had done over a century before, but his Welsh support never rallied, and the fated rising he led was in London, an attempted palace coup.

Essex's overweening demand for rewards fitting his extraordinary honour had excluded him from court and given power instead to Cecil and the 'base pen clerks' whose rise he had so resented. By her inability to restrain Essex, Elizabeth had lost that balance at court which had brought stability and assured her control; even Essex's fall could not restore it. Cecil, confiding court secrets, in code, to Sir George Carew (President of Munster) in Ireland, told of suspicions and jealousies. The adventitious alliance Cecil had made with Ralegh and Cobham against Essex now dissolved in renewed rivalry. Ambition, according to Eliza-bethans, was like the crocodile, which grew while it lived. The Queen's own will to power was undiminished, but she was haunted by Essex's betrayal, and feared that of others. She paced her Privy Chamber, sometimes thrusting her sword into the arras in rage, according to her godson, Sir John Harington. Now she kept few around her, except Lord Buckhurst, Burghley's successor as Lord Treasurer. As the natural end of her reign drew closer, her properties as goddess of the moon were no longer venerated, except publicly: privately it was said that 'she reigns as the moon in borrowed majesty'.

*

In November 1599 O'Neill, at the height of his power, issued a procla-mation to the Irish, a Catholic and nationalist manifesto. He set out twenty-two articles for the English, his terms for peace. His demands were extreme: the restoration of the Catholic Church, governed by the Pope, with an exclusively Irish clergy; all posts in the civil government, save the chief governor, to be held by Irishmen; O'Neill, O'Donnell, Desmond and their confederates to hold their ancient lands and privi-leges. If these demands were met, Ireland would be virtually an indepen-dent kingdom once again. Upon his copy of the articles Cecil wrote 'Ewtopia', but was it?

At this climacteric, it seemed as though Ireland would be reconquered not by the English but by the Irish. Essex had left, achieving nothing; his army, under the failing command of Ormond, was in disarray and the Dublin government on the point of collapse. Only the English Pale and the walled towns stood out against the rebels. O'Neill promised to pierce to the heart of the Pale, and even if he could not break the walls of the towns with artillery, he might undermine them by treachery within. The Pale itself was full of Gaelic settlers. Even if lords like the Earls of Thomond and Clanrickard, and Christopher Nugent, Lord Delvin, remained loyal, could they prevent their tenants and followers from joining the rebels? In Munster, the surviving New English fearfully awaited another massacre. Everyone expected a Spanish Armada to arrive.

The Anglo-Irish had, for the most part, not forgotten their English descent and their loyalty, but it was the hope of O'Neill and the fear of the English governors that they could be persuaded of a higher loyalty to Ireland and their Catholic faith than to England and a Protestant queen. O'Neill's whole purpose, he proclaimed, was to fight for the 'Catholic religion and liberties of our country'. With deliberate intent he wrote of 'Ireland' and 'we Irishmen', as though love of their native land would cause the Palesmen to forget their historical identity and difference from the Gaelic Irish who surrounded them. The Gaelic bardic poets, once employed to celebrate the renown of their own lords and lands, began to eulogize the whole land as the fatherland (*athardha*). In *Richard II*, Shakespeare had celebrated England's island state as 'This other Eden, demi-paradise, / This fortress'. Ireland was no less an island, no less Edenic: 'a fortress of paradise', wrote Maolmhuire Ó hUiginn (d. *c.* 1591). And within it, its two historical communities, Gaelic and Anglo-Irish, might now unite against the heretic Protestant newcomers.

Preachers, especially those fired by Counter-Reformation ideals – members of reformed orders, papal emissaries, Jesuits and seminary priests – insisted that the Irish fight for the faith; that to be Irish was to be Catholic. The papal legate preached in Munster during the revolt: 'What hath England to do with us? What right hath *their* queen over us, but by force?' Scotland, though confined within the same island as England, had her own king; why not Ireland? The rebels' reward would be a kingdom and liberty. What had they to lose but their lives? The preachers offered threats as well as promises: hell as well as heaven. The Catholic bishop of Cork and the Vicar-Apostolic, Owen MacEgan, threatened Viscount Barry with his 'soul's destruction' and his country's ruin if he did not join the rebels. Disingenuously, they told him they had a papal excommunication, but Pope Clement VIII never gave one to the rebels: instead on 18 April 1600 (n.s.) he gave a crusading indulgence to supporters of O'Neill, 'captain general of the Catholic army in Ireland'. The people stood in 'awful obedience', wrote Carew, the President of

Munster, to 'Romish priests' whose 'excommunications are of greater terror unto them than any earthly horror'.

In January 1600 O'Neill and his northern confederates marched south to Munster. It was a terrible winter journey. The Maguire bard, Ó Heóghusa, lamented the hardships suffered by his patron:

> Sad it is to me that Hugh Maguire, tonight in a strange land, lies under the lurid glow of showering, flashing thunderbolts, beneath the fury of armed savage clouds . . .
> When I think of his journey; enough to search my very heart is the pain of the icy weather.

Hugh Maguire never returned to Fermanagh. On 1 March he was killed by Sir Warham St Leger, whom he fatally wounded. O'Neill called his campaign a 'holy journey', and made a pilgrimage to the Holy Cross in Tipperary. But it was a journey more military than holy. He had made James Fitzthomas Earl of Desmond by proxy; now, in person, he created Florence MacCarthy the MacCarthy Mór, 'chief of the Irishry' of Munster. O'Neill threatened not only hellfire to those who refused to join him, but also the earthly hell of having his followers 'come and sojourn with you for a time'. News of Lord Deputy Mountjoy's move to plant a garrison on the shores of Lough Foyle on the north coast of Ulster sent O'Neill north, and he left the Munster rebellion in the command of Florence MacCarthy.

Mountjoy understood that it was upon the 'fortune of the north' that the reduction of the rest of the kingdom depended. All rested upon the defeat of O'Neill and O'Donnell. By May 1600 he and his lieutenant Sir Henry Docwra had established a fort on the shores of Lough Foyle. By lightning raids through the Midlands that summer, Mountjoy secured the Pale, and in October forced a passage through the Moyry Pass between Dundalk and Newry, the traditional gateway to Ulster. In August he had promised, 'I will hunt these squirrels even out of their strongest woods.' Not so easy. 'You have held,' wrote Cecil to Carew in September, that 'the war of famine must end the rebellion.' The destruction of harvests and the capture of herds were tactics used by both sides, sure and devastating. In the summer of 1600 Carew drove the rebels from Kerry: 'Now (I thank God) their harvest is ours.' If any objected that the loyal would suffer with the disloyal, the answer came that there were few enough of the former.

By the end of the year Sir George Carew had pacified most of Munster, at least outwardly. His means, as befitted Cecil's friend, were politic as well as military. His artillery undermined castles, and his playing upon their factions, spreading dissension and fear of betrayal, undermined the rebels. He and Cecil now determined to restore the old power structure, but tamed, and to supplant the *súgán* earl by the legitimate Desmond who had been in prison since his father's rebellion. Both the Queen and the poet Ben Jonson, who may have been Desmond's tutor in the Tower, were fearful. Jonson warned Desmond against 'politic pretext, that wries a state', and implored him to stand 'As far from all revolt, as you are now from fortune.' In October 1600 Desmond returned to Munster, the 'Queen's earl'. At first he was greeted with honour, but his Protestant faith was soon seen as an affront to his Geraldine blood, and he came back to England disappointed and dishonoured in the following spring. By the end of the autumn of 1600, Florence MacCarthy had submitted, the threat that he might become Gaelic overlord of Munster never fulfilled, and the next spring the fugitive *súgán* earl was captured. From the summer of 1601 both were in the Tower. Famine and military defeat undermined the rebellion in Ulster. As it became plain that O'Neill was not invincible, divisions appeared among the rebels, and his underlords, over whom he had ruled by the strong hand, began to drift away. Many Ulster lords sought pardons, and in Connacht Niall Garve O'Donnell formed an alliance with Docwra. Not that such agreements were adamantine. For Fynes Moryson, Mountjoy's secretary, the 'rebellion was nourished and increased by nothing more than frequent protections and pardons'. The rebels saw pardons only as a way of recovering themselves until they rebelled again, until the Spaniards arrived.

In September 1601 a Spanish fleet was sighted off the Old Head of Kinsale. At last, this was the significant landing the English had feared since the beginning of the war with Spain. Through November Mountjoy laid a tighter and tighter siege upon the Spanish in Kinsale as O'Neill and O'Donnell marched south, with great forces, plundering as they passed. The united Spanish and confederate forces, if joined by the Irish of Munster, might finally drive the English out of Ireland, and make Ireland a bridge for the invasion of England. Young English bloods, disporting themselves at Lecale garrison in Down, would remember the misery of Mountjoy's camp – 'intolerable cold, dreadful labour, and want of almost everything'; and, besieged as well as besieging, the uncertainty. O'Neill's tactic was always the waiting game; to let cold, despair and desertion drive away the English; O'Donnell's strategy was more heroic and impetuous, and it was his which prevailed. On Christmas Eve the Irish prepared to attack, and the English risked all on a dawn cavalry charge outside Kinsale. 'The dice were cast, the kingdom being ready to sway on that side that proved victorious,' wrote Carew. The Irish were routed. No one doubted the significance of the defeat. For the Four Masters, 'immense and countless was the loss in that place'; not in terms of lives lost, but

The prowess and valour, prosperity and affluence, nobleness and chivalry, dignity and renown, hospitality and generosity, bravery and protection, devotion and pure religion of the island, were lost in that engagement.

The Spanish departed in the spring. O'Neill withdrew to his Ulster redoubts, and on 27 December O'Donnell took ship to Spain, seeking further aid. An assassin followed him; not without Carew's connivance. O'Donnell's bard, Eoghan Ruadh Mac an Bhaird (Red Owen Mac Ward) feared for his chief as he sailed:

I . . . O'Hugh, am torn because of thy venture in the boiling wave of my mind.

The sea does not stir without bewildering me, the wind rises not but that my mind starts, the tempest does not alter the note of the stream without bringing anguish upon me, now thou art gone.

He was right to be fearful. O'Donnell died in Simancas, near Valladolid, in September 1602. His loss was disastrous for his cause. Soon after his brother's death the new chief, Rory O'Donnell, submitted.

Pacata Hibernia: Ireland pacified. As each Gaelic chief in turn received protection and made peace, the rebellion was broken and the war was over. But at a terrible cost for England. Elizabeth knew that the war had brought 'the alienation of our people from us'. Although in the Parliament of 1601 Cecil approvingly recalled the example of the women of Rome who gave their jewels to pay for the war against Hannibal, most felt resentment of the seemingly endless cost (of £2 million and more), the financial expedients and dodges – especially the 'great monster' of the sale of monopolies – practised to finance the Irish campaigns. 'That land of Ire has exhausted this land of promise', so a weary Cecil had written in 1600. Lives were lost fighting a war which the English, by their misunderstanding and mismanagement, had not prevented.

And for Ireland. The costs of rebellion and war were fateful. Ireland's population, unlike that elsewhere in Europe, had never grown during the sixteenth century. Now the depredations of war and the devastation of crops and herds brought famine to Ulster, as once before to Munster, and with it an inhumanity born of despair. Ulster was a wilderness. Debasement of the Irish coinage further undermined the fragile economy of the island. In defeat, the Irish fought among themselves. Bitter divisions grew as some made accommodation with the English and some fought on. As O'Sullivan Beare retreated from the rout of his forces at the siege of Dunboy, and made his desperate journey from Bantry to Leitrim, as many lords attacked him as sheltered him. When Niall Garve went over to the English, his wife Nuala, O'Donnell's sister, deserted him. The chief hope of those who yearned for Irish independence lay in the prospect of the Spanish returning; their principal fear, according to Lord Deputy Mountjoy, was that 'upon a peace will ensue a severe reformation of religion'.

Still O'Neill held out, and none among the Irish would, wrote Mountjoy sardonically, 'lay violent hands on their sacred prince ... their O'Neill'. In October 1602 the Queen was resolved not to give the arch-traitor 'grace in any kind'. But by 17 February 1603 she was resigned, and wrote authorizing Mountjoy to offer him life, liberty and pardon, on terms. He must renounce allegiance to foreign princes and the name of O'Neill. On 30 March O'Neill came to Mellifont in County Louth. Here in the first Cistercian abbey in Ireland, now converted into a fortified house, he submitted. What Mountjoy knew already, and O'Neill did not, was that the Queen who offered her rebel pardon, to whom he submitted, was nearly a week dead.

*

The pageants held in Elizabeth's honour in 1602 still venerated her as Cynthia, 'queen of love and beauty', as timeless, unchanging. At the last great festival of the reign, Cecil's entertainment for the Queen, held at Cecil House on the Strand on 6 December 1602, tapers burnt before Astraea's shrine, in honour of this 'saint', 'to whom all hearts devotion owe'. Astraea, the just virgin of Virgil's *Eclogues* whose return to earth brought a golden age of peace and eternal spring, was Elizabeth. Knowingly, her subjects practised a form of royal idolatry. But they knew that mutability must touch Cynthia, and feared the chaos which would follow if she withdrew her light from the world. The imperial virgin was tired, lonely and suddenly fearful, and the bonds between worshipped and worshippers grew strained. Her people were wearying of her reign and of her exercise of authority through insistence upon her loving concern. 'We did all love her,' so Sir John Harington remembered, 'for she said she loved us, and much wisdom she showed in this matter.'

By the middle of March 1603 Elizabeth was dying. She was restless, sleepless; she refused to take medicine, refused to eat, refused to go to bed. She sighed and sighed, as she had never done, except when Mary, Queen of Scots was beheaded. This was a dangerous moment for England, still at war with Spain. The Queen might become incapable of ruling. Even until her last hours she would never name her successor, lest her subjects' love and duty pass from her to the 'rising sun'. There were still, in 1600, at least twelve claimants for England's throne. The most formidable was the Infanta Isabella, wife of Archduke Albert, Governor in Flanders, the hope of Catholics loyal to the Pope. Henry VIII's line had at last failed (though lasting longer than he had feared); now Henry VII's direct descendant was James Stewart.

Although the Queen did not know it – and would have been enraged had she known – those who were 'most inward with her' had been most forward in communicating with the likely heir. Essex had kept a letter, purportedly from James VI, in a black purse around his neck. Listening to Essex's fevered suspicions that Elizabeth's councillors favoured a Spanish succession, and dazzled by his martial schemes, James had once thought that he would have to fight for his new kingdoms, and had persuaded the principal nobility of Scotland to enter a 'band' to defend his safety and his right. After Essex's death, wiser counsels – Cecil's counsels – prevailed, and James saw the wisdom of waiting upon 'God's time'. He now looked for his succession not by force but by right, 'with the favour of the people, and not as a conqueror'. Throughout the country, almost everyone acknowledged his claim, and those who did not kept silent. Leading figures wrote to James, their names encoded, in order to secure his safety, and their own; the kingdom's fortunes, and their own, 'when God should see His time'.

On the afternoon of Wednesday 23 March, speechless and dying, Elizabeth at last signalled that the King of Scots should succeed her. That night, so Robert Carey, Elizabeth's much younger cousin, recalled, her archbishop knelt by her in prayer, and told her 'what she was, and what she was to come to; and though she had been long a great queen here upon earth, yet shortly she was to yield an account of her stewardship to the King of Kings'. And when she did, she might have told Him what she had so often told her people: that England might have had a 'prince more wise', but would never have one 'more loving'; that 'in this world' she had desired nothing more than 'to preserve them in peace and to keep them from oppression and wrong'. She had asked her last Parliament, almost rhetorically, 'What am I as of myself, without the watchful providence of almighty God, other than a poor silly woman, weak and subject to many imperfections, expecting as you do a future judgement?' The time for judgement had come.

Epilogue

LOST WORLDS, NEW WORLDS

On the festival of Holy Cross in September 1607 the Earls of Tyrone and Tirconnell, and the chiefs Maguire and Magennis, with their families and followers, and leading Anglo-Irish families of north Leinster set sail from Ulster, pre-empting their arrest. They sought sanctuary in the Spanish Netherlands, for a time. O'Neill and Rory O'Donnell had been pardoned after Kinsale and confirmed in their vast estates with the titles of Earls of Tyrone and Tirconnell, yet they had never intended their submission to last. The fears and rumours among the English governors that the Earls were still in league with Spain, and that they were conspiring with the Anglo-Irish community to renew revolt in the name of the Catholic faith, were not unfounded. As official religious policy turned to repression, the Anglo-Irish, who had held back from joining Tyrone in rebellion before, now began to countenance it. The Four Masters lamented the Earls' precipitate decision: 'Woe to the heart that meditated . . . setting out on this voyage, without knowing whether they should ever return . . . to the end of the world.' They never did. Sanctuary became permanent exile.

With the flight of the Earls, the independent Gaelic order in Ulster, in Ireland, passed. The power of the Gaelic lords was broken, their great estates confiscated, their private alliances and armies disbanded, their followers leaderless. Ulster was reduced to submission by garrisons. Desolate and 'waste', it was at last the 'razed table' which English hardliners had advocated. Ireland lay open to colonizers, who not only enriched themselves but saw a right and a duty to impose law, civility and the Protestant religion. A new world of English and Scottish planters came to 'banish' Ireland.

As the Queen died, political and military conquest had not brought spiritual conquest. There were two contending Churches within the island: the Church of Ireland – official and Protestant – was taking over and stripping the parish churches, but not winning hearts and minds; the Church of Rome, whose priests celebrated unofficially in 'massing houses', held the people's allegiance. In Ireland, almost alone in Europe, the religion of the prince was not the religion of the people. The supremacy of the Queen was resisted; the primacy of the Pope upheld. The English language, which was, so the Speaker of the Irish Parliament had urged in 1569, the means whereby children could be taught in time to forget the 'affinity of their unbroken borderers', had not spread. And it was mainly in English that the new faith was evangelized. The Catholic faith was shared by both historic communities of the island, the Gaelic Irish and the Anglo-Irish, and their resistance to the Reformation came to temper their old animosity. While Elizabeth had not persecuted in matters of religion, the traditionally loyal Anglo-Irish community could reconcile compliance and obedience to the Crown with faith and conscience, but once aggressive attempts at reform began that loyalty would falter. It was the failure of the political orders to implement the official religion of the Queen of Ireland that had enabled the people to flout the laws and ignore her supremacy; it was their protection of priests and friars which allowed the sacraments to be celebrated. In Dublin a few patrician families had adopted the reformed religion, but this small Protestant coterie became isolated, alienated from the Catholic majority. Deeply attached to old ways and traditions, in religion as in civic life, Dublin's leading families turned to recusancy from the later 1580s and 1590s. Since chantries and religious guilds had never been suppressed in Ireland, older traditional practices were sustained. People worshipped still at the holy wells outside Dublin. The arrival of a small number of seminary-trained Catholic clergy confirmed the resolution of the citizens in their recusancy. It was the women of the city who were staunchest in their defence of the Catholic faith; they who protected the priests who celebrated Mass. The children of leading Anglo-Irish families were sent to study abroad; not only to English universities and the Inns of Court, but to the Irish Colleges founded in the 1590s at Douai and Salamanca. In 1593 Ralegh told the Commons that he believed that there were not six gentlemen in Ireland who were loyal in religion. A decade later, upon news of Elizabeth's death, the towns of Munster expelled the established clergy, tore up the service books, and installed outlawed Catholic priests to provide public celebration of the Mass. They demanded a religious freedom and toleration which no secular ruler, whose authority depended upon religious unity and a stable Church, could officially countenance.

A new world of reformed Tridentine Catholicism had brought religious revival to Ireland. Seminary priests, Jesuits and 'massing priests' said Mass, baptized children, ministered the sacraments in private houses, and played their part in animating the war in Ireland. From the 1560s onwards the papacy appointed bishops, establishing an alternative diocesan system, and sent to Ireland papal nuncios who were inspired by the ideals of the militant Catholic mission. Owen MacEgan, papal nuncio to Munster in the 1590s, had 'absolute power' and practised 'religious tyranny', according to Sir George Carew. Although Essex had told O'Neill, 'Thou carest for religion as much as my horse,' O'Neill, under the influence of the Jesuit James Archer, was increasingly committed to the principles and practices of the Catholic Reformation. The orders of friars who had brought spiritual renewal in the fifteenth century continued to inspire the people's devotion. In Connacht in 1574 there were twenty-one mendicant communities in Mayo, eleven in Sligo and twenty in Galway; and in 1594 there were still twenty monasteries and friaries in Ulster. These survived under the protection of the local lords who had always been their patrons. When in August 1601 Niall Garve O'Donnell betrayed his clan and his faith by garrisoning Donegal Abbey for the English, Hugh O'Donnell, outraged by the usurpation of the Franciscan 'sons of life', besieged it. As God willed to take 'revenge and satisfaction of the English' for the profanation, wrote the Four Masters, He caused their gunpowder to blow the garrison and the Abbey to pieces. This providence occurred on Michaelmas Day. In the moral distemper brought by rebellion and war God's hand was especially seen to intervene in the world to reveal His purposes. Ghostly armies were seen fighting battles in the sky. Even English soldiers were daunted by the faith of their Irish opponents. Sir John Harington wrote from Athlone in 1599: 'I verily think the idle faith which possesses the Irishry concerning magic and witchcraft seized our men and lost the victory.'

An older world of wonders and miracles lived on in Ireland. The traditional religion of saints' cults and pilgrimages, relics and images, continued. Sacred places, holy wells and high crosses stirred particular reverence. This was a world of devotion as far away from Tridentine Catholicism as from Protestantism. English attempts to destroy what they saw as idolatry failed. When O'Neill went on his 'holy journey' to Munster, he first visited the Cistercian Abbey of the Holy Cross, and its relic of the true cross was brought out to protect his army. In 1608 that relic was taken by the abbot to cure the infertility of fields in Kilkenny.

Catholic reformers determined to confine the miraculous to the Church, and to control the excesses of popular devotion. Edmund Campion, the Jesuit, devoted a chapter of his *Two Books of the Histories of Ireland* (written in 1571) to St Patrick's Purgatory at Lough Derg. People went to this supposed entrance of the nether world for penance, and reported on their return – if they returned – 'strange visions of pain and bliss', a 'sight of hell and heaven'. The Council of Trent had in 1563 disavowed the sensational apparitions associated with the doctrine of purgatory, and Campion insisted that the claims of miracles 'I neither believe nor wish to be regarded'. Yet the older world had a stronger hold on the popular imagination. Every section of Irish society – peasants or lords – believed that ghosts walked and diabolic spirits might appear.

In England, Catholics would talk of the return of their faith: 'We should have a new world shortly,' promised Babington and his fellow conspirators. Yet as the reformed faith slowly gained the victory, a world was lost which could not be restored. The adherents of the new faith had believed that they could, by bringing the Word to the people, transform religion and society. They had succeeded, at great cost. Reform brought physical destruction: the altars and shrines, dooms and roods of the parish churches were torn down; religious houses lay in ruins or were converted into gentry mansions. More traumatic than the desecration of treasures was the loss of the beliefs which they had symbolized; of mediation by holy helpers, of intercession by family and friends, of 'good works' which could make satisfaction for sin, if performed in state of grace. The community of the dead and of the living had been parted as the doctrine of purgatory was undermined. And if there was no intermediary world in the hereafter, no way of propitiation after death, then a starker judgement awaited Christians; of election or reprobation, heaven or hell. The world of shared faith was broken, and the Christian community divided. At the Reformation, the Christian was forced to choose between two Churches, each claiming to be the true Church, and sometimes to choose between private faith and public conformity. Most people did their public duty by conforming through all the Tudor reformations and, believing that the conscience of their prince was in God's hands, obeyed the royal will. In the way of things, most people, in most places, chose the anonymity of their households, the peaceful obscurity of their fields and workshops, the comforts of neighbourliness, to the lonely sacrifice that conscience and resistance to authority demanded. The claims of family life and the exigencies of making a living usually prevailed. There were many who, in lives of penury and drudgery, had little time and less energy to make a stand. Nevertheless, no one was left untouched by the great transformations which Reformation brought.

Time, the passing of generations, the gradual influence of education and evangelical preaching, and the entrenchment of vested interests had led to the retreat of traditional religion before the new. In some places, by 1600, the coming generation could look back upon the Catholic past as a lost world. In some places, but far from all. William Perkins, writing in about 1590, thought that most of the common people were still papist at heart. In the 'dark corners of the land', remote from the centre, the Gospel had hardly penetrated, and perennial reports came of unregenerate papistry, lingering idolatry and, above all, of benighted ignorance. Even the Prayer Book, the touchstone of conformity, was still haunted by remnants of medieval Catholicism; saints' days, kneeling, signing with the cross, and the language of priesthood remained to outrage the godly. Loyalty to the Prayer Book might even be taken as a sign of papistry.

Puritan evangelists despaired of Wales, that other Celtic borderland of the Tudor dominions, where the people were 'much given to superstition and papistry', they said. Certainly Wales was slow in true conversion to the Protestant faith. But the old faith's survival there was not a sign of political disloyalty. The people were in 'peace and good quiet', and their loyalty to the Queen was never in doubt. Reformation was not seen in Wales, as it was in Ireland, as an alien faith forced upon a reluctant nation. In Wales, unlike Cornwall and Ireland, the new faith was not imposed in English. A prudential decision was taken in Elizabeth's reign to present the new faith to the people of Wales in their own language, and once the scripture and service books had been translated into Welsh there were cultural and patriotic reasons for the faith to spread. Gradually, the reformed religion became associated in Wales with a double allegiance: to the Tudors (whose Welsh descent was not forgotten) and to Wales.

In Wales, as in England, the political orders had understood that order and stability, peace and prosperity, rested upon obedience to the Crown, the supreme head of a Church to which, whatever its failings, allegiance was also due. The Queen's duty was, under God, to maintain true religion, and her people were under a religious as well as a political obligation of obedience to her. For the gentry of Wales, as of England, their self-interest as well as their duty lay in conformity, for they had invested in the transformation in ecclesiastical authority; their lands included former Church lands, their patronage was once Church patronage. They had rallied in defence against the threat from international Catholicism. Steeped in the habits of obedience, the great majority dreaded the prospect of rebellion, in however good a cause. Allegiance to traditional religion could not extend to allegiance to Spain or to Rome. Indeed, resistance was countenanced, even urged against foreign tyrants, other nation's monarchs.

A wise prince understood, as Elizabeth had understood, that time, not coercion, was likely to bring conformity. She had, as Fulke Greville put it, 'let devout conscience live quietly in her realms'. With Elizabeth's death imminent, the 9th Earl of Northumberland wrote to the King of Scots: 'It were pity to lose so good a kingdom [England] for the not tolerating a Mass in a corner.' That a Percy, scion of so great a noble family, whose ancestors had in 1536 and 1569 led revolts in defence of the old ways, offered such politic advice marked another great transformation, another lost world. By the late sixteenth century the ancient nobility had been tamed, its power undermined. Martial honour and chivalry had been civilized. George Clifford, 3rd Earl of Cumberland, whose ancestor the 10th Lord Clifford (d.1523) and his knights had still performed the feudal ceremony of homage, was the Queen's champion of the tiltyard, and heroically spendthrift. In 1600 he appeared at the tilt as the Discontented Knight; discontented because the Queen had not given him the governorship of the Isle of Wight. This was a world away from the Cliffords' former integrity and independence in the far North. Clifford sold off his ancestral estates, although in the North, he knew, they measured 'honour by the acre', and the Clifford fortunes were only salvaged by the Queen's grant of a lucrative cloth-export licence.

The gentry, who had a century before followed their local lords and worn their livery, now held their offices and bought up their lands: such was the perception of those who considered the nature of royal power at the end of the century. The Tudors had succeeded in their ambition that loyalty to the Crown replace loyalty to the old nobility. The ancient nobility had yielded power – though very far from all their power – to a service nobility which owed its advancement to royal favour and employment at court. Essex was almost the last noble to dream of a throne. 'Well . . . he wore the crown of England in his heart these many years,' wrote his intimate, the Earl of Northumberland. But even Essex was a creature of the court, however unwillingly, and owed all to the Queen's favour.

The new world of the court had become the centre of power, patronage and stability, and everyone who mattered in the realm was drawn to it. It could be the fount of civility and courtesy. 'A virtuous court a world to virtue draws,' wrote Ben Jonson in *Cynthia's Revels* (1600), as though he hoped it were true. Yet the court was not the place to look for virtue. As John Donne wrote in *Satire 4*, the sort of satire which was banned in June 1599:

> No more can Princes' courts, though there be few
> Better pictures of vice, teach me virtue

The court was increasingly seen as a place of lies and spies, of 'privy whispering', where intrigue and treachery flourished, and where the truth was not to be found. The Queen, who had herself portrayed in gowns embroidered with eyes and ears, as symbols of her ceaseless vigilance over her people, might not know what happened around her. 'Greatest and fairest empress, know you this?' asked Donne in *Satire 5*: did she know of the corruption which surrounded her? The excesses of foreign courts and the extension of monarchical power in Europe was observed with alarm. Tyranny, which had threatened in England a century before, might come again if a prince fell from virtue, was misled by evil counsellors, or corrupted by a court, and now there were fewer curbs on royal power. As Elizabeth's reign drew to its natural close, there were reasons for unease. At this moment, not only of the Queen's 'declining age' but of what Greville called 'this crafty world's declining age', William Shakespeare wrote a play whose hero lamented that 'the time is out of joint'.

Hamlet was first performed, in London, in or just before 1600. Throughout the world of the play there is a dark questioning, some of the questions touching the world of the audience. Shakespeare's art is transcendent, Prince Hamlet's questions are for all time, but the play originated in a particular time and place, and its themes were quintessentially those of the Renaissance and Reformation. As Hamlet tells the players of the play within the play, the purpose of playing is to hold the mirror up to nature and show the 'very age and body of the time his form and pressure'. When the play begins, King Hamlet, the godlike prince of Denmark, is two months dead. Claudius has taken both the throne and his brother's widow, marrying her precipitately in scandalous profanation of the sanctions of decent mourning, and of the prohibitions upon incest. Prince Hamlet is in mourning and a mood of deepest melancholy. He has bidden farewell to love and cannot tell why he has of late lost all his mirth. He laments familial betrayal, the flight of his mother to 'incestuous sheets', and knows that kin is 'less than kind' and cousinage brings 'coz'nage' (deception). His greatest griefs are silent, inexpressible – 'But I have that within which passes show' – and he seeks dissolution.

To the distraught son his father's Ghost appears. Deep uncertainties attend the apparition of the Ghost – where it comes from, what it intends. Hamlet determines to speak to it.

> Be thou a spirit of health or a goblin damn'd,
> Bring with thee airs from heaven or blasts from hell.

The doubts about the Ghost's provenance expose the lasting divisions between the faiths; uncertainties which, for some, remained unresolved. Since for the reformed faith there is no purgatory, no spirits can appear, and ghosts can only be the Devil's conjurations. Later, Hamlet acknowledges his own susceptibility:

> The spirit that I have seen
> May be a devil, and the devil hath power
> T'assume a pleasing shape, yea, and perhaps,
> Out of my weakness and my melancholy . . .
> Abuses me to damn me.

Reformed Catholicism divorced the essential doctrine of purgatory from ghostly appearances. It is an older world of traditional Catholicism which haunts Hamlet in the form of his father's spirit.

> Doom'd for a certain term to walk the night,
> And for the day confin'd to fast in fires,
> Till the foul crimes done in my days of nature
> Are burnt and purg'd away.

The Ghost tells a chilling story and gives a dreadful command:

> If thou didst ever thy dear father love – . . .
> Revenge his foul and most unnatural murder.

King Claudius was his brother's assassin, and had dispatched him 'Unhousel'd, disappointed, unanel'd'. That horror of dying without the sacraments recurs throughout the play. The Ghost calls upon Hamlet's filial duty and love, but supernatural forces impel him to obey. He is 'prompted to my revenge by heaven and hell'.

Educated, like Faustus, at Wittenberg, Hamlet is trained to debate cases of conscience, to weigh the arguments for and against action. But he is preoccupied first by the universal mysteries of human existence, with the paradox in human nature which Renaissance minds especially meditated upon: man, endowed with 'godlike reason', is also, like a beast, 'passion's slave'; reason contends with appetite; sin with divinity. Hamlet is tormented by that human predicament: 'What should such fellows as I do crawling between earth and heaven?' He is obsessed with the pains of life – 'the heartache and the thousand natural shocks that flesh is heir to', 'the slings and arrows of outrageous fortune' – and with the pains of death and uncertainties of the afterlife. Resolution weakens with too much thinking – 'conscience does make cowards of us all' – and so does Hamlet's, as he delays his revenge.

When Hamlet accepts the duty commanded by the Ghost, his private revenge has public consequences. Hamlet is a prince at war with his assassin uncle. In *Hamlet*, as in late Elizabethan minds, moral contagion spreads from the fatal sin of the monarch. 'Something is rotten in the state of Denmark.' The people grow 'muddied, thick and unwholesome in their thoughts'. Claudius's court at Elsinore is the kind of court that the Renaissance thought a tyrant creates and deserves. Guarded by mercenary Switzers, advised by counsellors and flatterers who speak to please rather than to tell the truth, Claudius is unconstrained in his abuse of power. The mood is of distrust, dissimulation and fear. Spies, 'seeing unseen', lurk behind the arras; poison is at hand. Friendship is false. Hamlet's childhood friends, Rosencrantz and Guildenstern, have been suborned, 'sent for' by the King to spy on Hamlet, who resolves to trust them 'as I will adders fang'd'. When they die, victims of their own treachery, Hamlet's conscience is untroubled, for 'they did make love to this employment'. Reform may come from without. On the borders of Denmark Young Fortinbras of Norway marches at the head of a band of 'lawless resolutes'. Or it may come from within. Hamlet is a prince, born not only to endure, like other men, but to lead, 'to set it right'. Confronted by regicide, he is sworn to act. Here Hamlet's hesitations bear upon the dangerous contemporary debates about the limits of obedience and the duties of resistance. The necessary action demands ruthlessness.

Not until the final act of the play are Hamlet's doubts resolved and his conscience, which he has so painfully consulted, fully committed. 'Does it not, think thee, stand me now upon,' he asks, to remove the man 'that hath kill'd my king and whor'd my mother', and plotted against Hamlet's life.

> Is't not perfect conscience
> To quit him with this arm? And is't not to be damn'd
> To let this canker of our nature come
> In further evil?

For much of the play Hamlet, though deeply Christian, has seen humanity subject to Fortune, the pagan goddess, but at the end it is rather of divine providence of which he speaks:

> There's a divinity that shapes our ends,
> Rough-hew them how we will –

He has learnt, as the Ghost had told him, that some things must be left to heaven. He understands now that he can neither avert nor foreknow what will happen:

We defy augury. There is special providence in the fall of a sparrow. If it be now, 'tis not to come; if it be not to come, it will be now; if it be not now, yet it will come. The readiness is all.

Hamlet kills the king, but is himself killed. Dying, Hamlet approves the succession of Fortinbras, the prince from the North: 'he has my dying voice'. At the end of a century which has half shattered the old faith, which has opened new worlds of the mind and spirit, Shakespeare has Hamlet's friend Horatio salute the dead prince in words which, haunted as they are by the traditional Latin burial service, convey how lasting were ancient certainties:

> Good night, sweet prince,
> And flights of angels sing thee to thy rest.

Bibliographical Essay

In his *Defence of Poesy* Philip Sidney wrote of the historian 'loaden with old mouse-eaten records, authorizing himself (for the most part) upon other histories'. So it was, and is. This book rests only partly upon work on manuscripts, and is mainly dependent upon printed primary sources, transcribed, compiled and calendared by the heroic labours of editors, from John Foxe onwards.

A comprehensive bibliography of primary and secondary sources is found in *Bibliography of British History: Tudor Period, 1485–1603*, ed. Conyers Read (Oxford, 2nd edn, 1959). See also G. R. Elton, *England, 1200–1640* in the series The Sources of English History (London, 1969). A. W. Pollard and G. R. Redgrave, *A Short-Title Catalogue of Books Printed in England, Scotland and Ireland . . . 1475–1640* (2nd edn, 3 vols., London, 1976–91) is indispensable for a study of the contemporary literature. Many of the poems cited are to be found in *The Penguin Book of Renaissance Verse, 1509–1659*, selected by D. Norbrook and edited by H. R. Woudhuysen (London, 1993), a book for a desert island.

For Ireland, *A New History of Ireland*, vol. 2, *Medieval Ireland, 1169–1534*, ed. A. Cosgrove (Oxford, 1987), and vol. 3, *Early Modern Ireland, 1534–1691*, ed. T. W. Moody, F. X. Martin and F. J. Byrne (Oxford, 1976) include full bibliographies. R. W. D. Edwards and M. O'Dowd, *Sources for Early Modern Irish History, 1534–1641* (Cambridge, 1985) is an important survey of printed sources, with chapters on archival collections and historiography.

THE PRINCIPAL SOURCES

Fundamental are the calendars of the state papers. Every historian of Henry VIII's reign depends upon the great collection of *Letters and Papers, Foreign and Domestic, of the Reign of Henry VIII, 1509–1547*, ed. J. S. Brewer, J. Gairdner and R. H. Brodie (21 vols., London, 1862–1932), and the *State Papers . . . King Henry VIII* (11 vols., London, 1832–52). Calendaring the state papers, the editors divided them in ways that do not reflect the thinking of Tudor councillors, who had to consider policy as a whole: 'Domestic', 'Foreign', 'Scottish', 'Irish', etc. *Calendar of State Papers, Domestic Series of the reigns of Edward VI, 1547–1553; Mary I, 1553–1558*, ed. C. S. Knighton (2 vols., London, 1992, 1998); *Calendar of State Papers, Domestic: Elizabeth I*, ed. R. Lemon and M. A. E. Green (12 vols., London, 1856–72); *Calendar of State Papers, Foreign: Edward VI and Mary*, ed. W. B. Turnbull, (2 vols., London, 1861) and *Elizabeth*, ed. J. Stevenson *et al* (23 vols., London, 1863–1950); *Calendar of State Papers Relating to Scotland and Mary, Queen of Scots, 1547–1603*, ed. J. Bain, *et al*. (13 vols., Edinburgh and Glasgow, 1898–1969); *Calendar of State Papers, Venetian*, ed. R. Brown, *et al*. (9 vols., London, 1864–98); *Calendar of State Papers, Spanish*, ed. G. A. Bergenroth, *et al*. (13 vols. and 2 supplements, London, 1862–9); *The Acts of the Privy Council of England*, ed. J. R. Dasent (46 vols., London, 1890–1964). 'State' records were effectively private papers in this period, and remained in the councillors' families. Outstanding among the volumes published by the Historical Manuscripts Commission are: *Calendar of the MSS of Lord De L'Isle and Dudley at Penshurst Place* (3 vols., London, 1925–36); *Calendar of the MSS of the Marquess of Salisbury at Hatfield House* (24 vols., London, 1883–1976); and *Calendar of the MSS of the Marquess of Bath at Longleat* (5 vols., London, 1904–80).

For Ireland, the chief printed sources are the *Calendar of State Papers Ireland, 1509–1603*, ed. H. C. Hamilton, *et al*. (11 vols., London, 1860–1912); *Calendar of Carew MSS. . . at Lambeth, 1515–1624*, ed. J. S. Brewer and W. Bullen (6 vols., London, 1867–73); *State Papers, Henry VIII*, vols. 2 and 3 (London, 1834). *Irish history from contemporary sources, 1509–1610*, ed. C. Maxwell (London, 1923) is useful. The official Irish records formerly held in the Public Record Office, Dublin, were mostly destroyed in the destruction of the Four Courts in 1922. Most of the printed sources are by the English, about the Irish. For a remarkable edition of a remarkable collection of Irish annals compiled in the early seventeenth century, see *The Annals of the Kingdom of Ireland by the Four Masters*, ed. J. O'Donovan (7 vols., 3rd edn, Dublin, 1998). See also *The Annals of Loch Cé, 1014–1590*, ed. W. M. Hennessy, (2 vols., London, 1871).

GENERAL HISTORY

The most authoritative and recent general introduction to the Tudor period is John Guy, *Tudor England* (Oxford, 1988). See also, on the whole period, G. R. Elton, *England under the Tudors* (2nd edn, London, 1974) and D. M. Loades *Politics and the Nation, 1450–1660* (London, 1974). Valuable general works on part of the period are: C. S. L. Davies, *Peace, Print and Protestantism, 1450–1558* (London, 1976); G. R. Elton, *Reform and Reformation, 1509–1558* (London, 1977); A. G. R. Smith, *The Emergence of a Nation State: The*

Commonwealth of England, 1529–1660 (London, 1984); and P. Williams, *The Later Tudors: England, 1547–1603* (Oxford, 1995).

The best modern surveys of sixteenth-century Ireland are S. G. Ellis, *Ireland in the Age of the Tudors, 1447–1603: English Expansion and the End of Gaelic Rule* (Harlow, 1998) and C. Lennon, *Sixteenth-century Ireland: the Incomplete Conquest* (Dublin, 1994). Richard Bagwell, *Ireland under the Tudors* (3 vols., London, 1885–90) provides the most detailed political narrative. R. D. Edwards, *Ireland in the Age of the Tudors* (London, 1977) is a good general account. Nicholas Canny's *From Reformation to Restoration: Ireland, 1534–1660* (Dublin, 1987) is influential.

*

What follows is a select bibliography of works which I have used, collected chapter by chapter, and by themes within the chapters. Articles are cited where the research is not presented elsewhere.

Prologue

Thomas More's writings are collected in the great *Yale edition of the Complete Works of St Thomas More* (15 vols., New Haven and London, 1961–). I have preferred to use David Wootton's translation and edition of *Utopia, Thomas More: Utopia* (Indianapolis, 1999). Of the many biographies of More, the first, by his son-in-law, William Roper, remains the most compelling: *The Life of Sir Thomas More* in *Two Early Tudor Lives*, ed. R. S. Sylvester and D. P. Harding (New Haven, 1962). For a different view, see R. Marius, *Thomas More* (London, 1985). For *The History of King Richard III*, see *Complete Works*, vol. 2, ed. R. S. Sylvester (New Haven and London, 1963). For Richard III's reign, see C. Ross, *Richard III* (London, 1981), and R. Horrox, *Richard III: A Study in Service* (Cambridge, 1989).

1 Rather Feared Than Loved

Contemporary chronicles of Henry VII's reign are: *The Anglica Historia of Polydore Vergil, AD 1485–1537*, ed. D. Hay (Camden Society, London, lxxiv, 1950), and *The Great Chronicle of London*, ed. A. H. Thomas and I. D. Thornley (Gloucester, 1983). Francis Bacon's history is as revealing of his own times as of Henry VII's: *The History of King Henry the Seventh*, ed. J. Weinberger (New York, 1996). The standard studies of Henry VII and his reign are by R. L. Storey, *The Reign of Henry VII* (London, 1968) and S. B. Chrimes, *Henry VII* (London, 1981). For his exile and passage to Bosworth, see R. A. Griffiths and R. S. Thomas, *The Making of the Tudor Dynasty* (Gloucester, 1985).

The closest observer of the landscape of England and Wales was the great Tudor topographer, John Leland; see *The Itinerary of John Leland in or about the years 1535–1543*, ed. L. Toulmin Smith (5 vols., Carbondale, Illinois, 1964). See also M. W. Beresford and J. K. S. St Joseph, *Medieval England: An Aerial Survey* (2nd edn, Cambridge, 1979). The essential work upon rural society is *The Agrarian History of England and Wales*, vol. 4, *1500–1640*, ed. Joan Thirsk (Cambridge, 1967). Helpful introductions are found in D. C. Coleman, *The Economy of England, 1450–1750* (Oxford, 1977), and D. M. Palliser, *The Age of Elizabeth: England under the later Tudors, 1547–1603* (London, 1983). See also E. Kerridge, *Agrarian Problems in the Sixteenth Century and After* (London, 1969) and J. C. K. Cornwall, *Wealth and Society in Early Sixteenth Century England* (London, 1988). W. G. Hoskins illumines local society for the county where Henry VII seized his throne in *The Midland Peasant: The Economic and Social History of a Leicestershire Village* (London, 1957). His polemical study of English society, *The Age of Plunder: The England of King Henry VIII, 1509–1547 (London, 1976)* is important. For London, see G. A. Williams, *Medieval London: From Commune to Capital* (London, 1963).

For the nature of England's constitution and government, see S. B. Chrimes, *English Constitutional Ideas in the Fifteenth Century* (Cambridge, 1936); G. R. Elton, *The Tudor Constitution: Documents and Commentary* (2nd edn, Cambridge, 1982); S. J. Gunn, *Early Tudor Government, 1485–1558* (Basingstoke, 1995); *The End of the Middle Ages? England in the Fifteenth and Sixteenth Centuries*, ed. J. L. Watts (Stroud, 1998); P. Williams, *The Tudor Regime* (Oxford, 1979); and G. L. Harris, 'Political society and the growth of government in late medieval England', *Past and Present*, 138 (1993).

For 'Britain', see R. Davies, 'The Matter of Britain and the Matter of England', an inaugural lecture delivered before the University of Oxford on 29 February 1996 (Oxford, 1996). A revealing comparison between the societies and government of England, Wales, Scotland and Ireland is found in R. Frame, *The Political Development of the British Isles, 1100–1400* (Oxford, 1995). For Wales, see G. Williams, *Renewal and Reformation: Wales, c. 1415–1642* (Oxford, 1993); J. Gwynfor Jones, *Early Modern Wales, c. 1525–1640*(Basingstoke, 1994; and *The Marcher Lordships of South Wales, 1415–1536*, ed. T. B. Pugh (Cardiff, 1963). For Scotland, see R. G. Nicholson, *Scotland: the Later Middle Ages* (Edinburgh, 1974); G. Donaldson, *Scotland: James V to James VII* (Edinburgh, 1965); J. Wormald, *Court, Kirk and Community: Scotland, 1470–1625* (Edinburgh, 1981), and *Lords and Men in Scotland: Bonds of Manrent, 1442–1603* (Edinburgh, 1985). For the North of England, see A. J. Pollard, *North-Eastern England during the Wars of the Roses: Lay Society, War and Politics* (Oxford, 1990). A pioneering comparative study of the far north of England and the Irish Pale, two border regions, is found in S. G. Ellis, *The Frontiers of Noble Power: The Making of the British State* (Oxford, 1995).

For society and lordship in Gaelic Ireland in the later middle ages, see K. W.

Nicholls, *Gaelic and Gaelicised Ireland in the Middle Ages* (Dublin, 1972); *Land, Law and Society in Sixteenth-Century Ireland* (Dublin, 1976); and his chapter in *A New History of Ireland*, vol. 2, *Medieval Ireland, 1169–1534*, ed. A. Cosgrove (Oxford, 1987). For Anglo-Irish society, see R. Frame, 'Power and Society in the Lordship of Ireland, 1272–1377', *Past and Present*, 76 (1977); *The English in Medieval Ireland*, ed. J. Lydon (Dublin, 1984); C. Lennon, *The Lords of Dublin in the Age of Reformation* (Dublin, 1989); and D. Bryan, *Gerald Fitzgerald the Great Earl of Kildare, 1456–1513* (Dublin and Cork, 1933). For the Church, see J. A. Watt, *The Church in Medieval Ireland* (Cambridge, 1972), and C. Mooney, *The Church in Gaelic Ireland, 13th to 15th Centuries* (Dublin, 1969).

For a polemical reassessment of Henry VII's achievement, see Christine Carpenter's essay in *The Reign of Henry VII* ed. B. Thompson (Stamford, 1995), and her *Locality and Polity: a Study of Warwickshire Landed Society, 1401–1499* (Cambridge, 1992), Ch. 15–16. The first pretender rising is treated in M. J. Bennett, *Lambert Simnel and the Battle of Stoke* (Gloucester, 1987). For Henry's methods of government and treatment of the nobility, see B. P. Wolffe, *The Royal Demesne in English History: The Crown Estate in the Governance of the Realm from the Conquest to 1509* (London, 1971); G. R. Elton, 'Henry VII: Rapacity and Remorse', and 'Henry VII: A Restatement' in his *Studies in Tudor and Stuart Politics and Government*, vol. 1 (Cambridge, 1974); J. P. Cooper, 'Henry VII's last years reconsidered', *Historical Journal*, ii (1959); T. B. Pugh, 'Henry VII and the English Nobility' in *The Tudor Nobility*, ed. G. W. Bernard (Manchester, 1992); and J. R. Lander, *Crown and Nobility, 1450–1509* (London, 1976). For Perkin Warbeck and the 1497 rising, see I. Arthurson, *The Perkin Warbeck Conspiracy, 1491–1499* (Stroud, 1994), and his 'The Rising of 1497: A revolt of the peasantry?' in *People, Politics and Community in the Later Middle Ages*, ed. J. T. Rosenthal and C. F. Richmond (Stroud, 1987).

For Henry's last years, see M. M. Condon, 'Ruling Elites in the Reign of Henry VIII' and S. J. Gunn, 'The Courtiers of Henry VII' in *The Tudor Monarchy*, ed. J. Guy (London, 1997); D. A. Luckett, 'Crown Patronage and Political Morality in Early Tudor England: The Case of Giles, Lord Daubeney', *English Historical Review*, cx (1995); C. J. Harrison, 'The Petition of Edmund Dudley', *English Historical Review*, lxxxvii (1972); and S. Anglo, 'Ill of the Dead: The posthumous reputation of Henry VII', *Renaissance Studies*, i (1987).

2 Family and Friends

Of the four surviving English mystery play cycles, I have particularly concentrated upon and cited from *The N-Town Play: Cotton MS Vespasian D.8*, ed. S. Spector (Early English Text Society, supplementary series, 11–12, Oxford,

1991). The meaning and purposes of the plays are elucidated in V. A. Kolve, *The Play called Corpus Christi* (Stanford, 1966) and R. Woolf, *The English Mystery Plays* (Berkeley and Los Angeles, 1972).

Illuminating accounts of the Mass and the Christian community are found in J. Bossy, 'The Mass as a social institution, 1200–1700', *Past and Present*, 100 (1983), and *Christianity in the West, 1400–1700* (Oxford, 1985); E. Duffy, *The Stripping of the Altars: Traditional Religion in England, 1400–1580* (New Haven and London, 1992), Part 1; Bernard, Lord Manning, *The People's Faith in the Time of Wyclif* (Cambridge, 1919); and M. Rubin, *Corpus Christi: The Eucharist in Late Medieval Culture* (Cambridge, 1991). See also S. Brigden, 'Religion and social obligation in sixteenth-century London', *Past and Present*, 103 (1984). *The Lay Folks Mass Book*, ed. T. F. Simmons (Early English Text Society, original series, 71, London, 1879) is a revealing source.

The place of the dead is discussed in J. le Goff, *The Birth of Purgatory*, trans. A. Goldhammer (Aldershot, 1984); J-C. Schmitt, *Ghosts in the Middle Ages: The Living and the Dead in Medieval Society*, trans. T. L. Fagan (Chicago and London, 1998); R. Houlbrooke, *Death, Religion and the Family in England, 1480–1750* (Oxford, 1998); and *The Place of the Dead: Death and Remembrance in Late Medieval and Early Modern Europe*, ed. B. Gordon and P. Marshall (Cambridge, 2000). For the devotion to saints and their images, see *Mirk's Festial*, ed. T. Erbe (Early English Text Society, extra series, xcvi, 1905); M. Aston, *Faith and Fire: Popular and Unpopular Religion, 1350–1600* (London and Rio Grande, 1993); J. Huizinga, *The Waning of the Middle Ages* (Harmondsworth, 1955); E. Mâle, *Religious Art from the Twelfth to the Eighteenth Century* (London, 1949); R. C. Finucane, *Miracles and Pilgrims: Popular Beliefs in Medieval England* (London, 1977); and J. Sumption, *Pilgrimage: An Image of Mediaeval Religion* (London, 1975).

For the power of religion in the lives of the people, and the authority of the Church and priesthood, see J. J. Scarisbrick, *The Reformation and the English People* (Oxford, 1984); R. Swanson, *Catholic England: Faith, Religion and Observance before the Reformation* (Manchester, 1993); P. Marshall, *The Catholic Priesthood and the English Reformation* (Oxford, 1994); K. V. Thomas, *Religion and the Decline of Magic: Studies in Popular Beliefs in Sixteenth and Seventeenth Century England* (London, 1971); and T. N. Tentler, *Sin and Confession on the Eve of the Reformation* (Princeton, 1977). Illuminating contemporary accounts of Catholic morality are Richard Whitford, *A Werke for Housholders, or for them that have the gydynge or gouernaunce of ony company* (London, 1530); W. Harrington, *In thys boke are conteyned the comendations of matrimony* (London, c. 1517); and *The Tree of Commonwealth: A treatise written by Edmund Dudley*, ed. D. M. Brodie (Cambridge, 1948).

For English society generally, see K. Wrightson, *English Society, 1580–1680* (London, 1982); J. A. Sharpe, *Early Modern England: A Social History, 1550–*

1760 (London, 1987); P. Laslett, *The World we have Lost: Further Explored* (London, 1983); and J. Youings, *Sixteenth-century England* (Harmondsworth, 1984). For the English family and life cycle, see D. Cressy, *Birth, Marriage and Death: Ritual, Religion and the Life-Cycle in Tudor and Stuart England* (Oxford, 1997); R. Houlbrooke, *The English Family, 1450–1700* (Harlow, 1984); B. Hanawalt, *The Ties that Bound: Peasant Families in Medieval England* (Oxford, 1986); P. Laslett, *Family Life and Illicit Love in Earlier Generations: Essays in Historical Sociology* (Cambridge, 1977); and *Household and Family in Past Time*, ed. P. Laslett and R. Wall (Cambridge, 1972). For an intimate portrait of one family, see *The Lisle Letters*, ed. M. St C. Byrne, (6 vols., Chicago and London, 1981). See also *The Plumpton Letters and Papers*, ed. J. Kirby (Camden Society, 5th series, viii, 1996); *Memorials of the Holles Family, 1493–1656, by Gervase Holles*, ed. A. C. Wood (Camden Society, 3rd series, lv, London, 1937); B. Winchester, *Tudor Family Portrait* (London, 1955); and L. E. Pearson, *Elizabethans at Home* (Stanford, 1957).

On population, the pioneering and authoritative study is E. A. Wrigley and R. S. Schofield, *The Population History of England, 1541–1871: A Reconstruction* (London, 1981). See also J. Hatcher, *Plague, Population and the English Economy, 1348–1530* (Basingstoke, 1977).

For childhood and youth, see P. Ariès, *Centuries of Childhood: A Social History of Family Life*, trans. R. Baldick (London, 1962); I. Pinchbeck and M. Hewitt, *Children in English Society: From Tudor Times to the Eighteenth Century* (London, 1969); K. V. Thomas, 'Age and Authority in Early Modern England', *Proceedings of the British Academy*, lxii (1976); S. Brigden, 'Youth and the English Reformation', *Past and Present*, 95 (1982); and I. K. Ben Amos, *Adolescence and Youth in Early Modern England* (New Haven, 1994).

Marriage, and the making of marriage, are discussed in R. B. Outhwaite, *Clandestine Marriage in England, 1500–1850* (London, 1995); M. Ingram, *Church Courts, Sex and Marriage in England, 1570–1640* (Cambridge, 1987); R. H. Helmholz, *Marriage Litigation in Medieval England* (Cambridge, 1974); *Marriage and Society: Studies in the social history of marriage*, ed. R. B. Outhwaite (London, 1981); and A. Macfarlane, *Marriage and Love in England: Modes of Reproduction, 1300–1840* (Oxford 1986).

The last things and the art of dying well are explained in St Thomas More, *English Poems, Life of Pico* and *The Last Things*, ed. A. S. G. Edwards, K. G. Rodgers and C. H. Miller in *The Complete Works of St Thomas More*, vol. 1 (New Haven and London, 1997); R. Whitford, *A Dayly Exercyse and Experyence of Death*, ed. J. Hogg, Salzburg Studies in English Literature (1979); N. L. Beaty, *The Craft of Dying: The Literary Tradition of Ars Moriendi in England* (New Haven and London, 1970). For funerals, see *The Diary of Henry Machyn, Citizen and Merchant-Taylor of London, from AD 1550 to AD 1563*, ed. J. G. Nichols (Camden Society, original series, xlii, 1848); and C. Gittings, *Death, Burial and the Individual in Early Modern England* (London, 1984). For chantries and prayers for the dead, see J. T. Rosenthal, *The Purchase of Paradise* (London, 1972); and K. L. Wood-Legh, *Perpetual Chantries in Britain* (Cambridge, 1965).

For the sense of kinship and lineage among the nobility and gentry, L. Stone, *The Crisis of the Aristocracy, 1558–1641* (Oxford, 1965), J. Hughes, *Pastors and Visionaries: Religion and Secular Life in Late Medieval Yorkshire* (Woodbridge, 1988), and C. Carpenter, *Locality and Polity* (Cambridge, 1992) are indispensable. See also M. E. James, *Family, Lineage and Civil Society: A Study of Society, Politics and Mentality in the Durham Region, 1500–1640* (Oxford, 1974); and J. P. Rosenthal, *Patriarchy and Families of Privilege in Fifteenth-Century England*. The 'surnames' of the far north of England are described in G. MacDonald Fraser, *The Steel Bonnets: The Story of the Anglo-Scottish Border Reivers* (London, paperback edn, 1995); and R. Robson, *The Rise and Fall of the English Highland Clans: Tudor Responses to a Medieval Problem* (Edinburgh, 1989). For kinship in Ireland, see K. Nicholls, *Gaelic and Gaelicised Ireland* (Dublin, 1972). See also *Land, Kinship and Life-Cycle*, ed. R. M. Smith (Cambridge, 1984); D. Cressy, 'Kinship and Kin Interaction in Early Modern England', *Past and Present*, 113 (1986); and *Migration and Society in Early Modern England*, ed. P. Clark and D. Souden (London, 1987).

The character of gentry and noble households is described in D. Starkey, 'The Age of the Household: Politics, society and the arts, *c.* 1350–*c.*1550' in *The Later Middle Ages*, ed. S. Medcalf (London, 1981); K. Mertes, *The English Noble Household, 1250–1600: Good Governance and Politic Rule* (Oxford, 1988); F. Heal, *Hospitality in Early Modern England* (Oxford, 1990); and K. Simms, 'Guesting and Feasting in Gaelic Ireland', *Journal of The Royal Society of Antiquaries of Ireland*, 108 (1978). For the education of the sons of the nobility, see N. Orme, *From Childhood to Chivalry: the Education of English Kings and Aristocracy, 1066–1530* (London, 1984).

The families and households of merchants and the lower orders are studied in M. Spufford, *Contrasting Communities: English Villagers in the Sixteenth and Seventeenth Centuries* (Cambridge, 1974); M. K. McIntosh, *A Community Transformed: The Manor and Liberty of Havering, 1500–1620* (Cambridge, 1991); M. Pelling, *The Common Lot: Sickness, Medical Occupations and the Urban Poor in Early Modern England* (Harlow, 1998); and A. Kussmaul, *Servants in Husbandry in Early Modern England* (Cambridge, 1981).

A compelling contemporary account of a city is *A Survey of London by John Stow*, ed. C. L. Kingsford (2 vols., Oxford, 1908). The best studies of life in English cities and towns are found in S. L. Thrupp, *The Merchant Class of Medieval London, 1300–1500* (Ann Arbor, 1976 edn); C. Phythian-Adams, *Desolation of a City: Coventry and the Urban Crisis of the Late Middle Ages* (Cambridge, 1979); S. Rappaport, *Worlds within Worlds: Structures of Life in Sixteenth-Century London* (Cambridge, 1989); D. M. Palliser, *Tudor York* (Oxford, 1979); and G. Rosser, *Medieval Westminster, 1200–1540* (Oxford,

1989). For Ireland, see C. Lennon, *The Lords of Dublin in the Age of Reformation* (Dublin, 1989).

Parish, neighbourhood and fraternity are considered in I. Archer, *The Pursuit of Stability: Social Relations in Elizabethan London* (Cambridge, 1991); S. J. Wright, *Parish, Church and People: Local Studies in Lay Religion, 1350–1750* (London, 1988); *Disputes and Settlements: Law and Human Relations in the West*, ed. J. Bossy (Cambridge, 1983); and A. G. Rosser, 'Parochial Conformity and Popular Religion in Late Medieval England', *Transactions of the Royal Historical Society*, 6th series, i (1991). For parish fraternities, see H. F. Westlake, *The Parish Gilds of Medieval England* (London, 1919); *Parish Fraternity Register: Fraternity of the Holy Trinity and SS. Fabian and Sebastian in the Parish of St Botolph without Aldersgate*, ed. P. Basing (London Record Society, London, 1982); and C. Barron, 'The parish fraternities of medieval London', in *The Church in pre-Reformation Society*, ed. C. Barron and C. Harper-Bill (Woodbridge, 1985). The classic work upon the English religious houses is D. Knowles, *The Religious Orders in England* (3 vols., Cambridge, 1959). See also L. Butler and C. Given Wilson, *Medieval Monasteries of Great Britain* (London, 1979). For Ireland, see A. Gwynn and R. N. Hadcock, *Medieval Religious Houses in Ireland* (London, 1970); and B. Bradshaw, *The Dissolution of the Religious Orders in Ireland under Henry VIII* (Cambridge, 1974).

For the poor and outcast, and attempts to aid or control them, see P. Slack, *Poverty and Policy in Tudor and Stuart England* (London, 1988) and A. L. Beier, *Masterless Men: The Vagrancy Problem in England, 1560–1640* (London, 1985). On crime, see J. A. Sharpe, *Crime in Early Modern England, 1550–1750* (London, 1984) and *Crime in England, 1550–1800*, ed. J. S. Cockburn (London, 1977). On suicide, see M. MacDonald and T. R. Murphy, *Sleepless Souls: Suicide in Early Modern England* (Oxford, 1990).

3 Ways to Reform

John Foxe was the first to write the history of the Lollards and to collect the evidence of their trials; see *The Acts and Monuments of John Foxe*, ed. G. Townsend (8 vols., London, 1848–9), especially vol. 4. The most important study of the 'known men and women' is by Anne Hudson, *The Premature Reformation: Wycliffite Texts and Lollard History* (Oxford, 1988). Other revealing studies are M. Aston, *Lollards and Reformers: Images and Literacy in Late Medieval Religion* (London, 1984); A. Hope, 'Lollardy: The Stone the Builders Rejected?' in *Protestantism and the National Church*, ed. P. Lake and M. Dowling (London, 1987); and D. Plumb, 'The social and economic status of the later Lollards' and 'A gathered church? Lollards and their society' in *The World of Rural Dissenters, 1520–1725*, ed. M. Spufford (Cambridge, 1995). A. G. Dickens, *Lollards and Protestants in the Diocese of York, 1509–1558*

(London, 1959), and J. F. Davis, *Heresy and Reformation in the South-East of England, 1520–1559* (London, 1983) suggest links between Lollardy and the new religion.

For Christian humanism and hopes for reform in the Church, see the introduction by J. H. Hexter to *Utopia* in *Complete Works of St Thomas More*, vol. 4 (New Haven and London, 1965); M. M. Phillips, *The 'Adages' of Erasmus: A Study with Translations* (Cambridge, 1965); J. C. Olin, *Catholic Reformation: Savonarola to Ignatius Loyola* (New York, 1969); and D. Fenlon, *Heresy and Obedience in Tridentine Italy: Cardinal Pole and the Counter-Reformation* (Cambridge, 1972). For the lives and influence of Dean Colet and St John Fisher, see J. H. Lupton, *A Life of John Colet* (London, 1887); J. B. Gleason, *John Colet* (Berkeley, 1989); and *Humanism, Reform and Reformation: The Career of Bishop John Fisher*, ed. B. Bradshaw and E. Duffy (Cambridge, 1989). Outstanding critical accounts of More's *Utopia* are D. Baker-Smith, *More's 'Utopia'* (London, 1991) and S. Greenblatt, *Renaissance Self-Fashioning from More to Shakespeare* (Chicago, 1980). Key texts by Erasmus in translation are *The Sileni of Alcibiades* which is published in *Thomas More: Utopia*, ed. D. Wootton (Indianapolis, 1999); *The Education of a Christian Prince*, ed. Lisa Jardine (Cambridge, 1997); *Enchiridion Militis Christiani or The Manual of the Christian Knight* (London, 1905); and *Praise of Folly*, ed. A. H. T. Levi (Harmondsworth, 1993). See also *The 'Julius Exclusus' of Erasmus*, tr. P. Pascal, ed. J. Kelley Sowards (Bloomington and London, 1968). For revealing studies of Erasmus, see R. J. Schoeck, *Erasmus of Europe* (Edinburgh, 1993); J. K. McConica, *Erasmus* (Oxford, 1991); and L. Jardine, *Erasmus, Man of Letters* (Princeton, 1993).

Luther, his theological discoveries, and his challenge to the Church, are explained in R. H. Bainton, *Here I Stand: a Life of Martin Luther* (London, 1951); A. McGrath, *Luther's Theology of the Cross* (Oxford, 1985) and *Iustitia Dei: a history of the Christian Doctrine of Justification* (2 vols., Cambridge, 1986); and H. Oberman, *Masters of the Reformation* (Cambridge, 1981). For the Catholic position, and the defence against Luther in England, the following are indispensable: R. Rex, *The Theology of John Fisher* (Cambridge, 1991) and 'The English Campaign against Luther in the 1520s', *Transactions of the Royal Historical Society*, 5th series, 39 (1989); and *Responsio ad Lutherum* in *Complete Works of St Thomas More*, ed. J. M. Headley, vol. 5 (New Haven and London, 1969). Henry VIII's own theology is discovered in J. J. Scarisbrick, *Henry VIII* (London, 1968) and *The Reign of Henry VIII: Politics, Policy and Piety*, ed. D. MacCulloch (Basingstoke, 1995).

Important general works on the early Reformation in England are A. G. Dickens, *The English Reformation* (rev. edn, London, 1989), a pioneering study, and C. A. Haigh, *English Reformations: Religion, Politics and Society under the Tudors* (Oxford, 1993); and R. Rex, *Henry VIII and the English Reformation* (Basingstoke, 1993). For the evangelical 'brethren', see S. Brigden, *London and the Reformation* (Oxford, 1989) and 'Thomas Cromwell and the Brethren' in *Law and Government under the Tudors: Essays presented to Sir Geoffrey Elton on his retirement*, ed. C. Cross, D. M. Loades and J. J. Scarisbrick (Cambridge, 1988). For More's assault on the 'brethren', see especially *A Dialogue concerning Heresies* in *Complete Works*, vol. 6, ed. T. M. C. Lawler, G. Marc'hadour and R. C. Marius (New Haven and London, 1981); *Supplication of Souls* and *Letter against Frith* in *Complete Works*, vol. 7, ed. F. Manley, G. Marc'hadour, R. C. Marius and C. H. Miller (New Haven and London, 1990), *The Confutation of Tyndale's Answer* in *Complete Works*, vol. 8, ed. L. A. Schuster, R. C. Marius, J. P. Lusardi and R. J. Schoeck (New Haven and London, 1973), and *The Apology* in *Complete Works*, vol. 9, ed. J. B. Trapp (New Haven and London, 1979).

Tyndale's remarkable, fundamental scriptural translations from Greek and Hebrew are republished: *Tyndale's New Testament*, ed. D. Daniell (New Haven and London, 1989) and *Tyndale's Old Testament*, ed. D. Daniell (New Haven and London, 1992). For Tyndale's life, see Foxe, *Acts and Monuments*, ed. G. Townsend, vol. 5 (London, 1846); and J. F. Mozley, *William Tyndale* (1937).

4 Imperium

COURTS AND KINGS

The best edition of Wyatt's poems is *Sir Thomas Wyatt: the Complete Poems*, ed. R. A. Rebholz (Harmondsworth, 1978). For his life and work, see S. M. Foley, *Sir Thomas Wyatt* (Boston, Mass., 1990).

The world which Henry VIII created for himself is revealed in S. Thurley, *The Royal Palaces of Tudor England: Architecture and Court Life, 1460–1537* (New Haven and London, 1993); C. Lloyd and S. Thurley, *Henry VIII: Images of a Tudor King* (Oxford, 1990); J. N. King, *Tudor Royal Iconography* (Princeton 1989); J. Roberts, *Holbein and the Court of Henry VIII* (Edinburgh, 1993); and *Henry VIII: A European Court in England*, ed. D. Starkey (London, 1991). The political significance of the Privy Chamber is David Starkey's discovery. He has elucidated its workings in a series of important articles: 'Court and Government' and 'Representation through intimacy: A study of the symbolism of monarchy and court office in early modern England', in *The Tudor Monarchy*, ed. J. Guy (London, 1997); and *The English Court from the Wars of the Roses to the Civil War*, ed. D. Starkey *et al.* (Harlow, 1987). The first biography of Henry VIII is still valuable: Edward, Lord Herbert of Cherbury, *The life and raigne of King Henry the eighth* (London, 1649); and the account of his reign by his contemporary, Edward Hall, *The Union of the Two Noble and Illustre Famelies of York and Lancaster*, ed. H. Ellis (London, 1809) is indispensable. J. J. Scarisbrick, *Henry VIII* (London, 1968) is not only the best biography of the King but also the fullest political history of his reign. D. Starkey, *The Reign of Henry VIII: Personalities and Politics* (London, 1985) is a lively and perceptive account. For revealing studies of politics, war and court culture, see S. Gunn, 'The Accession of Henry VIII', *Historical Research*, 64 (1991) and 'The French Wars of Henry VIII' in *The Origins of War in Early Modern Europe*, ed. J. Black (Edinburgh, 1987); and 'Chivalry and the Politics of the Early Tudor Court' in *Chivalry in the Renaissance*, ed. S. Anglo (Woodbridge, 1980). Thomas Wolsey's spectacular career in church and state is studied in P. Gwyn, *The King's Cardinal: The rise and fall of Thomas Wolsey* (London, 1990); and *Cardinal Wolsey: Church, state and art*, ed. S. J. Gunn and P. G. Lindley (Cambridge, 1991). George Cavendish, the Cardinal's gentleman usher, wrote an intimate biography of his master, *The Life and Death of Cardinal Wolsey*, ed. R. S. Sylvester (Early English Text Society, original series, 243, Oxford, 1959).

The nature of Henrician politics is discussed in G. R. Elton, 'Tudor Government: The points of contact, Part 3, The Court' in his *Studies in Tudor and Stuart Politics and Government*, Vol. 3 (Cambridge, 1974). The extent to which Henry's court was dominated by faction has occasioned much debate. My own interpretation follows those of David Starkey and Eric Ives. See E. W. Ives, *Faction in Tudor England* (2nd edn, London, 1986). Eric Ives's thrilling biography of Anne Boleyn is important for the politics, religion and culture of the court: *Anne Boleyn* (Oxford, 1986); see also J. S. Block, *Factional Politics and the English Reformation, 1520–1540* (Woodbridge, 1993). For the political culture of the court, see D. Starkey, 'The Court: Castiglione's ideal and Tudor reality', *Journal of the Warburg and Courtauld Institutes*, 45 (1982); and F. W. Conrad, 'The problem of counsel reconsidered: The case of Sir Thomas Elyot', in *Political Thought and the Tudor Commonwealth*, ed. P. A. Fideler and T. F. Mayer (London, 1992). For women at court, see B. J. Harris, 'Women and politics in early Tudor England', *Historical Journal*, xxxiii (1990). Court entertainments and spectacles are studied in S. Anglo, *Spectacle, Pageantry and Early Tudor Policy* (Oxford, 1969).

ROYAL SUPREMACY

The starting point for study of Henry's 'Great Matter' remains J. J. Scarisbrick, *Henry VIII* (London, 1968). Virginia Murphy, 'The literature and propaganda of Henry VIII's first divorce' in *The Reign of Henry VIII: Politics, Policy and Piety*, ed. D. MacCulloch (Harlow, 1995), and H. A. Kelly, *The Matrimonial Trials of Henry VIII* (Stanford, CA, 1976) are also important. For Anne Boleyn as an evangelical, see Ives, *Anne Boleyn*, and M. Dowling, 'Anne Boleyn and Reform', *Journal of Ecclesiastical History*, xxxv (1984). Wolsey's fall is explained by E. W. Ives, 'The fall of Wolsey' in *Cardinal Wolsey: Church, state and art*, ed. S. J. Gunn and P. G. Lindley (Cambridge, 1991). For Thomas More as Lord Chancellor and opponent of reform, see J. A. Guy, *The Public Career of Sir Thomas More* (Brighton, 1980).

The authoritative account of the making of the political Reformation is G. R. Elton, *Reform and Reformation* (London, 1977). For Cranmer, see Diarmaid MacCulloch's commanding biography, *Thomas Cranmer* (New Haven and London, 1996). Thomas Cromwell's vision of a reformed commonwealth is studied in G. R. Elton, *Reform and Renewal: Thomas Cromwell and the Common Weal* (Cambridge, 1973). Fisher's stand is discussed in J. J. Scarisbrick, 'Fisher, Henry VIII and the Reformation Crisis' in *Humanism, Reform and the Reformation: The Career of Bishop John Fisher*, ed. B. Bradshaw and E. Duffy (Cambridge, 1989). The passage of the legislation through Parliament is studied in S. E. Lehmberg, *The Reformation Parliament, 1529–1536* (Cambridge, 1970). For the law of treason and its working, see G. R. Elton, *Policy and Police: The enforcement of the Reformation in the Age of Thomas Cromwell* (Cambridge, 1972) and R. Rex, 'The execution of the Holy Maid of Kent', *Historical Research*, 114 (1991).

Henry's own theology and his intentions for his Church are penetrated by D. MacCulloch, 'Henry VIII and the Reform of the Church' in *The Reign of Henry VIII*, ed. MacCulloch (Basingstoke, 1995). See also G. W. Bernard, 'The Making of Religious Policy, 1533–1546: Henry VIII and the search for the middle way', *Historical Journal*, xli (1998). For the connections between political Reformation and Reformation in religion, see S. Brigden, *London and the Reformation* (Oxford, 1989). The fall of Anne Boleyn is studied authoritatively in E. W. Ives, *Anne Boleyn*, and 'Anne Boleyn and the early Reformation in England: the contemporary evidence', *Historical Journal*, xxxvii (1994).

The magisterial and best account of the dissolution of the monasteries is D. Knowles, *The Religious Orders in England*, vol. 3 (Cambridge, 1959). J. Youings, *The Dissolution of the Monasteries* (London, 1971) is useful. On the Pilgrimage of Grace, the standard account remains M. H. and R. Dodds, *The Pilgrimage of Grace and the Exeter Conspiracy* (Cambridge, 1915). See also M. L. Bush, *The Pilgrimage of Grace: A study of the Rebel Armies of October 1536* (Manchester, 1996). C. A. Haigh, *The Last Days of the Lancashire Monasteries and the Pilgrimage of Grace* (Chetham Society, 3rd series, 17, 1969) and S. M. Harrison, *The Pilgrimage of Grace in the Lake Counties, 1536–7* (London, 1981) are important local studies. For a persuasive account of the revolt's causes, see C. S. L. Davies, 'Popular Religion and the Pilgrimage of Grace' in *Order and Disorder in early modern England*, ed. A. Fletcher and J. Stevenson (Cambridge, 1985).

For the evangelical animus and official campaign against images, see Margaret Aston's profound study, *England's Iconoclasts*, vol. 1, *Laws against Images* (Oxford, 1988). A revealing study is P. Marshall, 'The Rood of Boxley, the Blood of Hailes and the defence of the Henrician Church', *Journal of Ecclesiastical History*, xlvi (1995). For the reformers' own letters, see *Original Letters relative to the English Reformation*, ed. H. Robinson (2 vols., Parker Society, Cambridge, 1847). Theological developments and divisions among the reformers are examined in MacCulloch, *Thomas Cranmer* and C. W. Dugmore, *The Mass and the English Reformers* (New York, 1958). For the Act of Six Articles and Cromwell's fall, see G. R. Elton, 'Thomas Cromwell's Decline and Fall' in his *Studies in Tudor Politics and Government*, vol. 1 (Cambridge, 1974); S. Brigden, 'Popular Disturbance and the Fall of Thomas Cromwell and the Reformers, 1539–40', *Historical Journal*, xxiv (1981); and *The Examinations of Anne Askew*, ed. E. V. Beilin (New York, 1996). For Henry's last months, see S. Brigden, 'Henry Howard, Earl of Surrey, and the "conjured league"', *Historical Journal*, xxxvii (1994); and G. Redworth, *In Defence of the Church Catholic: The life of Stephen Gardiner* (Oxford, 1990). The subversion of Henry's plans for the regency and the rewriting of his will are discussed in Starkey, *The Reign of Henry VIII*; and E. W. Ives, 'Henry VIII's will – a forensic conundrum', *Historical Journal*, xxxv (1992).

5 Bearing Rule

LORDSHIP

For Fulke Greville's musings upon nobility, see 'A dedication to Sir Philip Sidney' in *The Prose Works of Fulke Greville, Lord Brooke*, ed. J. Gouws (Oxford, 1986). The most influential scholar of the late medieval nobility was K. B. McFarlane: *The Nobility of Later Medieval England* (Oxford, 1973). For the changing role of the nobility in the sixteenth and seventeenth centuries, see Laurence Stone's commanding study, *The Crisis of the Aristocracy, 1558–1641* (Oxford, 1965). C. Carpenter, *Locality and Polity: A study of Warwickshire Landed Society, 1401–1499* (Cambridge, 1992) anatomizes Midland society, with vital conclusions for the whole polity. See also J. M. W. Bean, *From Lord to Patron: Lordship in Late Medieval England* (Manchester, 1989). Important studies of individual families are found in C. Rawcliffe, *The Staffords, earls of Stafford and dukes of Buckingham, 1394–1521* (Cambridge, 1978); M. E. James, *Society, Politics and Culture: Studies in Early Modern England* (Cambridge, 1986); S. Gunn, *Charles Brandon, Duke of Suffolk, c. 1484–1545* (Oxford, 1988); G. W. Bernard, *The Power of the Early Tudor Nobility: A study of the fourth and fifth earls of Shrewsbury* (Brighton, 1985); and *The Tudor Nobility*, ed. G. W. Bernard (Manchester 1992). As a group the nobility are studied by H. Miller, *Henry VIII and the English Nobility* (Oxford, 1986); and the gentry by F. Heal and C. Holmes, *The Gentry in England and Wales, 1500–1700* (Basingstoke, 1994).

SOVEREIGNTY IN IRELAND

A compelling near-contemporary picture of the Gaelic lordships is found in *Annals of the Kingdom of Ireland by the Four Masters*, vols. 4–6, ed. J. O'Donovan (Dublin, new edn, 1998). Richard Stanihurst, the Dubliner (1547–1618) gave an account of Gaelic society, and an exploration of why it needed reform, in his chronicles of 1577: *Holinshed's Irish Chronicle*, ed. Liam Miller and Eileen Power (Dublin, 1979). The political structure of Gaelic Ireland is examined by K. Simms, *From Kings to Warlords: The Changing Political Structure of Gaelic Ireland in the Later Middle Ages* (Woodbridge, 1987) and 'Gaelic warfare in the Middle Ages' in *A Military History of Ireland*, ed. T. Bartlett and K. Jeffery (Cambridge, 1996); K. W. Nicholls, *Gaelic and Gaelicised Ireland in the Middle Ages* (Dublin, 1972); and M. O'Dowd, *Power, Politics and Land: Early Modern Sligo, 1568–1688* (Belfast, 1991). The power of the earls of Kildare is studied by S. G. Ellis in *Tudor Frontiers and Noble Power: The making of the British State* (Oxford, 1995). For Henry VIII's constitutional revolution, see B. Bradshaw, *The Irish Constitutional Revolution of the Sixteenth Century* (Cambridge, 1979) and *The Dissolution of the Religious Orders in Ireland under Henry VIII* (Cambridge, 1974); C. Brady, 'Court, Castle and Country: the Framework of Government in Tudor Ireland', in *Natives and Newcomers: The making of Irish Colonial Society, 1534–1641*, ed. C. Brady and R. Gillespie (Dublin, 1986) and *The Chief Governors: the rise and fall of reform government in Tudor Ireland, 1536–1588* (Cambridge, 1994). Reports by the governors on Irish affairs between 1515 and 1547 are found in *State Papers, Henry VIII,* vols. 2 and 3 (London, 1834).

JUSTICE

The magisterial and best introduction to English law and the legal system is *The Reports of Sir John Spelman*, ed. J. H. Baker (2 vols., Selden Society, 93–4, 1976–7). For the character of English law, see J. G. A. Pocock, *The Ancient Constitution and the Feudal Law* (Cambridge, 1987 edn). Important general material is found in E. W. Ives, *The Common Lawyers of Pre-Reformation England. Thomas Kebell: A case study* (Cambridge, 1983). For the treason law and those who suffered, see G. R. Elton, *Policy and Police: The enforcement of the Reformation in the Age of Thomas Cromwell* (Cambridge, 1972), Ch. 9. Wyatt's 'Defence' is printed in K. Muir, *The Life and Letters of Sir Thomas Wyatt* (Liverpool, 1963). For the development of equity jurisdiction, see J. A. Guy, *The Cardinal's Court: The Impact of Thomas Wolsey in Star Chamber* (Hassocks, 1977); A. Fox and J. Guy, *Reassessing the Henrician Age: Human-*

ism, Politics and Reform, 1500–1550 (Oxford, 1986); and W. J. Jones, *The Elizabethan Court of Chancery* (Oxford, 1967). Church courts and their juris-diction are studied in B. L. Woodcock, *Medieval Ecclesiastical Courts in the Diocese of Canterbury* (Oxford, 1952); R. A. Houlbrooke, *Church Courts and the People during the English Reformation, 1520–1570* (Oxford, 1979); and R. M. Wunderli, *London Church Courts and Society on the eve of the Reformation* (Cambridge, Mass., 1981).

For arbitration, see E. Powell, 'Arbitration and the law in England in the late Middle Ages', *Transactions of the Royal Historical Society,* 5th series, 33 (1983); *Law and Social Change in British History,* ed. J. A. Guy and H. G. Beale (London, 1984). See also J. G. Bellamy, *Bastard Feudalism and the Law* (London, 1989); and I. Thornley, 'The Destruction of Sanctuary' in *Tudor Studies,* ed. R. W. Seton-Watson (London, 1924). For March law, see R. Robson, *English Highland Clans: Tudor Responses to a Mediaeval Problem* (Edinburgh, 1989); R. R. Davies, 'The Law of the March', *Welsh History Review,* v (1970); 'The survival of the Bloodfeud in Medieval Wales', *History,* liv (1969); 'The Twilight of Welsh Law, 1284–1536', *History,* li (1966); and J. Wormald, 'Bloodfeud, Kindred and Government in Early Modern Scotland', *Past and Present,* 87 (1980). For brehon law, see K. Nicholls, *Gaelic and Gaelicised Ireland in the Middle Ages* (Dublin, 1972); K. Simms, *From Kings to Warlords* (Woodbridge, 1987); and N. Patterson, Gaelic law and the Tudor conquest of Ireland', *Irish Historical Studies,* xxvii (1991).

THE COMMONS

Tudor theories of obligation and of the social order are understood from contemporary treatises; for example, *The Tree of Commonwealth: A treatise written by Edmund Dudley,* ed. D. M. Brodie (Cambridge, 1948); John Cheke, *The Hurt of Sedition, 1549* (reprinted, Menston, 1971); 'Defence of John Hales' in *A Discourse of the Common Weal of this Realm of England,* ed. E. Lamond (Cambridge, 1954 edn); and *Humanist Scholarship and Public Order: Two Tracts against the Pilgrimage of Grace by Sir Richard Morison,* ed. D. S. Berkowitz (Washington, 1984).

The most accessible introduction to Tudor rebellions is A. Fletcher and D. MacCulloch, *Tudor Rebellions* (4th edn, London, 1977). See also R. B. Man-ning, *Village Revolts: social protest and popular dissent in England, 1509–1640* (London, 1988); and G. W. Bernard, *War, Taxation and Rebellion in Early Tudor England* (Brighton, 1986). For 'Evil May Day' and London's disloyalty, see S. Brigden, *London and the Reformation* (Oxford, 1989). For the North, see M. A. Hicks, 'The Yorkshire Rebellion of 1489 reconsidered', *Northern History,* 22 (1986); and A. J. Pollard, *North-Eastern England during the Wars of the Roses* (Oxford, 1990). For the divisions in Lincolnshire society in 1536, see M. E. James, 'Obedience and Dissent in Henrician England: The Lincolnshire Rebellion, 1536', *Past and Present*, 48 (1970), and S. Gunn's convincing rejoinder, 'Peers, Commons and Gentry in the Lincolnshire Revolt of 1536', *Past and Present*, 123 (1989).

For hierarchies and structures of power, see the essays in *The Experience of Authority in Early Modern England*, ed. P. Griffiths, A. Fox and S. Hindle (Basingstoke, 1996); and S. Hindle, 'The Problem of Pauper Marriage in Seventeenth-Century England', *Transactions of the Royal Historical Society*, 6th series, 8 (1998); for bondmen and their manumission, see D. MacCulloch, 'Bondmen under the Tudors' in *Law and Government under the Tudors*, ed. C. Cross, D. Loades and J. J. Scarisbrick (Cambridge, 1988).

For women in English society, see S. Amussen, *An Ordered Society: Gender and Class in Early Modern England* (Oxford, 1988); and *Women in English Society, 1500–1800*, ed. M. Prior (London, 1985).

6 Rebuilding the Temple

For Henry VIII's policy towards Scotland, see *State Papers, Henry VIII*, vol. 4 (London, 1836). For the possibility of uniting the kingdoms, see *Conquest and Union: Fashioning a British State, 1485–1726*, ed. S. G. Ellis and S. Barber (London, 1995); *The British Problem* c. *1534–1707: State Formation in the Atlantic Archipelago*, ed. B. Bradshaw and J. Morrill (Basingstoke, 1996); and *Scotland and England, 1286–1815*, ed. R. A. Mason (Edinburgh, 1987).

Edward's personality and political concerns are still best discovered in *The Literary Remains of King Edward the Sixth*, ed. J. G. Nichols (London, 1857). For his political education, see *The Chronicle and Political Papers of Edward VI*, ed. W. K. Jordan (London, 1966) and *Sermons and Remains of Hugh Latimer*, ed. G. E. Corrie. (2 vols., Parker Society, Cambridge, 1844, 1845). Original letters of Edward and Mary's reigns are printed in P. F. Tytler, *England under the Reigns of Edward VI and Mary* (2 vols., London, 1839); J. Strype, *Ecclesiastical Memorials, relating chiefly to religion under King Henry VIII, King Edward and Queen Mary I* (3 vols., Oxford 1822); and *The Letters of William, Lord Paget of Beaudesert, 1547–63*, ed. B. L. Beer and S. Jack (Camden miscellany, xxv, Camden Society, 4th series, 13, 1974). Important studies of Edward's reign are W. K. Jordan, *Edward VI: the Young King* (London, 1968) and *Edward VI: the Threshold of Power* (London, 1970); M. L. Bush, *The Government Policy of Protector Somerset* (London, 1975); D. Hoak, *The King's Council in the Reign of Edward VI* (Cambridge, 1976); and *The Mid-Tudor Polity, c. 1540–1560*, ed. J. Loach and R. Tittler (London, 1980).

For economic problems, and attempts to solve them, see *A Discourse of the Common Weal of this Realm of England*, ed. E. Lamond (Cambridge, 1954 edn); *Agrarian History of England and Wales*, vol. 4, *1500–1640*, ed. J. Thirsk

(Cambridge, 1967); D. M. Palliser, *The Age of Elizabeth: England under the later Tudors, 1547–1603* (London and New York, 1983); and C. E. Challis, *The Tudor Coinage* (Manchester, 1978). The rebellions of 1549 have been described in B. L. Beer, *Rebellion and Riot: Popular disorder in England during the reign of Edward VI* (Kent, Ohio, 1982); Julian Cornwall, *The Revolt of the Peasantry, 1549* (London, 1977). S. T. Bindoff, *Kett's Rebellion* (London, 1949) and D. MacCulloch, 'Kett's rebellion in context', *Past and Present*, 84 (1979) illumine East Anglian society.

Autobiographical accounts by evangelicals are found in *Narratives of the Days of the Reformation*, ed. J. G. Nichols (Camden Society, 1st series, 77, London, 1859). The advance of evangelical religion and the political man-oeuvrings are explored in D. MacCulloch, *Thomas Cranmer* (New Haven and London, 1996) and S. Brigden, *London and the Reformation* (Oxford, 1989). *Beware the Cat, by William Baldwin: The First English Novel* ed. W. A. Ringler and M. Flachmann (San Marino, 1988). For the crisis of 1553, see *The Chronicle of Queen Jane and Queen Mary*, ed. J. G. Nichols (Camden Society, 1st series, 48, 1850); *Vita Mariae Angliae Reginae*, ed. D. MacCulloch (Camden Miscellany, xxviii, Camden Society, 4th series, 29, 1984); and M. Levine, *Tudor Dynastic Problems, 1470–1571* (London, 1973).

For Mary, see D. M. Loades, *The Reign of Mary Tudor: Politics, Government and Religion in England, 1553–1558* (London, 1979) and *Mary Tudor: A Life* (Oxford, 1989). For her council and privy chamber, see *Revolution Reassessed: Revisions in the History of Tudor Government and Administration*, ed. C. Coleman and D. Starkey (Oxford, 1986); and S. Gunn, 'A Letter of Jane, Duchess of Northumberland in 1553', *English Historical Review*, cxiv (1999). The opposition to the Spanish marriage is studied in *A Machiavellian Treatise by Stephen Gardiner*, ed. P. S. Donaldson (Cambridge, 1975); E. H. Harbison, *Rival Ambassadors at the Court of Queen Mary* (London, 1940); D. M. Loades, *Two Tudor Conspiracies* (Cambridge, 1965); and J. Procter, 'The History of Wyatt's Rebellion' in *Tudor Tracts*, ed. A. F. Pollard (London, 1903).

For the restoration of the Catholic religion, see J. Loach, *Parliament and the Crown in the Reign of Mary Tudor* (Oxford, 1986); E. Duffy, *The Stripping of the Altars: Traditional Religion in England, 1400–1580* (New Haven and London, 1992); R. Pogson, 'Reginald Pole and the priorities of government in Mary Tudor's Church', *Historical Journal*, xviii (1975); and M. Aston, *England's Iconoclasts* (Oxford, 1988). The martyrs are chronicled and celebrated by John Foxe in *Acts and Monuments*, ed. G. Townsend, vols. 6–8 (London, 1846–9); see also D. M. Loades, *The Oxford Martyrs* (London, 1970). For theories justifying resistance, see J. Ponet, *A Short Treatise of Politic Power* (Menston, 1970); Q. R. D. Skinner, *The Foundations of Modern Political Thought*, vol. 2, *The Age of Reformation* (Cambridge, 1978); and *The Cambridge History of Political Thought, 1450–1700*, ed. J. H. Burns (Cambridge, 1991).

7 'Perils, Many, Great and Imminent'

The chapter's title is taken from one of William Cecil's memoranda on of the state of the realm, where England's peril is a constant refrain; in *A Collection of State Papers . . . left by William Cecil, Lord Burghley*, ed. S. Haynes (London, 1740). Elizabeth reveals something of herself in her letters: *The Letters of Queen Elizabeth I*, ed. G. B. Harrison (London, 1935). Biographies of the Queen abound: see especially J. E. Neale, *Queen Elizabeth* (London, 1938 edn); and W. T. MacCaffrey, *Elizabeth I* (London, 1993). The first full history of her reign, written by an historian who witnessed many of the events, is still enthralling: William Camden, *The History of . . . Princess Elizabeth* (3rd edn, London, 1675) and *The History of . . . Princess Elizabeth: Selected chapters*, ed. W. T. MacCaffrey (Chicago and London, 1970). See also *Annals of the first four years of the reign of Queen Elizabeth by Sir John Hayward*, ed. J. Bruce (Camden Society, London, 1840). Important studies of the first years of her reign are: W. T. MacCaffrey, *The Shaping of the Elizabethan Regime: Elizabethan Politics, 1558–72* (London, 1969); C. Read, *Mr Secretary Cecil and Queen Elizabeth* (London, 1955); *The Reign of Elizabeth I*, ed. C. Haigh (Basingstoke, 1984); R. B. Wernham, *Before the Armada: The Emergence of the English Nation, 1485–1588* (London, 1966); N. L. Jones, *The Birth of the Elizabethan Age: England in the 1560s* (Oxford, 1993); and S. Alford, *The Early Elizabethan Polity: William Cecil and the British Succession Crisis, 1558–1569* (Cambridge, 1998).

Letters of reformers about the state of the Elizabethan Church and religion are printed in *Zurich Letters, AD 1558–1602*, ed. H. Robinson (2 vols., Parker Society, Cambridge, 1847). The most convincing account of the making of the Elizabethan settlement is now N. L. Jones, *Faith by Statute: Parliament and the Settlement of Religion, 1559* (London, 1982). For the debates in Parliament, see *Proceedings in the Parliaments of Elizabeth I*, vol. I, *1558–1581*, ed. T. E. Hartley (Leicester, 1981).

Religious divisions and European politics are examined in N. M. Sutherland, *The Massacre of St Bartholomew and the European Conflict, 1559–1572* (London and Basingstoke, 1973); D. R. Kelley, *The Beginning of Ideology: Consciousness and Society in the French Reformation* (Cambridge, 1981); and *International Calvinism, 1541–1715*, ed. M. Prestwich (Oxford, 1985). Useful documents are collected in *Calvinism in Europe, 1540–1610*, ed. A. Duke, G. Lewis and A. Pettegree (Manchester, 1992). For Philip II of Spain, see G. Parker, *Philip II* (London, 1979); and H. Kamen, *Philip II* (New Haven and London, 1997). The Dutch revolt is studied by P. Geyl, *The Revolt of the Netherlands, 1555–1609* (2nd edn, London, 1958); G. Parker, *The Dutch Revolt* (Harmondsworth, 1977); A. Duke, *Reformation and Revolt in the Low Countries* (London and Ronceverte, 1990); and M. Van Gelderen, *The Political Thought of the*

Dutch Revolt, 1555–1590 (Cambridge, 1992). See also W. T. MacCaffrey, 'The Newhaven Expedition, 1562–1563', *Historical Journal*, xl (1997).

For the hopes of creating a united and Protestant British Isles, see J. Dawson, 'William Cecil and the British dimension of early Elizabethan foreign policy', *History*, lxxiv (1989); and S. Alford, *The Early Elizabethan Polity*. Scottish politics are discussed in G. Donaldson, *All the Queen's Men: Power and Politics in Mary Stewart's Scotland* (London, 1983).

The Queen's marriage and the succession are studied in M. Levine, *The Early Elizabethan Succession Question, 1558–1568* (Stanford, California, 1966); S. Doran, *Monarchy and Matrimony: The Courtships of Elizabeth I* (London, 1996); and M. Axton, *The Queen's Two Bodies: Drama and the Elizabethan Succession* (London, 1977). For courtship, see C. Bates, *The Rhetoric of Courtship in Elizabethan Language and Literature* (Cambridge, 1992).

Many letters to Sir Henry Sidney in Ireland are printed in *Sidney State Papers, 1565–1570*, ed. T.Ó Laidhin (Dublin, 1962). Sidney's own letters from Ireland are found in *Letters and Memorials of State*, ed. A. Collins (2 vols., London, 1746), I. His 'summary relation of all his services in Ireland', written for Sir Francis Walsingham in March 1583, is printed in *Calendar of Carew MSS, 1575–1588*, ed. J. S. Brewer and W. Bullen (London, 1868), pp. 334–60. In writing about Ireland in the 1560s, and of the mutual consequences of faction in Ireland and in England, I have relied on the important works of C. Brady, *The Chief Governors: The rise and fall of reform government in Tudor Ireland, 1536–1588* (Cambridge, 1994) and 'Faction and the origins of the Desmond Rebellion of 1579', *Irish Historical Studies*, xxii (1981); N. Canny, *The Elizabethan Conquest of Ireland: A pattern established, 1565–76* (Hassocks, 1976); and J. G. Crawford, *Anglicizing the Government of Ireland: The Irish Privy Council and the Expansion of Tudor Rule, 1556–1578* (Dublin, 1993). See also D. Edwards, 'The Butler Revolt of 1569', *Irish Historical Studies*, xxviii (1992–3). For Sir Humphrey Gilbert in Ireland, see *The Voyages and Colonising Enterprises of Sir Humphrey Gilbert*, ed. D. B. Quinn, (2 vols., Hakluyt Society, London, 1940); and T. Churchyard, *Churchyarde's Choise, a general rehearsal of warres* (London, 1579).

The sense and the reality of the dangers which beset the Elizabethan polity in the late 1560s are understood by reading *Calendar of State Papers, Domestic* and *Calendar of State Papers, Foreign, Elizabeth, 1566–8* and *1569–71*; and *Proceedings of the Parliaments of Queen Elizabeth I*, vol. 1, *1558–1581*. For the politics, see W. T. MacCaffrey, *The Shaping of the Elizabethan Regime: Elizabethan Politics, 1558–72*; C. Read, *Mr Secretary Walsingham and the policy of Queen Elizabeth* (3 vols., Oxford, 1925); S. E. Lehmberg, *Sir Walter Mildmay and Tudor Government* (Austin, Texas, 1964); and M. R. Thorp, 'Catholic conspiracy in early Elizabethan foreign policy', *Sixteenth Century Journal*, 15 (1984). For the crisis occasioned by the Darnley murder, and by Mary, Queen of Scots' abdication and flight, see A. Fraser, *Mary, Queen of*

Scots (London, 1989 edn); J. Wormald, *Mary, Queen of Scots: A study in failure* (London, 1991); G. Donaldson, *The First Trial of Mary, Queen of Scots* (London, 1969); and H. Villius, 'The Casket Letters: a famous case reopened', *Historical Journal*, xxviii (1985). The Norfolk match and the rebellion of the northern earls are described in William Camden, *The History of . . . Princess Elizabeth*, ed. MacCaffrey, Ch. 7; and M. James, 'The concept of order and the Northern rising, 1569' in his *Society, Politics and Culture: Studies in Early Modern England* (Cambridge, 1986). The choices faced by English Catholics are considered by E. Rose, *Cases of Conscience: Alternatives open to Recusants and Puritans under Elizabeth I and James I* (Cambridge, 1975). For the debates surrounding the punishment of Mary, Queen of Scots, see P. Collinson, 'The Monarchical Republic of Queen Elizabeth I' in his *Elizabethan Essays* (London and Rio Grande, 1994).

8 Wars of Religion

John Calvin's teachings are found in his *Institutes of the Christian Religion*, trans. H. Beveridge (2 vols, London, 1962); his teachings upon grace in Book Third of the *Institutes*. For the working of providence in the lives of the godly, see K. V. Thomas, *Religion and the Decline of Magic: Studies in popular beliefs in sixteenth and seventeenth century England* (London, 1971), Ch. 4. For English Calvinism, see P. Lake, 'Calvinism and the English Church, 1570–1635', *Past and Present*, 114 (1987); R. T. Kendall, *Calvin and English Calvinism to 1649* (Oxford, 1979); and N. Tyacke, *Anti-Calvinists: the Rise of English Arminianism, c.1590–1640* (Oxford, 1987). The Protestant understanding of history is explained by G. J. R. Parry, *A Protestant Vision: William Harrison and the Reformation of Elizabethan England* (Cambridge, 1987); see also R. Helgerson, *Forms of Nationhood: The Elizabethan writing of England* (Chicago and London, 1992); and K. R. Firth, *The Apocalyptic Tradition in Reformation Britain, 1530–1645* (Oxford, 1979).

Patrick Collinson has illumined the world of Elizabethan Protestants in a series of magisterial and indispensable works: *The Elizabethan Puritan Movement* (London, 1967), *Archbishop Grindal, 1519–1583: The Struggle for a Reformed Church* (London, 1979), *The Religion of Protestants: The Church in English Society, 1559–1625* (Oxford, 1982), *Godly People: Essays on English Protestantism and Puritanism* (London, 1983) and *The Birthpangs of Protestant England: Religion and Cultural Change in the Sixteenth and Seventeenth Centuries* (Basingstoke, 1988). Important documents, with commentaries, are printed in *Puritanism in Tudor England*, ed. H. C. Porter (London and Basingstoke, 1970). For the debates in Parliament, see *Proceedings in the Parliaments of Elizabeth I*, vol. 1, 1558–1581, ed. T. E. Hartley (Leicester, 1981). The interpretation of J. E. Neale, *Elizabeth I and her Parliaments* (2 vols., London,

1953–7) is questioned by G. R. Elton, *The Parliament of England, 1559–1581* (Cambridge, 1986). Biographies of each member of Parliament are found in *The House of Commons, 1558–1603*, ed. P. W. Hasler (3 vols., London, 1981).

For understanding English politics and England's place in Europe, the state papers are, as ever, indispensable: *Calendar of State Papers, Foreign*. See also *Relations Politiques des Pays-Bas et de l'Angleterre*, ed. Baron J. Kervyn de Lettenhove (11 vols., Brussels, 1882–1900); W. Murdin, *A Collection of State Papers relating to Affairs in the Reign of Queen Elizabeth from 1571 to 1596* (London, 1759); T. Wright, *Queen Elizabeth and her times* (2 vols., London, 1838). Important studies are C. Read, *Lord Burghley and Queen Elizabeth* (London, 1960) and *Mr Secretary Walsingham and the Policy of Queen Elizabeth* (3 vols., Oxford, 1925); W. T. MacCaffrey, *Queen Elizabeth and the Making of Policy, 1572–1588* (Princeton, 1981); R. B. Wernham, *Before the Armada: The growth of English foreign policy, 1485–1588* (Oxford, 1966); and C. Wilson, *Queen Elizabeth and the Revolt of the Netherlands* (London, 1970). B. Worden, *The Sound of Virtue: Philip Sidney's* Arcadia *and Elizabethan Politics* (New Haven and London, 1996) is a compelling study of the ethics and politics of the forward Protestants and of the way in which the world of politics infused literature.

For the events leading up to the massacre in Paris, see N. M. Sutherland, *The Massacre of St Bartholomew and the European Conflict, 1559–1572* (London and Basingstoke, 1973); B. B. Diefendorf, *Beneath the Cross: Catholics and Huguenots in Sixteenth-Century Paris* (New York, 1991); *Calvinism in Europe, 1540–1610*, ed. A. Duke, G. Lewis and A. Pettegree (Manchester, 1992); and G. Parker, *The Dutch Revolt* (Harmondsworth, 1977).

The structure of the court and the nature of its politics are analysed by S. L. Adams in 'Eliza Enthroned? The Court and its Politics', in *The Reign of Elizabeth I*, ed. C. Haigh (Basingstoke, 1984) and 'Favourites and factions at the Elizabethan Court', in *The Tudor Monarchy*, ed. J. Guy (London, 1997); P. Williams, 'Court and Polity under Elizabeth I', *Bulletin of the John Rylands Library*, 65 (1982–3). The letters in *Memoirs of the Life and Times of Sir Christopher Hatton*, ed. H. Nicolas (London, 1847) are revealing of life at court.

The 'Civil wars of the Church of God' are explained by P. Collinson, *The Elizabethan Puritan Movement* (London, 1967). For puritan attempts to transform society, see his *The Birthpangs of Protestant England* (Basingstoke, 1988) and 'The Puritan Character: Polemics and polarities in early seventeenth-century English culture' (Williams Andrews Clark Memorial Library, Los Angeles, 1989); and M. Spufford, 'Puritanism and social control?' in *Order and Disorder in Early Modern England*, ed. A. J. Fletcher and J. Stevenson (Cambridge, 1985). For an illuminating study of changing religious and secular rituals, see R. Hutton, *The Rise and Fall of Merry England: The ritual year, 1400–1700* (Oxford, 1994).

For understanding Ireland, C. Brady, *The Chief Governors: The rise and fall*

of reform government in Tudor Ireland, 1536–1558 (Cambridge, 1994); N.
Canny, *The Elizabethan Conquest of Ireland: A pattern established, 1565–76*
(Hassocks, 1976); J. G. Crawford, *Anglicizing the Government of Ireland: The
Irish Privy Council and the expansion of Tudor Rule, 1556–1578* (Dublin,
1993) are essential. For Edmund Campion's time in Dublin, see E. Campion,
Two bokes of the Histories of Ireland (1571), ed. A. F. Vossen (Assen, 1963).
Philip Sidney's views upon Ireland are found in *Miscellaneous Prose of Sir Philip
Sidney* eds. K. Duncan-Jones and J. van Dorsten (Oxford, 1973). For Spenser
in Ireland, see E. Spenser, *A view of the present state of Ireland in 1596*, ed.
W. L. Renwick (London, 1934, reprinted Oxford, 1970); *The Faerie Queene*,
Book V in *Spenser: Poetical Works*, ed. J. C. Smith and E. de Selincourt (Oxford
1912; reprinted 1989); A. Hadfield, *Spenser's Irish Experience: Wilde fruit and
salvage soyl* (Oxford, 1997); and important essays by C. Brady and R. McCabe
in *Spenser and Ireland*, ed. P. Coughlan (Cork, 1989). The hardening of English
attitudes to the Irish is best shown by J. Derricke, *The Image of Irelande*
(London, 1581); see also V. P. Carey, 'John Derricke's *Image of Ireland*: Sir
Henry Sidney and the massacre at Mullaghmast, 1578', *Irish Historical Studies*,
xxxi (1999); and A. Hadfield, 'Briton and Scythian: Tudor representations of
Irish origins', *Irish Historical Studies*, xxviii (1993). The plans for Ulster are
studied by H. Morgan, 'The colonial venture of Sir Thomas Smith in Ulster,
1571–1575', *Historical Journal*, xxviii (1985). For composition, see B. Cunning-
ham, 'The composition of Connaught in the lordships of Clanrickard and
Thomond, 1577–1641', *Irish Historical Studies*, xxiv (1984).

The nature and success of Elizabethan Catholicism have occasioned controversy. John Bossy's contention in *The English Catholic Community, 1570–
1850* (London, 1975) that the old Catholic Church died and a new community
was created was challenged by C. Haigh, 'The Continuity of Catholicism in the
English Reformation' in *The English Reformation Revised*, ed. Haigh (Cambridge, 1987). See also C. Haigh, *English Reformations: Religion, Politics and
Society under the Tudors* (Oxford, 1993) and 'From Monopoly to Minority:
Catholicism in early modern England', *Transactions of the Royal Historical
Society*, 5th series, 31 (1981). The attitudes of Catholics towards their position
are considered by P. Holmes, *Resistance and Compromise: The political thought
of the Elizabethan Catholics* (Cambridge, 1982), and A. Pritchard, *Catholic
Loyalism in Elizabethan England* (London, 1979). The best account of Cam-
pion's life remains R. Simpson, *Edmund Campion: A biography* (London,
1896). See also *Anthony Munday: The English Roman Life*, ed. P. J. Ayres
(Oxford, 1980).

For John Dee, see P. French, *John Dee: The world of an Elizabethan magus*
(London, 1984 edn). The crisis for the godly in the late 1570s is best explained
in B. Worden, *The Sound of Virtue* (New Haven and London, 1996); P. Collinson, 'The downfall of Archbishop Grindal and its place in Elizabethan political
and ecclesiastical history', and W. T. MacCaffrey, 'The Anjou match and the

making of Elizabethan foreign policy' in *The English Commonwealth, 1547–1640*, ed. P. Clark, A. G. R. Smith and N. Tyacke (Leicester, 1979); C. Marsh, *The Family of Love in English Society, 1550–1630* (Cambridge, 1994); and C. Wilson, *Queen Elizabeth and the Revolt of the Netherlands* (London, 1970). For Scotland, see G. R. Hewitt, *Scotland under Morton, 1572–80* (Edinburgh, 1982); and K. M. Brown, *Bloodfeud in Scotland, 1573–1625: Violence, justice and politics in an early modern society* (Edinburgh, 1986). For the alarm with which the Anjou match was viewed, read *John Stubbs's* Gaping Gulf *with letters and other relevant documents*, ed. L. E. Berry (Charlottesville, Virginia, 1968). For a Catholic condemnation of Leicester and his purposes, see *Leicester's Commonwealth: The Copy of a Letter written by a Master of Art of Cambridge (1584)*, ed. D. C. Peck (Athens, Ohio and London, 1985). Robert Persons' mission is uncovered by J. Bossy, 'The heart of Robert Persons' in *The Reckoned Expense: Edmund Campion and the Early English Jesuits*, ed. T. M. McCoog (Woodbridge, 1996). For a thrilling, and chilling, account of the world of spies, see J. Bossy, *Giordano Bruno and the Embassy Affair* (New Haven and London, 1991). The Bond of Association and its implications are explained by P. Collinson, 'The Elizabethan Exclusion Crisis and the Elizabethan Polity', *Proceedings of the British Academy*, 84 (1994).

9 The Enterprise of England

For Sidney's thwarted enterprise see 'A dedication to Sir Philip Sidney' in *The Prose Works of Fulke Greville, Lord Brooke*, ed. J. Gouws (Oxford, 1986). The pioneering historian of England's colonies in Ireland and America is D. B. Quinn: see D. B. Quinn and A. N. Ryan, *England's Sea Empire, 1550–1642* (London, 1983) and its bibliographical essay; and D. B. Quinn, *England and the Discovery of America, 1481–1620* (New York, 1974). Spain's contemporary reputation for oppression is studied in W. S. Maltby, *The Black Legend in England: The development of anti-Spanish sentiment, 1558–1660* (Durham, North Carolina, 1971).

For English colonial ventures, see the writings of the first propagandists of empire: Richard Hakluyt, *Discourse of Western Planting*, ed. D. B. Quinn and A. M. Quinn (London, 1993); *The Voyages and Colonising Enterprises of Sir Humphrey Gilbert*, ed. D. B. Quinn (2 vols., Hakluyt Society, London, 1940); T. Harriot, *A briefe and true report of the new found land of Virginia . . .* (London, 1588) in *The Roanoke Voyages, 1584–1590*, ed. D. B. Quinn (2 vols., Hakluyt Society, 2nd series, London, 1955); W. Ralegh, *The Discovery of the Large, Rich and Beautiful Empire of Guiana* in *Sir Walter Ralegh: Selected Writings*, ed. G. Hammond (Harmondsworth, 1986); *The Origins of Empire: British overseas enterprise to the close of the seventeenth century*, ed. N. Canny (The Oxford History of the British Empire, Oxford, 1998). Historians have noted parallels between English colonizing enterprises in Ireland and the New World: see D. B. Quinn, *The Elizabethans and the Irish* (Ithaca, 1966), especially Ch. 9; N. Canny, *Kingdom and Colony: Ireland in the Atlantic World, 1560–1800* (Baltimore, Maryland, 1988); *The Westward Enterprise*, ed. K. R. Andrews *et al.* (Manchester, 1978). Ciaran Brady has challenged the idea that Ireland was seen as a colonial frontier: 'The road to the *View*: on the decline of reform thought in Tudor Ireland' in *Spenser and Ireland*, ed. P. Coughlan (Cork, 1989). Sir Francis Drake's *West Indian Voyage, 1585–1586*, ed. M. F. Freeler (Hakluyt Society, 2nd series, 148, London, 1981).

For the coming of the war with Spain, see *Calendar of State Papers, Foreign*; W. T. MacCaffrey, *Queen Elizabeth and the Making of Policy, 1572–1588* (Princeton, 1988). K. R. Andrews, *Elizabethan Privateering: English privateering during the Spanish War, 1585–1603* (Cambridge, 1964) is an invaluable study of the war of plunder, and hence of sixteenth-century sea warfare in general. Leicester's progress in the Netherlands can be traced in *Correspondence of Robert Dudley, Earl of Leicester . . . 1585 and 1586*, ed. J. Bruce (Camden Society, xxvii, London, 1844). See also R. C. Strong and J. A. van Dorsten, *Leicester's Triumph* (Leiden and London, 1964). For Philip Sidney, as he lived and died, see K. Duncan-Jones, *Sir Philip Sidney: Courtier poet* (London, 1991).

The transformations in Elizabethan politics which came with war are explained by J. Guy, 'The 1590s: The second reign of Elizabeth I?' in *The reign of Elizabeth I: Court and culture in the last decade*, ed. Guy (Cambridge, 1995). The Babington plot is uncovered in *Calendar of State Papers relating to Scotland and Mary, Queen of Scots, AD, 1585–1586*; C. Read, *Mr. Secretary Walsingham and the policy of Queen Elizabeth*, vol. 3 (3 vols., Oxford, 1925). The debates in Parliament are found in *Proceedings in the Parliaments of Elizabeth I*, vol. 2, *1584–1589*, ed. T. E. Hartley (Leicester, 1995). See also P. Collinson, *The English Captivity of Mary, Queen of Scots* (Sheffield, 1987); and P. E. McCullough, *Sermons at Court: Politics and Religion in Elizabethan and Jacobean Preaching* (Cambridge, 1998).

A compelling and masterly account of the coming and the flight of the Spanish Armada, within the wider European context, is G. Mattingley's classic, *The Defeat of the Spanish Armada* (London, 1959). See also M. J. Rodriguez-Salgado and S. Adams, *England, Spain and the Gran Armada, 1584–1604* (Edinburgh, 1991); and C. Martin and G. Parker, *The Spanish Armada* (London, 1988). For the suborning of the English ambassador in Paris, see M. Leimon and G. Parker, 'Treason and plot in Elizabethan diplomacy: The "fame" of Sir Edward Stafford reconsidered', *English Historical Review*, cxi (1996). For the Armada's arrival in Ireland, see *Calendar of Carew MSS, 1575–1588*; R. Bagwell, *Ireland under the Tudors*, vol. 3 (London, 1885–90); and L. Flanagan, *Irish Wrecks of the Spanish Armada* (Dublin, 1995). Contemporary comments upon the defeat are found in *Calendar of State Papers, Domestic, 1581–90*; and *The Great Enterprise: The history of the Spanish Armada, as revealed in contemporary documents*, ed. S.

Usherwood (London, 1978). The Earl of Arundel's treason is described in W. Camden, *The History of . . . Princess Elizabeth* (London, 1675 edn) for 1589.

10 The Theatre of God's Judgements

The chapter title is taken from a work of 1597 which recounts a series of providential punishments: Thomas Beard, *The theatre of God's judgements: Or a collection of histories*. For the rumours in Essex of a vagrant army, see W. Hunt, *The Puritan moment: The coming of revolution in an English county* (Cambridge, Mass. 1983); and for the rising that did not happen, J. Walter, 'A "Rising of the people?" – the Oxfordshire rising of 1596', *Past and Present*, 107 (1985).

Population figures for England are drawn from E. A. Wrigley and R. S. Schofield, *The Population History of England, 1541–1871: A reconstruction* (London, 1981) and for London from V. Harding, 'The Population of London, 1550–1700: A review of the published evidence', *London Journal*, 15 (1990).

For the agrarian developments, see D. Palliser, *The Age of Elizabeth: England under the later Tudors, 1547–1603* (London, 1983); C. G. A. Clay, *Economic Expansion and Social Change: England, 1500–1700* (2 vols., Cambridge, 1984); *The Agrarian History of England and Wales*, vol. 4, *1500–1640*, ed. J. Thirsk (Cambridge, 1967); M. Spufford, *Contrasting Communities: English Villagers in the sixteenth and seventeenth centuries* (Cambridge, 1974); J. Youings, *Sixteenth-Century England* (Harmondsworth, 1984); J. A. Yelling, *Common Field and Enclosure in England, 1450–1850* (London, 1977); and C. Platt, *The Great Rebuildings of Tudor and Stuart England* (London, 1994).

The perception and the reality of the crisis of the 1590s is studied in R. B. Outhwaite, 'Dearth, the English Crown and the crisis of the 1590s' and P. Clark, 'A crisis contained? The condition of English towns in the 1590s' in *The European Crisis of the 1590s*, ed. P. Clark (London, 1985); J. Sharpe, 'Social strain and social dislocation, 1585–1603' in *The reign of Elizabeth I: court and culture in the last decade*, ed. J. Guy (Cambridge, 1995); I. Archer, *The Pursuit of Stability: Social Relations in Elizabethan London* (Cambridge, 1991); S. J. Watts, *From Border to Middle Shire: Northumberland, 1586–1625* (Leicester, 1975); A. L. Beier, *Masterless Men: The vagrancy problem in England, 1560–1640* (London, 1985); A. Appleby, *Famine in Tudor and Stuart England* (Liverpool, 1978); *Famine, Disease and the Social Order in Early Modern Society*, ed. J. Walter and R. Schofield (Cambridge, 1989).

For the plague and its consequences P. Slack, *The Impact of Plague in Tudor and Stuart England* (London, 1985) is indispensable. The godly understanding of God's will revealed in the natural world is explained in P. Lake, *Moderate Puritans and the Elizabethan Church* (Cambridge, 1982); and G. J. R. Parry, *A Protestant Vision: William Harrison and the Reformation of Elizabethan England* (Cambridge, 1987), Ch.7. Bacon's remarks upon the plague are found in

'Certain Observations made upon a libel published this present year, 1592' in *The Letters and the Life of Francis Bacon*, vol. 1, ed. J. Spedding (London, 1861).

Of the many works upon witchcraft and the witch craze in England, K. V. Thomas, *Religion and the Decline of Magic: Studies in popular beliefs in sixteenth and seventeenth century England* (London, 1971); and A. Macfarlane, *Witchcraft in Tudor and Stuart England: A regional and comparative study* (London, 1970) are particularly important. A good introduction is J. Sharpe, *Instruments of Darkness: Witchcraft in England, 1550–1750* (London, 1996). William Perkins, *A discourse of the damned art of witchcraft* is printed in *The Work of William Perkins*, ed. I. Breward (Abingdon, 1970).

I have studied the A-text of Christopher Marlowe, *Doctor Faustus*, ed. D. Bevington and E. Rasmussen (Manchester, 1993). For John Dee's life and thought, see his extraordinary diaries, *The Diaries of John Dee*, ed. E. Fenton (Charlbury, 1998); P. French, *John Dee: The world of an Elizabethan magus* (London, 1984 edn); and N. H. Clulee, *John Dee's Natural Philosophy: Between Science and Religion* (London, 1988). Humphrey Gilbert's visions are discovered in D. B. Quinn, *Explorers and Colonies: America, 1500–1625* (London, 1990), Ch. 12. For Elizabethan science and occult philosophy, see F. Yates, *Giordano Bruno and the Hermetic Tradition* (London, 1964) and *The Occult Philosophy in the Elizabethan Age* (London, 1979); and A. G. Debus, *The English Paracelsians* (New York, 1966). On Harriot, see especially *Thomas Harriot, Renaissance Scientist*, ed. J. W. Shirley (Oxford, 1974). Brilliant accounts of Christopher Marlowe, as he lived and died, are found in S. Greenblatt, *Renaissance Self-Fashioning: From More to Shakespeare* (Chicago and London, 1980); and C. Nicholl, *The Reckoning: The murder of Christopher Marlowe* (London, 1993 edn). For the Elizabethan cult of melancholy, see R. Strong, *The English Icon: Elizabethan and Jacobean Portraiture* (London, 1989). For one melancholic, see *The Poems of Robert Sidney*, ed. P. J. Croft (Oxford, 1984). The excesses of the nobility at court are described in L. Stone, *The Crisis of the Aristocracy, 1558–1641* (Oxford, 1965). For Fulke Greville and the arts of power, see D. Norbrook, *Poetry and Politics in the English Renaissance* (London, 1984), Ch. 6.

11 Court and Camp

For the horoscope, see H. Gatti, 'The Natural Philosophy of Thomas Harriot' (Thomas Harriot Lecture, Oxford, 1993). The image of the Queen and the devotion demanded of her subjects are explored in R. Strong's classic, *The Cult of Elizabeth: Elizabethan Portraiture and Pageantry* (London, 1999 edn) – here the identification of Essex with the *Young Man among Roses* is made. See also H. Hackett, *Virgin Mother, Maiden Queen: Elizabeth I and the Cult of the Virgin Mary* (Basingstoke, 1996 edn).

Ralegh and Essex reveal themselves in their letters and in their poetry: W. Devereux, *Lives and Letters of the Devereux, Earls of Essex, 1540–1646* (2 vols., London, 1853); *The Letters of Sir Walter Ralegh*, ed. A. Latham and J. Youings (Exeter, 1999); and *The Poems of Sir Walter Ralegh*, ed. A. Latham (London and Cambridge, Mass., revised edn, 1951). Essex's preoccupation with the cult of honour is examined in an illuminating essay by M. E. James: 'At a crossroads of the political culture: The Essex revolt, 1601' in his *Society, Politics and Culture: Studies in Early Modern England* (Cambridge, 1986). For Ralegh and the twelve-year war, see 'The Ocean to Cynthia' in his *Poems;* and W. Oakeshott, *The Queen and the Poet* (London, 1960).

To understand the preoccupations and politics of the 1590s, contemporary letters and memoirs are indispensable: the letters from his agents in London to Sir Robert Sidney in *Letters and Memorials of State*, ed. A. Collins (2 vols., London, 1746); *The Letters of Queen Elizabeth I*, ed. G. B. Harrison (London, 1935); *Calendar of the MSS of the Marquess of Salisbury at Hatfield House*, vols. 4–12 (London, 1883–1976); *The Letters of John Chamberlain* (2 vols., Philadelphia, 1939); *Manuscripts of the Earl of Ancaster preserved at Grimsthorpe* (Dublin, 1907); *The Letters and Life of Francis Bacon*, vols. 1–2, ed. J. Spedding (London, 1868); *The Memoirs of Robert Carey*, ed. F. H. Mares (Oxford, 1972); and *Letters and Epigrams of Sir John Harington*, ed. N. M. McClure (Oxford, 1930).

For the politics, foreign and domestic, of Elizabeth's last years, William Camden's *The History of . . . Princess Elizabeth* (3rd edn, London, 1675) is a vital source, for he witnessed many of the events. Important studies are W. T. MacCaffrey, *Elizabeth I: War and Politics, 1588–1603* (Princeton, 1992); R. B. Wernham, 'Elizabethan War aims and strategy' in *Elizabethan Government and Society*, ed. S. T. Bindoff *et al.* (London, 1961), *After the Armada: Elizabethan England and the Struggle for Western Europe, 1588–1595* (Oxford, 1984) and *The Return of the Armadas: The last years of the Elizabethan War against Spain, 1595–1603* (Oxford, 1994); C. Read, *Lord Burghley and Queen Elizabeth* (London, 1960); *The reign of Elizabeth I: Court and culture in the last decade*, ed. J. Guy (Cambridge, 1995).

For France as the 'theatre of misery' see Bacon's 'Observations made upon a Libel, 1592' in his *Letters and Life*, vol. 1; J. H. M. Salmon, *Society in Crisis: France in the Sixteenth Century* (London, 1979); P. Benedict, *Rouen during the wars of religion* (Cambridge, 1981); and H. Lloyd, *The Rouen Campaign, 1590–1592: Politics, warfare and the early modern state* (Oxford, 1973).

For the alleged *regnum Cecilianum* or kingdom of the Cecils, and the resentment of it, see J. E. Neale, 'The Elizabethan Political Scene' in his *Essays in Elizabethan History* (London, 1958), and N. Mears, 'Regnum Cecilianum? a Cecilian perspective of the Court' and P. E. J. Hammer, 'Patronage at Court, faction and the Earl of Essex' in *The reign of Elizabeth I: Court and culture in the last decade*, ed. J. Guy (Cambridge, 1995); and P. E. J. Hammer, 'The Uses of Scholarship: The Secretariat of Robert Devereux, second Earl of Essex, *c.* 1585–1601', *English Historical Review*, cix (1994).

Calendar of State Papers, Ireland and *Calendar of Carew MSS* contain important letters and reports upon Ireland. Essential for understanding the history of Ireland in the 1580s, and the failures of English governors there, are C. Brady, *The Chief Governors: The rise and fall of reform government in Tudor Ireland, 1536–1588* (Cambridge, 1994) and H. Morgan, *Tyrone's Rebellion: The outbreak of the Nine Years War in Ireland* (Woodbridge, 1993), which explains the origins of the greatest rebellion the Tudors ever faced. For the divisions at the English court which continued to undermine the governors of Ireland, see H. Morgan, 'The Fall of Sir John Perrot' in *The reign of Elizabeth I*, ed. J. Guy. The Munster plantation and the aspirations of the planters are explored by M. MacCarthy-Morrogh, *The Munster Plantation: English Migration to Southern Ireland, 1583–1641* (Oxford, 1986); and N. Canny, *The Upstart Earl: A study of the social and mental world of Richard Boyle, first Earl of Cork, 1566–1643* (Cambridge, 1982). Edmund Spenser's *View of the Present State of Ireland*, ed. W. L. Renwick (Oxford, 1970) is essential, and to understand how he came to it, C. Brady, 'Spenser's Irish crisis: Humanism and experience in the 1590s', *Past and Present*, 111 (1986). For the freebooters, see C. Brady, 'The captains' games: Army and society in Elizabethan Ireland' in *A Military History of Ireland*, ed. T. Bartlett and K. Jeffery (Cambridge, 1996); and M. O'Dowd, *Power, Politics and Land: Early Modern Sligo, 1568–1688* (Belfast, 1991).

The Queen's growing impatience with her puritan subjects was expressed in Parliament: *Proceedings in the Parliaments of Elizabeth I*, vol. 3, *1593–1601*, ed. T. E. Hartley (Leicester, 1995). J. Guy, 'The Elizabethan establishment and the ecclesiastical polity' in *The reign of Elizabeth I*, ed. Guy. The challenges from and to the puritans, and the development of presbyterianism are best explained in P. Collinson's classic *The Elizabethan Puritan Movement* (London, 1963). See also P. Lake, *Moderate Puritans and the Elizabethan Church* (Cambridge, 1982) and *Anglicans and Puritans? Presbyterianism and English Conformist Thought from Whitgift to Hooker* (London, 1988); H. C. Porter, *Puritanism in Tudor England* (London, 1970); *The Presbyterian movement in the reign of Queen Elizabeth as illustrated by the minute book of the Dedham Classis, 1582–1589*, ed. R. G. Usher (Camden Society, 3rd series, 8, 1905); and D. MacCulloch, *Suffolk and the Tudors: Politics and Religion in an English County, 1500–1600* (Oxford, 1986). For Martin Marprelate and his effect, see L. H. Carlson, *Martin Marprelate, Gentleman: Master Job Throckmorton Laid Open in his Colors* (San Marino, 1981); and P. Collinson, 'Ecclesiastical vitriol: Religious satire in the 1590s and the invention of puritanism' in *The reign of Elizabeth I*, ed. Guy. For the crisis of 1593, see P. Collinson, 'Hooker and the Elizabethan establishment' in *Richard Hooker and the Construction of a Christian Community*, ed. A. S. McGrade (Tempe, Arizona, 1997).

For John Donne, see *The Complete English Poems*, ed. C. A. Patrides (London,

1985); and J. Carey, *John Donne: Life, Mind and Art* (London, 1990 edn). Tresham's triangular lodge is described in N. Pevsner, *The Buildings of England: Northamptonshire* (2nd edn, Harmondsworth, 1973).

Robert Southwell's spiritual mission is explained in his *An humble supplication to Her Maiestie in answere to the late proclamation* (1595, reprinted Menston, 1973); see also *The Poems of Robert Southwell*, ed. J. H. MacDonald and N. Pollard Brown (Oxford, 1967). The ways in which Catholics considered their position are discussed in P. Holmes, *Resistance and Compromise: The Political Thought of Elizabethan Catholics* (Cambridge, 1982) and *Elizabethan Casuistry* (Catholic Record Society, lxvii, 1981); A. Pritchard, *Catholic Loyalism in Elizabethan England* (London, 1979); L. Wooding, *Rethinking Catholicism in Reformation England* (Oxford, 2000); and A. Walsham, *Church papists: Catholicism, conformity and confessional polemic in early modern England* (Woodbridge, 1993). One of the best local studies of Catholicism is J. C. H. Aveling, *Northern Catholics: The Catholic Recusants of the North Riding of Yorkshire, 1558–1790* (London, 1966). J. Bossy, 'The character of Elizabethan Catholicism', *Past and Present*, 21 (1962) is an illuminating study. For understanding the transformations in English Protestantism, H. C. Porter, *Reformation and Reaction in Tudor Cambridge* (Cambridge, 1958) and N. Tyacke, *Anti-Calvinists: The rise of English Arminianism, c. 1590–1640* (Oxford, 1987) are indispensable.

For Essex's 'violent courses', the correspondence in *Letters and Memorials of State*, ed. A. Collins and *The Letters and Life of Francis Bacon*, ed. J. Spedding are important. See also the essays by Mears and Hammer in *The reign of Elizabeth I*, ed. J. Guy; and R. McCoy, *The Rites of Knighthood* (Berkeley and Los Angeles, 1989). Essex's strategy in European affairs is discussed in P. Hammer, 'Essex and Europe: Evidence from confidential instructions by the Earl of Essex, 1595–6', *English Historical Review*, cxi (1996); and L. W. Henry, 'The Earl of Essex as strategist and military organiser (1596–7)', *ibid.*, lxviii (1953). The Cadiz expedition and the Islands voyage are described by Wernham, *The Return of the Armadas*; and P. E. J. Hammer, 'Myth-making: Politics, propaganda and the capture of Cadiz in 1596', *Historical Journal*, xl (1997). For Essex and his friends, M. James, 'At a crossroads of the political culture: The Essex revolt, 1601' and D. Wootton, 'Francis Bacon: Your flexible friend' in *The World of the Favourite*, ed. J. H. Elliott and L. W. B. Brockliss (New Haven and London, 1999); and R. A. Rebholz, *The Life of Fulke Greville, first Lord Brooke* (Oxford, 1971) are important. Camden described Essex's quarrel with the Queen in *The History of Princess Elizabeth*. Andrewes's minatory sermon is found in *Ninety-six sermons by the Rt. Hon. and Revd. Father in God, Lancelot Andrewes*, ed. J. P. Parkinson and J. P. Wilson (Oxford, 1843).

For the war in Ireland, the *Calendar of State Papers, Ireland; Calendar of Carew MSS, 1589–1600* and *1601–1603; The Itinerary of Fynes Moryson*, vols. 2 and 3 (Glasgow, 1907); *Ireland under Elizabeth ... by Don Philip*

O'Sullivan Bear, trans. M. J. Byrne (Dublin, 1903); and *Annals of the Kingdom of Ireland by the Four Masters*, ed. J. O'Donovan (3rd edn, Dublin, 1998) are essential. Important studies of the war are H. Morgan, *Tyrone's Rebellion: The outbreak of the Nine Years War in Ireland;* C. Falls, *Elizabeth's Irish Wars* (London, 1950); J. McGurk, *The Elizabethan Conquest of Ireland: The 1590s crisis* (Manchester, 1997); 'A Supplication of the Blood of the English most lamentably murdered in Ireland, cryeng out of the yearth for revenge', ed. W. Maley, *Analecta Hibernica*, 36 (1994); and A. J. Sheehan, 'The overthrow of the plantation of Munster in October 1598', *Irish Sword*, xv (1982–3).

Essex's moves to conspiracy and revolt are discovered in *Correspondence of King James VI of Scotland with Sir Robert Cecil and others in England*, ed. J. Bruce (Camden Society, 78, London, 1861); 'A declaration of the practices and treasons . . . by Robert, late Earl of Essex' in *The Letters and the Life of Francis Bacon*, vol. 2; Camden, *The History of Princess Elizabeth; Calendar of the MSS. . . at Hatfield House*, vol. 11; and M. James, 'At a cross roads of the aristocratic culture: The Essex revolt, 1601'.

For the end of the Nine Years War, see H. Morgan, 'Faith and Fatherland or Queen and Country? An unpublished exchange between O'Neill and the state at the height of the Nine Years War', *Dúiche Néill: Journal of the O'Neill Country Historical Society*, 9 (1994), 'The end of Gaelic Ulster: A thematic interpretation of events between 1534 and 1610', *Irish Historical Studies*, xxvi (1988) and 'Hugh O'Neill and the Nine Years War in Tudor Ireland', *Historical Journal*, xxxvi (1993); N. Canny, 'Hugh O'Neill, Earl of Tyrone, and the changing face of Gaelic Ulster', *Studia Hibernica*, 10 (1970); M. Caball, 'Faith, culture and sovereignty: Irish nationality and development, 1558–1625' in *British Consciousness and Identity: The making of Britain, 1533–1707*, ed. B. Bradshaw and P. Roberts (Cambridge, 1998); J. J. Silke, *Kinsale: The Spanish intervention in Ireland at the end of the Elizabethan Wars* (Liverpool and New York, 1970); and 'Bodley's visit to Lecale, County of Down, AD 1602–3', *Ulster Journal of Archaeology*, 2 (1854). Thomas Stafford, *Pacata Hibernia*, ed. S. O'Grady (2 vols, London, 1896) is an account of the suppression of the revolt in Munster by Sir George Carew, 1600–3. For the bards' laments for their loss, see O. Bergin, *Irish Bardic Poetry* (Dublin, 1970).

Robert Carey was present as the Queen was dying: see his *Memoirs*. The anxieties that attended her death and James's accession are described in *Correspondence of King James VI of Scotland with Sir Robert Cecil*, ed. J. Bruce.

Epilogue

For the flight of the earls, see J. McCavitt, 'The flight of the earls, 1607' in *Irish Historical Studies*, xxix (1994).

The history of the Reformation and Counter-Reformation in Ireland has occasioned much controversy. For a narrative framework, see R. D. Edwards, *Church and State in Tudor Ireland: A History of the Penal Laws against Irish Catholics, 1534–1603* (Dublin, 1935); and M. V. Ronan, *The Reformation in Ireland under Elizabeth, 1558–80* (London, 1930). For explanations of why the Reformation failed in Ireland and accounts of the vitality of the Catholic Reformation, see B. Bradshaw, 'Sword, word and strategy in the Reformation in Ireland', *Historical Journal*, xxi (1978); and 'The English Reformation and identity formation in Ireland and Wales' in *British Consciousness and Identity: The Making of Britain, 1533–1707*, ed. B. Bradshaw and P. Roberts (Cambridge, 1998). Bradshaw's original arguments were challenged by N. P. Canny, 'Why the Reformation failed in Ireland: *Une question mal posée*', *Journal of Ecclesiastical History*, xxx (1979). For the history of the Church of Ireland and of Reformation there, see A. Ford, *The Protestant Reformation in Ireland, 1590–1641* (Dublin, 1997) and *As by Law Established: The Church of Ireland since the Reformation*, ed. A. Ford, J. McGuire and K. Milne (Dublin, 1995). For the religious world of the people, see R. Gillespie, *Devoted People: Belief and Religion in Early Modern Ireland* (Manchester, 1997). The reaction of Dublin's patriciate to the Reformation is explored in C. Lennon, *The Lords of Dublin in the Age of Reformation* (Dublin, 1989).

For understanding the consequences of more than half a century of Reformations in England, the following are indispensable: Christopher Haigh, *English Reformations: Religion, Politics and Society under the Tudors* (Oxford, 1993); M. Aston, *England's Iconoclasts: Laws against Images* (Oxford, 1988); P. Collinson, *The Birthpangs of Protestant England: Religious and Cultural Change in the Sixteenth and Seventeenth Centuries* (Basingstoke, 1988); E. Duffy, *The Stripping of the Altars: Traditional Religion in England, 1400–1580* (New Haven and London, 1992); C. Marsh, *Popular Religion in Sixteenth-century England* (Basingstoke, 1998). For a magisterial study of Wales, see G. Williams, *Wales and the Reformation* (Cardiff, 1997). The best studies of the transformation of the Tudor nobility are Laurence Stone's classic *The Crisis of the Aristocracy, 1558–1641* (Oxford, 1965) and M. James, *Society, Politics and Culture: Studies in Early Modern England* (Cambridge, 1986).

For literature and the late Elizabethan court, see D. Norbrook, *Poetry and Politics in the English Renaissance* (London, 1984), especially Ch. 5–7, and B. Worden, 'Ben Jonson and the Monarchy' in *Neo-historicism*, ed. G. Burgess, R. Headlam Wells and R. Wymer (Woodbridge, 2000). The best edition of *Hamlet* is by Harold Jenkins (Arden edition, London, 1982). Stimulating works upon *Hamlet*, and the world in which it was written, are C. Devlin, *Hamlet's Divinity and other essays* (London, 1963), and R. M. Frye, *The Renaissance Hamlet: Issues and Responses in 1600* (Princeton, 1984).

Index